FOUNDATIONS OF CIVIC ENGAGEMENT

Rethinking Social and Political Philosophy

Ralph D. Ellis
Norman Fischer
James B. Sauer

University Press of America,® Inc.
Lanham · Boulder · New York · Toronto · Oxford

Copyright © 2006 by
University Press of America,® Inc.
4501 Forbes Boulevard
Suite 200
Lanham, Maryland 20706
UPA Acquisitions Department (301) 459-3366

PO Box 317
Oxford
OX2 9RU, UK

Library of Congress Control Number: 2006926969
ISBN-13: 978-0-7618-3535-6 (paperback : alk. paper)
ISBN-10: 0-7618-3535-0 (paperback : alk. paper)

Contents

PREFACE   v

CHAPTER ONE — REOPENING FUNDAMENTAL QUESTIONS   1

CHAPTER TWO — POLITICS AND VALUE THEORY:
  A COMPLEX RELATIONSHIP   19

CHAPTER THREE — FORMATIVE CONCEPTS FROM
  EARLY PHILOSOPHERS: PLATO AND ARISTOTLE   43

CHAPTER FOUR — HOBBES AND THE ORIGINS OF
  MODERN SOCIAL CONTRACT THEORY   71

CHAPTER FIVE — HOBBESIAN DIFFICULTIES AND
  LOCKE'S RIGHTS-BASED APPROACH   95

CHAPTER SIX — SOCIAL CONTRACT THEORIES,
  EQUALITY, AND LIBERTY: ROUSSEAU AND KANT   117

CHAPTER SEVEN — THE NORMATIVE BASIS OF MARXISM   155

CHAPTER EIGHT — CONTEMPORARY THINKING
  ABOUT JUSTICE: RAWLS AND NOZICK   175

CHAPTER NINE — CONTEMPORARY THINKING
  ABOUT JUSTICE: THE FEMINIST CRITIQUE   201

CHAPTER TEN — JUSTICE AS IF CONTEXT MATTERED:
  COMMUNITARIAN THEORIES OF JUSTICE   219

CHAPTER ELEVEN — BACK TO IMPARTIALITY AND
    BEYOND: EUROPEAN VOICES IN THE JUSTICE
    CONVERSATION   237

CHAPTER TWELVE — THE POSTMODERN RIPOSTE:
    CONTESTING UNIVERSALISM   265

CHAPTER THIRTEEN — PRIVACY AND THE PUBLIC LIFE   277

REFERENCES   319

INDEX   325

ABOUT THE AUTHORS   329

Preface

The three authors undertook this project for a very pragmatic reason. Each of us had been concerned that there was no single comprehensive textbook providing a critical overview of the entire field of social and political philosophy, exploring the basic arguments of the most important historical and contemporary figures, and at the same time covering the important themes that run through all periods and are in need of in-depth analysis. Moreover, the line between textbooks in this field and original theoretical proposals tends to be blurred. As for those that clearly are meant as textbooks, most consist of collections of isolated essays by important philosophers with little or no commentary, or else confine themselves to the contemporary period or to a single theme such as the social contract or liberalism or communitarianism. In addition, we were concerned that many texts, both primary and secondary, are quite difficult for the typical college student to read with good comprehension.

Accordingly, we have undertaken to combine historical and thematic methods of presentation, in order to be sure and include the most crucial arguments and criticisms associated with the most important trends and theories, with clear explanations of the basic concepts used by various social and political philosophers through history, addressing their overall arguments rather than isolated excerpts.

Perhaps the easiest way to get an overview of the scope and thematic approach of the book is by means of a quick survey of each of the thirteen chapters:

CHAPTER ONE: REOPENING FUNDAMENTAL QUESTIONS

This chapter defines some important terms, concepts and themes central to social and political philosophy, with preliminary exposition of several crucial problems, questions, arguments, and counter-arguments, especially addressing the issues of social contract; communitarianism; the question of the legitimacy of governments; the problematic notion of political "rights"; limitations on the powers of government; utility maximization; retributive justice; distributive justice; the various conflicts among all these basic political values; and the relation of these values to empirical realities.

CHAPTER TWO: POLITICS AND VALUE THEORY—A COMPLEX
RELATIONSHIP

The rational and critical examination of basic beliefs in social and political
philosophy are imperative in two common, everyday cases: First, when these
beliefs seem to conflict with each other. Second, when they seem to harmonize too
easily with the self-interest or the self-congratulatory pride of the person who
asserts them. However, when a person raises these questions, a more fundamental
question obviously presents itself: How can we demonstrate the truth of a principle
of social or political philosophy at all? What are the most basic assumptions and
modes of reasoning for this purpose? On what basis should we choose from among
the various conflicting frameworks for thought? Those questions will be
considered in more detail in Chapter Two. After that basic groundwork has been
discussed, we can then turn our attention to the more specific issues in social and
political philosophy.

CHAPTER THREE: FORMATIVE CONCEPTS FROM EARLY PHILOSO-
PHERS: PLATO AND ARISTOTLE

It is highly instructive to see how early theories of government that were
developed in Ancient times preliminarily explored many of the main arguments
that are still used in political discussions today. This chapter will examine Plato's
"tripartite" approach to the state and Aristotle's personalist-communitarian
approach. It is especially instructive to compare the Ancient thinkers' views of
human nature with those of modern times. The term "human nature" is a very
slippery one that tempts many philosophers to pack unquestioned presuppositions
into their definitions. An interesting part of the question involves whether human
nature is egoistic and hedonistic, and in what senses. Even the very concept of
"happiness" was understood very differently in Ancient times, so it is to be
expected that the role of government in Ancient Greek theories would also be very
different. Moreover, the Ancient Greeks already understood that questions about
human nature involve establishing cause and effect relationships in human
motivation and action. To what extent is human nature, as Aristotle argued,
"rational"? And to what extent are we by nature embedded in a community, or as
Aristotle said, "political animals"?

CHAPTER FOUR: HOBBES AND THE ORIGINS OF MODERN SOCIAL
CONTRACT THEORY

In this chapter, we discuss some of the assumptions regarding human nature
and ethics which ground the origin of social contract theory in early modern
philosophy. We will see how these assumptions can lead to some very different
political philosophies. Thomas Hobbes argues that human nature necessitates
absolute government for the preservation of life and property; John Locke, by
contrast, argues that a limited government would best serve this cause. In this
chapter, we focus primarily on the thinking of Hobbes, whose basic assumptions
form the crucial groundwork for subsequent social contract theories, but also raise
serious difficulties upon which later theories must improve.

CHAPTER FIVE: HOBBESIAN DIFFICULTIES AND LOCKE'S RIGHTS-BASED APPROACH

In this chapter, we first focus on the way Hobbes's assumptions lead to a justification for absolute government power. We then consider some major criticisms and unsolved problems of Hobbes's way of thinking. There is the danger that, by relegating human virtue to mere passions, and construing reason as merely in the interest of egoistic passions, Hobbes has failed to get around the difficulty that a social contract will enable "might to make right" in the final analysis. This criticism forms the transition to later contract theories, particularly to the rights-based approach of John Locke, which is considered in the second half of this chapter.

CHAPTER SIX: SOCIAL CONTRACT THEORIES, EQUALITY, AND LIBERTY: ROUSSEAU AND KANT

This chapter discusses those social contract theories that critique the theories of human nature underlying the previous chapters' thinkers, and hence lead to a much different theory of the origins of the social contract, emphasizing the connection between liberty and equality. We particularly emphasized in this chapter the social contract philosophies of Jean-Jacques Rousseau and Immanuel Kant.

CHAPTER SEVEN: THE NORMATIVE BASIS OF MARXISM

Many people, including some philosophers, believe that Marxism is no longer as important as it once was, given the collapse of the Soviet Union. However, this overlooks the huge place of China and many Latin American countries on the world stage. Moreover, most Marxist philosophers were always quick to point out that the Soviet Union was not a very good example of a Marxist government, since it was more characterized by fascist dictatorship than socialist equality. The important issues raised by Marx are still crucial, even if we end up reaching different conclusions about them from the ones Marx advocated. Also, the age of economic globalization returns to the forefront many questions regarding exploitation of workers by monolithic corporate entities that were not as pressing during the last part of the twentieth century. Finally, our view of Marx includes the "humanist" interpretations that were under-emphasized in the mainstream of Marxist interpretation during the past century. On this view, Marx is a philosopher of the human condition, not merely a critic of one particular economic system, i.e., the capitalist system.

CHAPTER EIGHT: CONTEMPORARY THINKING ABOUT JUSTICE: RAWLS AND NOZICK

Here we come to perhaps the most widely debated of all current topics: the concept of justice. We must consider the following: John Rawls's idea of "rational consent"; Robert Nozick's proposed distinction between "rights" and "entitlements"; the attempt to conceptually clarify the distinction between "liberals" and "conservatives" in contemporary political debates. This chapter sets up the basic language and concepts of justice theory. It then critically examines the two basic liberal justice theories of Rawls and Nozick.

CHAPTER NINE: CONTEMPORARY THINKING ABOUT JUSTICE—THE FEMINIST CRITIQUE

This chapter begins with the critique of Rawls's notion of "justice as fairness" by liberal feminists. Susan Okin and Drucilla Cornell are used as representatives of the position that liberal justice theory can be reconfigured to consider issues, problems and concerns of women, children and families. Cornell provides a bridge to feminists who argue for a more context-dependent approach to justice theory. The work of Carol Gilligan, Rita Manning, and Virginia Held are critically examined. The chapter attempts to open a conversation on gender and justice, and to explore the interrelations of justice, freedom, and the development of person, by examining feminist theory as a deeper critique of justice as rational consent.

CHAPTER TEN: JUSTICE AS IF CONTEXT MATTERED— COMMUNI-TARIAN THEORIES OF JUSTICE

The contextualism of a feminist ethics of care sets the stage for the context-dependent rationality of communitarianism. Alisdair MacIntyre and Michael Waltzer's justice theories are critically examined. The chapter concludes by returning to the impartialism and partialism debate in justice theory as a bridge to the "discourse impartialism" of Jürgen Habermas.

CHAPTER ELEVEN: BACK TO IMPARTIALITY AND BEYOND— EURO-PEAN VOICES IN THE JUSTICE CONVERSATION

This chapter begins with a short discussion of justice theory as it has gone forward on the continent of Europe. Students are introduced to the influences on European justice thinking that are too often ignored in the English-speaking arena. Jürgen Habermas' proceduralism is critically examined, along with Horkheimer, Adorno, and Apel. By using the work of American feminist theorist Iris Young, critical theory is linked back to North American conversations about justice. The chapter concludes with an examination of Paul Ricoeur's personalist justice theory, which mediates between procedural and contextual rationality as it applies to justice theory.

CHAPTER TWELVE: THE POSTMODERN RIPOSTE—CONTESTING UNIVERSALISM

No examination of the contemporary scene would be complete without considering developments in "post-modern" justice theory, of which the works of Michel Foucault and Jean-Francois Lyotard are especially illustrative. The chapter examines the problems with social constructivism and relativism for developing a theory of justice.

CHAPTER THIRTEEN: THE PUBLIC AND PRIVATE SPHERES

A crucial question in social philosophy is which kinds of human behaviors are appropriately considered part of the public political sphere at all. Many people believe that privacy itself is a political right, but beyond this, can we theorize about social philosophy in the realm of the private sphere? This seventh chapter will thus consider the ideas of privacy as a social value; the public protection of privacy; abuses of the private-public distinction; and critiques and rejoinders to the private-public distinction.

In this chapter, we also consider whether there can be compromises, combinations, bridges, or dialogues among some of the various theoretical options we have considered. This chapter explores ways in which such bridges might be possible by looking at mutual compatibilities. For example, liberalism and communitarianism become more commensurable when we consider the interrelatedness of communitarian, feminist, and classical liberal conceptions of the public-private relationship. Can communitarianism be reconciled with liberal justice thinking? There may be a crucial role to be played here by discourse ethics as a mediating principle.

We have quoted extensively from some of the political philosophers discussed in this book, and we are grateful to the publishers for their permission to do so. In particular, *To Empower People: The Role of Mediating Structures in Public Policy*, by Peter Berger and Richard Neuhaus, is quoted by permission of The American Enterprise Institute for Public Policy Research. Rita Manning's "Just Caring," from Eve Browning Cole and Susan Coultrap-McQuinn's *Exporations in Feminist Ethics*, is quoted with permission of University of Indiana Press. Drucilla Cornell's *At the Heart of Freedom* is quoted by permission from Princeton University Press. *The Structural Transformations of the Public Sphere*, by Jürgen Habermas, and Habermas' *Moral Consciousness and Communicative Action* are quoted through permission from the MIT Press. We also thank the University of Chicago Press for permission to quote extensively from Paul Ricoeur's *Oneself as Another*, and also Ricioeur's *The Just*. The University of Chicago Press also granted permission to quote Hannah Arendt's *The Human Condition*. Cambridge University Press allowed us to quote extensively from Michael Sandel's *Liberalism and the Limits of Justice*, and the University of Notre Dame Press was kind enough to allow us to quote from both Alasdair MacIntyre's *After Virtue* and MacIntyre's *Whose Justice? Which Rationality?*

Ralph D. Ellis
Atlanta, Georgia
January 9, 2006

Chapter One
Reopening Fundamental Questions

On September 11, 2001, terrorists bombed the World Trade Center and the Pentagon. Besides the extraordinary loss of property because of the bombing, they killed more than 3,000 people. The terrorists carefully targeted the buildings they bombed because they were symbols of American power and economic, military, and political dominance on the contemporary world stage. The act was politically motivated and had a political intention. If subsequent facts are correct, the act was intended not just to make a statement. It was calculated to damage the American economy and structure of national leadership.

The terrorists who carried out the bombings were a loose association of individuals united for a political purpose—to harm the United States, whom they regard as an enemy. They were not, however, carrying out the intention of any national government openly or covertly at war with the United States. The terrorists were not soldiers. Their actions were not associated with any nation state. Individually, they held citizenship in several different countries. Many of their countries of origin were U.S. allies or at least not hostile to the United States.

However, the terrorists did not act individually, but collectively through the encouragement and support of the *al-Qaida* network. This "network" sponsors terrorism throughout the world. It has an avowed policy to oppose the interests of the United States and its allies everywhere possible, using any means possible. *Al-Qaida*, the terrorists' sponsor, is not working for any nation state. As an organization, it was supported and sheltered in Afghanistan by a controlling government, the *Taliban*. While the *Taliban* controlled a significant area of Afghanistan, it did not control the whole country. Indeed, before September 11, only three countries recognized the *Taliban* as Afghanistan's "legitimate" government. After September 11, when it was clear that the *Taliban* was involved with the bombings, two of those countries withdrew their official recognition of the *Taliban*. Only one country, Pakistan, maintained its diplomatic ties because continued communication might contribute eventually to destroying *al-Qaida* and the *Taliban*.

The complicated facts and relationships in these events raise difficult and interesting social and political questions that many Americans have not thought about for a long time. What makes a state legitimate? What is the difference between being a terrorist and a soldier? What distinguishes criminal actions from justified political interests? The terrorists were not sponsored by any national interest, yet their actions were political. Should they be considered soldiers engaged in military action rather than terrorists? *Al-Qaida* has a political agenda that it has defined for itself. It enjoys considerable public support in the Muslim world. However, it is not a government nor an agent for any government. In spite of this, ought it to be considered a government agency if legitimate governments support its actions? These questions and others like them concern fundamental ideas about the meaning of legitimate political action and national identity. They also force us to think about what separates "legitimate" governments from armed bands, the nature of war versus police action against criminals, and the like.

Addressing such questions is not as simple as it seems at first. For example, what does it mean to say that a controlling faction is not the legitimate government of a country? May their actions be considered nonetheless as the acts of a legitimate government? More to the point, what criteria permit us to distinguish legitimate governments from regimes that are illegitimate? In Afghanistan, the *Taliban* controlled most of the country and exercised the functions of a government. However, internal warlords of other factions contested its control. Externally, only three countries recognized the *Taliban's* legitimacy. Thus, was *Taliban's* involvement with *al-Qaida* political or criminal? If *al-Qaida* were officially sponsored by the legitimate government of Afghanistan, would the bombings have been potentially justified acts of war rather than acts of terror?

Consider this scenario. Suppose a group of rebels engages in activities like bombing and hostage taking against their government. They are not officially supported by any government, but they have the unofficial support and cooperation of certain governments in whose interests they work. Are they terrorists, criminals, or government agents, and so in some sense soldiers? Would the fact that "sovereign" states sponsor their activities make their acts legitimate "acts of war" rather than "terrorism?" If it did, then one could argue that, since *al-Qaida* activities are condoned if not supported by some governments, they are acts of war and not terrorism.

The international community regards terrorist acts as criminal. Acts of war, under certain conditions, are military actions. Different standards regulate each. For example, if terrorist acts are acts of war, then "combatants" are governed under the articles of the Geneva Convention. If the acts are criminal, then national criminal codes cover them. So, the question stands, why should the acts of those associated with a network like *al-Qaida* be regarded as criminal rather than military? The difficulty in answering this question lies in determining what distinguishes the acts of the terrorists supported by *al-Qaida,* sponsored the *Taliban,* from legitimate military actions.

It does not seem sufficient to say that one group was the aggressor while the other was "only defending itself." This move does not adequately clarify the meaning of these ideas. For example, the terrorist group may insist that it is only defending itself against past imperialist aggressions by the official government against which they fight. This claim to legitimate self-defense may include previous wars or threats, in which it was debatable who was really the aggressor.

Similarly, it is really not adequate to try to define "terrorism" as criminal rather than military simply because it targets innocent civilians. Historically, armies have targeted an enemy's civilian population. For example, President Truman effectively ended World War II against Japan by dropping atomic bombs whose intended targets were two large cities full of civilians. Most people, even those who disagree with Truman's decision to drop the atomic bombs, would not say Truman was a "terrorist" in the same sense that members of the *al-Qaida* network are called "terrorists." *Al-Qaida* terrorists are considered essentially an international crime syndicate, not a nation engaging in legitimate warfare. One might object that Americans in 1776 used violent means to revolt against their Royal British governors. However, few people would consider this revolution an act of terrorism. Instead, many would say that it was a legitimate dispute over who should be the rightful government in the Americas.

Simply citing the facts cannot answer these questions and others like them. The underlying problems driving them are conceptual, not factual. Indeed, the concepts that objectify human experience of social and political relations are among the most basic and fundamental concepts we use to think about our relationships to others as individuals and communities of individuals. This is to say that they are philosophical questions. One does not answer philosophical questions by citing empirical facts of the particular cases. The mere fact that the U.S. is "only defending itself," even if true, is not the relevant criterion by which to decide that the opposing fighters are terrorists while the U.S. is a legitimate government. Nor is the fact that *al-Qaida* purposely targets innocent civilians, since the U.S. did that too, in Hiroshima and Nagasaki.

What we require is a more careful analysis of the ideas involved in thinking about the issues. This rethinking involves a careful examination of basic, fundamental questions in three areas. First, there are *moral* questions that address what ought to be done, by governments or anyone else. Second, there are *ontological* questions that concern the way reality is. Third, there are *epistemological* questions concerning how we know what we think we know or believe. These more basic questions are among the philosophical ones with which social and political philosophy concerns itself. Let us see how this occurs with a short introduction to the discourse of social and political philosophy related to the questions raised above.

1. The Concept of Social Contract

How can the potentially coercive power of government be justified or legitimated? This is one of the most fundamental problems of social philosophy. For most of human history, governments were justified as sanctioned or created by the gods or God. Human social and political orders were mirrors of a divine-sacred order. The power of the sovereign was derived from the power and authority of God. However, the consensus among modern thinkers is that the consent of the governed is what makes governments legitimate. Yet not everyone would consent to everything their government does, if given a choice. In fact, it is difficult to think of any governmental policy with which every single citizen would agree.

Contractarians—those who believe that government is justified only by a social contract—argue that people show this consent in two ways. One is through an implied or explicit "social contract," by which each person agrees with every other to the principles of government. Second, there is a political process through which each person participates in the making and enacting of laws for the common good. The second of these two points, the requirement for political participation, is an extension of the first. On a contractarian account of government and law, the social contract decisively separates people from a *state of nature*—a state without law—by binding people together into a civil society under law.

At the time of the *al Qaida* bombings of 2001, the idea of a *social contract* theory of government was out of fashion in many circles of social and political philosophy (see Lessnoff 1986). There seemed to be two reasons why this was true. First, social contract theory seems to have difficulty justifying its philosophical arguments with complete adequacy. Second, social contract theory did not seem relevant to the kinds of social and political problems that most thinkers were focusing on in the "post-modern" world. However, when the war began, the question of the difference between a social contract and a "state of nature" suddenly loomed large.

A "social contract" is taken to mean that the government operates not only with the consent of the governed, but also according to principles to which any reasonable citizen *would have* been willing to contractually consent, *if* there had been an explicit choice. Social contract theorists call this requirement for a legitimate social contract the principle of *tacit consent*. Even though there was no specific time at which any of us explicitly consented to be ruled by our government, we can be said to have "tacitly consented" if it can be shown that any reasonable person *would have* consented, given a choice.

For example, any reasonable citizen would want protection against being murdered. So if there had been an actual point in time when all of the parties worked out and negotiated a social contract, anyone presumably would have wanted a law against murder to be part of the contract. Moreover, they would have wanted the government to enforce such a law. Thus there would also be a tacit agreement that citizens would pay taxes to support police and a legal system in exchange for the resulting protection.

Analogously, a social contract theorist might argue that any reasonable person with an equal bargaining position would want certain *political rights* guaranteed by government. The reason is that a guarantee of such political rights would be better from each bargainer's point of view than to be continually in danger of losing them. These rights might include the right to vote and the right to a fair trial if accused of crimes. Such political rights are needed in order to protect us from losing the power to negotiate fairly with respect to any of our other rights.

By contrast, a reasonable person given a fair bargaining position would have been very reluctant to agree to enter a contract that allowed the government to burn witches or to dictate people's religious beliefs. In such a bargaining position, the individual would have had nothing tangible to gain by allowing the state to have these kinds of powers. Also, they might have much to lose if they should find themselves victimized by a government with too many powers over the lives of its citizens. Most social contract theorists will therefore conclude that governmental powers that are not needed in order to benefit anyone—such as the power to burn witches or dictate religious beliefs—can never be a part of any legitimate social contract.

We shall see later that social contract theory is not as simple as this example suggests. It is also open to several different kinds of objections. The point for now is that the kind of political theory that the U.S. government believes it represents includes a heavy component of "liberal" social contract thinking. "Liberal" here means giving priority to "liberties," or freedoms (see Sandel 1982).

This view contrasts sharply with the kind of government envisioned as the ideal by the *Taliban* in Afghanistan. They advocated government power to regulate personal beliefs and behavior based on religious doctrine. Accordingly, they prevented women from working or getting an education, required men to wear beards, and even supported international terrorists in the killing of innocent civilians. While some early social contract theorists, like Thomas Hobbes (1968), argued that the government ought to have the power to regulate religious beliefs, later contract theorists did not. They believed that such government powers were unjustified, because it would not be in the interest of the parties to a social contract to allow the government to have such absolute powers.

Contractarian thinkers often contrast the idea of a social contract against the notion of a *state of nature*. A state of nature exists, on this account, where there is no accepted government based on consent to a social contract that provides the justification for authority to act. Each person does whatever he or she has the power to do. Thus a powerful person could steal others' property, or kill them, or demand that they pay "protection money" in exchange for allowing them to continue in their lives free of this harassment. The powerful person's justification would be simply the power to act in this way. Similarly, if an overbearing majority wanted to enslave a small group, and had the power to do so, there would be nothing to prevent them from doing so. The small group would be subject to the power of the large or more powerful.

According to social contract theories, a government based merely on the power of terrorists and the armies of "illegitimate governments" would not be a social contract. Having power and the means to enforce it is not sufficient justification for being a state or government. Indeed, the actions of such a "government" would be more similar to a case of thugs imposing their will in a state of nature than to a contract. Similarly, most contract theorists would not consider a *theocracy* to be a legitimate government. A theocracy is not a state of nature. However, it is still illegitimate, according to contract theory, because it would allow the government to have powers—for example, punishing people for engaging in certain religious practices—that cannot be justified in terms that would have been acceptable to rational parties to a social contract, if each enjoyed a fair bargaining position in the working out of the contract (Beccaria 1963; Gutman 1986). Here again, such bargainers presumably would have nothing to gain by allowing the government to have such powers over them, and much to lose if they should end up on the wrong side of the government's religious rules.

Limitations of social contract thinking, and communitarian alternatives. Social and political philosophy, when taken seriously, forces us to think carefully about these kinds of concepts and assertions. Half the world's political systems allow the government to exercise powers, such as the power to regulate religious practices, that parties to a social contract probably would not consent to, on most interpretations of the theory. Moreover, the social contract concept itself is not as clear as it might at first appear. Muslim governments insist that it is in the interest of their people to have their religious practices regulated (Ibn Khaldun 1969). Regulation of religious beliefs and practices reinforces membership in the religious community. Membership in a strong religious community is a personal and communal value. Without a strong religious community, a single individual loses his or her sense of direction and purpose in life. Without direction, an individual is not as positive a contributor to the community. The resulting *anomie* and social dislocation affect the lives of others in the community. Thus, it is in the interest of all members of the community to allow the government to have this power.

Such an approach to government—where the community determines some of the moral beliefs and practices of individuals in the community—is an example of a *communitarian* approach to social organization (see Brightman 1945; Gutman 1986; Sandel 1982, 1984). In many Muslim countries, for example, a religious vision controls the view of the good life as one of harmony and salvation. Submission to the divine will as revealed in the *Qu'ran* and the intricacies of divine law are the basis of social order. In this framework, people believe that the community has a responsibility to foster harmonious behavioral tendencies for its members. Thus, they expect the community through its religious leaders to intervene in many different ways in people's daily lives.

A government may not necessarily have to resort to brainwashing or propaganda to achieve communitarian results. These results may also be achieved simply by allowing the government to financially support institutions that help people's self-development. Even in the U.S., there are many examples of communitarian policies, especially in relation to children: the government plays a role in educating children, trying to ensure that they are in the care of fit parents, providing child care facilities and welfare benefits, and even encouraging young people not to use harmful drugs, drink, or smoke cigarettes. Even government-sponsored TV ads encourage adults to use condoms to protect themselves against sexually transmitted diseases, to avoid using harmful drugs, or to eat a healthy diet. Authorities try to rehabilitate criminals when possible, and one of the purposes of government welfare assistance is to steer people in desperate financial straits away from crime (Ellis and Ellis 1989). So even the U.S. government is not completely based on a social contract, since it too includes some of these communitarian powers on the part of the government. Thus, some notions of community and community values are not inconsistent with a contractarian view of government.

In addition, there are serious questions as to whether a government *should* be a social contract type of government in the first place. Given a choice, many young men who were forced to fight in the Viet Nam war would not have chosen for their government to decide to wage war in the ways that such decisions are made in the United States. Likewise, they would not have agreed to risk their lives based on the decisions made by these types of procedures. For example, they might not have agreed that the Secretary of Defense should be allowed to make tactical military decisions against the advice of his own generals; or that the legislature should be able to authorize the President to make war just because a majority of their constituents (who are not in the draftable age group) support the war. Many argued that a majority of people supported the war in the early years only because so many citizens were ignorant of the facts. Complete information was purposely suppressed by the government. So consent for the war was in some measure secured based on distorted information. Yet a social contract theory would presumably insist that some such decision-making procedure *would have* won the tacit consent of any rational bargainer, if given a real choice. So it is questionable whether the government's power could ever, in real practice, be justified by a true social contract as defined by the theory.

In theory, a social contract requires obedience to the law. Such obedience is justified based on the assumption that, if given a real choice in the original bargaining position, citizens would agree at least to the political procedures by which those laws are made. Likewise, it is assumed that people would also consent to the government's power to enforce them once they are made. Not only are these assumptions questionable in the case of many laws; there is a further problem: to say that the government should conform to the shape of a social contract type of political system is to make a value assumption. It is to affirm that this type of government, all things considered, is the best type of government.

Part of the problem here is that if the governmental principles are limited only to those principles that every bargainer to the social contract would have supported, then the government's powers seem too limited to ensure justice in concrete policy matters. For example, it may be that not everyone in the original bargaining position would have agreed to give the government the power to collect taxes in order to create public parks, or to strictly regulate industrial pollution, or to provide health care for everyone, or to distribute generous welfare benefits to the needy.

This question raises the further question whether such a minimal government is really preferable to some other kind of government that perhaps would have still further powers. It is questionable, for example, whether a social contract would require that the government provide services to help minorities overcome discrimination if most of the voters, purely out of self-interest, do not support it. We could raise similar questions regarding welfare programs, unemployment compensation policies, and other "liberal" social programs. While most social contract theories would allow that a majority can vote for such programs it they want to, they would not necessarily require that there be such programs.

Moreover, these liberal programs would actually conflict with basic rights that social contract theorists assume are very important to the original bargainers. For example, property rights must be restricted if governments are to collect the taxes to support the programs, yet property is usually considered to be an important type of right that should be protected by a social contract system.

What our short discussion up to this point seems to show is that social and political philosophy cannot get off the ground without opening a discussion of basic value questions, which traditionally are the concern of ethics and moral philosophy. What are the requirements for a "justification" of any social practice? How do we decide whether a government ought to give priority to respecting individual rights over the value of doing whatever benefits a majority—even if the majority wish? For example, could a majority deny religious freedom to a minority? What happens if a vast majority of the people favor slavery, or wish to respect the right of employers to discriminate against minority groups? What if the majority favor legalized abortion, while a minority believe that abortion is murder? Would the situation be different if those opposed to abortion were in the majority? Or would this make no difference, just as it would make no difference whether those who favor slavery are in the majority or the minority? Here we confront a very basic "should" question: In what types of cases should the majority have the power to decide what should be done?

2. The Value Assumptions of Social and Political Action

Examining value assumptions. A major part of social and political philosophy consists of carefully considering basic "should" or "ought" questions. Dealing with basic value questions requires thinking about ethical theory. The rational inquiry into the nature and justification of value beliefs, as in any other area of philosophy, begins when the necessity for choice challenges those beliefs.

We may find ourselves in the position of having our fundamental beliefs challenged for several reasons. First, we may confront a situation that brings two or more of our fundamental beliefs into conflict with each other. For example, confronted with the decision whether to participate in a plot to assassinate Hitler during World War II to save millions of Jews from genocide, some conscientious Germans became persuaded that one should choose the course of action that produces the most desirable consequences. Thus, they chose to save the lives of the Jews, although to do so they had to violate the rule against murder and the normal constraint against taking the law into one's own hands. In the thinking of many, the notion that Hitler was an immoral person who deserved to be punished was not the relevant consideration. They were not engaging in the assassination plot for the purpose of punishing Hitler, but simply because removing him from power would have overwhelmingly beneficial consequences for humanity. Thus the action was judged purely by the *consequences* it produced, or was expected to produce. Most people would be reluctant to encourage ordinary citizens to take the law into their own hands to decide for themselves who ought to be assassinated, even in cases where it would be broadly beneficial to do so. However, in the case of Hitler, the decision seemed justified to many because of the number of death camp victims whom they could have saved.

But the question must be considered: do potential positive consequences justify defying the law? In a more difficult case, on April 8, 2003, Iraqi soldiers allegedly fired on U.S. troops from the al-Rasheed Hotel in Baghdad. The only way the Americans could stop the Iraqis from firing (if we are to believe the U.S. news accounts of the incident) was to fire heavy artillery at the hotel, resulting in the deaths of several journalists, who were already known to be operating in the hotel. Part of the justification of the decision to fire the artillery was that, if the Americans held their fire, the Iraqis would continue to fire from the hotel as well as from other civilian areas, confident that the Americans would not shoot back. So the reasoning was that firing the artillery would save more lives in the long run than it would destroy. To make a decision on this basis is to assume that actions should be judged in terms of whether the total consequences they produce are more beneficial or harmful in the final analysis. But the question is troubling to some: do such actions reflect the right kind of justification?

Someone using a purely *utilitarian* framework of moral reasoning might answer "yes," based on the utilitarian belief that one should choose the action that produces the best consequences in the given circumstances, rather than obeying a set of rules presumed to be valid no matter what the consequences. Utilitarians usually define the value of consequences in terms of how beneficial for people the results are likely to be, on the whole and in the long run. For some of those who participate in such decisions, however (for example, the theologian Dietrich Bonhoffer participated in a plot to assassinate Hitler), the decision is not so easy. Some also believe in other values, such as justice, obedience to laws, and the procedural issue of whether ordinary citizens are justified in doing whatever they like if they believe it to be beneficial.

President Truman, in his decision to use the atomic bomb to end World War II, also used the utilitarian principle of judging actions by their consequences. In his view, using the bomb was likely to save more lives in the long run than it would destroy, even though it involved purposely killing civilians. In spite of the common sense appeal of this utilitarian principle, problems begin to surface when we realize that essentially the same reasoning can be used to support the murderous activities of many terrorist organizations such as *Islamic Jihad* and *Hisballah* in the Middle East and elsewhere. These organizations, like those who attempted to assassinate Hitler, think that the deaths resulting from their acts will ultimately produce good consequences. These good consequences will outweigh the harm and the undesirability of the deaths of innocent people. Such consequences include relieving millions from starvation, misery and political tyranny in exchange for the death of a few. The terrorist challenges us to consider, for example, the number of deaths that occur each year among Palestinian and Afghani refugees because of inadequate medical facilities, poor nutrition, and generally impoverished conditions. These conditions exist, in their view, because of American foreign policies that allow Israel to drive Palestinians from their own land and which destabilized the government of Afghanistan in the 1990s. If they can save a large number from suffering through a few well-chosen killings, they may ask, then how can any clear-thinking utilitarian disapprove of the killings?

If the only criterion for such decisions is the utilitarian one of assessing consequences, then the actions of terrorists would seem to be just as justifiable, in principle, as those of Truman or of those who attempted to assassinate Hitler. The fact that Hitler was an evil person or merited punishment would not affect the decision process involved. If actions are to be judged by their consequences, then such considerations would seem to be irrelevant. On this view, even the punishment of ordinary criminals should be determined by the beneficial consequences produced by the deterrent effect of the punishment. However, in order to deter crime, the police must maintain high conviction rates, and this goal in turn often leads to making out-of-court deals and other such practices that result in distributive unfairness in the treatment of comparable offenders. All such examples highlight the crucial question: Can an action or policy be justified by its consequences?

Utility *versus* rights. What we see when we compare life experiences like the German situation during World War II and the contemporary situation involving terrorism is an ethical dilemma of the most fundamental kind. Should we decide what to do in a given situation based on which action might produce the most desirable consequences in the long run? Or are there certain rules of conduct that no one has the *right* to disobey for *any* reason, despite the overall consequences of that disobedience? Rights-talk is extraordinarily slippery. However, we usually define "rights" as rules of conduct that not only are beneficial for people, but also must not be violated even if doing so would benefit people more. For example, I may claim to have a "right" to free medical care. However, it is fair to question whether others have a duty to respond to my claim, even though receiving the free medical care would obviously benefit me. To say that I have a right to something is to assert more than simply that it would benefit me. In some sense, it is often believed that respecting rights is more important or mandatory than providing other kinds of benefits to people. The catch phrase is that rights in some sense tend to "trump" other kinds of benefits.

Does a political tyrant have a moral right not to be murdered, even if his murder might produce good consequences so extensive as to outweigh the life or death of one individual? Both alternatives seem to have their philosophical problems. If we choose utilitarianism, then terrorism seems defensible, at least in principle. On the other hand, if we choose against utilitarianism, then we seem committed to the strange position that it is sometimes all right to commit an action even if we know that it is going to produce disastrous consequences. This would be the case, for example, were one to allow Hitler to continue exterminating the Jews in order to respect his right not to be assassinated.

Moral conflict and absence of moral consensus. Another way people sometimes find themselves in the position of having to justify or defend their value beliefs occurs when the members of one culture develop a sophisticated knowledge about the variety of attitudes and lifestyles cherished by other cultures and subcultures. The diverse philosophical landscape of ancient Greece provides a good example. Ancient Greek cities were heavily involved in geographically extensive trading and military operations. As a result, they encountered a variety of cultural traditions very different from their own. This fact occasioned a lively debate about values and the meaning of ethics in Greek society. Indeed, one might make a case that the cosmopolitan and pluralistic nature of Greek society, together with its democratic political institutions that made the public debate of crucial issues popular, was one of the chief factors to promote the open-mindedness and radical reexamination of attitudes and beliefs for which the most famous of the Greek philosophers are noted.

For many Ancient Greek thinkers and citizens, the shock of discovering that different cultures had different ethical norms was so great that it led them to regard all ethical norms as only expressions of social conventions and customs. In other words, some Greeks doubted that values and ethical norms had any objective validity. Such a view was especially popular among the Greek Sophists, such as Lycophron and Protagoras. In our own time, some cultural anthropologists like Ruth Benedict (1958), William Sumner (1909/2002), and Edward Westermarck (1932), as well as logical-empiricist philosophers like A.J. Ayer (1936), have championed a similar view. This view can generally be called *ethical relativism.* Ethical relativism is the philosophical belief that, in principle, there is no objective validity to any basic ethical proposition. Indeed, in the view of ethical relativists, such beliefs are not really "beliefs" in the strict sense at all, because their contents are not really propositions about reality. Rather, they are expressions of the emotional preferences and customary attitudes that people are psychologically conditioned to adopt as they grow up in their particular culture.

Thus, according to ethical relativism, different cultures will make different basic assumptions about value issues. Consequently, there is no objective criterion that could make it possible to regard one value assumption as rationally more defensible than the others. A.J. Ayer, the well-known logical-empiricist philosopher, called his version of this view *emotivism,* because of his stress on the emotional character of value commitments. It was based on his epistemological assumption that the only sources of verifiable truth are deductive logic and empirical-scientific evidence, hence the term *logical empiricism.* On this account, neither deductive logic nor empirical evidence can be used to verify the objective truth of any value feeling. This assumption is an *epistemological* one—involving how we can know or verify different kinds of knowledge and belief. So political philosophy must clearly examine epistemological assumptions as well as ethical ones.

In essence, many Ancient Greek philosophers, such as Lycophron, championed ethical and epistemological relativism because of their knowledge of the variety of value systems in the different cultures about which they were knowledgeable (see Aristotle 1974, 119). Many of them believed also that human nature is essentially *hedonistic* and *egoistic.* Egoistic hedonism affirms that, ultimately, people value only their own happiness, and thus that the value beliefs they advocate are really only an indirect means of trying to attain as much happiness as possible.

Socrates, Plato and Aristotle devoted a great deal of philosophical effort toward refuting ethical relativism and egoistic hedonism. These philosophers believed that such beliefs were corrupting the leadership of Greek society and undermining the value-theoretic underpinnings necessary for a good political theory that in turn could provide the basis for a good government. We shall return to this issue below.

While relativism and egoism may result from the shock of encountering societies with vastly different ethical norms from our own, another consequence is that genuine philosophical thinking occurs. Such philosophical thinking helps further clarify the rational basis of ethical beliefs. Socrates, Plato and Aristotle exemplify this response to the challenge of culture shock. Rather than throwing up their arms and saying "It's all arbitrary," or "One person's opinion is as good as another's," these thinkers met the challenge by settling down to the hard work of weighing different theories against each other in terms of their comparative rational justification.

Questioning assumptions in changing times. A similar challenge for rethinking basic assumptions occurs when a political or economic situation changes so much that older value systems no longer seem to make as much sense as they once did. For instance, in nineteenth-century America, government intervention in the affairs of the business community not only appeared unnecessary in most people's opinion, but was actually considered a violation of the basic political and moral rights of businessmen. Today, such a generous notion of "rights" as including freedom by entrepreneurs to form trusts, cartels and monopolies, to fix prices, or to falsely advertize their products, no longer appears to make sense even to the most conservative of economic and political analysts. New experiences, resulting from the complexities of modern economic realities, forced people to reexamine their thinking on the "rights" of big business owners and operators. For example, in the early part of this century people discovered that monopolies, such as those common in the railroad and oil industries, diminished competition and artificially raised prices by manipulating scarcity. Because of this, a basic assumption—that government regulation of business is unthinkable—moved aside in favor of such legislations as the Sherman Anti-Trust Act.

A similar type of controversy occurred when the World Health Organization (WHO) in 1983 reported that the sale of infant formula to mothers in Third World countries caused as many as a million infant deaths per year (*Atlanta Constitution,* May 22, 1981, 10-B). American-based food companies, the WHO reported, gave mothers a few weeks' supply of the formula as a free sample. The free sample lasted just long enough for a mother's natural milk to dry up. By then, the mother was dependent on the infant formula. However, many mothers were not able to buy enough of the formula to support the child's life. The result was the death of many children due to malnutrition or because mothers mixed the formula with unclean drinking water. The WHO proposed that the United Nations do something to prevent this knowing exploitation by the food companies. President Reagan dissented from the almost unanimous opinion of world leaders on the issue. Reagan did not deny that the formulas were responsible for the deaths, which could perhaps legitimately have been questioned. Rather, he justified his refusal to support action against the food companies by appealing to the right of businesses to engage in "free trade." Thus he argued that companies ought to be free to continue their practices. Here, ethical issues joined factual and political issues to yield a decision and a justification of that decision.

In fact, political issues more often than not hinge upon more basic, underlying ethical questions. Politicians may try to make the issues appear factual. This is possible because their ethical presuppositions are usually implicit rather than explicit. Implicit presuppositions are more difficult to criticize. Therefore, they are safer for those who hold them, and often lend themselves more naturally to effective rhetoric than do explicit value assumptions, precisely because they remain beneath the surface, functioning as "hidden persuaders." If these presuppositions were more often brought out into the open, as they are in philosophical discourse, then the listener would feel invited to question their validity. Unfortunately, this is the last thing many political orators would want to happen. They therefore tend to shift the focus to the relevant factual controversies and away from the basic ethical ones.

At the same time, successful politicians, like successful business leaders, are aware of the importance of appearing to be morally upright in their practices. If for no other reason than this, they are therefore keenly concerned about ethical issues. This is an important point. Many people in recent years have become convinced that the study of the philosophical foundations of political and ethical beliefs is irrelevant to "real life" as far as business and political practices are concerned. What difference does it make, they may ask, whether the dealings of a multinational corporation in a Third World country are ethical or not? What corporations will do in such situations, like what governments will do to limit them, depends not on ethics, but rather on purely economic motives in conjunction with the power of the corporation or government to get away with whatever means it chooses toward the attainment of its economic ends. Similarly, they reason, politics is merely a game of power in which the stronger political entity uses its economic and military bargaining position to whatever advantage it can. Some Marxists, though not all, go as far as to claim that the entire concept of ethics is only a camouflage, a smoke screen to make the purely egoistic motives of the ruling class seem justifiable in the eyes of the very people they exploit (see Kamenka 1969).

This cynical view is short-sighted, for at least two reasons. First, the very fact that politicians and business people want to appear morally justified in their actions is an indication of the power that people's ethical beliefs have to influence or even control what happens in the "real world" of power politics and economic wheeling and dealing. Whether politicians are genuine or not in their ethical beliefs (and there are reasons to believe that they often are), they realize the necessity of convincing their constituents of the validity of these beliefs, even if they may more often do so through rhetoric than reason.

One frequently hears the argument, for example, that multinational corporations stimulate the economies of Third World countries. It is convenient for American-based corporations to make this argument, or even believe that it is true, since their activities in the Third World seem more morally justifiable. Both the ethical and the factual assumptions needed for this conclusion may be self-deceptive. The evidence may be subject to interpretation, which in turn is subject to bias. For instance, many studies suggest that the presence of multinational corporations in less-developed countries actually more often retards economic growth than accelerates it. It diverts capital investment away from the host country, since the investments are then channeled into foreign-owned companies, thus de-capitalizing the host country's own business and industrial enterprises. So it is often the case that the presence of the multinational is accompanied by a decrease in the average real income in the country (Bornschier 1981). Yet American business people with overseas interests may deceive themselves into thinking that their activities are beneficial when often they are not in reality.

There is a second and perhaps more fundamental reason for the short-sightedness of the cynical view that the philosophical legitimacy of value assumptions is irrelevant. It is logically impossible to hold a political-policy opinion without basing the opinion on one or more ethical presuppositions. A *policy*, we must remember, is among other things a resolution to act in certain ways. As such, a policy is valid only to the extent that the results of the action are considered either more worthwhile than the results of acting differently, or else the action itself is considered more worthwhile than any of the alternative actions. Either way, ethical assumptions, that is, assumptions about what kinds of things are more worthwhile than others, and in what contexts and circumstances, and for what reasons, are needed to support the policy position.

Ethical analysis alone, however, is not sufficient. Every policy belief also presupposes factual beliefs. For example, a policy that encourages multinational corporation expansion in the Third World, on the assumption that the multinational and the host countries will mutually benefit, is sound only if it is in fact true that the host country will benefit. This can be determined only through rigorous, empirical-scientific research following the methodological procedures deemed adequate in terms of the generally accepted logic of scientific research. The more the results of the factual inquiry are relevant to ethical and policy issues, the greater will be the danger that the researchers may become either purposely or unconsciously sloppy in their data-gathering procedures or in the way they draw inferences from data because of a bias or prejudice in favor of a particular outcome. In such cases, then, one must insist on the most scrupulously rigorous scientific methodology.

Every philosophy student is well aware that public debate too often yields to the temptation to "cheat" on the rules of good scientific reasoning, especially when presenting views to a scientifically unsophisticated audience. For example, a political candidate asserts that the economy got worse during the opposing party's term of office, or after the implementation of some tax bill with which the candidate disagrees. The speaker uses this evidence to claim that the opposing party's policies or the tax bill in question *caused* the economic downturn. This rhetorical device is a classic instance of the *false cause fallacy*. The fact that one event follows another one, or is concurrent with it, is never enough to establish any probability that there is a cause and effect relationship between the two events. Yet speakers who know better often use this ploy, many times with no awareness that they are guilty of such a fallacy. This tendency to self deception, which can lead to harmfully illogical ways of arguing in the public arena, underscores the importance of social and political discourse. The times when the stakes are highest are the times we most often allow our emotions to take control and rationality is diminished.

A policy position, then, depends on both factual and ethical assumptions. To neglect the critical examination of either type of assumption runs the risk of acting according to a philosophically unjustifiable policy. Whether the policy is philosophically justifiable or not is relevant because public opinion, which is based on both factual and ethical assumptions, affects the policies of politicians and business people. Likewise, the more democratic a society becomes, the more important it is that citizens teach themselves to be skillful in the critical evaluation of the rational justification of ethical and social-scientific beliefs.

Honesty and philosophical analysis. Another factor that often forces us to reexamine our philosophical thinking is the realization that many people seem dishonest in their philosophical views. We all have a tendency to be tempted toward championing just those moral principles that (1) allow us to pat ourselves on the back in smug moral complacence while condemning the behavior of others, or (2) allow us to pursue our own gain. An example of (1) is the attitude of the "self-made man" who believes that everyone has a moral obligation to "pull themselves by their bootstraps" with no help from others. It is convenient for the wealthy person to think of earning great wealth as a moral virtue, and to hold those who cannot as blameworthy. This view makes the wealthy person virtuous and provides self-congratulatory justification for his or her own good fortune.

An example of (2) is the senator who believes in the right of large corporations with vital political interests to make large campaign contributions to senators. As the beneficiary of the contribution, naturally, it is easy for the senator to believe in the moral rightness of such contributions. The use of moral rationalization to justify for self-interest is probably as old as the human race.

Of course, the fact that a principle works to the benefit of its proponent is not sufficient evidence that the principle is false. Someone's belief that stealing is wrong does not become false just because that person benefits by preventing other people from stealing his or her property. Yet almost everyone can think of instances in which the self-deceptive moral maneuvers of a morally self-righteous person were obvious to everyone but the self-righteous person him- or herself.

Indeed, examples of the happy coincidence between political policy beliefs and thinly-disguised self interest, or between political policy beliefs and self-congratulation, suggest themselves so obviously that it is only natural to ask ourselves whether our own value structures are free of intellectual dishonesty of a similar origin. To answer this question, we must ask about the rational justification for the beliefs in question. We then discover that such an inquiry is both important and difficult. The urgency of resolving it is perhaps matched only by the dangers of resolving it incorrectly.

Chapter Two
Politics and Value Theory:
A Complex Relationship

It is a fact of human existence that there are many different value systems. Does the variety of attitudes and value systems among the world's diverse people mean ethical relativism follows? Ethical relativists, of which there are many types, affirm that there is no objective truth to sort out differences of moral beliefs and values. Each person's or group's values and moral beliefs are "as good" or "as true" as another's. Thus, in the view of relativists, what is valuable, right and wrong, is determined by one's preferences or the beliefs of a group. There is no objective standard to affirm that one value is better than another or that one moral belief is true and another false. Actions can be right or wrong only relative to the customs and traditions of the group—hence the name "relativism" for this viewpoint.

Relativism and recognition of *cultural pluralism*—the diversity of moral points of view associated with different cultural traditions—often seem to go hand in hand. This does not mean, however, that one of the most basic social and political problems disappears. How are people who hold a diversity of values and moral beliefs going to live together? The events of September 11 are an extreme example of value conflict and the importance of value pluralism.

One solution to the problem is the "rule of the majority." For some Ancient Greek relativists, such as Lycophron, ethical relativism went hand in hand with a simple majority rule sort of democracy (see Aristotle 1974). Let the majority decide, they would say. Since a true ethical relativist believes that there is no objective truth regarding basic value assumptions—including concepts of fairness and individual rights—a relativist position seems to imply that moral values are only emotions or cultural conventions.

Problems with simple majoritarianism. Why did Lycophron and other relativists think that relativism entails majoritarian democracy? The simple answer is *value pluralism*. If values are only social conventions, then what causes the conventions to be adopted in the first place? What causes a culture to adopt one convention rather than another? Why, for example, do people in the Southern U.S. usually disapprove of public nudity, while people in certain South American tribes, where the weather is scarcely any hotter, routinely go naked? What is the cause of these conventions?

Since relativism holds that the conventions cannot be based on any objective ethical standard, many relativists explain the evolution of the conventions by positing that *mutual self-interest* is the basis of moral standards. For example, each person wants to prevent others from murdering him or her, so we all agree to condemn and punish murderers. In other words, all we mean by "Murder is wrong" is that this community agrees that murder is not something we are willing for people to do. Why do we want to prevent murder? Not out of altruism, but from selfishness. Why do we disapprove of nudity? Perhaps out of self-interest: people do not like for others to see *their own* wives and husbands naked.

But who decides what the conventions and customs in a society are going to be? Presumably, the majority. Therefore, the majority should rule. According to relativism, there is no ethical standard beyond the interests and preferences of the majority that establish whose concept of "right" should be applied. This idea that "right" is determined by or justified by the will of the majority has been an attractive one in Western culture. Social convention seems to be a powerful formative influence on our ideas of what is right and wrong. But this position has the interesting consequence that thinking about "rights" is also determined by the majority. On the view of a relativist, even beliefs about *inalienable rights* (i.e., rights that should not be alienated from a person unless they conflict with the more important rights of others) are only social conventions.

This view seems to lead to a *simple majoritarianism*—that is, a simple majority rule concept of democracy. The will of the majority is the basis of all the "rules" of the social and political institutions. However, there is a problem with this view. In the absence of any moral constraints beyond the preferences of the majority, there are no principles to limit the power of a potentially *overbearing majority*. Aristotle's criticism of this notion of democracy was very concise. In his *Politics* he argued that according to this idea it would not be wrong for the majority to enslave the minority (Aristotle 1974, 119). Time proved Aristotle correct. In some of the earliest experiments with democracy, including the U.S. system, slavery was a social fact justified as the will, if not the obligation, of the majority.

Arguments against ethical relativism. It is important to realize that there are serious logical errors in the justifications usually offered by ethical relativism for its central thesis that there is no objective truth about value issues. The relativist position is based essentially on two general kinds of assumptions. First, cultures disagree with each other about what is right and wrong. Second, there is no way to prove beyond doubt that any given ethical belief is correct. The first claim is factually true, at least to a great extent, but it is not true in all cases, and thus cannot ground the conclusion that there are *no* objectively true value statements. The second assumption is logically problematic in an important way that warrants careful attention.

Logic cannot prove an ethical statement, the relativists argue, because it is possible to deny any given "ought" statement without contradicting oneself. Furthermore, empirical evidence cannot prove an ethical statement, because a description of a state of affairs is never equivalent in meaning to a statement about what ought to be done about a state of affairs. For example, from the *fact* that some people own weapons and believe that they have a "right" to own them, it does not follow that one *ought* to own weapons or *has a right* to do so. So, if ethical statements cannot be deduced from empirical evidence, nor can they be proven by means of pure logic alone, then ethical relativists conclude that there is no way to prove any ethical statement as having more objective truth than any other.

Nevertheless, ethical relativism in its true and complete sense does not follow from either of these two arguments. The fact that different cultures disagree on value issues does not show that there is no objective truth about any value issues. In the first place, as Ralph Linton (1954) has noted, even if different cultures disagreed on all of the specific rules of conduct, they still might agree on certain very general values that the many disparate systems of rules of conduct are meant to promote. For example, a culture that practices human sacrifice may not seem to accept the basic value of human life. However, closer examination shows that such cultures do value human life. The "value" of a life is what makes it an object worthy of sacrifice. Moreover, under most circumstances, such cultures act to protect life. When they sacrifice life, it is only for the sake of what they believe to be a greater good. It does not follow that they do not value life. At least one of the value beliefs relevant here is accepted by all cultures: the belief that human life has value unless overridden by a more important value—that is, that human life has *"prima facie" value.*

Secondly, and perhaps more important, even if the majority of people in a society believe something, it still might be objectively incorrect. For example, most people in Western Europe once believed that the sun went around the earth. This did not mean that the belief was true. The sun's relation to the earth is what it is regardless of our beliefs. More careful science eventually corrected the mistake. Likewise, there was a time when the majority of people in the U.S. believed in segregation and unequal treatment for Blacks. This did not mean that the moral belief was true. Greater moral refinement eventually corrected that mistake too. In neither case can one conclude that people's beliefs erased the truth about the situation.

Nor does the assumption that no ethical principle can be proven necessarily imply that there are no objectively true ethical principles, as opposed to mere subjective emotions or social conventions. There are many scientific theories that have not been absolutely proven. In spite of that, we believe them to be true with a moderate degree of certainty. We even risk our lives based on them. We believe them and act by them because they make more sense than other theories we have come up with. Similarly, many ethicists insist that an ethical theory need not be proven conclusively. It only needs to be shown that it makes more sense to believe in one moral perspective than another. In other words, it makes more sense to believe that there is some correct system of value priorities than that there is no such thing as moral value.

If ethical relativism cannot serve as a solid justification for majority rule, then where does that leave the philosophical foundations of democracy? The problem of majority rule was a serious problem for the early social contract theorists who believed in some form of democracy. Rousseau seems somewhat to have skirted this issue in *The Social Contract* (Rousseau 1762/1977). He speaks of "the sovereign" as reflecting "the general will," without ever saying how "general" this "general will" must be. Is the feeling of the majority about their collective self-interest general enough to qualify as a general will, even if it entails enslaving or oppressing a minority? Must the will be absolutely unanimous? Rousseau does not say. This problem in Rousseau's thinking will be considered in a later chapter.

To illustrate the seriousness of this problem, consider again the many conflicts within our criminal justice system. On the one hand, we want to protect the rights of accused criminals. On the other hand, there are the interests of the police and prosecutors to convict criminals for the welfare of the majority of citizens, by maintaining high arrest and conviction rates and thus deterring crime. These interests are often opposed to each other. How can we balance the two? The most serious question that simple majoritarianism poses here is not whether the crimes that the majority considers immoral really are immoral. The more difficult and relevant question is whether the feeling of a majority—for example, that the comparatively just treatment of offenders is more important than deterrence, or that rehabilitation is more important than retribution—should be taken as a guiding truth simply because it is the feeling of the majority. It seems that neither ethical relativism, nor the associated concept of democracy as a simple matter of the majority getting whatever it wants, is adequate to ground a judgment about the relative importance of the general welfare on the one hand, and of rights and principles of fairness on the other. When these different values need to be balanced, people may disagree as to what the best priority system may be, but there is no guarantee that the majority's opinion on this matter will serve the interests of justice, as opposed to the oppression of minorities and of individuals whose specific interests happen to be of little concern to the majority.

1. Utilitarianism, Distributive Fairness, and Tyrannies of the Majority

Utilitarian decision principles. Many contemporary thinkers believe that utilitarianism offers a coherent solution to these dilemmas. Utilitarianism is the moral position that affirms that an act is right if in the long-run it produces the greatest benefit for the greatest number of people. In most instances utilitarianism does *not* advocate (as it might at first appear from the idea of "benefitting the greatest number") disregarding the interests of underdogs in the society simply because the majority's interests oppose their interests. Utilitarianism does not claim that acts, rules, principles, or policies should benefit only the majority. Its principle of social benevolence insists that a policy should benefit as many people as possible as much as possible. If a policy such as a welfare program benefits a only small number, but to a great extent, while costing most people relatively little, then on balance the policy does maximize aggregate benefits on the whole, and thus is favorable from a utilitarian point of view.

In spite of this fact, one might still argue that the best that utilitarianism can offer by way of resolving these conflicts is what amounts to a very complex *cost-benefit analysis*. We must simply weigh all of the longer-term positive and negative effects for the society as a whole of a proposed policy or act. If respecting accused criminals' individual rights is ultimately best for most of the people in the long run—because it makes them feel that police will not unduly harass them if they should ever end up being wrongly arrested (or even correctly arrested, for that matter)—then utilitarianism will respect those rights. But if not, then it will not.

For example, when Castro took over Cuba, he cleaned up organized crime in the country. He did this in part by refusing to respect the legal rights of suspected members of the crime syndicates that the legal system had long been unable to get under control. In Castro's view, this was what was best for the majority of Cubans on the whole and in the long run. To be sure, some may have worried whether their rights would be respected if they were falsely accused. However, in Castro's view, the benefit of cleaning up crime outweighed worries about false accusations and arrests. Castro can therefore be seen as a very straightforward utilitarian. He did what it seemed would produce the best possible human consequences, on the whole and in the long run.

This problem is not limited to Cuba. In the U.S., the frequent application of utilitarian reasoning on the part of police and prosecutors results in unfair treatment of individuals in comparison with each other in order to promote deterrence and ultimately the general welfare. This occurs in particular instances such as wiretapping; the use of the informer system; the plea bargaining system that allows defendants to trade state's evidence for reduced sentences; and the comparative treatment of different crime categories where the severity of punishment needed for deterrence purposes may not correspond with what is morally deserved—nor with a just distribution of punishments when we compare the outcomes of different cases with each other. The criminal who "rats on his buddy" receives a reduced sentence or goes free, while his more loyal colleague who committed the same crime receives a stiff sentence. Yet police and prosecutors need to make such deals in order to obtain enough convictions to make the deterrence system work, and thus protect ordinary citizens. Reducing crime rates has value in utilitarian terms, but when out-of-court deals must be made to ensure enough convictions to have a deterrent effect, unfairness often results.

To solve this problem, utilitarians often propose that, in the interest of the welfare of the people as a whole, the powers of government must be limited by principles of equality under the law and respect for the rights of all. This principle, utilitarians argue, holds even when those rights appear to conflict with some outcome that seems useful in the short run. The goal is long term maximization of people's welfare, not immediate short-term gains. John Stuart Mill (1806-1873), for example, argued from this vantage point. Based on this idea Mill advocated, among other things, equal rights for women, universal suffrage, the abolition of slavery and child labor, and many reforms for working class people whose rights had few champions in nineteenth century England or America (Mill 1859/1947). As a result, his political philosophy was considered radical for its time.

Intrinsic and extrinsic values. Notice that the value of all these rights and principles of equality, in the thinking of utilitarians, consists technically of only *extrinsic* or *instrumental* value. Presumably, for any type of philosophy, something has extrinsic value only if in the long run it is expected to bring about some *intrinsic* value. Intrinsic values, in turn, are valuable simply for their own sake. From the utilitarian point of view, respect for rights and equality derive their value only from the long term benefits they are expected to deliver. Strictly speaking, this means that a utilitarian does not value these rights and principles of equality *intrinsically,* or simply for their own sake, although of course they may constitute very important types of extrinsic values, when and if they are conducive to the long-term general welfare, as they often are in many respects. Other philosophers, by contrast, *do* attribute intrinsic and not merely extrinsic value to these competing considerations.

According to utilitarianism, the only intrinsic value is to benefit human beings as much as possible, on the whole and in the long run. But one must still ask whether, even in this case, a problem remains when the extrinsic values of equality and individual rights do in fact conflict with the long range goal of maximizing the general welfare. Then, according to utilitarianism, the general welfare theoretically *ought to take priority* over the merely extrinsic value of protecting individual rights or ensuring fair treatment. Some utilitarians, such as J.J.C. Smart (1956), frankly admit that this conflict sometimes demands sacrificing individual rights and fairness, while others, like Mill, deny in effect that such conflicts could ever occur. One of the empirical facts that must be assessed, therefore, is whether such conflicts between principles of fairness and the general welfare do in fact occur. We have already noted several reasons to believe that these conflicts are widespread in the administration of criminal justice and other political policies. As we move along, many more examples of this conflict will arise.

Many utilitarians in the first half of the twentieth century, and some more recently, have held that conflicts between fairness and utility can be resolved by means of the idea of *rule utilitarianism*. Rule utilitarianism holds that rules of conduct, including the laws of the society, should be formulated regarding what will best serve the general welfare (see Brandt 1971). Moreover, once the rules have been formulated, they should be enforced in a way that is very strict and consistent. Any exceptions must be clearly spelled out in the letter of the rule itself. The argument for this position is essentially that, if we allow exceptions to rules other than the ones that are clearly stipulated in the rules themselves, then we may as well abandon the rules and simply let each person determine in each case what he or she believes will best promote the general welfare under the given circumstances. However, allowing such individual discretion would not contribute to the general welfare on the whole and in the long run. Since rules must be enforced strictly according to this approach, rule utilitarians believe that this strictness will ensure fair and equal treatment under the law (for example, see Hearn 1971).

One of the most important objections to this position as an effort to resolve the conflict between fairness and the general welfare, is that the rules themselves may have to be riddled with the "clearly spelled-out" exceptions. Utilitarians answer that these exceptions, as utilitarian, will be formulated to promote the general welfare, not to promote fairness *per se*—except to the extent and in those instances where fairness indirectly leads to the maximal general welfare in the long run. For example, it has been argued that we should allow police to use electronic surveillance without obtaining a court warrant to do so, since such freedom to eavesdrop on suspects would help law enforcement. It is believed that many police departments in the U.S. do in fact still electronically eavesdrop without warrants, although the practice has been illegal since 1968 (Smith and Pollack 1972, 187). Thus there is widespread belief among police and the courts that the practice has utilitarian value.

But there is also a problem with this defense of the fairness of utilitarianism: The fact that a formally-stated rule allowed the practice of eavesdropping without a warrant until 1968 does not mean that the practice was any more *fair or unfair* than it is now. Those who believe that electronic eavesdropping without a warrant is unfair will hardly admit that "strict enforcement" of the rules that allowed it would make it fair. Strict enforcement may ensure more fairness than haphazard enforcement. Still, this strict enforcement of rules does not guarantee that the *rules themselves* are fair, even if they are effective from a utilitarian point of view.

Contractarian arguments for distributive justice. Because of the problems just discussed, many political theorists advance positions that try to ground an *intrinsic*, and not merely *extrinsic*, value for distributive justice, completely *independently* of any utilitarian value. This is one reason for the revival of social contract theory in the past century. Those contributing to this revival have attempted to reconfigure social contract theory to overcome the problems of the earlier social contract approaches of Hobbes, Locke, and Rousseau, some of which were mentioned above, and will be further explored later in this book.

Most contemporary versions of the social contract theory (with a few notable exceptions such as Robert Nozick 1974) insist that the only *just*, or "fair," social contract is the one that *rational bargainers* with *equal bargaining positions* would accept. John Rawls (1971) is a well-known example of a social contract theorist who argues for this kind of assumption. Rawls insists on the notion of a fair contract, interpreted in terms of the distribution system for all kinds of opportunities, resources, and rights that a rational reflector would prefer if in a position free from the biases that arise from our knowledge of our own self-interest. Rawls calls this hypothetical position of the initial bargainers, with complete objectivity and no biases toward any particular social position, the *original position.* Rawls derives the idea of an original position from a thought-experiment. Imagine, he says, that you know that you must occupy some position in the society, but know nothing about yourself that would indicate what position you are likely to occupy. From this position of ignorance, what rules would you consent to for the society in which you will live? This imaginary position is what Rawls calls the "original position." A contract worked out by people in the original position would be a fair one, because no one would be biased in favor of any individual's particular social or economic position. Also, everyone would want to make sure that no group or individual suffered a disproportionate burden.

The motivation for this argument is to put all bargainers in the same position. This is based on the idea that a social contract would not be a fair one if it consisted of an agreement between people who did not have equal bargaining power. A legitimate social contract is an agreement that any rational person would enter if such a person, deliberating from a completely neutral point of view, had no reason to believe that he or she would occupy any especially privileged position in the resulting society.

According to Rawls, for example, a true social contract is one that any rational and self-interested person in the "original position" would favor—or we might say a position in which this rational reflector does not know which of the various positions in the resulting society he or she will occupy. In the original position, rational persons would not favor unjust social relationships, because they would realize that they would be likely to be victimized by this injustice if it turned out that they had to occupy one of the less favored positions. It would not be "rational" to risk extreme hardship and lack of basic necessities for the chance of gaining luxury items or frivolous privileges.

We shall see as we go along that many problems of social contract theory stem from a poor fit between its theoretical assumptions and empirical reality in three main respects. First, the extent to which current governments resemble such "social contracts" is at best limited. So comparing specific existing governments with the ideal of a just social contract is difficult. Consequently, on this basis it is difficult decide how legitimate the powers of these imperfect governments actually are. For example, is a young man constrained to fight and possibly die in a war that he considers unjust, simply because an imperfect governmental system has decided that the war must be waged? Would the situation be any more just if the majority of his compatriots favored the war, or would this constitute still another unjust *"tyranny of the majority,"* as Alexis de Tocqueville (1945, 121) put it?

Second, making political decisions on a completely rational basis may be impossible in principle. For example, many people will choose to risk death fighting for their country even though such a decision may seem unreasonable from a logical risk-taking perspective. So it is difficult to decide how much of a role should be played by the logical risk-taking of the person in the original position to decide which distribution system is preferable. The person in the original position may realize that choosing a system that distributes goods somewhat unequally would create the risk of deprivation of some very important goods, if she should turn out to occupy one of the disadvantaged positions. Yet *how much* she is prepared to risk her most basic goods (in exchange for a chance to strike it richer if she should hit the jackpot) depends on how *daring or safe* a risk-taker she is. There is no logical formula for how daring a risk taker it is rational to be. People seem to violate the rules of rational risk-taking on a daily basis when they sacrifice hard-earned and badly needed money to buy lottery tickets with only a long-shot chance to win. Why, then, should we assume the person in the original position would be more rational in choosing how much to risk losing out on the most basic goods?

Third, and perhaps most important, it is difficult or impossible to say just what "rationality" would consist of in the context of social values and value priorities. For example, it is difficult to say how much inequality of income, opportunity and social position it would be rational for the person in the original position to favor. Would it be irrational for a person in the original position to accept the possibility of being economically destitute in exchange for the chance to be very wealthy? This seems like a fuzzy and irresolvable question. Yet in the contemporary type of social contract theory, the question what type of social contract would be acceptable in the original position presumably must be answered to justify any legislation or government power.

Notice that, if one accepts a social contract theory of this kind, such a contract leads to a theory of fairness that is somewhat at odds with a fundamentally utilitarian system of values in general. Equity in distribution would take priority over maximizing gains for the majority. Such a system would, however, allow the inclusion of *many* utilitarian values, since the rational reflector in the original position is to decide what social practices and institutions she would prefer to see implemented based on a calculation of the odds that she will end up benefitting or being harmed by those practices and institutions.

For example, the *deterrence of crime* typically ends up being one of the utilitarian values that are included in the recommendations of such social contractualist value systems. The rational reflector in the original position will place a high priority on being protected from crime and on giving everyone strong incentives to follow the rules of the society. She may, however, have enough of an interest in protecting herself against invasion of privacy, unfair interrogation and prosecution methods, etc., that she would want to ensure against the violation of the rights of the innocent. Thus, she may want to secure some of the more important rights of the guilty as well as the innocent, even in those cases where the interests of deterrence could best be served by policies that risk the violation of such rights.

A crucial question in criminal justice theory is whether such a concept of a fair social contract would imply that the severity of punishment for crimes should be proportional to the offender's **moral desert** or merit, in the interest of fairness, or whether on the contrary the severity of the punishment should be determined according to the severity *necessary to deter* a given type of offense. Moral desert is usually taken to mean that rewards and punishments should be directly proportional to the moral merit of an action. If this proportionality is taken to be a *intrinsic* value, and not merely extrinsic, then it would be valued *regardless of the consequences.* Yet, as far as crime *prevention* (deterrence) is concerned, it is entirely conceivable that the amount of punishment required to deter, let us say, embezzlement of large sums of money would be very *slight* when we remember that the threat of even mild punishments usually easily deters upper-middle-class offenders. Bank robbers, however, are very difficult to deter, even though the severity and certainty of punishment are very high and the average gain from bank robberies is very low compared with such crime categories as embezzlement (McPheters 1976).

If the gain from embezzlement is greater than that from bank robbery, then the harmfulness to society of embezzlement is also greater. Therefore most moral theories—and certainly contractualist theories of fairness such as Rawls'—would consider embezzlement a greater wrong than the bank robbery, more in need of prevention. So if the purpose of punishment is *deterrence*, then embezzlement does not need to be punished as severely as bank robbery, given that white-collar offenders are deterred very easily by mild punishments. But if retributive *fairness* based on moral desert is to be maintained in the proportion between crime and punishment, then the embezzler ought to get the stiffer penalty, since it involves stealing larger sums of money and is generally more harmful to society.

A moment's reflection will reveal that the same conflict occurs when comparing the deterrence and fairness considerations relevant to determining the penalties for many crime categories. The comparative penalties for the various kinds of crimes, offenders, and circumstances will apparently be different depending on whether we decide the severity of the penalty based on a notion of fairness, or based on a utilitarian advocacy of deterrence as the only relevant intrinsic value at stake.

The same problem is just as likely to occur if we want individual criminals who have committed the same offense to be treated fairly in *comparison* with each other. Suppose a small-time drug dealer can give evidence against the big-time dealer who supplies him. It appears that the conviction of the big-time dealer may often have more of a deterrent effect. If so, then it has more utilitarian value, since this would deter a more important class of offender. But if the small-time dealer is allowed to turn state's evidence, that is, trade evidence for a lighter sentence, then his punishment will end up being lighter than that of an *exactly similar* offender who is *not* in a position to turn state's evidence. Obviously, many such situations will result in unfairness if handled in a way that gives priority to the utilitarian value of deterrence.

Perhaps the most generally attractive way for a social contract theorist to get around this conflict between fairness and utility is by recourse to the distinction Rawls makes between fairness at the *"micro" level* and fairness at the *"macro" level.* Fairness at the micro level refers to what a rational reflector in the original position would choose as a distribution system for goods if she were to consider a situation *in isolation.* For example, she might ask herself what the fairest way to treat offenders would be *regardless of how this treatment affects other aspects of the society,* such as the well-being of potential victims of future crimes. By contrast, fairness at the macro level refers to what the rational reflector in the original position would choose as a distribution system for goods *considering all aspects of society and weighing them in relation to each other.*

Let's look at a concrete example using this distinction. If we consider the criminal justice system at the micro level, it might seem that such practices as assigning lesser punishments to greater offenses due to differences in the deterrability of the offenses, or allowing offenders to trade state's evidence, or the plea bargaining system, should be considered *unfair,* since similar offenders are not treated similarly. But Rawls' position is that fairness at the macro level must take priority over fairness at the micro level. In this case, the person in the original position must consider not only whether similar offenders should be treated similarly. She would also have to consider whether it is fair to the *potential victims* of future crimes to sacrifice general deterrence in favor of such considerations as fairness at the micro level. Rawls believes that the rational reflector would give priority to future potential victims in such a deliberation, because there are more of them. Also the potential losses to them are greater than those to the offenders. Therefore, she would have to weigh her odds of being victimized by crime against the odds of being victimized by inequality in the treatment of offenders.

James Sterba (1980) reinforces this conclusion. He argues that the person in the original position would give precedence to the interests of law-abiding citizens in her assessment of what is fair. The reason is that she would realize that, for the most part, all she has to do to avoid being victimized by inequality in the treatment of offenders is to avoid committing crimes in the first place. This does not mean that some degree of fairness in the micro sense should not be practiced in the criminal justice system. But this fairness must be balanced against fairness to the other members of society, with the latter getting a certain amount of priority.

In practice, however, this is a difficult position to apply. To what extent do offenders forfeit their right to be treated fairly at the micro level? How much priority should be attributed to the goal of deterrence over such fairness considerations? Should lesser offenders be treated "more fairly" (in the micro sense) than more serious ones? How do we measure the extent to which a person is treated fairly? Some of these problems, along with more deep-rooted problems with social contract theory, will be considered later.

2. Limiting Government Power

We have already seen that one of the main problems of political theory, and one whose practical applications are obviously very important, is the problem of determining the proper limits of government power. This was one of the main motivations behind the development of many of the social contract theories of the eighteenth century that influenced the framers of the U.S. constitution. According to many of the early versions of the social contract concept (notably Locke's theory, which was extremely influential), the government in a democracy does not have a right to exercise any more power over the individual than is necessary to preserve the democracy. Since a democratic society could not continue functioning as such if individuals were allowed to infringe each other's basic freedom and rights, it is necessary for the government to protect its citizens from such infringements. A clear example of this principle is the issue of slavery. Where slavery exists, the society is not really functioning as a democracy. Therefore, the government has the responsibility to prevent slavery from existing within its jurisdiction.

On the other hand, according to this theory, the government does *not* have a right to prevent people from practicing witchcraft, holding certain religious or political beliefs, or doing anything else they please insofar as such actions do not threaten the social contract itself. If such actions do seriously threaten the social contract, of course, then it might be argued that they must be regulated, as we shall see when we come to Hobbes. However, in the view of most modern thinkers, allowing the freedom of religious beliefs and other such personal philosophical worldviews does not threaten the contract itself. The important point is that there must be a clearly definable limit to the right of government to exercise power. Moreover, this limit must not be overstepped *even if the majority of the people desire it.*

Is there a place for retributive justice? The idea that the will of a majority cannot trump basic rights becomes especially controversial when we consider conflicts between *retributive* and *distributive* justice. Distributive justice refers only to fair distribution, without making an intrinsic value judgment as to who morally *deserves* greater or lesser benefits. By contrast, retributive justice does require rewarding and punishing relative to desert. To a great extent, the early Calvinist and Puritan settlers of North America believed that rewards should be determined by moral merit, and that the acquisition of wealth was a reward from God for practicing moral virtues such as hard work, parsimony, honesty, and moderation.

As an example of the potential conflicts between retributive and distributive justice, consider the social contract idea that the government can have no powers except those that benefit the original bargainers to the social contract. The limitation of a government's legitimate power is the basis of Cesare Beccaria's (1963) argument that the only purpose of punishment must be deterrence, as opposed to retribution. The reason is that the parties to the original social contract would have had nothing to gain by giving up power to the government merely to ensure that some offender receives a morally deserved punishment, merely because the punishment is deserved. On the contrary, the parties to the contract must gain something for every instance of power given up to the government. The only thing they would have to gain by punishing criminals would be the effect of deterring crime, so that they would be protected from crime victimization as much as possible. Thus the only legitimate purpose of punishment would be deterrence, not retribution. Moreover, parties to a social contract would also be concerned to limit even the power to punish for *this* reason, since they would want to ensure that their *own* rights would be protected in case they themselves should be accused or convicted of some crime.

Limited government and property rights. Still another example of a controversial implication of this severe limitation of government power arises from John Locke's highly influential idea that a social contract must treat citizens' *property* as a *basic right.* What Locke meant is that we have the right to keep our property and not have it taken away from us either by other private individuals or by the government, unless it is necessary for the government to assess taxes in order to ensure the preservation of the democracy and of the basic rights of others (see Railton 1985).

By this standard, my property could be taken from me in the form of taxation only if necessary for the preservation of the social contract, including respect for the basic rights for the sake of which citizens would be willing to give up power to the government. For example, the government can collect taxes to pay for an army, police, and courts, because these expenditures are necessary to defend people's lives, which is one of the basic rights for the sake of which people would give up power to the government.

But does the government have the power to infringe my basic right to keep my property, and collect taxes merely because having the use of my money would be *beneficial* to others? If the answer is no, then the social contract seems to advocate such a conservative form of government that it has the power to provide very few desirable social services. But if the answer is yes, then it seems that the government has been allowed to have powers that not every rational bargainer would have necessarily agreed to in the original working out of the terms of the contract. In either case, the question arises about what the *criterion* is for determining what kinds of benefits or protections for citizens are important enough to justify still further infringement of property rights, in the form of more taxation. Social contract theories have had a difficult time trying to spell out a clear-cut criterion for this kind of decision.

It is instructive to contrast this concept of limited government power with a simpler and more naive concept of democracy which would prefer to define democracy simply as "majority rule." One often hears the ordinary person, not well-versed in legal theory, speak as though democracy in the U.S. meant simply that the majority can enact whatever legislation or policy they please. Of course, the U.S. constitution is based on a theory of democracy much more complicated than this, and more resembling the notion of a social contract in which the government's powers are restricted in the ways mentioned above.

The point of stressing this limitation of the government in social contract theory is not to say that the legislature cannot or should not pass an unconstitutional law. The U.S. legislature can, in fact, amend the constitution with a two-thirds majority vote, or even call for a new constitutional assembly to rewrite the constitution. But the point is that social contract theory, as conceived by classic spokesmen such as Rousseau, Locke and Beccaria, does not justify the legislature passing just *any* law that is judged to be in the interest of the majority. This would be true even if a *vast or overwhelming* majority wanted it. Certain laws would be unjust even if in the majority's interest, because they would exceed the government's legitimate right to exercise power. Included in this category would be any punishment simply for the sake of retribution and having no deterrent effect. The fact that a behavior is morally contemptible does not, by itself, give the government the right to punish the behavior. However, as we will see in later chapters, there are many different ways to formulate a social contract theory.

3. Communitarian and Personalist Alternatives

The term "communitarianism" is used with a variety of social, political and rhetorical meanings. There is, however, a common element in the different uses. Since people's desires and interests are shaped in part by the community in which they live, the community should not neglect to take responsibility for the character and actions of individuals created by the community. This personality development itself has intrinsic value from the standpoint of a *personalist* value system. Not all communitarians are personalists, but they do stress this community responsibility. Social contract theories seem to neglect the idea that the interests of individuals are partly determined by aspects of their community. Social contract thinking seems to assume that the desires and interests of individuals are determined prior to their coming together to work out the social contract. After all, the satisfaction of those desires and interests in an effective and equitable way is the primary motivation of individuals bargaining together in the first place. But if the social contract itself is *already* in the process of *influencing* people's values and desires, then it is artificial to think that the social contract's only business is to satisfy the desires (Sandel 1982, 1984). It also partly determines *what the desires are* in the first place.

So the question arises whether the community is influencing the development of people's values and desires in a beneficial way or a harmful way. To say that it should not influence them either way is simply contrary to fact. It is inevitable that the form of community in which individuals grow up will influence their desires and interests. If they grow up in a community that rewards materialistic values, then they will tend to have more material values. If it rewards respect for others, they will tend to have more respect for others. Or, as feminists challenge, if it privileges male values, then male values will tend to be desired more than non-male or feminine values.

Until very recently, this communitarian idea had been undervalued by most Western social and political philosophers. Rousseau, in *The Social Contract,* foreshadowed subsequent political thinking in this regard when he wrote, "Taking men as they are and governments as they might be. . ." (Rousseau, 1862/1977, 49). Rousseau is often taken to be affirming here that the starting point of political thinking is "men as they are." Those who followed this interpretation of Rousseau and were persuaded by it took this principle to mean that the government should not undertake to manipulate people's thinking and values—although, as we will see later, Rousseau himself was highly ambivalent on this point. Unlike classical thinkers like Plato, Aristotle, and Aquinas, Rousseau does not seem comfortable with the idea that the values and personalities of the people should be largely predetermined by the nature of the social institutions under whose dominance and influence they grow up and function. Increasingly in social contract theories, *freedom of conscience* became a *basic right*. The relationship between individual and group thus becomes a one-way relationship. A number of originally separate individuals voluntarily come together and set up a government, not for the purpose of changing their personalities and values (it must "take men as they are," respecting their freedom of conscience), but simply for the purpose of arranging mutually-agreeable distribution systems for the values they do already have.

In the thinking of contractarians, if a vast majority of the people wish to have pornography legally available, the government's duty would not be to argue or psychologically condition people to oppose pornography due to its tendency to exploit women or corrupt people's moral character, but simply to make the pornography available as efficiently and as equitably as possible. It must "take men as they are," not try to remake them or contribute to their character development. On the other hand, if a vast majority think that pornography is harmful, then the social contract would provide for procedures allowing them to legislate against it.

The dispute between utilitarian and social contractarian conceptions of justice often has been framed in a way that bypasses this question. The *utilitarian* distribution system would distribute goods in a way that maximizes the happiness of the *greatest possible number* even if, in the end, this requires that a few must fall by the wayside or are treated unfairly. The *contractarian* distribution system, on the other hand, would distribute the goods in the way that is most *fair*, based on the nature of the agreement among the people that initially constituted the social contract (never mind, in the end, if the most "fair" distribution has negative consequences for the general welfare). But neither utilitarians *nor* contractarians would see the dominant social institution itself—the government—as having a responsibility to promote certain *conceptions of the good* or to counteract others, even to the modest extent of providing services whose purpose is indirectly to enable people to make rational decisions about values and the best ways to achieve them. For example, suppose the government were to provide more adequate re-employment, re-training and material support services for the chronically unemployed during periods of high unemployment, with the hope of steering people away from irrational attitudes that would lead to violence or property crimes. Communitarians would applaud such a policy, whereas most contractarians would worry that it gives too much power to the government to impact people's psychological development, which is not a proper power of the government in a social contract.

Communitarian theories (for example, MacIntyre 1981; Sandel 1982), by contrast, emphasize shaping community values to help people feel that they can expect some general connections between their behavior and the rewards they may receive. This would include promoting the view that society is interested in their well-being. Thus people would feel that they owe respect to its laws. According to data presented by James Short (1980) and others, such government services as work relief during the Great Depression had just such an effect on people's propensity to commit crimes. But, similarly, Roosevelt's programs are often accused of inhibiting such values as "freedom," property rights (especially the right not to be taxed to an unfair extent to support such programs) and individual responsibility—values that tend to have a high priority among Americans.

Continental European social thought more closely resembles such a communitarian perspective than does the Anglo-American tradition, especially in the area of criminal justice. According to the Norwegian criminologist Johannes Andenaes (1974), "In Continental legal literature the moral or educative influence of the criminal law is generally taken for granted and regarded as being of high importance" (Andenaes, 80). German criminologist Helmut Mayer says that "the basic general preventive effect of criminal law does not at all stem from its deterrent but from its morality-shaping force. . . . Nothing is so convincing to man as power, provided it appears as expression of a moral order" (Mayer 1936, 32). Notice, however, the danger with which communitarianism flirts here: The book quoted here was first published during the rise of Naziism in Germany.

Some recent European philosophical movements, which are particularly non-individualistic in nature—such as postmodernism and neo-Marxism, which will be discussed later—also tend toward communitarianism, and these also have in fact exerted some influence on legal theory (see Clark 1986). But even more traditional European social thought comes much closer to a communitarian perspective than does the Anglo-American tradition. Heidenheimer et al. (1982) point out that contemporary European governments tend to offer more extensive social services to help reorient the casualties of industrialized socio-economic structures, and part of the effect of these services is to maintain the integrity of the community, and to keep citizens oriented toward mainstream values and avoid letting them fall into an "underclass." In 1962, the Swedish economist Gunnar Myrdal warned that, because U.S. federal and state governments did not assume enough responsibility for providing reintegrative services for these casualties of urban-industrial society, a permanent underclass would develop of impoverished and hopeless ghetto-dwellers in American cities (Myrdal 1962). Government policies aimed at preventing crime in this way operate partly by indirectly affecting the *attitudes* of potential offenders. To influence the values and behavior patterns of citizens in this way goes beyond what is traditionally thought of as a social contractarian policy, and already begins to act in a communitarian way.

Paternalistic and non-paternalistic communitarianism. Many philosophers have argued against the communitarian perspective on social policy because of the difficulty of distinguishing between facilitating human development on the one hand and, on the other, controlling, regimenting and indoctrinating citizens through a *paternalism* that unwisely and unfairly limits their individual freedom(for example, see Sankowski 1985). What most contemporary communitarians propose, however, is not to take steps toward forcing a set of values on people, or toward indoctrination, but rather to try to ensure that citizens have opportunities and material support necessary to facilitate their finding an at least minimally satisfying non-criminal niche in the society. This type of communitarianism does not fall under the rubric of paternalism. It would, however, still conflict with certain current formulations of the responsibilities of the group toward the individual in terms of recent versions of social contract theory.

This conflict demands some detailed moral analysis that we will also have to address here. For instance, part of the responsibility of the community toward its individuals, in this approach, would be to help individuals toward constructive rather than destructive behavior in a number of ways. In relation to the criminal justice problem, for example, it would attempt to address those social problems that can be shown to cause people to develop (rational or irrational) criminal attitudes. For example, communitarians might support the idea of child protective policies that take children away from abusive or neglectful parents; the requirement that all citizens attain a certain level of education; programs designed to rehabilitate rather than merely punishing offenders; and the illegalization of certain drugs believed to cause drug users to become involved in serious crimes to support their drug habits, or to become unproductive members of society. Notice that all of these policies are practiced in Western democracies, but usually to a limited extent because of a fear of crossing the line to paternalism.

A communitarian approach could also discourage crime by making it easier for people to make legal choices simply by ensuring that crimes will be punished in a consistent way, perhaps combined with some rehabilitative strategies. Of course, there are conflicts between these two types of policies: consistent punishment for crimes does not fit easily with a rehabilitative system whose effectiveness may require that offenders be re-integrated into the community as smoothly as possible. Any minimally viable communitarian approach must include decision principles for these kinds of conflict situations.

4. The Importance of Racial and Ethnic Issues

Many modern political theories do not explicitly acknowledge a basic theoretical role for race and ethnicity in the foundation of socio-political principles. But the study of world history seems to suggest that racial and ethnic group membership do play significant roles in the development of social and political structures not only of early civilizations, but even of the most advanced countries. The importance of this factor is implicitly recognized when philosophers discuss the transition from the "state of nature" to the "social contract." The more a society resembles a state of nature, the more people naturally organize into clans and tribes based on relationships between family units. Aristotle sees the family as the most primitive political unit from which more complex structures are built.

We can vividly see racial and ethnic groupings playing pivotal roles, not only in terms of racism and in both intentional and de facto racial discrimination, but also in the way societies break down when a government loses its ability to govern, and thus becomes a *"failed state"*—as Iraq is on the verge of doing at the time of this writing. Very quickly, citizens turn to local militias for protection, and these militias are usually organized around tribal, religious or ethnic affiliations. People look for protection and assistance to organizational groupings based largely along ethnic or religious lines. Another clear example is the situation of war-devastated Lebanon in the 1980s, when most police and military power fell into the hands of the private militias employed by owners of large marijuana fields. In contractarian terms, this situation seems to be somewhere in the no man's land between a state of nature and a social contract. The local or sectarian militias resemble organized crime syndicates, but also take on many of the functions of government. Here again, people tended to trust only the groups that were organized around their own ethnic and religious affiliations for protection.

Cornel West, the influential African American political philosopher, suggests in his book *Race Matters* (2001) that the way the United States has dealt with racial issues both reflects and has driven many of the changes in socio-political philosophy throughout the history of the country. In the beginning, the authors of the U.S. Constitution were heavily influenced by the thinking of John Locke, whom we shall discuss in detail later. In Locke's view, property ownership is essential to survival in all but the most primitive hunting and gathering societies. Thus the right not to have one's property stolen is just as fundamental a right as the right not to be murdered. As a result, Locke believed that the rights of life, liberty, and property are equally important. Since slaves were the property of plantation owners in early America, the right to retain these slaves, in the view of some, was considered to be just as important as the slaves' liberty rights. In fact, it was sometimes argued that property and life are *more* important than liberty, since when we form the social contract we are willing to trade some of our liberties in exchange for the protection of life and property.

With further scrutiny of the suffering and misery caused by the institution of slavery, however, a new attitude developed in the early to middle 1800s. This attitude went hand in hand with the rise of the philosophy of utilitarianism, which held human happiness to be the only intrinsic value. The utilitarian philosopher John Stuart Mill became a strong advocate of abolishing slavery, not simply because it caused suffering and misery, but also because in his view liberty is the most important of all basic human rights.

Mill argued this position purely on utilitarian grounds. No one can be happy in a state of perpetual intimidation by bullies. Consider what it would be like to live in a neighborhood dominated by street gangs, and to be perpetually afraid of being beaten, humiliated, or robbed by the gangs. The loss of liberty creates just such a situation; it places us at the mercy of the power to which we have given up our liberty. Thus, in Mill's view, slavery should be abolished, not only because the slaves' misery outweighed the slight increase of the plantation owners' happiness due to their increased profits; but more importantly, the value of liberty can outweigh even the value of life and property. We would and do risk our lives to preserve liberty (for example, in fighting wars), but in Mill's view, we may not value even life itself so strongly if it must include too much suffering and misery. Liberty, then, takes priority over the property of the slave-owners, because basic liberties are required for a happy life and a society that can create long-term happiness for its citizens. This argument led to an increasing popularity of utilitarian approaches to all kinds of political problems, and utilitarian reasoning still plays an important role in many government policies, from the way criminals are prosecuted to the way the environment and business practices are regulated by the government.

The utilitarian view of political thinking on the problems of minority groups, as well as many other problems, prevailed until the middle of the twentieth century. At that point, racial issues again drove further rethinking of philosophical assumptions. It became clear that liberty and the maximization of human happiness do not guarantee still another value that must be considered in its own right: the value of *equity,* or *distributive justice.* Even though African Americans were technically free, they did not have an equitable share of the opportunities and resources needed to use that freedom. As the "black power" advocate Theodore Cross (1984) put it, both a rich man and a beggar are equally free to sleep under a bridge, but this does not give them equal power.

The Civil Rights Movement in the U.S. dramatically illustrated the fact that a society that maximizes human happiness across the board may do so by treating a small minority unjustly, and therefore still may be a fundamentally unjust society. It forced philosophers to take seriously the problem that distributive justice cannot be regarded merely as an *extrinsic* or *instrumental* value, a mere means toward the end of maximizing human happiness, as Mill and the other utilitarians had believed. There is the possibility of genuine conflict between these basic values, and if maximizing the general happiness—on the whole and in the long run—is considered to be the only *intrinsic* value, then it may *sometimes* lead to a "tyranny of the majority."

As Bernard Boxill points out in *Blacks and Social Justice* (1992), taking this problem seriously led to the development of new theories of distributive justice and new social contract theories in the second half of the twentieth century. A paradigm of this type of theory was developed by John Rawls (1971) in *A Theory of Justice.* For many years, Rawls had worked within a utilitarian framework, but he finally became convinced that it could not accommodate this type of issue adequately. For many years, Rawls taught at the Harvard Law School, and influenced a generation of legal thinking on civil rights issues. He specifically developed the idea that "affirmative action" is needed to bring the social structure closer to the most just possible society as spelled out in his social contract theory, which we shall consider in detail in a later chapter.

African American issues drove still another movement in academic social-political philosophy beginning with the late twentieth century. The radical transformation of American cities by the forces of industrialization and rapid economic development disrupted long-standing Black communities . Despite the limited financial resources of these communities, they had managed to maintain a social structure capable of nurturing each subsequent generation in constructive ways, and in large measure preventing the growth of organized crime in their neighborhoods. With the rapid upheaval of middle-to-late twentieth century urban development, these communities tended to be destroyed. Philosophers like Martin Luther King and Cornel West therefore began to take a personalist and communitarian perspective on these kinds of community problems. The fabric of community must be preserved if a society is to provide the resources needed by each new generation.

This point too illustrates a basic fact about the role of sectarian, tribal and ethnic groups throughout history. When governments do not provide badly needed social services such as education, help for the unemployed, medical care for the aged, and protection from organized crime, there is a strong tendency for smaller groups such as religious organizations or tribal warlords to take over this role. One of the reasons for the spread of Christianity during the Roman Empire was that the Church took over the role of providing these basic social services in local communities when the government was not willing or able to do so.

As we noted earlier, Martin Luther King was very impressed with this personalist communitarian philosophy. He studied philosophy at Morehouse College, and then went on to philosophy graduate school at Boston University, which at that time was a stronghold of personalism, including Edgar Brightman, who as we have already mentioned specifically argued for communitarian social policies on personalist philosophical grounds.

During the same period of history, some Black philosophers adopted a more cynical view. For example, Lucius Outlaw (1996) argued in favor of an extreme ethical relativism. Outlaw's reasoning is that the dominant power group tends to control universities, where philosophy students work out the *epistemological criteria* for truth. Those criteria are then taken over by other sciences and applied to all types of information gathering, resulting in a body of belief that is consistent with that particular epistemology. Since the leading universities tend to be populated by the sons and daughters of the power brokers of the society, this means that the dominant philosophy of a society will be skewed toward the prejudices and blind spots of that elite group. Only the truths that fit their preconceptions will be recognized, and truths that come from areas of life that they have not experienced, or that they do not value, will tend to be left out.

Outlaw is referring to a problem long recognized by philosophers. It is the problem of the *"hermeneutic circle."* The term "hermeneutics" means "interpretation," usually in relation to texts, but in philosophy it is used to mean our interpretation of reality. The reason this interpretive limitation is a *circle* is that it may seem superficially that the natural way to overcome it would be to examine ourselves and observe how our prejudices, preconceptions, and category structures tend to influence the way we see reality. But the problem with this solution is that, when we look at ourselves in order to see what our prejudices and limitations are, we see ourselves *through the same* distorting sunglasses that also distort everything else we look at. Hence the riddle which asks: why can racists not see that they are racists? Answer: because they are racists. The same category system that distorts our view of external reality will also distort our view of ourselves. Thus we *cannot* overcome the hermeneutic circle simply by examining our own prejudices and preconceptions, because they themselves will prevent us from understanding *ourselves* accurately.

Cornel West sharply criticizes Outlaw's use of this problem to justify an extreme ethical relativism. While West acknowledges that the hermeneutic circle is a legitimate problem, he sees Outlaw's extreme ethical relativism as an over-reaction. What the hermeneutic circle implies is not relativism, in West's view, but rather a need for diversity within philosophy. African American philosophers, for example, may have prejudices and blind spots; but they are not the *same* prejudices and blind spots that limit the philosophical thinking of the well-to-do ruling elite (or at least comfortable bourgeoisie) that have almost completely dominated academic philosophy throughout its long history.

West's response to the hermeneutic circle is therefore to recommend a *philosophical pluralism* within the philosophical community of scholars. The idea here is that, when people with a diversity of category systems engage in dialogue, each will see the problems in the *other's* viewpoint more clearly, and the result will be a philosophical community that, on the whole, moves closer to the truth, although it will never perfectly attain it.

West's call for further diversity is especially striking at a time when minority groups are dramatically under-represented in academic philosophy. The irony is that, because of affirmative action theories of the kind that John Rawls advocated, almost all U.S. universities are now desperately trying to attract Blacks and other minorities to their graduate programs, and are prepared to offer handsome scholarship packages. Yet at the time of this writing, only two percent of the doctoral degrees in philosophy go to African Americans, who represent about 13 percent of the U.S. population. And the number of Blacks entering the field of philosophy has only recently increased from one to two percent.

Finally, we should not overlook the relationship between racial and ethnic groupings and the problems caused by economic globalization. We mentioned earlier that many studies show that the operation of multinational corporations in impoverished countries in most instances not only does not seem to help the masses of people in those countries, but actually tends to further suppress their living standard. As Robert Perkins (2004) points out, one reason for this effect is that corporations in a global economy are now large enough to be able to afford to bribe government officials and threaten to financially back organized attempts to overthrow their governments. The result is that the government capitulates to unfair trade relations, resulting in the further impoverishment, pollution, and using up of the natural resources of the country. In many instances, the eventual result is a "failed state," and the country devolves into sectarian and ethnic strife because, here again, the only provider of the resources and security that are now so desperately needed is the local tribal or sectarian warlord or militia. This problem of economic globalization is one of the emerging problems of social and political philosophy, and we shall return to it later in this book.

We have already noted that a defensible social or political theory must depend not only on value assumptions, but also on factual assumptions involving human nature and human behavior patterns. These assumptions may be the result of philosophical considerations, based on the rational analysis and clarification of concepts. They may also depend on empirically verified social-scientific information, or some combination of the two. Some of the earliest philosophers whose political theories have come down to us were keenly aware of this problem, notably Plato and Aristotle. Both of these philosophers were especially sensitive to the need to balance utility-maximizing policies against retributive and distributive justice issues, as well as communitarian concerns. The next chapter will consider the contributions of both of these Ancient Greek philosophers.

Chapter Three
Formative Concepts from Early Philosophers: Plato and Aristotle

Many people are initially surprised to learn that Socrates (469-399BC), although he was perhaps the most famous of all philosophers in history, never wrote anything down. Any philosophical theories to which Socrates may allegedly have committed himself are not even known to us except that his student Plato (427-347BC) wrote philosophical dialogues in which Socrates was usually a principle character, playing the role of a "gadfly" by pressing interlocutors to defend their basic assumptions. To what extent the views expressed by the Socrates of the dialogues match those of the real Socrates is a matter of scholarly speculation and wide-open controversy.

What seems clear is that Socrates' main purpose was not to espouse theories and doctrines. It was to ask penetrating and useful questions about people's philosophical presuppositions—especially political ones. This was the real reason for Socrates' eventual execution for the alleged crime of "corrupting the youth." When the most basic assumptions of a society or a political system are questioned, a great deal is at stake, and people tend to become very defensive. In fact, throughout history, societies have much more often persecuted those who ask serious philosophical questions than they have tolerated them. Luckily for us, however, the work of Socrates led to subsequent generations of careful philosophical thinking about political philosophy. This chapter focuses on two of those thinkers: Plato, who was Socrates' student, and Aristotle (384-322BC), who in turn was a student of Plato.

Part of the fascination of studying the Ancient Greeks is that their political thinking was so different from our own. They tended to endorse what we nowadays would call "personalist" and "communitarian" views (as defined in the previous chapters), and did not place great emphasis on the idea of a social contract. On the other hand, they were aware of many of the theoretical alternatives that modern philosophers find attractive, such as social contract and ethical relativism. For the most part, they found these alternatives inadequate. Yet their thinking defined many of the main political questions with which we are still grappling today.

1. Platonic Political Philosophy: The Republic

The interpretation of Plato's texts involves a difficulty that we will not find in most works of philosophy. The problem is that Plato does not speak in his own name. Instead, we find a primary speaker (most often, but not always, Plato's mentor Socrates) in dialogue with others of various sorts. In this respect, the dialogues resemble plays more than philosophical treatises. And like plays, the primary concern is not speech in some theoretical manner, but speech as a mode of action. What *happens* between the characters bears a complex relationship to the content of the speeches, taken in themselves. In reading any Platonic dialogue, the theoretical content of Socrates' or any other character's speech must be accounted for with the question in mind as to what each speaker desires or wishes to accomplish. For example, in many instances, Socrates has no intention of advancing a theoretical standpoint, but rather in motivating his interlocutors to question their own. This makes interpretation of these texts more complex than a straightforward treatise.

The following reading of one of Plato's most famous dialogues, *The Republic*, can only begin to touch on these complexities, and so is necessarily introductory. However, the primary issues of the dialogue—the nature and desirability of justice—are easily approached from even a surface reading. The focus of what follows is to see how the dialogue attempts to provide some rudimentary answers to these issues.

Book One: Justice and injustice debated. The *Republic* begins with Socrates and his young friend Glaucon returning from a religious festival at the port of Piraeus, to Athens. There, they are accosted by a group of young men including Glaucon's brother, Adeimantus, and his friend Thrasymachus, who is a teacher of rhetoric, or **sophist** (literally in Ancient Greek: "possessor of wisdom"). This group persuades Socrates to come to the house of one of the young men, Polemarchus, in order to observe a race on horseback later that night, and to converse with the young men. The horse race is soon forgotten, and what results is a conversation about justice that lasts all night.

The conversation begins with Socrates asking Polemarchus' father about the advantages of being old, and some light conversation about whether the old are more just. In his typical fashion, Socrates turns from this question to ask about the nature or definition of *justice itself*. Polemarchus' father, Cephalus, replies that justice can be defined as *telling the truth and returning what is borrowed to those from whom one has borrowed.* As soon as Socrates begins to raise difficulties for this definition, Cephalus retires to make sacrifices to the gods, and his son, Polemarchus, takes up the conversation.

Polemarchus reinterprets his father's definition in a more "war-like" way, befitting his name (which means "war-lord"). Justice, he says, means *returning good to one's friends and harm to one's enemies.* Socrates questions this definition. First, he shows that Polemarchus' answer begs the question about whether justice primarily involves harm as well as good. Socrates argues that if justice is to be a good, then it must always do good, or at least do no harm. Second, and more important, Socrates raises questions as to whether friendship or enmity can be a proper criterion for justice, or whether it actually must work the other way around—that justice is a criterion *for* friendship in the first place. One would wish to have "true" rather than "false" friends, and justice seems a necessary element of this concern. Friendship as a criterion therefore begs the question regarding the nature of justice. If justice is required for a friendship to be a "true" one, then we cannot know who our true friends are until we first know *what justice is.* The definition of justice, then, cannot presuppose that we already know who our friends are.

This small exchange between Socrates and Polemarchus sets up two important characteristics of justice that should not be overlooked: first, that it seeks primarily to benefit (or at least do no harm); and second, that it must be prior to questions of private friendship. Those who ignore these characteristics will tend to become more interested in the question of *power* than that of justice. They would be more concerned with benefitting their supposed friends than with the question of who *ought* to be benefitted and how—the real question of justice. Thus Socrates concludes his discussion with Polemarchus by pointing out that the idea of "justice" as friends and enemies is likely to be the opinion of a man who is overly impressed by his own power to accomplish great tasks (Plato 1979, 336a).

At this point, Socrates and Polemarchus are interrupted by a verbal barrage from Thrasymachus, who begins by insulting them, calling them naive sycophants in argument. After some effort, Socrates finally persuades Thrasymachus to give *his* definition of justice. Thrasymachus replies confidently that justice is *"the advantage of the stronger."* This means that those who rule in a particular community make laws to maximize their own advantage. Hence, in a democracy, the majority rule for their own advantage, but in a monarchy, the king rules to his own advantage; both of these are called justice.

We can see the influence of Thasymachus on his young pupil Polemarchus (the "war-lord") in this "might-makes-right" definition. To refute Thrasymachus' definition, Socrates asks him, first, whether rulers ever make mistakes. If they do, then the laws they make would not necessarily be to their advantage, and hence those laws could not be just. Thrasymachus avoids this conclusion by stating that the ruler, properly speaking, is one who does not err, but always acts "with perfect art," or knowingly.

Socrates accepts this definition of ruler, but asks in response whether the practitioner of an art acts for the benefit of himself, or for the benefit of those for whom he performs the art? So, for example, a doctor, cares for the sick, not himself; and the captain of a ship cares for his sailors, not primarily himself. In all the arts, properly speaking, the artist benefits those whom he serves, not himself. The purpose of rulership (and justice, by Thrasymachus' definition) therefore seems *not* to be the advantage of the ruler (the stronger), but instead the advantage of the ruled. Justice involves a service to others. This crucial idea shapes the entire dialogue that follows. It begins to make explicit that the topic of the *Republic* will be twofold: not only is there a concern with the *definition* of justice, but also a concern with the question as to *why* we should be just. If justice is *another's* advantage, then why should any individual, interested in his or her own good, be concerned with it?

Thrasymachus accepts Socrates' conclusion, but now makes a striking reversal. He says that simple justice is indeed the pursuit of someone else's good, but that this means that *injustice* is what rules, and indeed is better than justice. To make this argument, he uses the example of a shepherd: while a shepherd appears to be looking after the good of his sheep, his real purpose is to fatten them up for his own good or that of his master. The unjust man, seeking his own advantage, says Thrasymachus, is always able to get the better of the just man, who seeks the advantage of others. He will always benefit and get more than his share; hence the unjust man lives a better life (Plato 1979, 343b-344d).

Socrates responds that, while the ruler in the precise sense acts for the sake of the ruled, just as a shepherd rules for the sake of his sheep, it is still necessary that the shepherd be paid for his work. He must therefore partake in two different arts at the same time—the art of money-making, *and* the art of rulership, in order to be persuaded to benefit those whom he serves. Hence, rulers are usually paid or honored in order to be persuaded to benefit others by their rulership.

Furthermore, even decent men are persuaded to rule by a similar logic. Since they fear the consequences of the rule of bad men, they decide to seek office themselves. All of these considerations do not, however, refute Thrasymachus' contention that the unjust life is inherently superior to the just; in all of these cases, the just life is pursued for individual advantage, and so the advantage of the ruler, or injustice, is preferred to the advantage of the ruled, or justice. Even decent people are more concerned with their own good (avoiding the suffering of injustice) than with justice for its own sake. In essence, Thrasymachus advocates an *egoistic-hedonist* view of human nature, which foreshadows the views of Thomas Hobbes, whom we shall discuss in the next chapter.

This issue about egoistic hedonism, as Socrates says, is a "far bigger thing" than what they first considered. Now the *definition* of justice is not the only concern, but also whether justice itself is *good* (Plato 1979, 347b-e). For the rest of the dialogue, these two questions will prove inseparable. Socrates will have to convince his interlocutors that justice is a good thing, not only for others, but *for the person who acts justly*.

Socrates attacks Thrasymachus' claim in several different ways, none of which turns out to be satisfying, even to Socrates. First, he points out that Thrasymachus calls justice foolishness and injustice wisdom. The unjust man's seeking to get the better of everyone (as a tyrant does) actually resembles the activity of one who is not at all interested in knowledge. After all, a knower does not seek to get the better of other knowers. Knowledge or Wisdom seems to be similar to justice in this way: both grant a type of *equality*. This does point out a difference between wisdom and injustice, which shames Thrasymachus, since Thrasymachus claims to be a wise man. He claims to be wise *for teaching injustice*; yet in this respect he seems to contradict himself: why should he teach everyone how to get the better of others by acting unjustly? If he would teach them to be just, then according to his account, he could then act unjustly and get the better of *them*. This does not, however, resolve the question ultimately, since one might still choose the benefits of injustice over those of wisdom.

Socrates next takes on another aspect of Thrasymachus' claim—that injustice is more *powerful* than justice since the unjust man or tyrant, not limited by any obligations to others, can therefore do what he wants to secure his own advantage. Socrates points out that this is not necessarily so by showing that any unjust enterprise requires common action between people. And common action involves obligations to others, or justice. The tyrant, in order for his injustice to be effective, must have an alliance of advisors and subordinates whom he must treat more or less justly. If not, faction arises, and the ruler is overthrown (as we see so often in the history of the Roman Emperors). Justice, then, is a precondition of injustice. Furthermore, Socrates points out, even within an individual person's life, there must be a sort of concord or justice; if my own desires are at odds *with each other*, then I will be subject to an internal conflict that precludes acting powerfully.

While this argument seems somewhat more persuasive than the earlier ones, it does not resolve the fundamental question raised by Thrasymachus' objection. If justice is valuable for the sake of power, does this not still mean that the end or goal is my own (selfish) good, and not an obligation to others? The gap between individual happiness and the common good remains.

Finally, having established in the first argument that justice requires wisdom and virtue, not injustice, Socrates shows that this implies that the just man will lead the "good life," that is, will have happiness and fulfilment, since the good life is defined by the *proper functioning* of a person, and the proper functioning of a thing is identical with its virtue. However, notice that this argument relies on the dubious conclusion of Socrates' first argument. Even if the pursuit of wisdom is different from the pursuit of injustice, this does not imply that wisdom is *the definitive virtue* for a human life, nor that it is the same as justice. As in so many of Plato's dialogues, Socrates' sparring partners are not mere "straw men," and Socrates cannot knock them down quickly or easily.

While these arguments do not ultimately convince, and perhaps fail to establish either the desirability or the nature of justice, they do clarify the lines upon which these two issues are related. If justice is the other person's good, then how can justice be an excellence of the individual himself? Does the best or most desirable human life involve an essential obligation to the good of others? And how does the life of philosophy or wisdom fit into this?

Glaucon and Adeimantus. At this point, Glaucon and Adeimantus, the two young brothers, express dissatisfaction with Socrates' arguments, and proceed to defend different aspects of Thrasymachus' position. First, they try to force Socrates to speak more plainly as to nature and benefit of the just life. This forces the explicit question of what kind of thing justice is; how can it be both our own good and yet involve an apparent subordination of one's own good to that of others?

Glaucon begins most boldly, by asking Socrates not to defend justice as something chosen merely *as a means* to some other good (a merely *extrinsic* value), but rather as something worthy of choice by the person who wishes the highest or most noble good for himself (i.e., an *intrinsic* value). First, he notes that most people think justice to be chosen as a means to an end. People choose it, not because it is desirable in itself, but because of limitations upon their power. To make this point, Glaucon tells a story from mythology, the story of the *ring of Gyges*. A shepherd named Gyges discovers a ring that makes him invisible. Using this ring's power, Gyges seduces the king's wife, kills the king, and becomes a successful tyrant. Glaucon says that every person would act the same as Gyges if given the chance. But because we do not have this strong an advantage over our fellows, we choose justice—not because it is the most desirable in itself, but because what we hate is to be victimized by injustice at the hands of our fellows, which is inevitable without justice, for most people. Here we have an early foreshadowing of a kind of *social contract* theory.

Second, Glaucon claims that even within society's conventions of justice, the unjust person leads a better life. The completely unjust man, as part of his injustice, will connive to have a false *reputation* for justice, and so will receive the benefits of this reputation. By contrast, the simply just man will choose justice for its own sake, not for extrinsic benefits such as reputation, wealth, or power. But then the just man will be unjustly accused and will suffer from such accusation and reputation, yet still choosing justice. Glaucon then asks: given these descriptions, who would choose the life of the just man over that of the unjust? Is not injustice the life of happiness, and thus worthy of choice? Glaucon seems to think that if the just life is to be defended, it must be defended as worthy of choice even if all other goods must be sacrificed. This is a strong challenge to the compatibility of our obligation to others and our choice of a happy life for ourselves.

Adeimantus supplements Glaucon's opinion that justice is chosen only as a means to other goods. He points out that the myths and stories of the heroes and the gods do not make justice worthy of choice *for itself*, but only worthy of choice because of the rewards that it might bring. Justice is hard, but it leads to pleasurable and honorable rewards. Furthermore, the traditional stories are not even clear on this, for it seems that it is the *appearance* of justice that is rewarded, not its reality. Moreover, even those who are unjust can avoid punishment and reap the rewards of justice, since the gods can be bought, and men are easily corruptible.

Thus Adeimantus seconds his brother's demand to hear why justice should be considered praiseworthy *in itself*, not merely for the other consequences it might bring. The question is whether justice is an *intrinsic* and not merely an *extrinsic or instrumental* value.

Before moving on to Socrates' reply to these objections, it is worth pointing out the insightfulness of Glaucon and Adeimantus on two related points. First, our obligation to others cannot be simply reduced to our own pleasure or honor; if it is to be tied to a desire to our own excellence, there must be a different understanding of our individual good than is available in the notions of pleasure and honor. It is precisely this which Socrates must strive to develop, and to which ultimately the practice of philosophy, the love of wisdom, answers. Second, Socrates must address the common assumption, particularly evident in Adeimantus' thinking, that justice is a hardship and not an excellence of human action. Not only the stories of ancient times favor this opinion—one need only look to the ethical attitudes of our own time and the stories we tell as to the character of the happy life to see the difficulty of this problem.

The city and the soul. Socrates' response to the two brothers' challenge is a strange one. Rather than engaging in dialectical argument against their positions, as he had done with Polemarchus and Thrasymachus, he rather proposes that they look for justice's nature (and its goodness), not in the case of the individual, but in the case of a *city* (in Greek, *polis*, from which we get the word "politics"). Socrates says that it is much harder to see justice in the individual, but much easier to do so in the city. Thus he proposes that we should see it first in the city, and then go back to the individual soul.

This procedure is, to say the least, quite strange. Socrates appears to beg the question as to the relationship of the city and the individual. Why should we suppose that the relationships between individuals in a political community somehow give us a clue as to how the happiness of the individual is constituted? What are we to assume is the relationship between the constitution of a city and the various powers of individual persons?

An obvious example of this difficulty, as we shall see in detail as we go along, is what scholars have labeled Socrates' *"tripartite theory of the soul."* Socrates divides the soul into three main parts: the *rational* part, the *"spirited"* (or courageous) part, and the *"appetitive"* part (the part that has desires and appetites). The correct *balance* of these three parts, he argues, is *justice* as far as the individual soul is concerned—thus leading to the four classical Greek virtues:

wisdom, courage, temperance, and justice. Correlatively, the *polis* or society can be divided into three parts: the intellectual/scientific, the military, and the business communities, and the correct balance among these three consists of justice for the society as a whole. But this raises a problem with Socrates' view: if all persons in the city possess reason, courage, and desire, how is it that any one class of persons within the constitution of the city—for example, the military or the intellectual/scientific community or the business community—could represent only reason, or only courage, or only desire?

What, then, is the rationale for this procedure of understanding the individual by comparison to the *polis* as a whole? Near the end of this dialogue, when Socrates is asked whether the ideal city that the speakers have created in their imaginations could ever come to be, Socrates expresses grave doubt—a doubt which makes one think that the proposals that he gives may not be intended as practical political proposals. However, he does say that this ideal city, even if impossible in practice, has a role as a paradigm for the individual soul, and anyone who seeks happiness will build such a city *in his soul*. The purpose of looking at the city is not primarily political, although it may impart lessons as to the nature of political reality along the way, insofar as politics is relevant to the choiceworthy nature of justice for the individual.

In this way, Socrates answers to Glaucon's demand that the just life be *happy*, or in accordance with the nature of human desire. This concern with the city begins an understanding of political life that we later see taken up by Aristotle, and much later by certain communitarian thinkers. The city does not exist for its own sake, but for the sake of the perfection of its citizens' natural capacities. The speakers in the dialogue actually enhance the condition of their own souls by creating a good city, even if only in their imaginations. Thus scholars often speak of Ancient Greek moral and political theory as forms of **eudaimonism** (from the Greek word *"eudaimonia,"* which means happiness or fulfillment). Eudaimonism is the theory that a good person is happier (in the fullest sense of "happiness") than an evil person.

Secondly, and more subtly, in moving the discussion from individual happiness to that of civic happiness, he makes Glaucon and Adeimantus' own happiness complicit with the happiness of others, of those they rule in speech. In other words, Socrates begins to habituate the young men towards acting justly, or for the good of others, by making them *founders* of an imaginary city in speech. As founders of this city, they must (as Socrates had earlier pointed out) concern themselves, not with the happiness of themselves, nor of merely a favored part of the community, but with the community as a whole. Socrates creates, that is, a public-spirited and selfless concern that is at the heart of the very justice that they are seeking. The young brothers are convinced *in practice* that their own ambition for something great and noble is not at odds with the concern for the good of others, but involves it in its very essence. This is reflected in the development of the city in their conversation. There is a development in interest among the interlocutors from the most selfish to the most comprehensive concern.

During the earliest stages in the development of a city, it is ruled without any comprehensive concern at all, which is to say that it runs like *nature*, where every organism concerns itself primarily with *its own good*, yet everything works out for the system *as a whole*. This is the city that Adeimantus and Socrates initially construct in their imaginations, what Socrates calls the "truthful" city. In it, there is simple economic exchange, and people have easily fulfilled desires rather than great or luxurious ones. A moment's reflection reveals that this simple city, in which everyone exchanges simple goods and services without any government or administration, is in its way the most "selfish" of the stages of development. It is not selfish in a harmful way, since no one concerns themselves essentially with anyone else's goods. The reason is that people's desires are very simple in this primitive or first city. The fulfillment of one's own desires is never contraverted by the fulfillment of any other person's, because there is no scarcity, given the simplicity of people's desires. Justice is not to be found in this city, because there is no need for it: thus it is dominated completely by private hedonistic concerns. Here we have Socrates' vision of what might be compared to a *"state of nature"* in later social contract theories.

However, Glaucon immediately calls this city a "city of pigs," because there are only simple pleasures. The complex pleasures of human civilization are absent, notably those of fine art, music, and the industrial arts of metalworking and such that make these fine arts possible. Socrates admits these in, even though it changes the city from one that is "healthy" to one that he calls "feverish." The consequence for such a city, is, ultimately, that it will expand in size, for it will be needing more. Socrates points out that this will necessitate conflict and contact with neighboring cities. Such conflict and contact necessitates some sort of government, or at least an *armed force* (of the kind that their friend Polemarchus, the "war-lord" represents). The discussion for the rest of the dialogue has to do primarily with the nature of this government or armed force, whom Socrates calls *"guardians."* With government, the question of the appropriate self-definition of the city arises (and by analogy, the order of powers in the soul—especially the appetitive, rational, and spirited powers which we discussed above). It is in the interaction of the city with other cities that this concern of self-definition arises, and it is perhaps in the same way that the individual's concern with self-definition always arises. This issue of justice, then, is always a concern of *our own* good.

While it might seem regrettable for Socrates to allow in Glaucon's desire for feverish pleasures, we can see in Glaucon's desire itself, as well as in their response to this desire, a more comprehensive concern encouraged by Socrates. The simple desires of the "truthful city" (i.e., the primitive way of life) allow the members not to be concerned one way or the other with the good of others, since nature provides for them all. By contrast, the complex desires of the "feverish city" necessarily involve a concern with the good of others, even if at first in a negative manner. If the city is to expand, this means that other cities may need to be infringed upon, or war may be necessitated. This is true, not only in the city's external relations, but internally as well. The feverishness of desire means that I look at my fellow citizen as an obstacle or tool for my own self-interest as well. Both internally and externally, the question of justice is now explicit, since what I owe to others now potentially conflicts with my own desire. A precondition of a concern with justice, then, is a more complex desire that transcends the simple natural satisfactions of the earliest city.

But the response to the feverishness of human desire even further indicates Socrates' encouragement of the brothers' concern for justice. The emphasis of the ensuing discussion is on the development of the type of person, or class of persons, *who are by their very profession concerned with the good of the city as a whole*, the people who are called "guardians." If the brothers, in their desire for the best life for themselves, are encouraged to focus their attention on those in the city whose concern is for the city as a whole, this implies that the concern for the best life will essentially involve a comprehensive concern, not only a concern for one's own.

The remainder of the *Republic's* account of the city in speech is largely devoted to the development of this class of guardians. There is a twofold function of such guardians; to protect the city from those hostile to it, and to refrain from becoming hostile to the city as a whole themselves. The discussion centers on what sort of education is necessary to provide the character for fulfilling these two functions. Socrates advocates a form of *censorship* regarding literary, musical and physical education, since these are the things that influence character. The guardians of the city should be encouraged to be both brave (to protect the city from hostile attack), and moderate (to refrain from taking from their fellow citizens, and thus being corrupted in their role as guardians).

However we might object to such radical censorship in politics, it is clear that for Plato (and Aristotle following him), our character is formed by what we take pleasure and pain in, and the encouragement of certain passions as painful and pleasant is crucial to the formation of an appropriate character. Even modern democracies, which as much as possible refrain from censorship in the public sphere, recognize the right of parents, churches, and other smaller communities to regulate character. Furthermore, democratic citizens, precisely because of the encouragement of private liberty, require the encouragement of these virtues. If democratic citizens do not have both courage and moderation in their decision-making, they are likely to concern themselves excessively with their private good to the detriment of the good of the community as a whole.

At the end of this educational discussion, Adeimantus raises the question as to whether the guardians themselves will be happy. Socrates reminds them that a guardian's concern is not with individual happiness, but with the happiness of the city as a whole. Yet even those whose responsibility is to concern themselves with the city as a whole—perhaps particularly those—may take themselves to merit *all* of the city's goods, instead of those that are appropriate to themselves. In this they would act unjustly, in taking their private good to be the comprehensive good.

As a response to this difficulty, Socrates goes on to further elucidate other characteristics of the guardians' lives. The guardians will live in utter *communism*—communal ownership of their goods and services—since their concern is not to be for anything private, but only the community as a whole. This concern involves not only property, but more radically, women and children as well. Children of the guardian class are to be raised in common, so that none of them will form a private attachment to a family, but will be concerned only with the. common good. Furthermore, the guardians will be tested in various ways to resist any attempts at depriving them of this public devotion; those who pass the most rigorous tests will be not only called guardians, but rulers. Even within the guardian class, then, there comes to be a distinction between those whose knowledge of the public good is unassailable, and those whose opinion is correct, but whose knowledge is subject to decay. This is the distinction between the rulers and the guardians.

There are, then, three classes within the city: the rulers, the guardians (i.e., military), and the various craftsmen or ordinary citizens who devote themselves and their work to their own good (the business community). We must, however, recall that the purpose of the this discussion is not primarily political reform, and Socrates indicates that his discussions of utter communism, especially regarding the raising of children, are to be taken somewhat poetically. The function is to better understand justice's nature, and so that the young men become desirous of justice as an essential virtue for human happiness.

Thus, at the end of his discussion of the guardians' education and living arrangement, Socrates returns to the primary question of the dialogue: where is it that we find justice in the city they have constructed? He embeds this question in a discussion of the four cardinal virtues according to tradition; courage, wisdom, moderation and justice. The first three of these virtues correspond roughly to the three social classes in the city—artisans, guardians, and rulers. The necessary virtue of the rulers is *wisdom*, since they must command with knowledge of the principles of the city. The virtue of guardians is primarily *courage*, which assists the rulers in the application of the principles of the city. The virtue of the artisans or craftsmen is *moderation*, because without moderation, the business community would take over the government and turn all its functions to private gain, leading to corruption.. Moderation is not unimportant, but crucial; if the artisans are not themselves moderate, then the rule of the wise will be more by force than by persuasion. Moderation therefore ties the entire city together, and can be found in various ways in the other classes of the city as well.

Finally, Socrates discerns as the principle of *justice* the very *ordering* of the other virtues of the city, by which every type of person does their job, and their job alone, not pretending to do that of the other classes. Those who are interested in private business affairs, or the artisans, do not rule, or take the private good to rule the public; neither are the rulers interested in private gain, as is appropriate to the artisans. Nor does the interest in defense of the city (the primary characteristic of the guardian class) entitle the guardians to a claim of either ruling wisdom, or to private goods. These conclusions address the concerns of the two brothers, whose earlier speeches in defense of injustice emphasized the use of the public merely for private gain.

Socrates then applies this structure of the city to the individual soul. The point of this is to indicate to Glaucon that justice is an ordering of the soul that is appropriate to the satisfaction of human nature. Just as with the city, the just human being is now defined as one for whom wisdom rules, with the help of courageous spiritedness, and for whom desire is moderated. In this way, each part of the human soul is doing its appropriate job, and such a person is now said to be happy.

As in the case of the city, the key part of the person that is addressed is the part for which courage is the virtue; it must be subordinated, not to desire as such, but to reason or wisdom. What is meant by this is indicated much later in the *Republic*, when Socrates discusses the deficient types of cities and their corresponding souls. The worst type of soul—the opposite of the just person—is the tyrant. The tyrant is a slave of unlimited desire, and his spirit or courage is entirely in service to this unlimited desire. Wisdom, which would limit desire in order to impose a rational order upon a person's desires, is entirely enslaved in such a person. In this way, Socrates hopes to have persuaded Glaucon and Adeimantus that justice is good for the individual because it involves an ordering of the individual's powers and capacities in such a manner as to guarantee the human being's fulfillment. Justice, even if it involves an essential concern for another's good, also fulfills the individual who acts justly. This notion, that justice and human virtue in general lead to fulfillment of the individual human being's natural capacities, is taken up and developed systematically by Plato's student Aristotle. We shall discuss Aristotle's development of this idea in the following section.

At this point, Socrates may seem to have fulfilled the task that was set up when the two brothers challenged him to defend justice, or a concern with the good of others, as essential to the happiness of individuals. However, this is not yet clear. Even if justice is a certain ordering of the capacities so that reason rules spirit and desire in the individual, it still is not clear how *this* excellence of the individual *essentially* involves a concern for the good of others. It is clear that the man who is moderate in his desires (as is the individual who mirrors the city in speech) will have less occasion to conflict with others. Such a person will refrain from the harm of others, since he has no need from others for his own good; his own good is entirely in the order of his own soul. *But this is precisely the difficulty*. If he has no need of others, he will appear to be indifferent to their good. While he will have little motive to harm others, this does not yet translate into a positive concern with the good of others, or of rulership as it was defined in the early conversation with Thrasymachus. As Socrates had observed in this discussion, the decent human being will not intrinsically concern himself with looking out for others' good, which is the function of rulership or *political* activity. There appears to be a tension between two sorts of notions of justice—that which involves the ordering of the soul of the individual, on the one hand, and that which involves a service to others. What needs to be somehow explained, in order to satisfy the brothers' demand, is some way of understanding that the appropriate functioning or ordering of the soul is accomplished only in a concern for the good of others.

Philosophy and politics. From today's standpoint, it is very interesting to notice in a little more detail Socrates' views regarding the *role of women* in society and politics. Polemarchus and Adeimantus wish to have Socrates go into more detail regarding his proposed "communism of women and children." Socrates does this in a playful manner, and then adds something for which they did not ask. He calls the discussion of the communism of women and children the "female drama," since the crucial issue there is of the role of women in political community. Socrates takes a radical and self-consciously controversial step here: he eliminates what we might call the uniquely female role in human life, in two different ways. First, he says that women should play identical roles to men in the life of the guardian and ruling class. The difference between man and woman is to be no different from the difference between bald and non-bald men. Secondly, he says that children are to be raised in common, not by individual parents; every child will be the ward of the state.

What these two reforms have in common is that they ignore the different roles of men and women in child-bearing and child-raising. Socrates' intent seems to be to destroy any sort of allegiance that one might have to a particular family or child. Yet the love of family seems crucial for the irreducible value of the individual human being. This sense of the individual's singularity was tradition-ally considered the province of the female, and is closely tied to the woman's role in the creation of individual human life. Thus we often say that a *mother's* love is a primary source of the sense of the unconditional worth of a person's life.

What could be the point of Socrates' dangerous and extreme reforms? Ultimately, it is to increase the unity of the community, and remove any obstacle to the guardians' and rulers' allegiance to the common good, as opposed to one's own. In Socrates' discussion of these familial reforms, another source of attachment to one's own is rooted out: sexual activity is treated merely as a mode of breeding. Humans are to be treated no differently from the way dogs are by breeders; sexual partners are to be arranged by their ability to produce suitable offspring for the benefit of the city as a whole, and Socrates takes great care in describing an elaborate procedure for doing this without the knowledge of those who are undergoing it. Romantic or erotic love attaches us to particular men or women, whose lives become our lives; this, too, is an obstacle to the unity of the state, as we see in the many great pieces of literature that associate romance and law-breaking. Therefore, it too must be carefully eliminated in the name of the overwhelming sanctity of the political community as a whole.

Were these reforms to be taken non-poetically, they would run into several important objections, all of which come down to what we have seen to be the crucial issue of the *Republic* from the beginning. We might argue that these reforms would ultimately be self-defeating, since it is precisely from familial and erotic relationships that we gain a sense of the value of our individual lives, and that this sense is a precondition for any sort of political allegiance and concern for our own self-development by means of character education to begin with. A political community that persecuted romance and the family would ultimately, therefore, destroy the very possibility of the guardians that are necessary to its preservation. For a political community ultimately to be human, it must do justice to those relationships that are fundamentally non-political, yet meaningful. In Socrates' reforms, we reduce the individual's significance to that of an *interchangeable part* whose significance is only in their contribution to the whole. The distinction between political community so conceived and slavery seems difficult to discern.

This points to a more essential criticism, one that was implicit in the earlier objection of Adeimantus. In making men political, it seems that we make them ultimately unhappy. We also might wonder whether, in making our allegiance to the political community absolute in this way, we are making it inhuman. If the city is seen as if it were some sort of natural whole, as if *it* were the living being, then this seems to make a concern for individual happiness—*either of ourselves or of any other*—illegitimate. Individuals become merely means for the purpose of the unity of the state; and one ought to wonder whether this can be the principle of justice, justice either to ourselves or to others. It is the playfully blunt ignorance of this issue that makes one wonder whether these reforms can be meant as serious political suggestions.

The fundamental intent of Socrates seems to be to preserve the possibility of perfect justice. And who can deny that the greatest obstacle to justice may be the particular attachments that we have to family and those whom we love? These things tend toward making us value the good of those who are close to us as infinitely of greater value than that of our fellow citizens. Particular attachment tends to narrow our focus when it comes to an appreciation of the good of others, by making it identical to or coincident with our own good. Once again, a tension arises between individual happiness and justice as a service to others. It is because of this difficulty that Socrates proposes his ludicrous reforms. As opposed to real cities, the city in speech seeks to reduce the difference between private interest and the public good to nothing.

Socrates then discusses the possibility of such a city coming into being, and it is in this context that he makes a bold and startling claim—that there could be one change in actual cities that would "bring the city to our kind of regime" (Plato

1979, 473b-c). This change would be, startlingly enough, that *philosophers would become kings*. This strange supposition calls into question the previous reforms. If philosophers could come to rule actual regimes, and actual regimes do not themselves have these radical reforms, then would it be necessary at all to engage in the radical forms of communism and elimination of the family that were just discussed? Or would it be that the rule of philosophers would itself substitute adequately for such reforms? The text of the *Republic* is not entirely clear on this question.

However we resolve this issue, the notion that what is essential to the just political community is the rule of philosophers (lovers of wisdom) is itself a curious suggestion—perhaps, Socrates suggests, even more problematic than the other reforms. In the *Republic* itself, this proposal meets with two types of objections—one from the side of the ordinary people, and another from the side of the philosophers themselves. Before we look at these substantial objections, it is crucial to understand why it is that a *philosophical* type of rulership is a solution to the problem of justice as it has been formulated.

If we recall, the difficulty seems to be the one that was presented first by Thrasymachus, and then more fully by the two brothers: the best life for an individual seems to involve justice, or our duty to others only instrumentally or accidentally; justice, they argued, cannot really be an *intrinsic* value. Justice is either not at all worthy of choice for the self-interested person, or it is only good as a *means* to some individual self-interest. The unsatisfactory nature of the earlier discussion with Thrasymachus, as well as Socrates' apparent "solution" to the difficulty in the earlier analogy between city and soul, is that the decent man seems to view his obligation to others as something external to his concern for his own good. The question raised here, then, is this: how does the specifically *philosophical* concern rectify this difficulty, if at all?

In order to address this, two things must be done. First, the philosophical concern must be established as the highest good that is achievable by the individual. Remember that in Ancient Greek "philosopher" meant simply "lover of wisdom"—that is, the person who seeks truth above what it is convenient to make people believe. Secondly, this philosophical concern must essentially be seen to involve the type of rulership that Socrates had identified with the virtues of the various arts in his opening discussion with Thrasymachus—it must be concern itself essentially with the good of others. This double function calls attention to some objections to philosophical rule. The first is the objection raised by ordinary people, who take the philosophical task to be either useless or harmful; it can be neither fit to rule nor individually satisfactory.

In response, Socrates compares the situation of the philosopher in actual cities to how things are in a disorganized and unsuccessful ship. The philosopher—the lover of truth—is like the navigator, who can read the stars, the winds, and the maps in order to guide the ship successfully to its proper destination. But, Socrates says, think what would happen if a ship were ruled in its course, not by the proper navigator, but by some group, whether a minority or a majority, of sailors who did not know what they were doing? Would they not ridicule the navigator's gazing at the sky and observing the meteorological conditions? And, Socrates says, is this not the condition of things in most cities—that the wise do not rule, but rule seems to be haphazard by those who think themselves wise without being so? And, would a city not be better ruled by those who were concerned, not with *appearing* to be wise, but with those who are concerned with *actually* being wise? This difference of concern is what distinguishes all true philosophers from those who are concerned merely to seem to be wise, whom Socrates calls **sophists**. Most actual cities, Socrates says, are ruled by those who are sophistic in this way; the city is the "greatest Sophist"(Plato 1979, 493a-d).

To complement this insight, Socrates says that what distinguishes the philosophic nature is a true love of learning—one that is not content with how things appear, but seeks knowledge of their true **essence**. This true essence is referred to as the "form" or "shape" (*eidos*) of the thing—the set of crucial features that actually define what the thing is. The form or essence is what makes the thing investigated the type of thing that it is—it is the definitive nature the thing. This essential knowledge, which is irreducible to mere perceptions of the thing, is what the philosophical nature seeks.

Socrates describes this experience in a strange image, the famous *"analogy of the cave."* In this analogy, the human (and political) condition is compared to being chained to a wall so that one's head only looks forward, and one is engaged in trying to predict and identify the shadows that pass on the wall. These shadows are actually the shadows of certain statuettes held in front of a fire by certain men (the poets and politicians); the statuettes cast shadows on the wall as these men pass by. These things that cast the shadows, being human creations, are not necessarily reflective of the truth about their subjects. Socrates describes the philosophical education as the painful escaping from the cave, which must be accomplished, he says, by compulsion, since one who was raised in the cave will not wish to believe that there is any other reality. Philosophy is painful, because it means that we must set aside that which has become dear to us merely by the fact of its familiarity, in the search for the truth. This story reflects the earlier communitarianism in that we have the need to escape that which is "our own" in order to understand the truth of things.

The philosophical prisoners, once they are forced to look around, escape from the cave and gradually become accustomed to the sunlight. Outside the cave are the true essences of things, not merely the haphazard opinion of the poetic and political statue-makers. Socrates notes that just as the fire allowed things to be seen in the cave, so does the sun make possible the vision of things outside the cave. Something analogous to the sun makes possible true knowledge of things, just as the sun makes possible clear vision. Socrates calls this thing "the Good," and knowledge of the Good is what the philosopher ultimately seeks. But "the Good" cannot be glimpsed directly, just as the sun cannot. The best we can do is see its image in things that it might illumine, just as we can look at the sun through its image in water or other such things.

It is also important to note several things here about the realm of the cave and that of the outside world. First, they seem to be alike in one important respect: there is an attempt to illumine the nature of things by the construction of a fire in a dark place. Furthermore, when Glaucon expresses wonder at Socrates' image of the cave and the prisoners there, Socrates points out that such prisoners are "like us." This seems to indicate that Socrates' image-making activity is itself not something done "in the light," but itself is done in the cave. Perhaps what is indicated by this is that we simply are, as men, engulfed by the realm of opinion and images, the realm of what "seems to be." However, the meaning of the content of Socrates' image is that even if this is the case, to say so only becomes meaningful if we suppose a realm of the truth about things, a realm "outside the cave," toward which we must strive to move. The realm of images only becomes meaningful if we assume the presence of the fundamental reality of which they are the images. This does not mean, of course, that we can ever dispense with this realm of shadows (and hence politics and the fine arts), if we know ourselves as human beings.

The philosophical type, having escaped the realm of images to the realm of reality, does not wish to return to this realm. Why would we, since the philosophical nature is so finely attuned to desiring to know the essence of things? Why would we find images at all attractive, after we have escaped to the real, and so (as Socrates says) have achieved a divine thing while still alive? At this point, however, Socrates points out that the philosopher must be compelled to go back down into the cave of political life, and that this is justice. This is justice because in the city that Socrates and the two brothers have constructed, each man subordinates his own good to the good of the city. The philosopher, the lover of truth, despite a strong desire to reside with the essences, is the one best equipped to guide the construction of and identification of the images within the cave. Philosophers, unlike those who have not sought outside of the cave, have a memory of the essential nature of things to guide them.

The unwillingness of the philosopher, the lover of wisdom, to return to the care of political life returns us to the question as to the relation of individual happiness and the service to others. Suppose philosophy responds to the ordering of the soul by the truth of things, which is the deepest desire of human being, and that the height of philosophical activity is the apprehension of the essences of things along with the Good that makes their knowledge possible: in this case, is the demand of *justice,* which returns the philosopher to the cave, not itself opposed to individual happiness? It seems that again we have an inevitable tension, even at the deepest part of the Platonic teaching, between our service to others and our individual happiness. Does Socrates at all accomplish the defense of justice that he promises at the beginning?

There is serious scholarly dispute regarding this question. One school of thought has it that the teaching of the *Republic* is that there is an inevitable and irrevocable tension between the interest of philosophy (or individual happiness) and the interest of politics (or of care for other human beings). This school of thought has on its side the prevalence of the difficulty throughout the dialogue. As we have seen, at crucial points, when an apparent conclusion to the construction of the city in speech arrives, this question reappears, just as it had at the conclusion of the opening discussion in Book One. Insofar as there is any reconciliation with the political community, it takes the form of the philosopher's *indifference* to political concerns. Like Glaucon, philosophers are ambitious; but their ambition is not political, and so they are of no danger to their fellow men, but rather treat them with characteristic moderation. The city is only just insofar as it imitates this moderation. However, the foundation of the most just community involves a fundamental injustice, in that it forces the philosophers to rule, that is, to enter the cave, which can only be a second-best activity for them. In so doing, it must violate the very principle that constitutes its justice—that every person do what he or she is best capable of, and nothing else (Bloom 1968, 401-412).

While this school of thought makes a good argument, there is another side to the question (for example, see Dobbs 1985, 809-22). The first thing to consider is this: because philosophers are compelled to return to the cave, does this necessarily make this act unjust from the point of view of the philosophers themselves? Could it be that the philosophers, in the desire for the essences of things, actually are deficient in theior own wisdom in some manner, and for this reason must be compelled to concern themselves with political issues?

Some of the things we have noted above indicate that this may be. First is Socrates' description of the philosopher's self-image outside of the cave; he seems to have thought he was in the Blessed Isles while still alive. The Blessed Isles are mythically the place for those men who have lived good lives, that is, for those whose goodness is complete. Socrates' claim that they reach it while still alive is suspect, because it is questionable whether their good life is complete, given that their life is not yet complete. There is something deficient in their knowledge of themselves.

Second, Socrates says that the Good is itself the proper study of philosophers. Yet the Good is described, not simply as the intelligible light that illuminates the pure essences, but as the source of anything just and beautiful and the cause of rational action for both ourselves and our city. It seems that a true study of the Good must account not only for its action in knowing, but also in any other human activity. A knowledge of the good abstractly, without considering it as the source of all things just and beautiful, would seem to be an incomplete knowledge (Plato 1979, 517b-c). Knowledge that is merely of the pure essences is not a full or comprehensive knowledge of the good. The seeking out of the good, in all of its appearances and images, is a worthwhile activity and not to be slighted. It is precisely in the political concern that this becomes visible. A philosopher, that is, must have a *comprehensive* concern with the good, not merely an abstract one in the purity of the essences. If philosophers were merely to pursue the latter, they would repeat the mistake that Adeimantus had earlier made—treating one's own good as if it were the only good worthy of attention.

This insight takes account of two things we noticed earlier: that the good is not entirely absent in the cave (there is a light in the cave by fire), and that the prisoners in the cave are "like us." If we are like the prisoners in the cave, then we are not *ever* in the pure light of the outside world, and we are restricted to observations of the shadow on the wall. Yet, we may be ourselves *oriented* by the outside world of pure essences in our discussion or identification of the images upon the wall. We do not take for granted, that is, that the opinions and speeches given in the city are themselves the pure essences of things. There is an element of our intelligence that wishes to measure them by truth. But these opinions are not of themselves *without* sense entirely, and by seeking the truth, we do not seek to replace the realm of opinion with some other realm, but rather to measure opinion by the truth. The political realm cannot ever be forsaken, since our place is not simply on the outside, but in conversation with others. This seems to point to a much closer connection between Aristotle's description of humans as both "rational" and a "political" animals.

A close look at what Socrates says regarding the philosopher's return to the cave bears out this interpretation. One may be tempted, he says, to laugh at the philosopher in his return to the city, since he will stumble around at first, as one who goes from sunlight into a cave might. But what is of interest here is that the philosopher ought to be congratulated, not in ascending from the cave, but in descending back into it. The reconciliation between the individual's own interest and justice as the good of others, according to this account, is of the essence of philosophy. Philosophy seeks out the good, not merely for the philosopher, but comprehensively. This necessarily means that the philosopher must submit to residing in "the cave" of political life, because this cave is not so simply divorced from a concern with the good, but is essential to a proper understanding of it.

The two understandings of the *Republic* that we have considered here represent somewhat different views of the activity of philosophy. The first, which emphasizes an irresolvable *tension* between philosophy and the political community, philosophical activity is seen as an essentially *solitary* activity. Because it can be accomplished in a solitary gaze upon the intelligible essences of things, sociality of any sort is extraneous, and must be regarded fundamentally as merely an instrument to philosophical activity. The second viewpoint, in which there is some sort of *reconciliation* between philosophy and community, supposes the activity of philosophy to be essentially friendly or to take place *between* human beings. If this were the case, then there would ultimately always be an element of friendship or community in philosophical activity that would be the ground of philosophy's political responsibility. Philosophy would consist precisely of dialogue, as informed by an honest love of truth.

Whichever of these views one accepts as final, with the discussion of the role of philosophy in politics we reach the high point of *The Republic*. The rest of the dialogue concerns itself with the devolution of forms of rule from the rule of philosopher-kings. This devolution ends in the worst of regimes, the mirror opposite of philosophical rule—the rule of a tyrant. Tyrants, although sharing the philosopher's comprehensive desire, make this desire into a desire that subordinates the good of all others to their own private good. As such, their rule is the opposite of justice. Socrates takes great pains to point to the *unhappiness* of the tyrant's life; his soul is disordered, and so he is a slave to his irrational desires. Also, his preoccupation with lording it over all makes him ultimately a slave in his own kingdom.

The final book of the dialogue returns briefly to the question of poetry. Shortly after warning of the seductions of poetry in its tragic guise, Socrates demonstrates its necessity by ending the conversation with a myth about the afterlife. This myth shows that philosophy is the only true defense against injustice and unhappiness. The end of the dialogue thus concurs with its height; the only way to choose well is to have a comprehensive and ruling concern for the good.

Conclusion. These last considerations have apparently taken us a bit far afield. What can we say the *Republic* as a whole teaches about the political good?

We have emphasized that the dialogue raises what is the fundamental question about the nature of justice: what is the ground of our concern for the good of others? The position of the dialogue as a whole is that justice must answer to the deepest concerns for individual happiness. The political implication is that the political community exists to shape character so as to produce fulfilled human beings—a decidedly *communitarian* viewpoint. This is reflected in the notion of justice that defines the city in speech; each person is to do the task that they are by nature most fit to do. But the question of the dialogue is whether this works reciprocally as well: does the satisfaction of the individual involve an allegiance to the community? In any case, we see the concern with character formation that runs throughout the dialogue, and this concern forms the basis of Aristotelean political philosophy that will be discussed in the next section. This does not mean that the details of political structure that Socrates discusses in the *Republic* are the only way to manifest this concern. Aristotle himself will keep this concern while criticizing many of the Socratic institutions, particularly the communism of women and children, as defeating the overall political purpose of character formation, for reasons similar to the objections we considered above.

A crucial consideration here that modern political theories tend to neglect is the importance of character for decent political community. Whereas modern political theories tend to emphasize the importance of certain *institutional* arrangements, the emphasis for both Plato and Aristotle is on the *type of person* who is in the position of rule. No matter what type of institution is present, if those who make decisions for the political community are not possessed of a good character (possessing the virtues of justice, moderation, wisdom and courage), then the political community will come to harm. In this respect, ancient political philosophy can act as a complement or corrective to modern political thought.

This said, there is a tendency in the *Republic* to treat the individual human being as merely a "part" of the political community, something that would offend modern political sensibilities, in two respects. First, if individual human beings are valued for their own sake, then any political philosophy that treats them as if they were merely a part in a larger political body would be inherently unjust. If we avoid the excesses that Socrates proposes in his communism and breeding, it seems that the concern of character formation can accommodate this criticism. In demanding that individuals form their character in a rational and socially responsible manner, one does not mean to shortchange the value of the individual. On the contrary, one is committed to individuals developing their natural capacities so as to fulfill the nature of their being as rational and political animals.

Secondly, modern political theorists will argue that it is the individual's *freedom* and *rights* that are to be protected by the political community. Ultimately, behind this is a notion of what the dignity of a rational individual requires. This criticism becomes a major source of disagreement between modern and ancient political thought. Plato and Aristotle would argue that freedom is of secondary importance to what we might call *human fulfillment*. Liberty might be a necessary condition of such fulfillment for Aristotle, as something implicit in the excellence of choice that is characteristic of the mature individual—but it is not itself inherently an excellence of choice, and so is not sufficient for fulfillment. In fact, for freedom or rights to be completed requires a certain kind of habituation of one's passions, and such habituation requires precisely that one be ruled by others in one's choices. Freedom is not, for the ancients, the primary political good. In *The Republic*, this is manifested by the fact that democracy, the regime of freedom, is not considered to be the best regime. The more serious conflict between ancients and early modern thought is over this question of freedom.

2. The Normative Basis for Aristotle's Political Philosophy

In order to understand the normative component of Aristotle's political philosophy, it is necessary to begin with an area of his philosophical thinking that initially seems far removed from political issues—Aristotle's concept of "purpose" in living organisms. Superficially, this discussion might sound more relevant to biology than to ethics or politics, but such is the interrelatedness of philosophical issues as they pertain to questions about meaningful human activities.

Although Aristotle's book *Politics* is considered to be the classic statement of his political ideas, the basic assumptions of the *Politics* are supported in a more specific way in Aristotle's primary ethical work, *Nicomachean Ethics*. In this book, and also in Aristotle's *De Anima* ("on the soul"), the concept of "*organism*" is carefully defined; it is clear that this concept is the backbone of Aristotle's understanding of human personality and the purpose of human existence. An organism is a type of **natural whole**, in Aristotle's sense— a particular kind of collective entity in which the "whole is different from the mere sum of its parts," as the now somewhat overworked expression goes. To be more precise, an organism is an entity that exhibits two properties:

(1) The parts of the entity function in such a way as to further progress toward the realization of the goals of the *whole* entity, rather than each part's merely working toward its own particular goals. For example, the cells of the human body work together in order to further the aims of the body as a whole; if one type of cell should work only to realize its own advantage, even at the expense of thwarting the purposes of the body as a whole, the result would be cancer, an abnormal condition which ultimately would cause the organism to cease being an organism at all and revert to a mere mass of inorganic matter.

(2) The other essential distinguishing feature of organisms is that, within certain limits, the whole may maintain the same identity and continue functioning in the same way even when all or most of the parts have been replaced. For example, almost all the cells in the human body are replaced every seven years, yet John Smith remains essentially the same person he was eight years ago. He can even still remember experiences he had eight years ago. Moreover, in organisms, if one part changes in such a way as to disrupt the purposive functioning of the whole, then the whole may cause some of its other parts to change in such a way as to compensate for the change in the initial part which had led to the disruptive tendency. In this way, the organism strives to maintain continuity of purposeful function among its various parts, even though the parts themselves may change. A particularly clear twentieth century exposition of this point was given by the psychologist and neurologist Kurt Goldstein (1938) in his important book *The Organism*.

Because organisms can rearrange their parts in order to serve the purposes of the whole, they also have the capacity to *act* rather than just *react*. Thus, in the case of humans, there is a capacity for responsibility: "Man is the source of his actions" (Aristotle 1962, 62).

The principle that the whole is sometimes different from the sum of its parts, or that the whole sometimes causes its parts to be governed by different rules from those which would govern them in other contexts, has been given the name "*holism*." Some philosophers and scientists believe that holism is a confused and misleading concept—that the functioning the whole, even in the case of organisms, can be explained perfectly well in terms of the mechanical interactions of the parts, each governed by the laws of physics as they would apply to the same parts in any other context. In its extreme form, this latter view would be called "*atomism*"—the principle which says that atoms or particles behave in the same way (i.e., according to the same physical laws) in one context as in another.

"Atomism" is also used on a more metaphorical basis to describe the same thesis as pertaining, not to atoms or particles in a literal sense, but to the individual parts that make up any given whole. More moderate varieties of atomism might allow that the same individual phenomenon does indeed behave differently in different situations, but always by the same physical laws, which specify how it will react in various circumstances. This moderate form of atomism would therefore not deny that organisms function in a unified way and that they exhibit the two features mentioned above; it would assert, however, that no further explanatory hypothesis is needed beyond those which would explain the motion of the parts. Aristotle was an extreme organicist or holist in terms of this controversy; but there may be the possibility that his theory would have similar ethical and political implications even if he had described the phenomenon of organic unity in the context of a modified atomism.

Aristotle believed that an organism or natural whole cannot be understood aside from the concept of *purpose*. Without mentioning the fact that an organism has its own unified purpose, one could not distinguish an organism from an inorganic object in terms of the two features of organisms mentioned above. He goes on to say, more specifically, that the most general purpose of any organism, the one that provides the overall unity of its functioning, is growth toward the mature status appropriate to the particular kind of organism in question. For example, any description of an acorn would be incomplete if it omitted any mention of the fact that the acorn has as its purpose to grow into an oak tree. Aristotle therefore defined the "*soul*" (the Greek word was *psyche*—that which distinguishes living from non-living things) as the "principle of growth" in something. This concept of the unified purpose of organisms gave rise to the notion of "*teleology*"—that at least some processes in nature are guided toward the achievement of natural purposes or goals.

Aristotle therefore concluded that all "value"—even moral value—must be derivative from this concept of purpose. Only in relation to organisms does value exist. Value results when an organism achieves its most general purpose, which is maturity and mastery of the mature virtues of the particular kind of organism in question. The implications of this doctrine for value in human life are obviously not hedonistic in the modern sense (in the sense discussed by Hobbes, for example) because if the organism is to achieve its mature status, momentary satisfactions must often be sacrificed for the attainment of this goal; once the mature status is attained, momentary satisfactions also must often be sacrificed in order to *maintain* the condition of maturity. Maturity is not guaranteed by mere physical age, but is rather a specific quality of well-functioning that must be achieved by the organism.

In the case of human beings, the ultimate goal has two facets, corresponding to the two facets of the essence of what it means to be a complete human being: (1) Man is the *rational animal*; (2) because he cannot attain and maintain a state of rationality apart from a social community, it is also necessary and essential to man's mature status that he be a *political or social animal*. In a mature state, then, a person will have cultivated the kinds of habits, through self-conditioning, that make him or her into the kind of person who derives more pleasure from *rational and socially constructive* activities (for example, rationally thought-out, non-criminal career goals, and community service) than from other kinds of activities (such as overindulging in destructive, self-destructive, or socially non-productive forms of pleasure).

Aristotle writes in his *Nichomachean Ethics:* "As regards the pleasures, pains, appetites and diversions, . . . It is possible to be the kind of person who is overcome even by those which most people master; but it is also possible to master those by which most people are overcome" (Aristotle 1962). Which type of person one is, according to Aristotle, depends on conditioning or habit—a hypothesis strikingly congruent with most modern psychological theories of learning, particularly those of Hull and Spence. But whether or not someone has cultivated this habit or that habit depends in turn on what kinds of moral training they have had, and on what kind of training and conditioning they have imposed on *themselves.* If someone wishes to be the kind of person who enjoys reading, for example, then one will begin by reading frequently, in full knowledge that eventually one will reach the point where one enjoys reading.

In this way, we choose our own needs and desires, by cultivating them in ourselves through conditioning. But if it is possible to cultivate *our own* needs and desires, it is also possible to train ourselves to be the kinds of people whose needs and desires do not conflict with moral responsibility. It therefore remains within our power to act in accordance with ethically derived moral principles, because it is within our power to shape our needs and desires in such a way that those needs and desires do not interfere with the performance of our duty. In fact, in Aristotle's view, "None of the moral virtues is implanted in us by nature, for nothing which exists by nature can be changed by habit" (1962, 33).

To be a "rational animal," in Aristotle's sense, it is not enough to be intelligent. What Aristotle means by "rationality" is that we are intelligent enough to understand the principles of our own psychology and then to apply those principles to our own habit development, thus cultivating desirable virtues in ourselves. Which virtues are desirable, in turn, is defined by the second property of human beings—that we are "social or political animals." While other kinds of animals might be socially gregarious and cooperative, only humans are able to understand their own psychology well enough to condition ourselves to be what we think we should be. It would be absurd to hold a dog or cat responsible for such self-development.

A simple example of this Aristotelian concept of "rationality" occurs in an episode of a popular TV show, *Gunsmoke.* A sheriff's deputy is offered a banana by the owner of the local general store in a rural nineteenth-century town. When the deputy, who has never before tasted a banana, discovers that the bananas cost five cents each (an outrageous sum of money in those days), he refuses even to try a free sample, saying "I don't want to cultivate an appetite I can't afford." Similarly, one might say (roughly) that Aristotle suggests that we refrain from "cultivating appetites we can't afford"; but rather than offering this principle as a means of *saving money,* Aristotle offers it as a way to avoid having needs and desires that conflict with our status as socially constructive members of society.

The basic point is that needs and desires do not necessarily prevent us from conforming to moral principles and cultivating moral and political virtues. We can condition ourselves (within certain limits) to desire and need to perform just those kinds of actions that we know are socially constructive and morally virtuous, and we can de-condition ourselves from desiring and needing to perform immoral or counterproductive actions.

But Aristotle also recognized that, in order to achieve these outcomes, we need for the society to provide us with certain needed resources, Aristotle believed that these needed resources are fairly extensive. A person must have access to educational opportunities, must have a certain amount of economic security, and also must live in a community that encourages cooperation and political participation. In this regard, Aristotle was a strongly *communitarian* type of thinker. He believed that the community must take responsibility for the kinds of citizens it produces, through its educational system, its laws, and its attention to the economic needs of the people. In his *Politics,* Aristotle writes: "If the whole body be destroyed, there will not be a foot or a hand. . . . We thus see that the polis [community] exists by nature and that it is prior to the individual. The proof of both propositions is that the polis is a whole, and that individuals are simply its parts" (Aristotle 1974, 6).

Aristotle argues that his principle of rationality—the possibility of molding one's own desires, by means of self-conditioning—overcomes the problem of egoism in ethics. The society, especially as represented by its government, has according to Aristotle a corresponding duty to its citizens which in modern times has been generally de-emphasized. Besides being a vehicle through which the people ensure services and protections for themselves, besides being a mere "social contract" for the sake of mutual self-interest, the Ancient Greeks also envisioned the government as having the duty to *produce* good people. The total society must be arranged in such a way as to help people achieve the goal of maturity. The government was to be educator and trainer of people, not just provider for their material needs.

An extreme example of this principle, in the thinking of both Plato and Aristotle, has to do with censorship. Both Plato (in *The Republic*) and Aristotle (in his *Nichomachean Ethics* and in his *Politics*) go on at great length and in endless detail even about which *musical modes* young people should be allowed to listen to. To the Greeks, this was no small point, because building character depends on channeling the emerging *passions* into constructive directions. In music, this mean that the stalwart Dorian mode should be encouraged, while the wildly frenetic Phrygian mode was all but censored. If Aristotle were alive today, one cannot help but wonder whether he would recommend the censorship of popular music—not because of its lyrics, but because of the emotional content of the *musical scales* it uses!—in order to help adolescents (and adults) to cultivate more constructive passions by listening to jazz and classical music. Everything we listen to, after all, is playing a part in making us into the kind of persons we shall become.

This concept of Aristotle's could be applied more seriously to contemporary controversies around the issue of censorship. Should people be free to cultivate socially harmful emotions which they could just as happily live without if they had never cultivated them in the first place? (Remember, Aristotle believes that with the appropriate conditioning, we can get just as much pleasure out of Beethoven as a boorish person gets out of TV violence.) Should only those who have already attained the state of maturity be free to read pornographic literature? Or should pornography be censored in general, based on the premise that it tends to thwart the development of good habits and socially constructive attitudes? In Aristotle's thinking, if a person still has not cultivated the most socially constructive emotions possible for that person, then by definition he or she has not yet reached maturity and therefore should be helped by the society to continue developing toward the mature form of human existence.

Again, this would make sense only in terms of a value theory that places priority on the *existence of the human soul in a certain condition* (i.e., its mature state, which consists of rationality and constructive contribution to society) —a value system that considers this mature condition of the soul to be even more important than pleasure. This, finally, is what sets Aristotle apart from both utilitarianism and modern theories of justice. Neither the consequences of actions nor their conformity to rules is of ultimate concern, but rather the total *condition of the soul* in its activity congruent with man's proper essence. Human existence itself, in the full sense of "human" existence, is the goal. This implies such existence for all who are capable of it, and therefore we must all work together to help everyone achieve it insofar as possible, because of the "socially constructive" requirement inherent in the definition of the mature status.

One of the disconcerting aspects of Aristotle's theory, for the modern reader, is that he apparently did not believe that all people were capable of maturity; and he suggested that those who were absolutely incapable of reaching maturity should be "natural slaves." Some scholars contend that Aristotle only meant to include in this category the mentally retarded, and certain types of criminals who are incorrigible because of brain diseases, such as sociopaths and violent schizophrenics or violent types of bipolar disorder. Others insist that Aristotle meant to include many people in the slave class, that he was a totalitarian and an oligarch, blinded by the aristocratic prejudices of his day. Some mean between these extremes was probably the case. It may be that Aristotle was impeded on this point by his own cultural and historical setting. Slavery was still the norm at the time of Ancient Greece, and most of these slaves had been captured in the aftermath of wars, where the enemy's women and children would typically be taken as slaves.

But, whichever interpretation one gives to Aristotle's views on "natural slavery," the important point for our purposes is that it seems inconsistent with Aristotle's own overall theory to hold that *any* human being is incapable of maturity, except perhaps those with brain damage or mental diseases. If the *essence* of a human being is to be capable of growing to achieve such-and-such a mature form, then *all* people must be inherently *capable* of achieving the mature form, unless prevented by external circumstances or organic brain problems. And by Aristotle's own definition of man as the rational and social animal, any man must be inherently capable of achieving these outcomes.

Still another criticism of Aristotle also relates to his apparently "aristocratic" tendencies: While the notion that society should assume the responsibility to educate its people and ensure their opportunity for self-development seems plausible when considered in the abstract, political experiences such as those in Nazi Germany have convinced many people that, in a concrete political situation, Aristotle's plan would not work the way he envisions it as working. It is often suggested that Aristotle's view is too *paternalistic*. It sets up the government to train and indoctrinate people to be the kinds of people who will fit smoothly into that particular type of political system. This problem of paternalism in turn is one of the most serious criticisms of communitarian approaches to political philosophy in general.

Many contemporary philosophers of criminal justice, for example, would agree with Aristotle that rather than just building more prisons to punish criminals, we should realize that the society as a whole is creating the criminals themselves, because of certain socio-economic conditions. Removing these conditions might go a long way toward removing the crime. But most contemporary thinkers on these issues would stop short of Aristotle's notion that the society should mold the passions of its people by means of censorship. The feeling is that the philosophy of Aristotle, even if valid in an abstract sense, would end up very differently when placed in the hands of politicians and bureaucrats; that it would lead to arbitrary and reactionary limitations of people's freedom, and to dictatorial control of public opinion by means of censorship of the press.

On the other hand, defenders of Aristotle say that people must be rational and educated if democracy is to work. Thomas Jefferson, for example, stressed that intellectually underdeveloped people are putty in the hands of propagandists and therefore cannot make rational political decisions. The society must at least assume the responsibility to educate its people and to arrange social conditions as much as possible in such a way that people will have the opportunity to develop their full potentialities. An uninformed electorate cannot make intelligent choices when electing representatives in a democracy. Aristotelians strongly emphasize this communitarian requirement, and insist that the society therefore must not tolerate social conditions that thwart and inhibit the individual's development toward self-actualization.

Perhaps the most frequent criticism of Aristotle's theory of value is that it commits the *"naturalistic fallacy."* That is, it begins with the premise that human nature is such that we strive to realize such-and-such a purpose, and then concludes that we *should* strive to realize such-and-such a purpose. But if it is valid to infer from the fact that something *is* the case to the thesis that it *ought* to be the case, then it would follow that everything which is, ought to be. Therefore, there would be no possibility for any normative statements at all. There would be no difference between what is and what ought to be.

Aristotle is often accused of committing this "naturalistic fallacy"—the fallacy of equating a naturalistic situation with a morally desirable one. The twentieth century ethical theorist G.E. Moore (1900/1956), for example, famously argued that one cannot derive an Ought from an Is in the way that Aristotle attempts to do. If we derive what ought to be from what is, we only end up asserting that whatever is the case ought to be the case.

But this criticism is not really decisive against Aristotle. Aristotle does not hold that everything that is natural is automatically right. Human existence has a purpose, but the achievement of the purpose is not guaranteed by nature. Whatever gets in the way of its achievement is morally bad, simply because it is the purpose itself which gives the notion of moral value its ultimate meaning. This is far from entailing that whatever is, ought to be.

Chapter Four
Hobbes and the Origins of
Modern Social Contract Theory

1. Transition from Ancient to Early Modern Thought: The New Mechanistic Worldview

Social Contract theories of justice have been the dominant paradigm for the way we think of our relations to each other in political community during the modern period of history. There seems to be an appeal for modern people of the central principle at the heart of all such theories—the liberty of the *autonomous individual*. G. W. F. Hegel forecasted that this principle would not be merely a passing phenomenon, but would become a world-wide necessity: "When individuals and nations have once got in their heads the abstract conception of full-blown liberty, there is nothing like it in its uncontrollable strength, just because it is the very essence of spirit" (Hegel, 1971, 240).

This quotation reveals both Hegel's approval and his critique of the notion of the autonomous individual, a dual attitude shared by his most famous pupil, Karl Marx (whom we shall discuss later). Liberty's power makes it seem to be the *essence* of being human—our essential or defining property—yet the conception of liberty as that of the *individual* human is "abstract," not concrete or fully real. For both Hegel and Marx, liberty is actualized only in a certain sort of *political community*. In some sense, then, it is the community which is free, and the individual is free only derivatively.

This notion reflects, in the much later thinking of Hegel and Marx, the presence of a political philosophy where individual liberty, conceived of as the liberty of the "autonomous individual," is *not* the greatest concern of political community. In this respect, the thinking of Hegel and Marx is more like the philosophy of the ancient world than is the thinking of Hobbes and Locke. But all these modern thinkers share one common theme: they all emphasize the central importance of freedom.

It is highly instructive to contrast this emphasis against the thinking of Ancient Greece. The clearest statement regarding the objection of ancient philosophy to the priority of the autonomous individual is by Aristotle:

> That the city is by nature, and prior to each individual, then, is clear. For if the individual when separated from it is not self-sufficient, he will be in a condition similar to that of the other parts in relation to the whole. One who is incapable of participating or who is in need of nothing through being self-sufficient is no part of a city, and so is either a beast or a god. Accordingly, there is in everyone by nature an inclination toward this sort of partnership (Aristotle 1984, 1253a24-30).

In Aristotle's view, it is not in the nature of the individual to be simply autonomous. An individual human is not by nature *self-sufficient*. In his way of thinking, a god might be self-sufficient, because there would be no inherent vulnerability to create a need for a city; and a beast could be self-sufficient, because it is incapable of discussion about the just. But a human being cannot be self-sufficient. Thus it is in the nature of the human individual to seek association as an inherent element in human completeness.

In political community, as we saw in the previous chapter, the Ancients also believed we could overcome our inherent *partiality*—the inability to agree with value statements unless they fit our prejudices or are in our own self-interest. Aristotle believed that political association grounded the potential for impartiality by making possible the activity of human speech and reason:

> That man is much more a political animal than any kind of bee or any herd animal is clear. For, as we assert, nature does nothing in vain; and man alone among the animals has speech (logos). . . . Speech serves to reveal the advantageous and the harmful, and hence also the just and unjust. For it is peculiar to man as compared to the other animals that he alone has a perception of good and bad and unjust and just and other things of this sort; and partnership in these things is what makes a household and a city (Aristotle 1984, 1253a7-18).

In the view of the ancients, a being whose reason takes the form of speech necessarily will long for political community. Reason aims at the universally true, and the universally true is a public, not a private, good. For example, the truth of the statement "2+2=4" is not reducible to my individual act of perceiving it to be so; hence, the truth is available to all who possesses reason. As an individual, however, I am not the beginning or source of what is true. The evidence for this is the incompleteness of individual human reason, which becomes evident when we make mistakes.

In Ancient Greece, Socrates' wisdom was considered to consist precisely in his recognition of the *lack* of self-sufficiency in individual human reason. Because none of us is self-sufficient with respect to reason, particularly in regards to the standards of our own good, we must reason in common, i.e., in speech or dialogue. What constitutes a political community, then, is dialogue about the human good. Insofar as our desire is inflected by the desire to know, and we are by nature incomplete to satisfy this desire, the city is by nature a remedy for and a reminder of such incompleteness. This, of course, does not imply that *every* city is an adequate remedy for such incompleteness; however, it does point to a continuity between the city's nature and the fundamental human concern with living well.

Ancient philosophers were familiar with social contract theories of politics, as is revealed by certain of the sophists in the Platonic dialogues, and also by the sophisticated speech that Glaucon uses to challenge Socrates to defend justice in the *Republic*. The crucial point is that, in all contract theories, "the just" is identified with an *agreement* that is instrumental to the interests of autonomous individuals. Thus, according to social contract approaches, justice (and the political community itself) is not a natural pursuit of man, but merely a *means* for pursuing our autonomously determined goals. The dismissal of this view as inadequate by Plato and Aristotle is highlighted by the somewhat cynical manner in which Glaucon, in *The Republic*, speaks of social-contract justice. *Injustice*, he says, is what is natural to man; so then what forces us into society is not a love for justice as such, but a lack of power. Contract theory, for the ancients, was not a concern with justice, but precisely with *injustice*—the acquisition and safeguard of individual power.

By contrast, these power relations are the issues that Thomas Hobbes (1588-1679), the originator of modern contract theory, finds primary in thinking about politics. Hobbes actually uses as his starting point the thinking of the *pre-Socratic* philosophers. In the ancient world, the presuppositions about human desire and the origins of political society that grounded social contract ideas were linked to pre-Socratic natural philosophy. Before Socrates appeared on the scene, the atomism of Democritus and the notion of mind as an efficient cause in Anaxagoras were both linked to a *mechanistic* view of causation. In that view, natural phenomena are indifferent to the Aristotelean notion of *teleology*. Teleology refers to a purpose-guided process as opposed to a mechanistic causal chain. In the mechanistic view, everything, including human behavior, is caused by something that happened previously—not by an Aristotelian "essential nature" that could pull it toward fulfillment of a purpose.

Teleological concepts represent a standard of completeness in nature: they suggest that natural phenomena, especially living ones, tend to complete themselves through a self-organizational process of growth. By contrast, a cursory examination of the mechanistic doctrines of the pre-Socratics makes clear both their emphasis on autonomous individuality, and Aristotele's objection to both. If nature consists of atomic entities, which are randomly attracted to one another and disperse from one another, then there is no intelligible *end* or *purpose* of the motions of these atoms; and everything, of course, consists merely of conglomerations of atoms. There can be no judgment as to defect or perfection of beings that are mere conjunctions of atoms. One conjunction of atoms is as good as any other.

In the thinking of many of the pre-Socratics, which is picked up by Hobbes, we can see humans as just another example of these motions of nature. The desires or wishes of any given person are merely the result of a random conjunction of atoms, and are as good as any other set of desires. If this is so, then the only question remaining for desire is not the *worthiness* of the desire, but whether or not it can be satisfied. This, too, is just a matter for mechanistic causation to resolve. The question here is not a question of right, but of might, or *power*.

This line of reasoning roughly parallels Hobbes' psychology, which is based on an egoistic hedonism, and grounds his entire political philosophy. There is a crucial sense in which, even while rejecting the political consequences of this psychology, those who follow Hobbes accept the irrelevance of teleology—of purposefulness in nature—and hence further develop the mechanistic and hedonistic notions of psychology that Hobbes finds crucial.

Liberty and absolute sovereignty in the thinking of Thomas Hobbes. For Hobbes, certain mechanical motions constitute human activity. Our ordinary physical motions are what he calls *"vital."* Other motions, arising from sensation and imagination, are called *"voluntary";* this latter he also calls *"endeavor,"* of which there are two types: *desire,* and *aversion,* according to whether they move toward or away from the object that causes the motion. *Love* and *hate* are corresponding words used by Hobbes to describe desire and aversion, but love and hate direct attention to the *objects* that cause the motion, i.e., the objects of love and hate. Since these motions are natural and unguided by teleology; it follows that each person is legitimately the judge of good and evil. By nature, what is "good" and "evil" for us is merely what we desire or are averse to. Laws for good and evil that hold for all persons do not exist in nature, but are only the result of a *public will or authority* (Hobbes, 1968,120-21).

Since motion has no teleological direction by nature, it also follows that, when it comes to human action, no teleological direction can be given to desire, which is simply another kind of motion; it is *emotion*, or e-motion. Implied in this natural philosophy, then, are certain of the assumptions of another mode of thought that Socrates, Plato and Aristotle had much earlier critiqued—*sophistry*. The Sophists had claimed to be not only "lovers of wisdom" (philosophers) but actually "wise men" (sophists), and the wisdom they had taught to the young future rulers of their society was a somewhat cynical one: Politics is only a mechanisms whereby self-interest is sought. The Sophists had taught that this cynical view is grounded in the natural philosophy of the pre-Socratics. Pre-Socratic natural philosophy has implications, not only for nature, but for that which *reveals* nature—human speech or reason—and these implications are "sophistic." If nature gives us no guide to the direction in which desire is to be *Reason* focused, then the discernment of this direction can no longer be seen as reason's *takes* primary task. Reason is no longer to find the structures of being *teleologically* in *emotion* natural motion. Rather, it takes the direction given by *emotion* as authoritative, and calculates the means to make sure that the emotion is satisfied, given the other motions which it can discern in the world. These emotions are random consequences of previous motions, and therefore are not open to question regarding their primary direction. They must be simply granted as justified by their natural existence, in the same way that a cat's eating a mouse is justified.

Reason, then, is no longer primarily the discernment of natural ends, and thus reason can no longer be said to rule the desires or passions. Reason is merely concerned with the calculation or analysis of possible outcomes. It is no longer primarily about ends, but is fundamentally about means; it is "endless" or hypothetical. Modern science, as opposed to the Aristotelean, is inherently hypothetical. Reason no longer supplies the ends, but only the means to ends; as such, reason becomes subservient or a tool or function of desire or emotion. Since in modern physics motion always prolongs itself unless there is an obstacle, reason will merely become a means of the prolongation of the motion particular to humans or other animals—desire or emotion. At this point, we are very close to the assumptions of Hobbes regarding the nature and function of reason:

> When a man *Reasoneth*, hee does nothing else but conceive a summe total from *addition* of parcels; or conceive a Remainder, from Subtraction of one summe from another; which if it be done by Words, is conceiving of the consequences of the names of all the parts, to the name of the whole and one part, to the name of the other part. . . . The Logicians do the same in *Consequences* of words; adding together two Names, to make an Affirmation; and two affirmations, to make a Syllogisme; and many Syllogismes to make a Demonstration; and from the summe, or Conclusion of a Syllogisme, they subtract one Proposition, to finde the other . . . in summe, in what matter soever there is place for addition and subtraction, there also is a place for Reason; and where these have no place, there Reason has nothing at all to do.
>
> Out of all which we may define (that is to say determine) what that is, which is meant by this word Reason, when wee reckon it amongst the Faculties of the mind. For Reason, in this sense, is nothing but Reckoning (that is, Adding and Subtracting) of the Consequences of generall names agreed upon, for the marking and signifying of our thoughts (Hobbes 1968, 110-11).

For Hobbes, reason is inherently calculative, and does not have to do with the ends of reasoning. An important consequence of this point immediately follows—that reasoning is inherently hypothetical or indeterminate, and can gain certainty or determinacy only by subservience to authority. Here is what Hobbes says, in his characteristically colorful language:

Not but that Reason it selfe is always Right reason, as well as Arithmetique is a certain and infallible Art: But no one mans Reason, nor the Reason of any one number of men, makes the certaintie; no more than an account is therefore well cast up, because a great many men have unanimously approved it. And therfore, as when there is a controversy in an account, the parties must by their own accord, set up for right Reason, the Reason of some Arbitrator, or Judge, to whose sentence they will both stand, or their controversie must either come to blowes, or be undecided, for want of a right Reason constituted by Nature; And when men that think themselves wiser than all others, clamor and demand right Reason for judge; yet seek no more, but that things should be determined by no other mens reason but their own, it is as intolerable in the society of men, as it is in play when trump is turned, to use for trump on every occasion that suite whereof they have most in their hand. For they do nothing else that will have every of their passions as it comes to bear sway in them, to be taken for right Reason, and that in their own controversies: bewraying their want of right Reason, by the claym they make to it (Hobbes 1968, 111-12).

This passage takes issue with the medieval definitions of "Right Reason," which derive from Aristotle's conception of the function of reason, and are rejected by Hobbes. For Hobbes, reason is inherently calculative and hypothetical, and it is in one sense "right" when it calculates well; but this is *not* what is meant by Right Reason in the older Aristotelean philosophy with which Hobbes quarrels. "Right Reason" in the philosophy of the Middle Ages had been taken to mean the discernment of ends or goals for action; Hobbes denies this explicitly when he says that all these matters must be subjected to a judge "for want of a right Reason constituted by Nature." Duty will be *conventional*, not granted *by nature,* or by a reason which discerns such a natural duty. Only social convention can dictate what our duties are, and the social conventions in turn are determined by an interplay of the self-interest of those who established the conventions.

However, the subservience of reason to undirected or liberated "desire," in this sophistic and pre-Socratic paradigm, is only one side of the story. The ancient sophists did not interpret this subservience to desire as implying a subservience in the sense of subservience to authority. They interpreted it rather as liberation, notably a liberation from the customary. The most famous expression of this liberation is ascribed to the sophist Protagoras who famously said that "man is the measure of all things."

This subservience of reason to desire is experienced as a release from a greater subservience of reason that existed in the Aristotelean paradigm. If, as Aristotle believed, there were a constraint of natural teleology on the mind, this constraint would put a natural limitation on the calculative action of the intellect. But with this notion of teleology out of the way, the mind is liberated to engage in infinite formal manipulation. An interest with the discernment of "forms," in the sense used by Plato and Aristotle, is replaced by a fascination with the process of formation or formal manipulation. This is the significance of the view of René

Descartes, the "father of Modern philosophy," that all other animals—and perhaps the human body itself—are merely *machines*. Machines are not natural, but beings whose formal determinations are entirely dependent on the desires of those who build them. Machines do not, in principle, place any limitation on the calculative action of the mind, but are the result of such calculative action. By contrast, Aristotle's "forms," along with the correlative ideas of "natural beings," "natural wholes," and "natural purposes," were not supposed to be the result of any calculative activity. So, for Hobbes, the human being is no longer constrained in his intellectual activity by the finite ends given in nature; his measure becomes the "measure of all things," or in the language of Descartes, he becomes "master and possessor of nature."

This brief discussion of ancient non-Aristotelean philosophy can be helpful as a groundwork for looking at the modern assumptions about human nature that give birth to the "social contract" theories to be discussed below. Modern philosophy defines itself precisely in opposition to the Aristotelean principles that dominated the medieval schools. Everywhere in the early modern thinkers, beginning with the 1600s, we find disdain for the thought of these Aristotelian "schoolmen." Hobbes himself is one of the harshest critics. In the modern period, we find a return to and profound deepening and development of the atomism and corresponding sophistry that had been a minority opinion in the ancient and medieval worlds.

One result of this development is the interpretation of the human being as the autonomous or liberated individual. The consequences of this for political theory are crucial: since nature holds no standard or "law" by which the individual is obliged to live, we are free to pursue what we will. When Hobbes uses the term "natural law," he makes it clear that they are not really laws of nature in the sense of physics, but are only means to the satisfaction of an antecedent desire. The individual is, by nature, a law unto himself, or autonomous. Reason too is autonomous, and thus reason is liberated to be our guide. Reason no longer rules the individual in accord with "natural form" or "natural law"; instead, the individual rules nature with reason as his infinitely adaptable weapon of calculation to make war upon all the obstacles to his desire.

2. The New Grounds of Political Obligation—The State of Nature

In ancient philosophy, social contract theory was judged to be mere *"conventionalism."* It was equated with the theory that there are no moral principles or natural constraints to what is desirable other than convention. It would therefore imply that whatever the majority , or those who ruled, accepted as agreeable was by definition "the just," and there was variation from city to city as to whether a majority or a smaller ruling faction determined the rules of this "justice." Hence, justice is entirely conventional, a result of *implied consent* or social contract. This is why sophistry in the ancient world, or the primacy of the art of rhetoric, is associated with conventionalism. A rhetorician does not primarily concern himself with whether the desires of the members of political community, and hence the agreements of these members, are "just" independently of the agreement itself. Rather, he accepts these agreements as just for the sake of persuasion regarding the consequences of the principles. The Platonic and Aristotelean tradition of political philosophy rejects this rhetorical indifference to convention and hence the social contract theory that lies concealed behind it. The classical formulation of this rejection is once again Aristotle's:

> Whoever takes thought for good management, however, gives careful attention to political virtue and vice. It is thus evident that virtue must be the care for every city, or at least every one to which the term applies truly and not merely in a manner of speaking. For otherwise the partnership becomes an alliance which differs from others- -from remote allies- -only by location. And law becomes a compact and, as the sophist Lycophron says, a guarantor among one another of the just things, but not the sort of thing to make the citizens good and just. . . . For even if they (the households who are allied in such a compact) joined together while participating in this way, but each nevertheless treated his own household as a city and each other as if there were a defensive alliance merely for assistance against those committing injustice, it would not by this fact be held a city by those studying the matter precisely (Aristotle 1984, 1280b5-13 and 23-28).

Two things should be noted about this quotation: one, the city is not merely a compact or contract, but exists for the sake of "living well," as Aristotle says. And secondly, the priority of the city to compact is grounded in its promotion of virtue, of "making citizens just and good," which is the ruling consideration in "living well." In this way, the city is by nature a necessary constituent of human happiness. This is, to say the least, a complex matter. Despite the priority of the city to the individual by nature, the city itself has a purpose, which is the development of virtuous human beings, who are, of course, individuals. We might explain this somewhat paradoxical turn by saying this: on the one hand, the city is prior to "each household and each one of us" by nature (in its concern for the good or just per se and the development of all citizens). But on the other hand, the city itself is subject to the standard of the "complete individual," because it exists to help develop that individual to be able to rule in the city. The city does exist for the individual, but its purpose cannot be exhausted in this function, since the individual as such is incomplete, or not free. the city, then, exists for the complete individual whose individuality includes membership in the best city possible. It is only insofar as the potentially complete individual does not happen to be in the best city that there may be a tension between the individual and the city.

It is because the city has a natural function or purpose that Aristotle is able to judge cities better or worse and to set up both the best type of city absolutely and discuss the best city possible or the "practically" best city. Cities that foster the development and rule of virtue more completely than others are "better" than these others. As we saw in the previous chapter, this is derivative from Aristotle's conception of nature: since the city is not artificial, it too may be judged according to whether or not it achieves its purpose for being, much as we would judge an oak tree's development by a natural standard of the flourishing or full-grown oak. Nature for Aristotle is purposive, and the city is natural to man; hence it can be judged better or worse, healthy or stunted, by whether and how much it has achieved its purpose, which is to develop virtuous citizens and promote their activity. Again, this is obviously a communitarian view, and is in sharp contrast to the social contract thinking of Hobbes and most subsequent modern Western philosophers.

(In order to avoid the charge of "mere conventionalism"—which appears to be the necessary result of social contract theory in the ancient world—the modern advocates of social contract theory also have to appeal to some standard outside of the contract, in nature, or at least analogous to nature. This is the function of the *"state of nature"* in social contract theories.) This concept, however, must be radically distinguished from the Aristotelean idea of "nature" as the standard by which cities are judged. Natural motion and desire are not teleological. If there is no natural end or tendency of motion in nature, then there is no natural end or tendency of human desire. Any human desire is as good as any other: "What *any* man desireth he calleth good." The discernment of good and evil is conventional, that is, rooted in particular pursuit and avoidance. If any desire is valuable per se, then there would seem to be no way to judge regimes better or worse according to the desires which they encourage or discourage. Again, we seem left with conventionalism. One convention or social contract is as good as another, since they are all contracts. The solution to this difficulty cannot come from some notion of natural human perfection, but it does come from a reflection on what we might call the necessary conditions for the satisfaction of any desire. This is what can be reflected upon in man "in nature," or prior to society.

This change in the status of the political community leads to a corresponding change in the status of law. For Aristotle, law had been comparable to "intellect without passion," and hence stood for an objective and dispassionate notion of the common good, discernable by reason, to which the desires of individuals conform and by which they are judged. With the aforementioned change in the role of intellect and passion in modern philosophy, intellect and hence law can no longer be the ruler of human beings *per se*. Rather, any common good or law must come from a convergence or coincidence of private passions. Law is therefore the result of a **contract** of private individuals operating under their desire to promote their individual ends. Political philosophy, then, is a description of the conditions under which such a contract—the social contract—becomes necessary, and an analysis of what *individual* goods the social contract must promote.

In sum, political society becomes a tool of "enlightened self-interest." Different contract theorists are distinguished by their notions of what conditions must be present in order for self-interest to be fulfilled. What is common in them, however, is an appeal to what every and each individual, *prior to political society*, would find desirable or avoidable. Hence, the contract theorists presuppose a "state of nature" prior to all political society, in order to discern a common ground of self-interest.

This last feature is necessary to ground any sort of substantive moral judgments as to the legitimacy of political regimes. Without some notion of man's natural interest, what is right would be a function merely of self-interest as *perceived* (wisely or unwisely) by the individuals involved, and the sort of moral atomism would lead to a mere conventionalism. To put it more simply; in order for a political philosophy to be more than merely a description of political phenomena, but a set or recommendations for judging the relative value of actual political phenomena, there must be a standard of what is truly or fully real or actual to ground such a judgment. If not, we have a mere acceptance of the current conventions, with an inability to call them better or worse, legitimate or illegitimate.

For the Aristoteleans, nature possesses moral significance in the teleological goal of human perfection. For the social contract theorists, by contrast, morality is dependent on the contract, and thus would not seem to be based in nature at all. However, implicit in the contractarian's natural indifference to perfection there is a different type of standard of "perfection." This becomes clear if we reflect on the general *structure* of desire, rather than a specific object of desire with the specific end that it aims at. Desire, as such, wishes for the acquisition of its object. Hence, even if there is no qualitative distinction to be made between specific objects of desire, there is still a better or worse state relative to desire in general: to be able to acquire the object of desire is better than to not be able to acquire it. Acquisition, therefore, is the implicit value in the notion of liberated desire. As Aristotle himself understood, the liberation of desire from teleological nature leads to an unlimited desire to acquire (Aristotle, 1984, 1257b17-1258a18). Now this is not a "definite" end or perfection of desire; rather it is indefinite, since it is not limited to any specific set or ordering of desires; all desires, of which there are an infinite number, imply the desire for unlimited acquisition. This is the nature of unlimited desire.

Reflection on the desire to acquire makes one realize that the condition for the pursuit of the object of this desire is *power*. And since the desire for acquisition is limited only by desire itself—not by an objective *telos* or end—the desire for power is in principle limitless or infinite. Thus Hobbes says:

To which end we are to consider, that the Felicity of this life, consisteth not in the repose of a mind satisfied. For there is no such Finis ultimus (utmost ayme) nor Summum Bonum (greatest good) as is spoken in the Books of the old Morall Philosophers. Nor can a man any more live, whose Desires are at an end, than he, whose Senses and Imagination are at a stand. Felicity is a continuall progresse of desire, from one object to another, the attaining of the former, being still but the way to the latter. The cause whereof is, That the object of mans desire is not to enjoy once onely, and for one instant of time; but to assure for ever, the way of his future desire. And therefore the voluntary actions, and inclinations of all men, tend, not only to the procuring, but also to the assuring of a contented life; and differ onely in the way; which ariseth partly from the diversity of passions, in divers men; and partly from the difference of the knowledge, or opinion each one has of the causes, which produce the effect desired.

So that in the first place, I put for a generall inclination of all mankind, a perpetuall and restlesse desire of Power after power, that ceaseth only in Death. And the cause of this, is not alwayes that a man hopes for a more intensive delight, than he has already attained to; or that he cannot be content with a moderate power; but because he cannot assure the power and means to live well, which he hath present, without the acquisition of more (Hobbes 1968, 160-161).

The next step follows from the fact that happiness is not the Aristotelean state of perfection (or "repose"), but of "restlesse desire." If the end requires limitless power, then what is evil for all is anything that limits that power, and that which is good for all becomes that which enhances the power of acquisition. Happiness as restless desire "ceaseth only in death"; hence death is the ultimate evil, because it is the final limit on the acquisition of power. Or, put more positively, the necessary condition of the pursuit of acquisition power is life; this power makes possible all others. Liberated desire or enlightened self-interest requires more than anything the glorification and sanctification of the instinct towards self-preservation, or conversely, the fear of death.

When Hobbes speaks of this fear of death, however, he does so in the context of the conflicting desires of individuals. This fear is no mere fear of natural death, but the fear of a *violent* death at the hands of enemies or murderers. This implies a violation by others in their pursuit of power. Since others, too, are interested in the limitless pursuit of power, there is necessarily going to be conflict. The limitation that another's desire or will puts on one's grasping for power is only completely avoidable by the death of the other, or the cessation of the other's autonomous power—or vice versa. Infinite desire is confronted by a necessary obstacle in another's infinite desire. Conflict is unavoidable because of the limitless nature of one's pursuit; some limited good cannot be possessed by two unlimited wills. There cannot be more than one who successfully pursues power limitlessly—another person is a limit; hence, all others must be conquered or put to death. Hobbes' natural state, the state of the autonomos individual, is therefore a state of war, and a war of all necessarily against all.

Nature hath made men so equall, in the faculties of the body, and mind; as that though there bee found one man sometimes manifestly stronger in body, or of quicker mind than another; yet when all is reckoned together, the difference between man, and man, is not so considerable, as that one man can thereupon claim to himself any benefit, to which another may not pretend as well as he. For as to the strength of the body, the weakest has strength enough to kill the strongest, either by secret machination, or by confederacy with others that are in the same danger as himselfe.

And as to the faculties of the mind. . . . I find yet a greater equality amongst men, than that of strength. For Prudence, is but Experience; which equall time, equally bestowes on all men, in those things they equally apply themselves unto. That which may perhaps make such equality incredible, is but a vain conceipt of ones owne wisdome, which almost all men think they have in greater degree, than the Vulgar; that is, than all men but themselves, and a few other, whom by Fame, or for concurring with themselves, they approve. . . . For they see their own wit at hand, and other mens at a distance. But this proveth rather that men are in that point equall, than unequall. For there is not ordinarily a greater sign of the equall distribution of any thing, than that every man is contented with his share.

From this equality of ability, ariseth equality of hope in attaining of our Ends. And therefore if any two men desire the same thing, which nevertheless they cannot enjoy, they become enemies; and in the way to their End (which is principally their own conservation, and sometimes their delectation only,) endeavor to destroy or subdue one an other. And from hence it comes to passe, that where an invader hath no more to feare, than an other mans single power; if one plant, sow, build, or possesse a convenient Seat, others may probably be expected to come prepared with forces united, to dispossesse, and deprive him, not only of the fruit of his labour, but also of his life or liberty. And the Invader again is in the like danger of another. And from this diffidence of one another, there is no way for any man to secure himselfe, so reasonable, as Anticipation; that is, by force, or wiles, to master the persons of all men he can, so longe, till he see no other power great enough to endanger him. And this is no more than his own conservation requireth, and is generally allowed. . . .

Hereby it is manifest, that during the time men live without a common Power to keep them all in awe, they are in that condition which is called Warre; and such a warre, as is of every man, against every man. . . . Whatsoever therefore is consequent to a time of Warre, where every man is Enemy to every man; the same is consequent to the time, wherein men live without other security, than what their own strength, and their own invention shall furnish them withall. In such a condition, there is no place for Industry; because the fruit thereof is uncertain and consequently no Culture of the Earth; no Navigation, nor use of the commodities that may be imported by Sea; no commodious Building; no Instruments of moving, and removing such things as require much force; no Knowledge of the face of the Earth; no account of Time; no Arts; no Letters; no Society; and which is worst of all, continnuall feare, and danger of violent death; And the life of man, solitary, poore, nasty, brutish, and short.

It may seem strange to some man, that has not well weighed these things; that Nature should thus dissociate, and render men apt to invade and destroy one another; and he may therefore, not trusting to this Inference, made from the Passions, desire to have the same confirmed by Experience. Let him therefore consider with himselfe, when taking a journey, he armes himselfe, and seeks to go well accompanied; when going to sleep, he locks his dores; when even in his house he locks his chests, and this when he knows there bee Lawes, and publike Officers, armed, to revenge all injuries shall bee done him; what opinion he has of his fellow subjects, when he rides armed; of his fellow Citizens, when he locks his dores; and of his children, and servants, when he locks his chests. Does he not there as much accuse mankind by his actions, as I do by my words? But neither of us accuse mans nature in it. The Desires, and other Passions of man, are in themselves no Sin. No more are the Actions, that proceed from those Passions, till they know a Law that forbids them; which till Lawes be made they cannot know: nor can any Law be made, till they have agreed upon the Person that shall make it (Hobbes 1968, 183-87).

These last few paragraphs connect us from Hobbes' beginnings in human nature to the status of humans in the "state of nature." No passion is a "Sin"—desire or passion is liberated from natural constraint. This leads, however, to the grave situation of the war of all against all. Man is not naturally a political animal, but a tyrant, that most apolitical of rulers. The causes of this are the desire for Power and the love of the opinion that we are the end of all, or most powerful; we must note that Hobbes adds Reputation to Power, as motives for jealousy. While not strictly the same, Hobbes appears to consider reputation only insofar as it allows for liberty to do what one will; it is a uniquely human aspect of power, closely related to the power of speech. In any case, the problem that Hobbes sets for himself is this: not how to convince a potential tyrant of virtue, but to find peace preferable to war on the terms of natural tyranny.

Hobbes believes the solution to this problem lies in the fear of violent death. What liberated desire knows and respects is a power clearly greater than itself. In the state of nature, each autonomous individual is under much more severe constraint than when living under a social contract. Without the constraints that society provides, each individual is constantly threatened with the utter frustration of natural desire for power by the threats of death or enslavement. Now, one may say here that this is true in society as well as in nature; all people die, and even in society people do face the possibility of violent death. This is undoubtedly true; however, the degree to which this is so is radically different in the state of nature and in society. In the state of nature, acquisitive ventures are always done in the shadow of the threat of violent intervention by others; in society, this shadow is shortened by the power of a common authority—the political sovereign.

Nature therefore has a double function in Hobbes and the social contract theorists who follow him. On the one hand, the natural condition, the "state of nature," is thought to be cruel and brutish. So in this respect the condition of nature is no standard by which to judge the human end, except perhaps as something to be avoided. Nature acts in this way as a negative motive; the natural *condition* is not a standard for happiness. On the other hand, in another way, nature is a standard. If not, it could hold no positive recommendation for political society and its function. There would be no way of judging political entities better or worse, legitimate or illegitimate. But since human nature is guided only by natural desire, we can judge different forms of society as being better or worse as ways to reach mutually beneficial outcomes.

The natural human desire for unlimited acquisition is completely frustrated in the natural condition. Human nature, which pursues unlimited acquisition, or what the American founding fathers were to call the "pursuit of happiness" (not the achievement of happiness, which would limit pursuit, but the pursuit itself, which is in principle unending) is the standard by which we judge political society more or less good. Nature is, for the modern social contract theorist, something to be avoided as a condition so that natural desire can be fulfilled as much as is possible. Human nature conflicts with our natural condition—we are naturally alienated or homeless. Hence, we must create a second nature, or society, in order to house our ambitions. Hobbes and other social contract thinkers inherited this notion that our aspirations conflict with our condition from their medieval Christian forebears; what is different is only their response to this condition.

3. Hobbes: Right and Law

Hobbes is the first thinker to thematize the primacy of the autonomous individual, and therefore may be considered to be the great founder of political liberalism. His liberalism, however, seems to lead inexorably and paradoxically to absolute government. As such, Hobbes faces rather squarely the problematic nature of political authority, once one assumes the liberated individual as the starting point. If individuals are in principle radically self-interested, must not every contract have a judge who is *external* to any disagreement between individuals, and whose judgment is beyond the recall of any one person or several people? If not—if each individual's self-interested judgment can recall the judge—then there is no public authority, and any agreement reached is in principle temporary and arbitrary.

Hobbes therefore faces up to the abandonment of a common good which reason can judge to be the fabric of society, and realizes that there must be a very powerful common judge; otherwise there would be no "*common*-wealth." The ruling political entity, the **sovereign**, must be a *real* unity. Hobbes replaces the common good with the authoritative voice of a ruler whose power resembles that of a mortal God. Without such an absolute, we are subject to the relative judgments of private individuals, and this means that our lives are in the hands of others who do not share our interest. To avoid this state of things, we must contract to enter political society. The avoidance of death therefore leads us to a public judgment not reducible to a mere collection of private judgments. We contract to get beyond the status of mere contract—to an authority that has enough teeth to subdue conflicting private interests.

The picture of the natural human condition, and relevant considerations in human nature that have been sketched above are taken from the first thirteen chapters of Hobbes' masterwork, *Leviathan*. Let us summarize before continuing. Natural human autonomy is grounded in an atomistic physics; the individual's desires are simply another confluence of the mechanistic motions of the universe. Two motions in particular need to be emphasized: the passions are in themselves justified, or liberated, since there is no sin in any passion. In fact, in the state of Nature, it would be impossible for there to be any justice or injustice whatsoever, since there is inherently neither common good, nor what Hobbes will replace it with, common power.

The second crucial human motion is reason. Reason is not authoritative as discerning the common good (since good is entirely private or desire is liberated from such a reason), but it provides the means to increasing power, which is necessarily the constant goal of each as an autonomous individual. Reason is liberated to be an infinitely adaptable instrument of desire. As such, it may be an instrument to get the individual out of the natural human condition. The natural condition (the state of nature) is a war of all against all, since individuals are nearly equal in their ability to be killed, and in their opinion of what they deserve. In such a state, life is "solitary, poor, nasty, brutish, and short." Further, in such a state, there is no property, "no dominion, no mine and thine distinct." This last point is of crucial import; if the goal of our desires is to increase our "mine," and there is no way to do this effectively in the state of nature because of the threat of violent death, then the state of nature will not satisfy for anyone, and reason's task is to find a solution to this difficult situation. Hobbes notes this movement away from nature:

> And thus much for the ill condition, which man by meer Nature is actually placed in; though with a possiblity to come out of it, consisting partly in the Passions, partly in his Reason. The Passions, that encline men to Peace, are Feare of Death; Desire of such things as are necessary to a commodious living; and a Hope by their Industry to obtain them. And reason suggesteth convenient Articles of Peace, upon which men may be drawn to agreement. These Articles are they, which otherwise are called the Lawes of Nature (Hobbes 1968, 188).

We must note here that for Hobbes it is not merely life which is desired, but more positive modes of dominion for each—a "commodious living" and the ability to acquire goods by means of "industry" or hard work. We shall see that these concerns become more systematically incorporated into political theory by Hobbes' successors, notably Locke, Rousseau, and Marx. For Hobbes, however, the "right to life," which opposes the fear of death, is more fundamental than any other right; it is the most necessary condition of the pursuit of happiness. Loss of property, or other liberties, does not constitute the absolute loss of the pursuit of power that the loss of life does. Hence, self-preservation is a different kind of right from the others, however much the others may be natural to humanity.

Hobbes, however, leaves a loophole in his argument which expands self-preservation beyond the mere preservation of life. This "loophole" is actually the logical consequence of the natural desire for acquisition, and will eventually lead to a critical difficulty in Hobbes' political theory, perhaps inherent in all social contract theory. We shall turn to this loophole a bit later, but we can indicate it by quoting something which we spoke of earlier. When speaking of the dangers of the state of nature, Hobbes says that we all desire, *for the sake of self-preservation*, to acquire all that we can. Further, when it comes to our own life, we are the judge as to what is required for such preservation; and finally, this right to self-preservation cannot be contracted away, but rather is the *purpose* of the contract. All these points taken together do two things: (1) they connect the preservation of property to the preservation of the right to life, and (2) they undermine the absolute authority of the sovereign in regards to both of these rights. John Locke will further elucidate these conclusions against Hobbes, but they might be seen as implicit in Hobbes' own premises.

In any case, for Hobbes, self-preservation is the fundamental right, since it is the right which opposes the greatest evil, death. It is what Hobbes calls the "Right of Nature."

> The Right of Nature, which Writers commonly call Jus Naturale, is the Liberty each man hath, to use his own power, as he will himselfe, for the preservation of his own Nature; that is to say, or his own Life; and consequently, of doing any thing, which in his own Judgement, and Reason, hee shall conceive to be the aptest means thereunto.
>
> By Liberty, is understood, according to the proper signification of the word, the absence of externall impediments; which Impediments, may oft take away part of a mans power to do what hee would; but cannot hinder him from using the power left him, according as his judgement, and reason shall dictate to him.
>
> A Law of Nature (Lex Naturalis) is a Precept, or generall Rule, found out by Reason, by which a man is forbidden to do, that, which is destructive of his life, or taketh away the means of preserving the same; and to omit that, by which he thinketh it may be preserved. . . . And because the condition of Man (as hath been declared in the precedent chapter) is a condition of Warre of every one against every one; in which case every one is governed by his own Reason; and there is nothing he can make use of, that may not be a help unto him, in preserving his life against his enemyes; It followeth, that in such a condition every man has a Right to every thing; even to one another's body. And therefore, as long as this naturall Right of every man to every thing endureth, there can be no security to any man (how strong or wise so ever he be) of living out the time,

which Nature ordinarily alloweth men to live. And consequently, it is a precept or generall rule of Reason, *That every man, ought to endeavor Peace, as farre as he has hope obtaining it; and when he cannot obtain it, that he may seek, and use, all helps, and advantage of Warre.* The first branch of which Rule, containeth the first, and Fundamentall Law of Nature; which is, to seek Peace and follow it. The Second, the summe of the Right of Nature; which is, by all means we can, to defend our selves.

From this Fundamentall Law of Nature, by which men are commanded to endeavour Peace, is derived this second Law; *That a man be willing, when others are so too, as farre-forth, as for Peace and defence of himselfe he shall think it necessary, to lay down this right to all things; and be contented with as much liberty against other men, as he would allow other men against himself.* For as long as every man holdeth this Right, of doing any thing he liketh; so long are all men in the condition of Warre. But if other men will not lay down their Right, as well as he; then there is no Reason for any one, to divest himself of his: For that were to expose himself to Prey (which no man is bound to) rather than to dispose himself to Peace (Hobbes 1968, 189-90).

There are two inseparable aspects of the Right of Nature. Each, by nature, can use his own power to preserve his life, and secondly, each can use his own judgment as to the means to this goal. Now, it is of course the latter aspect of the right of nature which is the cause of the difficulties in the state of nature. In the state of nature, the lack of a common judgment and the lack of a common power leads to the war of all against all; thus the remedy for this difficulty is an authoritative judgment and public power external to the radically private or interested judgments of the individuals. The externality of this judgment is necessary, since it prevents the sovereign from being himself a part of the contract, or merely a natural individual who acts from self-interest. It is this that grants the sovereign *absolute authority.*

This would seem to leave political community entirely to an external force. Since our judgment is radically privatized, how could we be persuaded to accept such an external force which creates a public judgment? It might seem that people would have to be driven into society like animals for their own benefit. Fortunately, this is not entirely so. People can be persuaded to accept this external authority *based on their own reasoning* in consideration of their interest. This part of Hobbes' argument is essential, since naturally no person or people is sovereign, given the relative equality of power in the state of nature and the non-existence of the notion of a common or highest good by which to measure a person's worth. Hobbes' sovereign is undoubtedly absolute and external to the contract, yet must be the *result* of this contract—a contract which must be found persuasive to the reason of all in the service of each individual's desire for acquisition. Hobbes appeals to this *"enlightened self-interest"* to ground both the original social contract and the agreement to keep such contracts. The passions incline us toward society; reason suggests to these passions the means to their satisfaction. These suggestions are the "Lawes of Nature," the fundamentals of Hobbes' social contract.

(The Right of Nature moves the individual to act; the Laws of Nature are the *means* to the achievement of the end present in the Right of Nature. Since the Right of Nature grants any act necessary to self-preservation, the Laws restrict action in the interest of self-preservation. Hence, these laws are not opposed to the Right of Nature, but are a result of it. The relation of right to law is reflected generally in the first law of nature; the Right of Nature is embedded within that law. Their relation reflects the priority of the autonomous individual. It is the individual who judges what is necessary to self-preservation; there is no common judgment by nature to arbitrate any such disputes.)

The second law of nature is the ground for the social contract. Thus, when other people are willing to cooperate in a mutual agreement, it is in the interest of each person's natural desire to lay down the individual's right to all; this mutual refraining from action is motivated by the interest of self-preservation or fear of violent death. Hence, in the interest of the desire for acquisition, each person renounces the right to *unlimited* acquisition. This mutual transferring of right is called contract and covenant. In the remainder of our discussion, we explore the way Hobbes lays out the conditions under which covenant is possible or violated. The only violation of these conditions is when a given proposition or proposal becomes logically self-contradictory. The root of all such self-contradictions is that we cannot be understood to contract away our own life, since the purpose of the contract is to preserve it.

A covenant reached or decided to through fear, however, is not invalid; quite the contrary, since the original motivation for entering into the social contract is fear, contracts that are entered into under fear are not a violation of contract, but a manifestation of the presence of the inalienable Right of Nature.

The third law of nature is necessary for the effectiveness of the first two; it states that when the agreement of the second law occurs, such a contract must be followed. It is here where justice and injustice arise, for they consist of nothing but the following or not following of the contract established. All the other laws of nature that Hobbes discusses can be derived as necessary conditions for or consequences of the first three. They are all meant to preserve the motive for peace from the obstacles that are natural to humanity in the state of nature: vengeance, pride, ingratitude, arrogance, judging in one's own case, etc. Hobbes sums all these by saying.

> And though this may seem too subtle a deduction of the Lawes of Nature, to be taken notice of by all men; whereof the most part are too busie in getting food, and the rest too negligent to understand; yet to leave all men unexcusable, they have been contracted in to one easie sum, intelligible to even the meanest capacity; and that is, *Do not that to another, which thou wouldest not have done to thy self;* which sheweth him , that he has no more to do in learning the Lawes

of Nature, but, when weighing the actions of other men, with his own, they seem
too heavy, to put them into the other part of his balance, and his own into their
place, that his own passions, and selfe-love, may adde nothing to the weight; and
then there is none of these Lawes of Nature that will not appear unto him very
reasonable (Hobbes 1968, 214-215).

Note here the negative way of stating what at first appears to be some version
of the "golden rule" of the New Testament, "do unto others as you would have
them do unto you." This "negative" statement coincides more with the intent of
the laws of nature in general than does the positive version of the golden rule. The
emphasis is on a *mutual refraining from judgment of others* (which is the source
of the difficulties in the state of nature), so as to allow each some room for the
pursuit of acquisitive action (the aforementioned "Industry" and "Commodious
Living"). The positive "golden rule," by contrast, involves precisely the judgment
of another's worth that the laws of Nature are meant to prohibit. If I wish to do
unto others as I wish to have done unto me, this means that I wish to provide a
universal standard of value by which to judge both another's activity and my own.
This means arrogating to oneself the judgment of the worth of another's actions,
and it is precisely this arrogation, or arrogance, that Hobbes' laws of nature are
meant to combat.

4. The Origins of Sovereignty

The origin of the titles of Just and Unjust are subject to an important caveat:
since all the "Laws of Nature" are not truly "Laws" without a sovereign, there is
no true Just or Unjust without the institution of the sovereign. Justice, then, is the
enforcement and interpretation of the contract by the sovereign.

But because covenants of mutuall trust, where there is fear of not performance
on either part (as hathe been said in the former Chapter) are invalid; though the
Originall of Justice be the making of covenants; yet Injustice actually there can
be none, till the cause of such feare be taken away; which wile men are in the
naturall condition of Warre, cannot be done. Therefore before the name of Just,
and Unjust can have place, there must be some coercive Power, to compell men
equally to the performance of their Covenants, by the terror of some punishment,
greater than the benefit they expect by the breach of their covenant; and to make
good that Propriety, which by mutuall Contract men acquire, in recompence of
the universall Right they abandon: and such power there is none before the
erection of a Common-wealth. And this is also to be gathered out of the ordinary
definition of Justice in the Schooles: For they say, that Justice is the constant
Will of giving to every man his own. And therefore, where there is no Own, that
is, no Propriety, there is no Injustice; and where there is no coercive Power
erected, that is, where there is no common-wealth, there is no Propriety; all men
having Right to all things: Therefore where there is no common-wealth, there

nothing is Unjust. So that the nature of Justice, consisteth in the keeping of valid Covenants: but the Validition of Covenants begins not but with the constitution of a Civill Power, sufficient to compell men to keep them: and then it is also that Propriety begins (Hobbes 1968, 202-203).

Natural law is naturally in a precarious position. On the one hand, natural law is the reasonable outcome of our primary desires, which do *not* demand a reform of this desire, but only a *prudential practice* of it. On the other hand, our natural desire is of such a sort that reason does not possess force. Reason, that is, is a mere instrument, and, like all other instruments, it cannot use itself; rather, the passions must first be engaged so that reason may be listened to or seen as itself an instrument worthy of use. The desires must therefore require enlightenment, both by force and by persuasion. The natural condition is clearly not enough to keep the advantages of the social contract before the eyes of natural human beings.

The reason for the weakness of contract in nature should by now be fairly obvious: it is the partiality of each person's reason. Let us say that all have agreed to lay down their right to all, on the conditions that all others also have done so. This involves the resignation not only of the physical acts and instruments of taking all (for example, weapons and militias), but more crucially, an individual's own judgment of what needs be taken according to the Right of Nature. Each must subject private judgment to some public judgment. This points to the need for an arbiter for discerning *what is the public judgment*—that is, what the original contract demands and requires for its application. Since the legitimacy of the contract under mere natural law is conditional (*if* others are willing to do so, I am required by reason to renounce my right to all), it is necessary that someone's judgment decide whether others *are* willing to and *have* done so. And in the transition from the state of nature, it is precisely this judgment which is left in the hands of each contracting individual. If *I* interpret that some one or some group of my fellow contractors has voided the contract, then I have every right against this one or group to renounce the contract myself and reclaim my "right to all" from nature.

Therefore, given each individual's natural proclivity to discern any act of another as a threat to one's own honor or power, the social contract will fail in the first act under its auspices. The parties will interpret the contract to their own advantage, and will accuse the others of misinterpreting and disobeying it, thus justifying their own disobedience. In the state of nature, the partiality of individual judgment prevents the effectiveness of the laws of nature, to everyone's detriment. Hence, what is needed is the correction of this state of radical privacy in the interest of making actual the desire for private acquisition. As Hobbes says, a real unity is needed, not merely a hypothetical one. It is to provide this real unity that the sovereign is necessary. Justice and injustice are established, not simply by the contract which brings about society and sovereignty, but by the enforcement of that covenant by sovereign authority. By doing this, Hobbes establishes a distinction between general principles and actual law; law's primary being is in force, in particular acts by the sovereign, not in thought alone. Prior to sovereignty, they are "mere words."

To say the least, this introduces a complexity into Hobbes: some have seen this as an inconsistency. The sovereign has an authority beyond the will of those who contract, yet its authority is constituted precisely by an act of these wills of the contracting parties. If the sovereign has an authority beyond that of the individuals who covenant, or if law is a command beyond perceived self-interest, on what authority does the command reside? Locke, by contrast with Hobbes, answers this question in the negative. In his view, the *people* are the authorities under which the sovereign always operates. In this way, Locke may appear more consistent than Hobbes; law is nothing but the result of self-interest *as it is judged by those who contract.*

Despite this difficulty, what Hobbes gains is a real unity of society, whereas we may say that in some way Locke only has consent or agreement. If we were to remain at the level of mere agreement, there would be no actual transcendence of private wills, and hence no public will or sovereignty. If there is no public will, then we are once again, in principle, in the state of nature. Hobbes makes it quite clear that the mere fact that many agree is not adequate for the constitution of political society, without a sovereign will above these other wills "to keep them in awe": mere agreement or concord will not do for political unity.

Hobbes, then, would accuse Locke's ideas of promoting civil war, which is most definitely opposed to political society. The grounds of political society, that which gives political society its definite character or law, must come from outside the contract and be in some way irreducible to private consent, because of the *partiality* of private individuals in interpreting the laws of nature. Hobbes, that is, takes seriously the problematic nature of the common good, since humans by nature differ from other social animals in that the common good is not contained in the private interest of each individual considered separately. Furthermore, speech does not rectify this situation but only exacerbates it. Therefore, it seems necessary that the common purpose come from outside of the covenant and its contracting members.

> It is true, that certain living creatures, as Bees, and ants, live sociably one with another (which are therefore by Aristotle numbered amongst Politicall creatures;) and yet have no other direction, than their particular judgements and appetites; no speech, whereby one of them can signifie to another what he things expedient for the common benefit: and therefore some man may perhaps desire to know, why Man-kind cannot do the same. To which I answer,
>
> First, that men are continually in competition for Honour and Dignity, which these creatures are not; and consequently amongst men there ariseth on that Ground, Envy and Hatred, and finally Warre, but amongst these not so.
>
> Secondly, that amongst these creature the Common good differeth not from the Private; and being by nature enclined to their private, they procure thereby

the common benefit. But men, whose Joy consisteth in comparing himselfe to other men, can relish nothing but what is eminent.

Thirdly, that these creatures, having not (as man) the use of reason, do not see, nor think they see any fault, in the administration of their common business: whereas amongst men, there are very many, that thinke themselves wiser, and abler to govern the Publique, better than the rest; and these strive to reforme and inovate, one this way, another that way; and thereby bring it into Distraction and Civill warre.

Fourthly, that these creatures, thought they have some use of voice, in making knowne to one another their desires, and other affections; yet they want that art of words, by which some men can represent to others, that which is Good, in the likenesse of Evill; and Evill, in the likenesse of Good; and augment, or diminish the apparent greatnesse of Good and Evill; discontenting men, and troubling their Peace at their pleasure.

Fifthly, irrationall creatures cannot distinguish betweene Injury, and Dammage; and therefore as long as they be at ease, they are not offended with their fellowes: whereas Man is then most troublesome, when he is most at ease: for then it is that he loves to shew his Wisdome, and controule the Actions of them that governe the Common-wealth.

Lastly, the agreement of these creatures is Naturall; that of men, is by Covenant only, which is Artificiall: and therefore it is no wonder if there be somewhat else required (besides Covenant) to make their Agreement constant and lasting; which is a Common Power, to keep them in awe, and to direct their actions to the Common Benefit (Hobbes 1968, 225-227).

Political authority, it seems, is ultimately external to individuality. Much of the debate in current political life is couched in terms of this opposition—the tension between private and public interest, or the conflict between "individual" and "society." Relative to the private interest, Hobbes says that the sovereign is a "mortal God" or "Leviathan " Our relation to this "mortal God" is similar to that of the immortal God in Christian doctrine, and confirms the idea of the absolute authority of the sovereign. If God's will coincides with human happiness, it does so in a way beyond human understanding. Thus God's authority for the human good transcends human consent. Likewise, the sovereign's authority must transcend human consent or covenant, but it does so *in the interest* of the happiness of humans. This is what is necessary for a true, as opposed to merely conventional, human good.

However, the fact that the sovereign's authority is in accord with what reason can discover about the conditions of human happiness reveals that this is not the entire story. If the source of the sovereign's authority is in accord with what reason can discover, then sovereign's authority lies in the judgment of the individual members who contract to form political society. This would seem to indicate that the sovereign's judgment is in some sense not absolute after all. Being the result of individuals who can see the benefit of such a sovereign, this means that the sovereign is not fully independent of the contracting individuals. This tension in

Hobbes' thought may indeed be irresolvable; we see this manifest itself again when he speaks of the rights of sovereign and subject.

5. Absolute Government: Rights of Sovereign and Subject

The real unity of the commonwealth means that each has escaped the natural condition (the state of nature), which is the condition of private judgment and power, and has entered into a new condition of existence—the realm of public judgment and public power. A new, non-natural being has been created, and the nature of its being demands that its authority be absolute. Hobbes does not defend monarchy per se; an *assembly* of people can and must have absolute authority if it is to be entitled "sovereign." What Hobbes defends is not monarchy, but authority or sovereignty. We might put Hobbes' opinion best this way: there is no contract between individuals and the sovereign, for the sovereign is not a private individual or subject, or even a collection of private individuals. A mere collection of individuals, no matter how large, is no commonwealth, and has no sovereign; it is no better than a merely temporary alliance.

The sovereign cannot be another natural individual with whom one contracts. Hobbes' reasoning for this is fairly straightforward: if the sovereign were an individual, then he, as well as all other individuals, would be the holder of a merely private will, and hence, like all other individuals without a public will between them, his opinion would be subject to dispute without end. The sovereign would be in a state of nature with those individuals he rules, and there would not be civil society, but only the war of all against all. Or else the sovereign, like all other individuals, would have to submit to a common judge who is other than himself; in either case, the sovereign would be no sovereign, but rather a natural individual or subject.

To say that the sovereign is outside of the contract means that, in a profound way, he *is* the contract; the sovereign is "the Essence of the Common-wealth." The sovereign represents the person of every individual who has contracted, for the purpose of the contract. And the major purpose of the contract is the setting aside of the right to all, which essentially involves the forsaking of one's own judgment of "mine and thine" in favor of a public judgment of these issues. This forsaking of individual judgment is the ground of the sovereign's absolute authority. In Hobbes' view, rebellious subjects who interpret their relation to the sovereign as one of a contract *with* the sovereign are contradicting themselves. Since the intent of the contract was to set up a public authority and judgment which is separate from the radically interested judgments ruling in the state of nature, it would be contrary to this purpose to act and speak as if the status between the public person and private person were one of equal individuals. This equal status of judgment, leading to the war of all against all, is precisely what the contract is meant to avoid. This is why Hobbes returns, in the case of such dispute, to a reminder that any harm caused by public authority is much less than that received in a state of nature.

> But a man may here object, that the Condition of Subjects is very miserable; as being obnoxious to the lusts, and other irregular passions of him, or them that have so unlimited a Power in their hands. And commonly they that live under a Monarch, think it the fault of Monarchy; and they that live under the government of Democracy, or other Soveraign Assembly, attribute all the inconvenience to that forme of Common-wealth; whereas the Power in all formes, if they be perfect enought to Protect them, is the same; not considering that the estate of Man can never be without some incommodity or other; and that the greatest, that in any forme of Government can possibly happen to the people in generall, is scarce sensible, in respect of the miseries, and horrible calamities, that accompany a Civill Warre; or, that dissolute condition of masterlesse men, without subjection to Lawes, and a coercive power to tye their hand from rapine, and revenge: nor considering that the greatest pressure of Soveraign Governours, proceedeth not from any delight, or profit they can expect in the dammage, or weakening of their Subjects, in whose vigor, consisteth their own strength and glory; but in the restiveness of themselves, that unwillingly contributing to their own defence, make it necessary for their Governours to draw from them what they can in time of Peace, that they may have means on any emergent occassion, or sudden need, to resist, or take advantage on their Enemies. For all men are by nature provided of notable multiplying glasses ,(that is their Passions and Self-love), through which, every little payment appeareth a great grievance; but are destitute of those prospective glasses (namely Morall and Civill Science) to see a farre off the miseries that hang over them, and cannot without such payments be avoyded (Hobbes 1968, 238-39).

The absolute nature of sovereignty is clearly the lesser of two evils, and necessary to avoid the harshness of the rule of radically private judgment. It requires re-emphasis that the absoluteness of authority for Hobbes is a necessity, given the radically private nature of rationality when it comes to the ends of society. Since reason cannot come to a public conception of the good in principle, this conception must come from outside of individual judgment, even when its ultimate purpose is the long-term interest of individual desire. This judgment must come from outside of individual judgment because of the weakness of reason in regards to the human desire for acquisition.

Chapter Five
Hobbesian Difficulties and Locke's Rights-based Approach

1. Criticisms of Hobbes

The thinking of John Locke (1632-1706) can best be understood as both an extension of and a critique of Hobbes. When Hobbes discusses the question of the liberties of subjects, serious difficulties arise with his theory, related to the problems involving the origins of the commonwealth (from the state of nature) and the basic relationship between the sovereign and the subjects (in which the sovereign is almost all-powerful). We might divide the liberties of subjects for Hobbes into two classes: liberties *consistent with* the unlimited power of the sovereign, and liberties which one may have *against* the sovereign.

Liberties consistent with the power of the sovereign would include liberties that the sovereign explicitly permits as well as those on which sovereignty is silent. The subject's liberty in this case consists merely in not being prevented from doing whatever is not forbidden by the sovereign—in other words, whatever is not illegal. Hobbes notes also that the liberty of the subject is not compromised in any way by the sovereign's command. Since to be a subject means to have given over one's right to the sovereign, the sovereign's limiting of one's own power is a limitation that one has authorized oneself. A limit that is *self-imposed* is not really a limit on one's liberty, but rather the *outcome* of one's liberty. This sense of liberty—defined as whatever the sovereign commands or does not command—is for Hobbes the primary sense of the subject's liberty. This even extends to the subject's own life under law or sovereign command:

> Nevertheless we are not to understand, that by such Liberty, the Soveraign Power of life, and death, is either abolished, or limited. For it has been already shewn, that nothing the Soveraign Representative can doe to a Subject, on what pretence soever, can properly be called Injustice, or Injury; because every Subject is

Author of every act the Soveraign doth; so that he never wanteth Right to any thing, otherwise, than as he himself is the Subject of God, and bound thereby to observe the laws of Nature. And therefore it may, and doth often happen in Common-wealths, that a Subject may be put to death, by the command of the Soveraign Power, and yet neither does the other wrong: As when Jeptha caused his daughter to be sacrificed: In which, and the like cases, he that so dieth, had Liberty to does the action, for which he is nevertheless, without Injury put to death (Hobbes 1968, 264-65).

In sum, the subject's liberty *is* the sovereign's command, whether it is against the subject's natural liberty or explicitly or implicitly permits it. *Civil* liberty thus differs in principle from natural liberty (liberty in the state of nature) through the constraint of sovereignty.

A more interesting type of liberty acknowledged by Hobbes consists of liberties *"against* sovereign command without injustice"*:

To come now to the particulars of the true Liberty of a Subject; that is to say, what are the things, which though commanded by the Soveraign, he may nevertheless, without Injustice, refuse to do, we are to consider, what Rights we pass away, when we make a Common-wealth; or (which is all one,) what Liberty we deny ourselves, by owning all the Actions (without exception) of the Man, or Assembly we make our Soveraign. . . . First, therefore, since Soveraignty by Institution, is by Covenant of every one to every one; and Soveraignty by Acquisiton, by Covenants of the Vanquished to the Victor, or child to the Parent; It is manifest that every Subject has Liberty in all those things, the right whereof cannot by Covenant be transferred. I have shewn before in the 14th Chapter, that Covenants, not to defend a mans own body, are voyd. Therefore,

If the Soveraign command a man (though justly condemned) to kill, wound, or mayme himselfe; or not to resist those that assault him; or to abstain from the use of food, ayre, medicine, or any other thing, without which he cannot live; yet hath that man the Liberty to disobey (Hobbes 1968, 268-9).

There is something naturally prior to the sovereign, and that is the self-defense of the individual's life. Where individuals feels themselves threatened, they have the right to resist the sovereign command. This is because, as Hobbes notes:

Whensoever a man Transferreth his Right, or Renounceth it; it is either in consideration of soe Right reciprocally transferred to himself; or for some other good he hopeth for therby. For it is a voluntary act: and of the voluntary acts of every man, the object is some Good to himself. And therfore there be some Rights, which no man can be understood by any words, or other signes, to have abadoned, or trasnferred. As first a man cannot lay down ther right of resisting them , that assaulth him by force, to take away his life; because he cannot be understood to ayme therby, at any Good to himselfe. The same may be sayd of Wounds, and Chayns, and Imprisonment; both because there is no benefit consequent to such patience; as there is to the patience of suffering another to be wounded, or imprisoned: as also because a man cannot tell, when he seeth men proceed against him by violence, whether they intend his death or not. And lastly, the motive, and end for which this renouncing, and transferring of Right is introduced, is nothing else but the security of a mans person, in his life, and in the means of so preserving life, as not to be weary of it (Hobbes 1968, 192).

Since the origin of the contract is in the intention to preserve individual life (and evidently also liberty, as indicated by Hobbes' words regarding imprisonment), no person can seriously be construed as authorizing the sovereign's taking his or her own life; thus any sovereign's command to do so would be against the contract. While the sovereign must be taken to be the contract itself, (since public judgment must supercede private judgment of right), in the end this can be justified only by the intention of the contract, which is preservation of life and liberty themselves, and this means *the individual's life and liberty*. In this respect, Hobbes and Locke are not so far apart; Locke adds "property" to the list of contractual purposes, through a complex relation to the rights of life and liberty which we shall consider in the next section.

The difficulty this leads to with the notion of absolute government becomes apparent in the following clarification which Hobbes gives on the right of a subject *against* the sovereign:

Again, the Consent of a Subject to Soveraign Power, is contained in these words, *I Authorise, or take upon me, all his actions*; in which there is no restriction at all, of his own former naturall Liberty; For by allowing him to *kill me*, I am not bound to kill my self when he commands me. 'Tis one thing to say, *Kill me, or my fellow, if you please*; anothing thing to say, *I will kill my selfe, or my fellow*. It followeth that. . . . No man is bound by the words themselves, either to kill himselfe, or any other man; And consequently, that the Obligation a man may sometime have, upon the Command of the Soveraign to execute any dangerious, or dishonourable Office, dependeth not on the Words of our Submission; but on the Intention; which is to be understood by the End thereof. When therefore our refusall to obey, frustrates the End for which the Sovereignty was ordained; then there is no Liberty to refuse; otherwise, there is (Hobbes 1968, 269).

The difficulty arises in the last sentence of this quotation. If the subjects are to know when they have liberty to disobey the sovereign, then it is the *subjects'* judgment that in this case is the ruling judgment. That is, subjects are the final authority as to whether their lives and liberty have been violated by the sovereign. Thus when it comes to the preservation of one's own life (which is the crucial case for the foundation of commonwealth), *in the end the private judgment of individuals is authoritative, not the public judgment of the sovereign*. It is up to the individuals who enter into the contract to decide on whether the sovereign is acting in accordance with the intent and purpose of the contract.

From this standpoint, the authority of the sovereign is not absolute, because it is not independent of the collective individual wills of the contracting individuals. Rather, the sovereign is merely a pragmatic power that can be modified by the contracting individuals according to their own definition of what their self-defense requires. From a theoretical point of view, this seems to point to a contradiction in Hobbes' idea of sovereignty. By granting the implications of rights against the sovereign, "Hobbes in fact admitted that there exists an insoluble conflict between the rights of the government and the natural right of the individual to self-preservation" (Strauss 1953, 197).

As we have noted since the beginning of this discussion, the cause of Hobbes' difficulty is in the lack of a conception of the common good. If we radically privatize reason, the only justification for a common authority is merely instrumental. Hobbes himself reflects this when he calls the Sovereign, his Leviathan, an "artificial man." As in the case of all artifice, the sovereign in principle has no source of motion within himself; this must be supplied from without, by the will and judgment of those who create him, i.e., by the intentions of the parties to the contract. All intentions, for Hobbes, are inherently *private* and *self-interested*. In the case of the political creation, the social contract, this means that the judgment of the contracting individuals has priority over the judgment of the sovereign. and it seems to follow that the sovereign can never claim absolute authority. It may be a *pragmatic or instrumental* good to *give* the sovereign unlimited authority; but this judgment is not the judgment of the sovereign himself; it must be the judgment of each one in the state of nature. This is a difficulty for Hobbes' absolutist doctrine; it must justify itself before the court of each individual's judgment.

Furthermore, for Hobbes, people are naturally inclined to forget this truth, even on a pragmatic level. If so, it appears that people are *not* naturally inclined toward society, but rather society must be artificially instituted. Or, if people already live in a society, the sovereign's authority must be re-instituted in every age. But the people's interest in doing so must itself be artificially generated, since people are naturally inclined to forget the consultation of reason. Here again, this would seem to require a sovereign with force *outside* of the contract to enforce the contract. Moreover, it may not be entirely a matter of force, but of persuasion.

In the end, Hobbes' sovereign must submit himself to the court of each person's opinion, so his absolutism requires the consent of the governed. In order for the governed to so consent, they must be persuaded that it is *in their interest* to always have a sovereign whose authority is considered to be absolute. People are self-interested for Hobbes, and this itself is no sin; what is needed is for them to act out of *enlightened self-interest.* Paradoxically, the condition of human beings requires that for this satisfaction it is necessary to have an absolute government. What is truly needed for society, then, is not merely one who would be the "artificial man," but one who will *speak* for this artificial man, one who can *enlighten* the self-interest of those who are to be governed. This, for Hobbes, is the task of political philosophy.

The crucial question regarding Hobbes' theory must therefore be this: is it valuable to have an authority who has an interest independent of private self-interest? The answer is clearly, yes. It is for this reason that Hobbes' theory has persuasive power to this day. If we glance at international politics, where there is clearly no common authority outside of the self-interests of the nations at hand, we can see the value of the notion of a state whose authority must lie outside of selfish interest. International politics does seem to be a thinly veiled *"war of all against all"* that begs for a common authority not bounded by the interests of any contracting members. A look at the ineffectiveness of such institutions as the United Nations makes clear the requirement of a strong sovereign external to the contracting members if there is to be lasting peace. Hobbes warns of the danger of the rule of private judgment—that, taken to its logical extreme, it leads to great harm, and in the end to the harm of private interest.

Correlatively, Hobbes points out an inevitable conflict between *political authority* and *private judgment*—an issue that defines political debate in the modern world, and hence raises the question as to the political requirements of individual liberty. It is in response to this conflict that all of Hobbes' most profound critics—Locke, Rousseau, Kant and Marx—have tried to rethink the issue that moved Hobbes. They all agree with the basic question—what individual liberty requires from political institutions—however much they *disagree* about the answers to this question and the meaning of liberty.

Finally, we should say this much in Hobbes' favor: he faces squarely the question of the origin of political authority. If, in the end, we agree that the liberty of acquisitive power is the ultimate political good, then must the end not be a "war of all against all"—a natural disjunction of individual ends, with only temporary alliances? Can we conceive of political authority as mere temporary political alliances of convenience? Hobbes realizes that this cannot be so, and given the radical conflict between people's natural desires, what will be necessary is an absolute will outside of nature to *forge* political unity. In the end, this foreshadows the criticisms of certain notions of natural liberty that we see in Rousseau and Marx: the natural individual cannot be taken to be fully free, but must be transformed by civil culture, or in Rousseau's famous phrase, "forced to be free."

Hobbes' thought, moreover, presents a difficulty with which all future social contract theories will have to grapple: the radical privacy of reason. Reason, we may recall, is incapable of discerning a common natural good by which we can judge political communities more or less good. The question to be raised here is this: can we abide by a conception of reason as private, and still have a basis for distinguishing between legitimate and illegitimate regimes? There are a couple of ways in which this problem comes up in relation to Hobbes and Locke in particular, but also in Rousseau. The first might be put this way: is there a distinction to be made between *procedural* legitimacy and *substantive* legitimacy?

That is, can we conceive of a law that is impartially fair (procedurally legitimate) without endorsing particular values and conceptions of justice (substantive legitimacy)?

To take Hobbes, for example; it would appear that Hobbes has a substantial standard by which we could distinguish between legitimate and illegitimate regimes. Legitimate regimes preserve life and protect individuals from one another, thereby promoting a more peaceful and commodious living by establishing an absolute sovereign to do this. But the difficulty arises from the paradoxical issue of the rights of the subject against the sovereign: *who is to be the judge* of the success of a particular society in fulfilling these goals? If the judge is to be the people, then we no longer have absolute authority, and Hobbes' system seems to contain an inevitable tension; further, it is unclear whether in Hobbes' theory we have any sort of political authority at all, but only a temporary contract, resulting from an alliance of convenience.

The criticism of Hobbes to be mounted by Locke therefore centers around the following problem: Hobbes' sovereign is in actuality only a private individual. And, since a private individual's judgment in the state of nature (the sovereign is not himself part of society) is inherently self-interested, why ought we to trust *his* judgment as to whether the substantive goods of society (self-preservation and liberty) are truly being promoted and protected? Hobbes' sovereign, while absolute, is also subject to the judgment of individuals regarding the requirements of these substantive rights. If this is the case, then what makes a government legitimate is the sheer fact that people have agreed to it out of their "enlightened self-interest." This, of course, runs into a similar difficulty as to whether the Hobbesian sovereign has "truly" understood what is required to protect the substantive rights of its members. Will this itself not be a matter of conjecture?

Locke's answer is instructive here: when the majority (or at least the powerful or propertied) has decided upon a new government, only then will we know. Locke's doctrine of *"limited government,"* or his distinction between civil society and government, is meant to put the power of interpretation back into the hands of the people; the government is subject to the will of the people. But then it becomes clear that only what a *majority* would have agreed upon at any given time (under conditions of fair bargaining in working out the contract) can be considered legitimate. In the thinking of Locke and Hobbes, legitimacy is either the result of the contracting parties (in Locke) or of some individual outside of the contract (Hobbes); but in both cases, the right is subsequent to *some* private judgment.

Thus, again as for the Ancient Greek sophists, it would seem that the right is merely *conventional.* In the thinking of the early contract theorists, the "legitimate" seems to mean simply what the people (or the sovereign, in Hobbes' terminology) believe to be legitimate. What "rights" involve (or even *are*) is simply a matter of agreed upon interpretation, whether by the majority or the absolute monarch. The question of *who decides*—that is, the question of "procedural" right—is prior to the question of *what is decided*, or of "substantive" right. It is true that certain procedural questions may indeed imply substantive results; but insofar as the procedural question is prior, the substantive question will remain fundamentally undecided. In order to avoid this difficulty, there must be some notion of a substantive idea of liberty that is prior to the judgments of particular individuals who have sovereignty. Rousseau, Kant, and Marx will later make this argument, against both Locke and Hobbes.

If the standards of legitimacy are merely the unquestionable will of either the collection of individuals or one representative individual, then legitimacy is merely conventional; it corresponds to what some happen to desire. If this is true, then any government that exists is legitimate, as well as any revolution against this government which proves successful. The inevitable conclusion would seem to be that might makes right after all; justice follows from power. And if so, then political philosophy becomes mere political history—a recording of the various substantive claims to legitimacy, justified by the fact of victory in a certain time and place. Right is no longer inherent in the substance of things, but is historical.

This difficulty is reflected in still another problem regarding the source of political obligation. If my allegiance to society is contractual, then in Hobbes' own view, this allegiance can extend only so far as it is advantageous to my "self-preservation," taken broadly to include liberty, property and honor. Thus, if at any time I can violate the contract without the contract being abandoned entirely, what would stop me? If one argues in Hobbesian fashion that violation of it would lead to a war of all against all, the reply would be that this would be true only if a substantial and powerful number of people violated the terms of the contract. But if I could get away with violation of the laws and commands of the sovereign, all the while promoting *general* obedience to it—perhaps even using the rhetoric of Hobbes where convenient to create general political stability—then what would stop me? This encapsulates part of Glaucon's objection to the social contract notion of justice in Plato's *Republic*, and it leads to the formulation of the "perfectly unjust man" possessing the reputation for justice while committing injustice as the happiest or best human being. It seems that Hobbes' egoistic psychology would justify such a portrait. Again, without a notion of reason that can discern a legitimately common good, a person interested in the most advantageous life possible would be allied to the political order only when it was expedient, and only for private gain.

Both of these difficulties arise from Hobbes' notion of the relation between reason and passion: the individual is primarily self-interested, and the passions are liberated from any obligation to others that is not grounded in a desire for acquisitive power. This being so, any obligation that we have in common with others is derivative from our private self-interest. Once a situation arises in which the allegiance to others is contrary to private interest, the allegiance to others seems to become groundless. Political society is inherently artificial for Hobbes. Reason is of no help in establishing a common ground with others, since it is entirely instrumental to private interest.

The inability to establish legitimacy is a function of the inability of reason to objectively assess a common good. Even if one grounds legitimacy in some notion of what people desire, it hardly answers the question as to whether these people desire what is in fact their *common* good. It may be pleasant to them, but it is at least philosophically questionable whether the pleasant is equivalent to the good. So Hobbes' social contract theory leaves us with at least as many unanswered questions as it answers. The radically private notion of desire precludes any sense of justice that is not merely temporary and conventional. It is largely in light of these criticisms that John Locke takes it upon himself to improve on the thinking of Hobbes.

2. Locke's Theory of Individual Liberty and Property

Our discussion of John Locke's political philosophy is largely taken from Locke's *Second Treatise of Government*, in which he systematically develops his objections to Hobbesian absolute rule into a new theory of government. Locke's theory has been influential on the politics of Europe and America, and indirectly (through Western influence) on the rest of the world. For Locke, liberty is grounded in and almost coextensive with property rights; this contrasts sharply against Rousseau, as we shall see in the next chapter. Locke and Rousseau, with their contrasting versions of liberty, set the ground for much of political debate in modern liberal countries.

State of nature and state of war. Like Hobbes, Locke looks to a state of nature to ground his theory of political society. In contrasting Locke against Hobbes, one is immediately struck by the differing ideas about the priority between individual rights and "natural law" (which in the language of the time referred to *natural "moral laws"*—moral laws that exist in the state of nature). In Hobbes, individual rights are prior to any law. In his view, a person has liberty to the means of self-preservation, however each individual understands these means. "Laws of Nature" (that is, any moral laws that may have existed in the state of nature) were mere maxims derived from a reflection on the natural condition in which this unfettered exercise of the right of nature occurs; hence, moral laws were derivative from individual rights.

By contrast, Locke starts with the coexistence of individual rights and moral law; all possess perfect freedom in the State of Nature, but freedom is *naturally* within the bounds of a natural moral law.

> Though this be a state of liberty, yet it is not a state of licence: though man in that state have an uncontroulable liberty to dispose of his person or possessions, yet he has not liberty to destroy himself. . . . The state of nature has a law of nature to govern it which obliges every one: and reason, which is that law,

teaches all mankind, who will but consult it, that being all equal and independent, no one ought to harm another in his life, health, liberty, or possessions (Locke 1980, 9).

There is not merely a right, but a *duty* to preserve oneself. Further, since each has an equal duty to self-preservation, each is bound to preserve the rights of another, when the duty of self-preservation does not come into conflict with those rights.

In the state of nature, because each is bound to this law of nature, and free to uphold it, each is also free to enforce it: "the execution of the law of nature is . . . put into every man's hands" (9). When, in a person's estimation, the law of nature has been violated, that individual has the right to punish the transgression, either for reparation (specific to one's own case) or for restraint (for others in general) (7-11). For example, if someone murders my brother, or the brother of a neighbor, I as an individual have not only a right, but also in some cases a *duty*, to hunt down and punish the offender. This duty to oneself and to others—as well as one's own goods, which are a necessary condition for liberty— is a natural one. It exists even in the state of nature, prior to society and its conventions.

The existence of these natural moral laws gives us a way to determine whether a government is "legitimate" or not, because the moral law grounds the substantive rights of *life, liberty and property*. The actual content of these rights, however, is not given much determination by Locke, and it is unclear that there is any substantive guarantee of these rights in Locke's theory, given his majoritarianism. At the very least, there might be a conflict between the procedural rights of the majority and any substantive interpretation of these fundamental rights encoded in the law of nature prior to majority rule. At this point, let us just say this much: if a society fails to uphold the duties of the laws of nature, then this society can be judged worse than those that do uphold them.

If there are any substantive rights—and Locke's discussions of slavery, property and absolute government seem to suggest there may be—this seems to be a remedy for a deficiency in Hobbes, whose doctrine of the radical privacy of reason's power seems to preclude any notion of a common substantive good. For Hobbes, as long as the social contract protects us from the harms of the state of nature, its power is legitimate. For Locke, the social contract must also guarantee us some substantive rights: it must protect our life, our liberty, and our property.

There is, however, a difficulty with Locke's "law of nature," or moral laws that already exist in the state of nature. It is not clear how these laws are justified. Hobbes has a fairly meticulous deduction of the laws of nature from the rights that people possess in nature; in Locke, we are not presented with any such deduction. There appear to be two candidates for the justification of the law of nature. First is religion: the duties of the law of nature are the result of God's wisdom in having made us. There are some obvious difficulties with this explanation, however. First of all, Locke does not emphasize this in the *Second Treatise*. In fact, it is scarcely mentioned. Second, what of those who are atheists, deists, or non-Christians?

Third, what he says about the relationship between reason and Scripture elsewhere makes any such claim problematic, because he seems to emphasize a separation between the two. And finally, there appear to be some serious discrepancies between Locke's *Second Treatise* and the Biblical teachings regarding family and property. It scarcely seems defensible to say that the Bible sanctions unlimited acquisition of property or a merely pragmatic attitude towards family loyalty, both of which Locke advocates.

More directly, Locke says that the law, as well as the standards of the enforcement of the law, are clear to the light of reason *independent* of revelation—they are clear to "any rational creature, and a studier of that law"(12). We are not, however, in the work at hand given such a study, nor a discussion of why these duties naturally bind us. They are merely asserted without argument. This does not mean, of course, that they are merely asserted as such; the claim that they would be evident to any "studier of the law" makes it clear that there may be such a discussion or deduction, but that it is not directly presented here. One can imagine such a deduction being made from the two claims about humanity in the state of nature in which Locke agrees with Hobbes—that all are free to do as they please, and that all are basically equal.

The ground of the law of nature may be *implicitly* present in what Locke says about the enforcement of the law of nature and the "state of war." Locke says that, in the state of nature, we all have the right to interpret and enforce the law as we see fit. Locke calls this doctrine a "strange" or "novel" one, because it seems so easily open to a Hobbesian objection. Is it wise, one might wonder, to allow people to be judges in their own case? Tellingly, *Locke does not deny the substance of the objection*—he denies only that the Hobbesian conclusion of absolute sovereignty necessarily follows from a reflection upon this objection:

What exactly is the Remedy?

> I easily grant, that civil society is the proper remedy for these inconveniences of the state of nature, which must certainly be great, where men may be judges in their own case. . . but I shall desire those who make this objection, to remember, that *absolute monarchs* are but men. . . . I desire to know what kind of government that is, and how much better it is than the state of nature, where one man, commanding a multitude, has the liberty to be judge in his own case, and may do to all his subjects whatever he pleases (Locke 1980, 12).

Locke seems to agree with Hobbes that the state of nature is an inherently unstable place, and for the same reason as Hobbes—the inherently self-interested nature of private judgment. If there is a law of nature, it is quite fragile and ineffective when in the state of nature. From this point of view, Locke appears to grant Hobbes' premises regarding the end result of the state of nature, and perhaps the fundamental motive of self-preservation, which for Locke explicitly involves liberty and property. The law of nature, even if "present" or "obliging" in the state of nature, is, as Hobbes might say, "mere words" in the absence of an empowered referee to enforce it.

Locke deduces from these Hobbesian premises, however, not absolute sovereignty, but *limited* authority. The argument is simple; if government's aim is to protect life and its requirements, liberty and property, then any absolute sacrifice of liberty to a sovereign is against the purpose of government. Absolute government is therefore incompatible with civil society. In absolute government, we would be giving up the means to preserve ourselves—the final function of government. It follows that absolute government would be a violation of the primary duty in the law of nature, and thus cannot be sanctioned by any social contract. The "law of nature" (the moral law which exists even in the state of nature) therefore has a very important function in Locke's theory: the existence of a pre-political duty that restricts sovereignty. Absolute government and slavery are in fact the same, and an absolute governor (or slaveowner) may be said to be in a state of war against his subjects, insofar as the subject's life and liberty is in the hands of another. If the sovereign is outside of the contract (as Hobbes insisted), then the sovereign in a state of war with the subject.

> And hence it is, that he who attempts to get another man into his absolute power, does thereby put himself into a state of war with him; it being understood as a declaration of a design upon his life . . . he that, in the state of society, would take away the freedom belonging to those of that society or commonwealth, must be supposed to design to take away from them every thing else, and so be looked on as in a state of war (Locke 1980, 14).

The state of war, therefore, differs from the state of nature. The state of nature exists where there is no common judge and may necessarily end in a state of war; but the state of war exists anytime someone uses force over another *without right*. This is a crucial distinction, since the state of war can exist not only in the state of nature, but in political society as well. Tyranny and absolute government create a state of war, but so does the mere invasion of my property and liberty by another individual even where there is no government.

This distinction also implies, against Hobbes, that there is force *with* right in the state of nature. For Hobbes, force has no moral status whatever in the state of nature; it only becomes legitimate by the command of a legitimate sovereign. In practice, this might be less of a distinction than one thinks. For Hobbes, the laws of nature, too, are binding in the state of nature, but only in "conscience"; they have no force, and hence are not truly law, because of each person's self-interested judgment. One person cannot unilaterally give up any advantage to another in the state of nature, so moral beliefs are impracticable.

But it seems that things are not much different on this score for Locke. In reality, a state of war is inevitably the result of the state of nature, because of the inability of people to judge properly in their own case. "Every least difference" seems to end in the Hobbesian war of all against all. In the state of nature, there is only an "appeal to heaven"—to abstract laws of nature, but without force. This makes one wonder whether the law of nature exists as a law in the state of nature; or whether it is not merely a deduction from self-interest, as in Hobbes. Each person's self-preservation requires respecting the right of others only when those rights do not conflict. Law is not prior to interest, but ultimately derivative from it.

However this may be, Locke's presentation of law as prior to interest, or naturally guiding interest, lends it a different function from what Hobbes recognized. For Hobbes, law simply was the will of the sovereign independent of self-interested interpretation. For Locke, the law exists as a standard by which to judge the will, not only of individual citizens, but of the sovereign as well. Rulers, as well as subjects, are human beings—so they too should be subject to the judgement of this law. The difficulty that still must be resolved, however, is this: if not the sovereign governor, then *who is to be the judge* of the requirements of the law of nature—especially since people tend to judge poorly in their own case? Before considering Locke's answer, we need to look at the way Locke construed self-preservation (which society is constituted to preserve) as including the preservation of private *property*.

Property. Leo Strauss has summarized the argument of Locke's doctrine regarding property in this way:

> If the end of government is nothing but "the peace, the safety and the public good of the people"; if peace and safety are indispensable condition of plenty, and the public good of the people is identical with plenty, and plenty requires the emancipation of acquisitiveness; and if acquisitiveness necessarily withers away whenever its rewards do not securely belong to those who deserve them—if all this is true, it follows that the end of civil society is 'the preservation of property (Strauss 1953, 244-5).

If it is true that Locke's doctrine justifies unlimited acquisitiveness (the guarantee of property rights to all an individual can acquire), the question is how it is that Locke comes to this conclusion in pre-political society from the very humble law of nature, which at first glance would seem to deny such unlimited acquisitiveness. If the law of nature allows for or even promotes this acquisitive sense of property, and political society exists to safeguard the law of nature, then political society will exist to safeguard the acquisition of private property. Locke, on Hobbes' basic premises, and with a similar content of the law of nature, will limit government so that it can increase property for each individual's own benefit. In what follows, we discuss Locke's argument under three headings: i. the origin of property; ii. the value of property; iii. the introduction of money.

i. The origin of property. Private property, according to Locke, is sanctioned by the law of nature. At first, however, it is limited by the law of nature. The law of nature gives each the duty to self-preservation. In order to do so, each must appropriate certain goods of nature, whether it be merely nuts and berries or the furs of animals, or agricultural products as a result of art. Hence one gains title of ownership to whatever one acquires *by one's labor*, in the beginning, it is labor alone which grants property. In beginning times, this limits the individual substantially, and likewise limits social conflict. Nature is generous when it comes to mere preservation, and in early times there were few people to share the immense bounty of nature. The law of nature prescribes only what is necessary for self-preservation; if someone acquires beyond this amount, they violate the law, for then they take away from nature that which could be used for the preservation of another. In the beginnings of natural property, the law of nature commands: do not appropriate what you cannot use. It forbids *waste*.

In this way, property in nature (especially of the non-durable goods on which life largely depends) is limited. Anyone who is industrious enough to produce from nature, can easily supply what is needed before it spoils or is wasted. The obstacle to unlimited acquisition, therefore, is that waste which would deprive others of their necessities. If this could be overcome, then unlimited acquisition would be within the bounds of the law of nature.

ii. The value of private property. Locke next tries to show the immense potential benefit for satisfaction of human desire that private ownership can have. He says that although God gave the world to people in common," he gave it them for their benefit, and the greatest conveniences of life they were capable to draw from it, (so) it cannot be supposed he meant it should always remain common and uncultivated. He gave it to the use of the industrious and rational, not to the fancy or covetousness of the quarrelsome and contentious" (Locke 1980, 21).

The desire to acquire private property, by inducing people to labor, increases the potential of the earth's benefit. In some sense, then, the earth is not plentiful, but poor; it is human labor that makes the earth plentiful. Nature is not, in fact, absolutely either plentiful or poor; it is a *potential* for plenty, which the motive of acquiring private property actualizes.

As evidence for the advantages of private property to humankind, Locke compares the productivity of undeveloped and developed land. Developed lands are ten or even a hundred times more productive, and "a king of a large and fruitful territory there [in undeveloped North America] feeds, lodges, and is clad worse than a day laborer in England" (Locke, 25-26). In England, the free acquisition of property is beginning to rule the day. Private property has helped to overcome the scarcity of nature for even the lower classes of society because of the sheer ability to produce more goods. It seems as if, at this point, we have satisfied one of the conditions of the law of nature: each can acquire more goods than is possible without private property, and private ownership does not decrease, but actually increases the ability of others to acquire enough for their own self-preservation and happiness. As Locke says,

> He who appropriates land to himself by his labor does not lessen, but increase the *common* stock of mankind: for the provisions serving to the support of human life, produced by one acre of inclosed and cultivated land ten times more than those which are yielded by an acre of land of an equal richness lying waste in common. And therefore he that encloses land, and has a plenty of the conveniences of life from ten acres, than he could have from an hundred left to nature, may truly be said to give ninety acres to mankind (Locke 1980, 23-4).

Potential Use → **iii.** ***The introduction of money.*** There is still, however, one condition of the law of nature which must be satisfied. If there is waste of my produce in the acquisition of private property, then I might still be accused of a violation of the law of nature. The goods I produce are perishable, so if I do not use them or trade them to another for their immediate use, then I can be rightly accused of depriving others of goods that they might be using to preserve themselves. It is the introduction of money, the accumulation of gold and silver (which are non-perishable) that overcomes the difficulty of waste. What gold and silver do is to give substance to my capacity to acquire, without this power actually being in immediate operation (bringing me goods that I cannot use, hence violating the command against waste). As long as someone agrees to take my surplus for this non-perishable power to acquire, I can acquire as much as I will.

What money represents is the unlimited capacity to acquire, or property without perishability. One might heap up as much of these durable things as one pleases, since "the exceeding of the bounds of just property does not lie in the largeness of possession, but the perishing of any thing uselessly in it" (Locke 1980, 28). Money thus makes possible the unlimited development of all lands, whereas before, the amount of land to be developed would be limited by what could be immediately used. But since I can now receive money for my surplus, I can be encouraged to develop as much land as will turn me a profit, thus increasing the wealth and benefit for all in the material goods necessary for happiness. Crucially, the agreement on the use of money is prior to society; hence the private and potentially unequal possession of the earth is granted by tacit and voluntary consent prior to civil society in the strict sense. When government is formed, it will be to preserve this pre-societal institution of property.

If, then, government is to be in the interest of the public benefit, it will encourage private property and its advantages. By means of a profit incentive, civil society at large will benefit, and all in accordance with the law of nature, since my building of wealth is "without injury to anyone."

A question to refine Locke's doctrine. According to Locke, the protection of unequal private property is justified because it fulfills the law of nature, since self-preservation is promoted without the detriment (and in fact a benefit) to that of others. Locke writes this before the development of industrialization in England and its attendant horrors which inspired the criticism of both bourgeois and communist socialists. However, Locke's theory can be seen as justifying the pursuit of wealth which gave birth to the industrial age. The objection of socialist critics to an absolute right to property is that, under industrialization, social conditions arise which harm the ability of many individuals to acquire goods, even when "industrious and rational"; and thus this right needs to be curbed in some way by a concern for a reasonable amount of equality to guarantee opportunities for reward for industry. If this is true, then under certain conditions we could use Locke's own principle to argue against his conclusions; unlimited acquisition would be a violation of the law of nature. This assumes, perhaps quite reasonably, that Locke's argument for unlimited property acquisition is based on its utilitarian value (even though Locke's entire theory is not purely utilitarian).

There is, however, another way of reading Locke's discussion which would argue against this conclusion. The law of nature says that I should further another's good *only insofar as it does not conflict with my own preservation*. Now, with private property comes the right to judge in my own case, and hence it may be possible for me to always judge that any forsaking of private property is opposed to my "self-preservation"; thus in principle I would have no concern for any others, since their interest always conflicts with my own. In other words, in order to make the critique that the socialists make within Locke's own framework, there needs to be some *objective* limit to my acquisition, beyond which I must turn myself to the concern of not obstructing the self-preservation of others. With the introduction of money, which allows acquisition beyond my current capacity to use without waste, it is at least questionable whether there is any such objective standard, in nature or elsewhere. This assumes a much closer tie between private property and liberty than the previous utilitarian interpretation, and would underlie the claim to a substantive right of private property in Locke.

Limited government and legislative power. With the addition of the right to property, Locke's theory of the origin of civil society follows much the same path as Hobbes; however, he uses the premises of Hobbes to argue for a *limited* government rather than a virtually all-powerful one. It could be argued that this conclusion is implicit in certain of Hobbes' thoughts on the rights of subjects against the sovereign. For Hobbes, the sovereign is absolutely authoritative because it is the will of each individual, and so its decree is like a rule over oneself in accordance with the right to self-preservation. However, since no one can be thought to give the right to another of violating self-preservation, the authority of the sovereign cannot extend to violation of self-preservation, and thus the subject holds this right *against* the sovereign.

Locke follows this reasoning to the point of making it the foundation of his theory of government. We enter society for self-preservation, and hence cannot be understood to rationally have agreed to any institution or practice that substantially endangers the goals of life, liberty and property. Locke's political theory is set up to ground a government of the sort that accords with these goals.

Locke emphasizes that the *consent of the governed* is the ground of authoritative government. Since the purpose of the law of nature is to protect individuals, it is only through consent that government not only arises, but is maintained. This contrasts strictly with Hobbes, for whom government, although formed as the result of consent, is irreducible to such consent or agreement. The sovereign is a "real unity of them all" that transcends the contract.

Locke's emphasis on consent is thus a safeguard against the independence of government from the contracting members of society. If a government is independent of the contracting individuals, it can be indifferent to the purposes for which it is formed. Such a claim to independence puts the government in a state of war against the contracting individuals. This kind of government would have arbitrary and absolute authority. Arbitrary authority may sometimes be *by chance* beneficial, but its claim is not thereby legitimate.

Consent, for Locke, can be either explicit or implicit. Implicit consent is termed *tacit consent*. Locke's doctrine flows from the purpose of society, namely to safeguard property. "Every man, that hath any possessions, or enjoyment, of any part of the dominions of any government, doth thereby give his tacit consent, and is as far forth obliged to obedience to the laws of that government, during such enjoyment, as any one under it"(Locke 1980, 64). If one has property in a nation, one has tacitly consented to abide by the laws of the land. However, this mere tacit consent is not enough to *make one a member* of a civil society; this for Locke requires *express* consent.

Once a community has been formed by consent, there must be a decision as to the form and extent of legislative authority. This decision to institutionalize the community in order to have a common judge, according to Locke, must be done *by majority*. Universal consent is impractical, and any other form of consent is unfair. The fairness of majority rule follows from the equality present in the state of nature; since we all have an equal right to the preservation of our property, each one has an equal part in this decision. Majoritarianism, by treating each voice as equal, respects this equality.

This may breed worries about the *"tyranny of the majority,"* which we discussed earlier. The majority may unjustly persecute a minority or an individual against the requirements of the law of nature. There are two possible responses that one could make in the Lockean spirit. The first would be to grant the point, insofar as majority rule can be shown to be in danger of infringing upon individuals' basic rights to property, life and liberty. Hence, it might be in the interest of each to safeguard these rights against majority infringement. One can see this concern in the thought and practice of the founders of the republic of the United States in America. Certain aspects of the U.S. Constitution are meant to weaken the capacity of the majority to act quickly and in an organized fashion against a minority or individual (the division of powers, for example, or federalism); others may be read as absolute protections of individual rights (the Bill of Rights, for example) against an overzealous majority.

It is curious, however, that Locke does not concern himself in the *Second Treatise* with such problems. There may be an explanation for this omission: if we were to ignore the majority will in favor of a minority or individual, this would actually result in a *deprivation* of each individual's equal procedural right to self-rule. Even in cases where a "substantive" violation of property may have occurred, if the majority sanctions it, is it Locke's position that the minority has *tacitly sanctioned* this "violation," simply by being a member of that community?

That this may be Locke's actual position is indicated by his notion of the dissolution of government. A violation of property is judged to have occurred, and therefore a judgment that the government is illegitimate, *when the majority has judged it to be so.* It is the people (i.e. the community prior to the institution of government, which rules by majority) who are the first authority above any legislative power. In being a member of this community, the individual is bound to the decisions of the majority, since only in majority is the procedural equality and liberty of the individual preserved.

This subordination of government to the community and its function—the preservation of private property—ultimately leads to a doctrine of limited governmental authority. Locke states this doctrine in four basic limits upon legislative power:

1. no absolute or arbitrary power NO secret laws
2. the government must rule by promulgated and standing laws
3. no taxation without consent
4. no transference of legislative power without the consent of the majority.

Locke thinks that the second, third and fourth limits follow from the first. That is, he thinks that law is opposed to arbitrary decree by its being *general,* and thus less likely to reflect a passing or particular interest. (It will be generally interested, not particularly. Further, the emphasis on "standing" law means this: law cannot, at the whim of the legislature, be ignored in a special case where there is a personal passion or grudge.) This helps to safeguard the people against arbitrary and absolute rule, since there cannot be any particular persecution.

The third limit requires interpretation. When Locke says that taxes cannot be taken without consent, he means, not necessarily that the individual must expressly give personal approval, but that by abiding in the community, the individual tacitly consents to the decisions of the legislative representatives appointed by the community. This accords with Locke's previous doctrine on "tacit consent. It seems to allow for quite a range of taxation, as long as the tax is consented to by the governed: "It is true, governments cannot be supported without great charge, and it is fit every one who enjoys his share of the protection should pay out of his estate his proportion for the maintenance of it. But still it must be with his own consent, i.e. the consent of the majority, giving it either by themselves, or their representatives chosen by them" (Locke 1980, 74).

A historical example will help to explain Locke's point. Recall that the American colonists at the time of the American Revolution were not bothered by the king of England taxing them as such; they revolted only because of "taxation without representation." That is, they object to taxation without consent. Taxation is not disallowed as such, but arbitrary appropriation of property by the community is illegitimate.

The fourth limit clearly manifests the authority of the people over the government. The legislature cannot alter itself or transfer itself without the consent of the majority. If it were able to do so, it would be claiming a root of sovereignty other than in the people. The American Republic follows this in one significant way. The branches of government can be altered only by *amendment* to the constitution, which must win the approval of the people before going into effect.

Limited government essentially means that the people—that is, the pre-governmental civil society—is ultimately sovereign. "There remains still in the people a supreme power to remove or alter the legislative, when they find the legislative acts contrary to the trust reposed in them" (Locke 1980, 77-8). Next in line is the legislative authority, since it is in law that the people's will is most directly expressed. Finally, the executive is subordinate to the legislature as the people's will. It is true that in some governments the executive calls the legislature into session, but it would be a usurpation of the people's will if the executive were to prevent the legislative body from meeting when it wanted to; by doing so, the executive would be declaring war on the people, who are the ultimate authority as to how government is to meet or be altered.

Revolution and dissolution: Lockean difficulties. Locke's explicit discussion of the dissolution of government follows from his discussion of tyranny, and it consists of two points. First, he defines "tyranny" as the *execution of power beyond right;* tyranny is a declaration of a state of war by a ruling body upon the people. Tyranny is both (a) action beyond the duly constituted law, or alienation of the legislature, and (b) action against the basic purpose of society and government—the preservation of property. In the first type of tyranny, the executive or legislature may decide to alter the form of government, by changing the meeting times of the legislature, or election rules, or by delivering the people into the hands of a foreign power, or abandoning executive power, all *without the consent of the people.* Once again, the people's consent is the crucial issue; political society is prior to any particular form of government, and is not dissolved with a change in government. Rather, it is authoritative over all such changes.

How does a legitimate change of government come about? Must the people only react to government change, once it is completed, or must they themselves actively oppose the government and change it if they see a breach of trust or property occurring?

Locke argues that the people are to be vigilant and have the right to change the government, since the governors are merely the deputies of the people. The main purpose for the formation of the social contract is the preservation of property and liberty, so therefore, "whenever the legislators endeavor to take away, and destroy the property of the people, or to reduce them to slavery under arbitrary power, they put themselves into a state of war with the people, who are thereupon absolved from any farther obedience" (Locke 1980,111).

In discussing the vigilance of the people, Locke decides to answer more fully a Hobbesian objection. This objection should be familiar in tone from our consideration of the people in Hobbes; the people are easily discontented and ignorant of their own interest, and so easily moved to revolution and civil war when there are only trivial causes. Locke's first answer is direct: the people are actually more or less stable, and they are not easily moved to great changes unless a clear and consistent pattern of threats to their interest are present. In this sense, they are more conservative by nature than Hobbes supposes. Moreover, they *are* capable of knowing their interest, broadly conceived;

> . . . . such revolutions happen not upon every little mismanagement in public affairs. Great mistakes in the ruling part, many wrong and inconvenient laws, and all the slips of human frailty, will be born by the people without mutiny or murmur. But if a long train of abuses, prevarications and artifices, all tending the same way, make the design visible to the people, and they cannot but feel what they lie under, and see whither they are going; it is not to be wondered, that they should then rouse themselves, and endeavour to put the rule into such hands which may secure to them the ends for which government was at first erected (Locke 1980, 113-4).

To this, a Hobbesian may raise a second objection—that the doctrine of Locke itself may foment rebellion. Perhaps the reason people do not rebel or have the character that Locke ascribes to them is the *result* of a lack of exposure to such doctrines as Locke's—doctrines that flatter their own knowledge of their interest. Locke responds to this more sophisticated argument by turning the tables on the objector; the promulgation of the doctrine will actually *decrease* rebellion because it will keep the people more vigilant about their interest broadly conceived. Governments will be less inclined to violate the property of a vigilant populace than they would of a less vigilant people; hence there will be less *cause* for revolution than under an absolutist regime. Locke points out that saying the *people* are rebellious is to misspeak: the authority for government, after all, lies in the governed, so the people cannot "rebel." Rather, it is the tyrannical ruler who is the true rebel. This is why Locke says that the government is *dissolved* by the betrayal of a tyrant, not by the people. The acts of the tyrant are already a violation of government. The people are only defending the law against the tyrant.

Finally, the Hobbesian apologist might raise a third objection: perhaps the proper use of Lockean doctrine would be permissible, but are not the people subject to influence of unscrupulous rhetoricians who would deceive them as to their interests? Locke's reply is twofold. Once again, he reaffirms his faith in the people. Secondly, he grants that he supposes such a rhetorician could possibly move the majority of people against their interests; but, he says, history shows that these cases are much rarer than the cases of a tyrant with absolute authority riding roughshod over the people's interests. All in all, then, relying on the people is a more stable way of preserving the interests of the people, as defined by the preservation of property, life and liberty.

One might wonder whose prudential judgment is most accurate regarding the ambition of the people with respect to their own interest—Hobbes' or Locke's. Might the increased vigilance that Locke suggests, along with people's natural self-interestedness, lead to the sort of instability Hobbes finds inevitable under limited government? One need only recall that Locke's work was revered as sacred text by those who planned the bombing of a federal building in Oklahoma City in 1998. Locke might argue that this will only be a fringe element, and the influence of the doctrine on the more stable majority will be less radical or extreme. This, however, might still seem to raise the question: is the contentedness of the majority a result of a correct judgment of interest by a vigilant population? Or is it the result of a Hobbesian calculation of the necessity of submission for the sake of law and order, even if it appears against one's interest? Further, it is unclear whether Locke can give any sort of convincing reasoning for a minority not to revolt, whereas the Hobbesian calculus does give a reason for submission—that any inconvenience is better than civil war.

This dispute hinges on the question of who is to judge whether a breach of the contract has been committed by the government. Hobbes, we recall, had been led by the incapacity of the people to judge in their own cases: for this reason, he put the final judgment in an absolute sovereign. Without this, we are still in a state of war. Furthermore, any actual government hoping to have authority in fact *must* claim this; no individual or faction can be above the law, whose essence is the will of the sovereign. This problem had caused a possible tension in Hobbes, since no one can contract away the right to life and its conditions—liberty and property; and with these, the judgment as to what is necessary to the preservation of life. Locke tries to resolve this tension by making the commonwealth prior to the government. The people are the judge (as a majority) over the government, without a return to the state of nature. Individuals are bound by their contract to society, but there is no contract between society and government; the government is the people's deputy, whom they can recall if they choose.

In fairness to Hobbes, we may say with him regarding this original contract that "a contract, without force, is but mere words." That is, it may be wondered whether a reversion to society is really any different from a reversion to a state of nature, because the contract at the level of civil society is merely an agreement to agree, without content. Locke himself admits that the legislative authority is "the essence and union of society," the "soul which gives it life, form and unity" (Locke 1980, 105). If society, then essentially dissolves with the legislative power, is the society really anything but a discontinuous and inactive (i.e., dead) body? In other words, when people consent to society, they consent to a kind of self-rule; but without this kind of self-rule, is there any real *content* to their consent?

The Hobbesian point can be put more simply: mere consent does not make unity. What prevents an individual or minority from withdrawing at any time from such a society and government, claiming wrongdoing according to the purposes of the contract? If an individual's judgment suggests that there has been such a violation, it appears that nothing can authoritatively prevent such a withdrawal. Consent, Hobbes would say, does not clearly remove us from the state of nature as to what is a violation of one's right to property, life, and liberty. Locke finally acknowledges this by saying that "every man is judge for himself, as in all other cases, so in this, whether another hath put himself in a state of war with him" (Locke 1980, 123).

Hobbes' worries about the corruption of the people's judgment by an appeal to ambition causes him to propose absolute authority. Locke's sanguine opinion regarding this same issue causes him to propose an opposite conclusion. The principles, however, are agreed upon from the start. And these principles are in perpetual tension. For Locke, once we consents to society, we are *bound* by majority decision. But what if the majority passes legislation that threatens our property, or life, or liberty, or even that of our fellow citizens? Whose judgment will settle the dispute? This same sort of question arose before when we were discussing Locke's doctrine of majoritarianism.

The question of sovereignty for Locke seems to be merely displaced to a tension between the majority of individuals and the individual taken separately, or between "society" on the one hand and the individual on the other. The resolution of this tension between individual liberty and governmental judgment is a task that Rousseau sets himself in his political philosophy: "all men are born free, but everywhere they in chains. The question is how to make these chains legitimate" (i.e. in concert with individual liberty). Rousseau's resolution is that we could consent only to a government whose will and law is itself constituted to guarantee our liberty.

In this way, Rousseau tries to resolve this tension in and between the views of Locke and Hobbes. Contra Locke, he takes the ultimate authority in political matters out of the hands of natural individuals: the "general will" is irreducible to either the will of all or that of the majority, and membership in political community will require the complete "alienation," or removal, of one's goods to the community. This does not mean, for Rousseau, the complete loss of individual liberty in the hands of an absolute sovereign individual, as in Hobbes. This is because the "general will" expresses the absolute conditions for individual liberty; hence, it guarantees certain rights and duties coincident with liberty. The preservation of substantive individual rights requires a "general" will authoritative above all particular wills—including the will of those who are the particular governors of a state. This is where Rousseau argues against Hobbes: the "general will" requires the subordination of government to a certain idea of right; a king or any other kind of ruler cannot be the final authority for the rules of society.

From this perspective, the problem with Hobbes' ruler is that he is a king—an actual individual. He is not, as it were, outside the contract *enough*, even though his will is the essence of the community. His will is merely a *particular* will, not a general one, and hence it is subject to the corruption that concerns Locke. Of course, this solution raises a difficulty: if neither the contracting individuals nor the particular sovereign determines what is lawful in society, then who makes this general will actual?

Rousseau's answer is (both like and unlike Hobbes): a true "mortal God"—*the Legislator*. The legislator, as opposed to a particular ruler, is not interested in actual rule, but is comparable to an engineer who sets the machine of society in motion and then *steps aside*.

Here, it seems, we reach the limits of social contract theory generally. The contracting members of society do not have procedural authority, but rather must abide by certain rules that are *derivative from the concept of liberty itself*. It is here that we see the tie between Rousseau and Kant: for both of these third-generation contract theorists, moral rules are not result of what people actually desire, but rather *from the concept of the freedom of the will itself*. This may be implicit in Hobbes' "laws of nature" from the beginning, but for Hobbes, laws become actual through enforcement, and have no reality without it; this is what leads to the conflict between what we have called "procedural" and "substantive" right noted in Hobbes and Locke. In Rousseau, and in Kant, this conflict is still present, but the clear emphasis is on the subordination of procedural right to a *substantive* notion of right. The difficulty for these later thinkers (and for their greatest interpreters, Hegel and Marx) becomes the reconciliation of the procedural with the substantive rights. If they cannot be reconciled, then Rousseau says that the people must be "forced to be free"—that society may be inherently *chains*, but chains that can be made "legitimate" by being the substantive content of liberty.

Chapter Six
Social Contract Theories, Equality, and Liberty: Rousseau and Kant

1. Rousseau and Social Liberty

Jean Jacques Rousseau (1712-1788) was one of the most influential men of letters in modern European history, not only in political thought but in literature as well. In his political work, Rousseau argues that liberty in community requires a radical understanding of human equality. This insight defines for him both the nature and the limits of social contract theory. In the work entitled *The Social Contract*, he advocates the "complete alienation" (i.e., transference) of all natural rights to society.

Recall that in the earlier social contract theories of Locke and Hobbes such an alienation of natural liberty was incomplete or conditional. We saw this in the difficulty of the subject's "rights against the sovereign" in Hobbes, and in the pre-political "law of nature" in Locke (i.e. the moral law that applies even in the state of nature). Both of these notions are rooted in a desire to preserve ourselves against others, who are viewed as potential obstacles to our own life, liberty, and property.

Rousseau asserts that as long as self-preservation *against others* is the ground of civil society, civil society will be both unstable and unfree. For Rousseau, the movement into legitimate political society requires a more radical break with what Hobbes and Locke take to be the natural desire for power and property. Whereas Hobbes and Locke had counted on the manipulation of self-interested desire for power and property to keep people within the bounds of law, Rousseau believes that such a desire must itself be sacrificed for the sake of liberty.

When Rousseau looks to the state of nature, he finds a "nature" that is prior to the desire for self-interest against others. It is his admiration for this state that grounds his ideas for legitimate political community. In order to fully understand

Rousseau's political theory as it is propounded in *The Social Contract*, it is necessary, just as with Hobbes and Locke, to examine his idea of the original state and the relationship of this original state to the function of politics. This requires that we begin with a different book of Rousseau's, his *Discourse on the Origin of Inequality*.

The original condition. In reading Rousseau's *Discourse on the Origin of Inequality*, we must ask this question: how is its account of the original human state useful for political theory? This question is forced on us by the radical difference that Rousseau proposes between humanity in the state of nature and in the civil state. If our original state is radically different from our civil state, then the original state would seem to be irrelevant. In sharp contrast to Hobbes, Rousseau says that the original state was one of happiness, and the current state one of misery. By studying original humanity and its devolution into social humanity, we can learn the causes of current misery and what sort of existence is, by contrast, happy. However, it also seems that this is a state to which we can never return; once the innocence of the original condition is lost, it is lost forever.

Showing us a condition that is happy, yet beyond our capacities to recapture, might superficially seem to be a recipe for discontent. However, the original state may reveal a remedy for the defects of current society without any need to actually return to the hazards of that state. What appears as merely a "loss" could then be understood as a "gain," if we can learn in what sense we have become "lost."

What characterizes human beings in the state of nature for Rousseau is complete *independence*. This independence is different from what is called "liberty" in Hobbes or Locke. In Hobbes and Locke, there is already an implicit social nature to liberty, in that it is always defined relative to one's concern with others. For Rousseau, by contrast, original independence is *solitary*. Rousseau's argument for this position is a refinement of Hobbes' reasoning, in which Hobbes argued that political society is artificial, not natural. In Rousseau's view, Hobbes does not go far enough.

Even though stable society in Hobbes' view is not present in the state of nature, Hobbes' pre-political condition is one of concern with the actions of others, and our own happiness is always dependent on subduing or earning the respect of others. In this sense, Hobbes' individual is dependent. As Hobbes himself indicates (and Locke concurs), the greatest obstacle to our own independence is others. We require of others, at least, the approval or acceptance of the value of our own acts, property, and power. This approval can be acquired either peacefully or through force, but in either case, the acquisition of another's recognition becomes necessary for one's satisfaction. Thus, as Rousseau is fond of saying, even in becoming the master of another, we becomes their slave. This seeking the recognition of others is, as Hobbes himself admits, an infinite task, or one that is never fully accomplished. But in Rousseau's view, this is an admission of the misery of Hobbes' human condition. For Hobbes, to be a social being means to look outside oneself to define oneself in relation to others; Rousseau's natural individual, by contrast to the one envisioned by Hobbes, is *indifferent* to external factors for satisfaction.

Natural human independence is a result of solitude. Thus Rousseau rejects as "natural" all passions that are associated with need or defect in relation to others or to nature. An individual human in nature is strong, not merely physically, but more importantly, in psyche. In fact, we might say that humanity in the natural condition is "care-free"; this defines the freedom there. What cares there are, are fleeting and simple, and easily sated; thus the individual appears not to be essentially in need. Rousseau never tires of contrasting the self-sufficiency of natural man to the dependence of social man.

> But without having recourse to the uncertain testimony of history, does anyone fail to see that everything seems to remove savage man from the temptation and the means of ceasing to be savage? His imagination depicts nothing to him; his heart asks nothing of him. His modest needs are so easily found at hand, and he is so far from the degree of knowledge necessary to make him desire to acquire greater knowledge, that he can have neither foresight nor curiosity. . . . His soul, agitated by nothing, is given over to the single feeling of his own present existence (Cress 1987, 46).

Explain

The passions that are present in the state of nature reflect this independence. Regarding oneself, one has the sweet sentiment of existence itself. This is what both grounds the later desire for self-preservation and is yet essentially different from it. Whereas the sweet sentiment of existence is indulging in the present, the concern for self-preservation is essentially concerned with the future, and a concern with the future arises only in the context of the experience of the weakness of the self, and this is foreign to the independence of nature. In the original state, nature itself facilitates the carelessness for the future, since nature provides in plenty for our limited and immediate desire. No future planning is necessary when the moment the stomach grumbles, food is present, and love is merely a physical desire that is easily sated.

Rousseau's doctrine of human intelligence in this natural state coincides with his doctrine of passion. The natural individual is able to adaptively imitate the industry of other beasts, because we humans have no particular instincts that are our own. However, in the original state of solitary plenty, there is no need for the sustained development of this intelligence in the direction of what may be called "reasoning." This development would only accompany the foresight necessitated by self-conscious need. Rousseau says a similar thing for the development of speech; on this point he concurs in part with the classical understanding of speech found in Aristotle. Speech, for Aristotle, is what distinguishes humans because of the need for discussion about the good or the just. This presupposes that the question "What is to be done?" is an intelligible one, and the intelligibility of this

We imitate others, he isn't giving human any credit.

question depends on the need for foresight. It is this that Rousseau denies to the human in the state of nature. Deliberative and communicative speech is not "natural."

Neither can there be what we would call "choice" in the state of nature. Choice is not, for Rousseau, a sign of independence but a sign of dependence. Choice is a choice *between* goods, both of which seem in some sense desirable, and decision occurs because both cannot be had (which implies a consciousness of *need*), and because one is more desirable than the other (which implies *foresight*). Choice and a consciousness of our need (and hence our misery) are directly linked. While Rousseau at first says that the freedom of the will distinguishes humans from the beasts, he at the same time emphasizes that in nature a person is close to being such an innocent beast. For this reason, Rousseau backs off of his claim that natural individuals possess freedom of the will. Rousseau says that "the will speaks when nature is silent," but for Rousseau, nature is not silent in our natural condition; in the state of nature, we act from the "simple impulse of nature" (Cress 1987, 45-6).

What Rousseau does preserve is what he calls human "perfectability," which is closely related to the imitative adaptability of intelligence. This notion throws a crucial complexity into the picture of natural humanity. For all that has been said about natural independence, a being that is capable of being "perfected" is not an essentially independent or self-sufficient being; rather, it is an incomplete or dependent being. When speaking of original independence, then, we are not really speaking of human "nature"— that is, a condition peculiar to the state of nature—but rather of the human condition in general. In the original condition, we is independent; but we are "dependent" on nature for this independence.

The lack of natural instincts means that the human is the animal that is most exposed to changes of circumstances or natural accidents. What we lack in the original condition, compared with our later existence in society, is a *consciousness* of dependence. This lack of consciousness is because of the beneficence of nature; the lack of awareness of dependence on the generosity of nature is the character of original "independence." Ignorance is bliss, and the human is an innocent beast, but one who, given perfectability, is subject more than any other to a loss of this innocence. When Rousseau praises original goodness, he really means that the human is "innocent" of the choice between virtue and vice.

The role played by this portrait of the sate of nature in Rousseau's eventual political theory is as follows: the independence of natural humanity is *unstable*, which is to say, that it is not truly independent. In fact, given that people in the state of nature are at the mercy of natural bounty, we might say that this state is a great deal less "independent" than we are in civil society, at least in respect to nature. Rousseau indicates this by claiming that humanity leaves the state of nature not by choice, but due to chance accidents of nature that force us to count on others—accidents that were not necessarily bound to happen, but simply did happen. The result of such chance events is to make humans dependent on each other. Nature had initially produced plenty for solitary individuals, whereas now it produces both scarcity and social dependence.

The question of political community then comes down to this: given that we now cannot escape self-consciousness and choice, which have arisen with need and desire, how can we shape this situation in such a way as to regain the independence that was present in the original condition? In praising natural human innocence, Rousseau is wise enough to see that we cannot return to the original innocence, since any return to innocence at this late date would itself not be "innocent," but rather a matter of choice. But precisely for this reason, the return to innocence might actually be *better* than the original state, since in political community the preservation of such independence would be the object of conscious choice, not a mere gift of nature's bounty. Our independence would not be subject to a condition given by nature, but instead would result from conditions *chosen* as our own.

Rousseau's praise of the natural condition is in stark contrast to Locke and Hobbes, who considered this condition as either inconvenient or terrible. Yet Rousseau's idealization of the original condition is also meant to relieve us from the condition of being subject to others, which in turn is a result of nature's chance operation. As Rousseau sees it, Hobbes and Locke have not escaped enough from the "natural"development of dependence on others.

We can sees this in Rousseau's comments on private property in the *Discourse*. Here he has in mind Locke's notion of private property. Recall that, in Locke's doctrine of property, the right is established, *prior to government,* as a necessary condition for self-preservation in the state of nature; it is an extension of the law of nature—a moral law that holds even in the state of nature. For Rousseau, by contrast, the pre-political possession of private property involves a *limitation* on liberty: originally, we ate as we wished, and the whole world was open for consumption, but when people begin to claim private property, the owner of private property must then always be concerned with *exercising that right against others*—that is, defending and expanding the property. The recognition of others is the ground of our property rights becoming real. This is how social existence, for Rousseau, encourages dependence on other particular individuals. In the original state, a common benefactor (God) grants to each without feeling the opposition between "mine" and "thine," and hence without a consciousness of lacking. By contrast, in the social state, there are property rights against others and thus a consciousness of weakness and dependence on the other's will. The question, then, regarding property within political community will be this: can something like the "beneficence of nature" be *re-instituted* within the bounds of society?

Rousseau argues that the only way to accomplish this aim in regards to property would be to eliminate or subordinate the idea of private property. Property must become *public*; thus the *system* of private property would become entirely derivative from and dependent upon the *public will.* In a way, this is what Hobbes says that *all* governments do. Private possession only becomes just when it is under the will of the sovereign, who is responsible for making actual the distinction between "mine" and "thine." Recall that for Hobbes, the will of the sovereign is not a private will, but the public will, as it is expressed in a representative body such as a legislature. The difficulty for Hobbes from Rousseau's point of view is that this public will is still embodied in private individuals. Rousseau's solution to this problem will be considered in due course, when we discuss his other major work *The Social Contract* below.

In making private property into a function of public will, we see the priority of social or general will over the particular will of the individual. This priority will constitute the primary emphasis of Rousseau's theory of legitimate government. Such a *public* notion of property would mean that, as in the state of nature, my usage of property would not deprive another of an equivalent usage, and hence I would not be opposed to or dependent on another individual's will for my preservation, nor *vice versa*.

In discussing Rousseau's picture of the original condition, we have emphasized the "independence" of this condition. This might seem to neglect Rousseau's emphasis on the other natural passion in human feeling—compassion for others. Rousseau says that this compassion is the ground of all the social virtues that bind us to each other in society. Perhaps, then, there is some evidence in nature of an awareness of mutual dependence that Rousseau seems to otherwise describe in the *Origin of Inequality* as a sort of slavery. It is clear, however, that natural compassion for Rousseau is quite different from "social virtue." Rousseau describes this natural sentiment, literally, as a *natural* passion; it does not involve the sort of *self-evaluative* dimension that all social duties do, but has the fleeting and not-lasting character of all passions in the state of nature. We naturally befriend our friends, but also hate our enemies. Such natural passions are entirely physical or mechanical, much like the cry of pain that elicits them. Natural compassion, that is, is not equivalent to a social duty that constrains our evaluation of others and ourselves, because in the original condition, there is no such evaluation.

A social virtue, then, is a duty that we have towards another; this presupposes both that it opposes some of our social passions, and also that we are mutually dependent on each other. Neither of these conditions are present in the state of nature. Rousseau describes the "maxim" by which natural compassion operates in such a way as to deny any claim or duty that the other has on us: "Instead of the sublime maxim of reasoned justice, 'Do unto others as you would have them do unto you,' compassion inspires all men with another maxim of natural goodness, much less perfect but perhaps more useful than the preceding one: 'Do what is good for you with as little harm as possible to others'"(Cress 1987,55).

Rousseau clearly distinguishes this formula from the "Golden Rule" of Jesus. It is important to understand the difference between the two. The Golden Rule ties my fate to that of others absolutely; Rousseau's maxim preserves indifference to (and hence independence from) others. What really prevents natural humans from harming others is *ease*, or natural plenty. If other means to our simple desires are available, we are moved by compassion to refrain from harming others, as a *secondary* priority. This does not, of course, cover the case where other means are *not* readily available. So Rousseau's rule of natural compassion contrasts with the Golden Rule, which is absolute. In fact, precisely *because* of this conditional nature of our duty to others in natural compassion, Rousseau allows for the development of the difficulties of society when natural plenty vanishes: the Golden Rule is a response to these difficulties. The Golden Rule, although based in compassion, is exceptionless; hence it is *more perfect* than natural compassion, which is unsteady and thoughtless. In the Golden Rule, we perfectly escape our natural condition in our solidarity with the other; but this first requires a concern with the difference between self and other that only arises in social relations.

The Golden Rule, therefore, is an example of "reasoned" and "social" justice. It is an example of the inherent superiority of the social state to the natural state, despite Rousseau's emphasis on the ruin of humanity when society, with all its conflicts, emerges out of the blissful state of nature. In society, compassion is made exceptionless, or independent of natural circumstances, whereas in Rousseau's account natural compassion (in the state of nature) is imperfect by being dependent on circumstances. The Golden Rule takes what is imperfect or conditional in nature and makes it perfect or absolute in society.

Corruption and unequal society. Before Rousseau turns to an account of the way humans moved from the original condition to the social condition, he notes two crucial points:

First, he reminds us of the crucial difference between the original and the social conditions. *Social inequality* is not present in the state of nature, but arises only in the social condition, because it arises from the situation of mutual dependence. Nature provided what was needed without others in the state of nature, and we were thus free in the original condition. If there are changes in this condition, however, human nature also must change. This is a result of the previously discussed perfectability of humans. We are not nailed to any particular nature, but can adapt to different natures.

Secondly, Rousseau emphasizes that human corruption is a series of *accidents,* that is, the changes are not rationally directed by human decision. The accidental nature of these causes exposes human independence in the state of nature as incomplete. Furthermore, the contingent nature of these causes points to the fact that *human nature can be shaped by external causes and conditions.* If we can harness these accidental causes, we can change the conditions of existence so as to *reform* society in the image of original liberty. Rousseau treats humans much in the same way that the modern natural scientist and engineer treat the natural world—as a result of external causes and conditions that occur accidentally, but which can be brought under human control precisely *because* they are accidental and not necessary.

It is not necessary here to go over every detail of Rousseau's account of human development; we shall here only point out a few of the more crucial steps in this development that reveal its overall character. The first step in this development is from solitary nature to primitive society. Primitive society is still largely equal, and Rousseau makes an explicit point that there is still no true social labor; each of us provides everything for our own subsistence, and so have no need of others for the conditions of our own existence. Even this society, however, sees the development of the conditions for inequality in the comparison of abilities, skills, appearance, and power that occurs when people live in close proximity. From this origin, notions of esteem and honor develop, even among the simplest societies.

However, since such inequalities are not tied to the need of others for purposes of our own preservation, or social labor, Rousseau describes this primitive society as a relatively happy condition. Each is still independent of others when it comes to self-preservation. Social inequality, or need of others' approval, is not yet tied to economic need. It is the development of this tie that causes the transformation from relatively equal and happy primitive society to modern *unequal* society. This, too occurs by accidental developments: the accidental discovery of the arts of agriculture and metallurgy and the forging of iron lead to two crucial developments. The first is the ***division of labor***; in metallurgy, people do work that does not directly contribute to their individual self-preservation. If I work on iron all day, I need *someone else* to provide the food I need, since I cannot eat the products of my own labor. Agriculture develops as a response to this need, since it makes possible the production of more than we needs for ourselves. In exchange between the surplus of the land and the tools of iron, we see the end of economic independence.

Second, with the development of agriculture, we develop a "sense of entitlement" to the land that we work. This is the origin of ***private property***. Rousseau says that, if labor is the ground of property, then property should be private only when it is being used; while lands lay fallow during the winter, there is no labor and hence no property. But private ownership of lands illicitly develops into a *permanent* ownership, so that people engaged in agriculture can develop a more steady stream of production for themselves. After all, if I let anyone squat on lands I had previously worked, then I can hardly be expected to be able to use this land for production the following year. Private property introduces competition for land.

Under these new conditions, the inequalities in natural talent, which had little opportunity to develop in the natural state of plenty, become manifest and lead to economic inequalities. The result is a society in which inequality and mutual dependence are the rule of the day; and the great inequality is between rich and poor, or economic, since this economic inequality is what is relevant to the desire for self-preservation.

The final step in Rousseau's vision is the development of political society. Rousseau sees the fundamental conflict as the conflict between rich and poor—between those who have private property and those who threaten it. In this economic concern, Rousseau's account is a variation of Locke's theory, in which society comes into being to protect private property as the right to an unfettered accumulation of wealth. For Rousseau, this means that political community is an act of the rich to protect their property from the poor. The wealthy need protection because their property without law can easily be taken from them. Rousseau does not, by saying this, deny that the poor do not gain something through the cessation of violence among themselves and between rich and poor. They gain some protection for their life; but in doing so, they are reduced to a kind of economic servitude. In this, inequality takes on the name of "justice."

It would be easy, although mistaken, to read the development from the original state to the inequality of modern society as simply a negative development in Rousseau's view. The fact that there is nothing in nature to prevent what happens means that there is an implicit approval of it. Also, the development of society offers a certain advantage that makes up for the disadvantages caused by destruction of the natural condition. The advantage is that the independence from nature's scarcity has become itself a conscious goal of humanity: we wish to make ourselves independent, but more perfectly so than is possible in the original state, where liberty was merely given, and was not the result of our own decisions. If freedom must become a conscious object, this consciousness reveals that freedom is unstable; yet this has *in fact* always been the case. Since nothing prevents the development of inequality in nature, this means that freedom was always, from the beginning, unstable. In our later socialized condition, we have knowledge of this, and this knowledge is a greater advantage than what was lost.

It is also important to note that the *obstacle to freedom* changes with the development from the state of nature to society. On the whole, external nature is the main obstacle to liberty, but after society develops out of the original condition, the greatest obstacle to liberty is *other people*. In this, Rousseau comes into partial agreement with Locke and Hobbes. Both Locke and Hobbes see the purpose of political society as a remedy for the inconvenience of having to protect our own life and liberty from the encroachments of others. Thus their political theories, from Rousseau's point of view, are already socialized to servitude. That is, they look at humans as *inherently in the condition of competition* for life, liberty, and property as scarce goods. Such competition is essential to the human condition for Hobbes and Locke, whereas for Rousseau it is the result of chance accidents in nature, and therefore is not essential. It can be altered, given other circumstances. The individuals of Hobbes and Locke are still operating under the assumptions of "nature" in terms of scarcity. Rousseau holds up a picture of human independence where nature is not a condition of scarcity, but of plenty. And the purpose of this point is to counter the notion that we must be content with a picture of humanity in which we inevitably contend *against* others for our liberty.

The re-institution of freedom within society requires a re-institution of the original condition, but within the self-conscious bonds of society. This condition, we recall, emphasizes independence from others. The reason there is no conflict in this condition is that others are not perceived as any sort of threat. The difficulty to be overcome in society is the "personal" or "private" nature of will or freedom, which is enshrined in Locke's notion of a private property that can exist prior to society, and in Hobbes' "right of nature" (the rights we possess in the state of nature), which cannot be "contracted away" to society. This private or personal liberty is not a freedom from a concern with others, but precisely as a freedom held *against* others. Only when we overcome a concern with liberty as "private"—as actualized only in opposition to the liberty of others—can we become capable of true "freedom." This condition imitates the original largess of the state of nature, in which no person's independent satisfaction interferes with any other's.

Liberty, then, must be entirely social. One person's right must not be derived from that person as opposed to others, but must apply to all generally, *as it is in the original condition*. Private liberty must be utterly alienated to a "general will." The problem of modern society is not the ambition to be free, but the fact that this freedom is wrongly interpreted under the condition of natural scarcity. In Rousseau's view, my private will is the architect, not of my liberty in opposition to others, but of my liberty in *coincidence* with others. This view of liberty re-institutes the condition of the state of nature. And it does so more securely by being the conscious intent of our will (as supported by the force of the state), and not the result of chance conditions in nature.

The social contract: Individual will and general will. From the *Discourse of the Origin of Inequality*, two major points are relevant to the purpose of the political society argued for in *The Social Contract*. First, in the original human condition we are independent from the judgment of others; in the ensuing development of society, our worth is dependent on the judgment of others. Natural independence is gone forever, and servitude, even for the masters of slaves, is the rule of society. Second, there is something inherently defective about original liberty. To be sure, this side of things is much less stressed in the *Discourse on the Origin of Inequality*, but it is implicit in Rousseau's account of human susceptibility to chance accident; the defect of natural liberty is precisely this susceptibility to accidents external to will. In the *Social Contract*, Rousseau is a great deal more explicit about this defect: "To the preceding acquisitions could be added the acquisition in the civil state of moral liberty, which alone makes man truly master of himself. For to be driven by appetite alone is slavery, and obedience tot the law one has prescribed for oneself is liberty" (Cress 1987, 151).

It is in nature that we are driven by appetite, not in society. The independence that we can claim in the original condition is merely "caprice," whereas in society, we are subject to the will and property of others. This, too, turns out to be mere caprice (the whim of others), until subjected to the law of political community, or the *general will*. If it were not for the fact that the general will is abused, humanity would thank forever the day it left behind nature.

Rousseau's solution to the difficulty of what he calls the "abuse" of society comes from a rejection of the primacy of what we might call the "natural individual" (following Rousseau's own distinction between natural and social liberty). The natural individual is one who reserves, *against others*, a *particular* right to treat them as means to his own preservation. For both Locke and Hobbes, this right cannot ever be given up, or alienated. Rousseau, by contrast, consistently emphasizes the alienation of particular rights to the community. He stresses that I must forsake the private nature of my own concern, in which I necessarily put myself into conflict with others, and thus become dependent upon them. *It is precisely this privacy of concern that is the source of dependence and hence the greatest obstacle to liberty.*

Rousseau begins the *Social Contract* speaking of the illegitimate grounds of society. Right is not equivalent, first, to might, nor is slavery the ground of society. Whereas Locke had opposed slavery because its deprivation of liberty would be opposed to self-preservation, Rousseau emphasizes that liberty itself is the ground of opposition to slavery: renouncing liberty is renouncing dignity as a human being. This allows Rousseau to avoid legitimizing voluntary slavery, entered into for the sake of self-preservation—a condition that Hobbes had allowed.

This emphasis on liberty means that the origin of any political society which is legitimate must be in a convention universally agreed upon—each person's liberty is sacred. As opposed to Locke, *majoritarianism* is not necessitated by universal agreement, but is itself a *result* of a prior universal agreement. This is a small but crucial point, for it shows that Locke preserves the primacy of the particular individual over what Rousseau would call the citizen. In Locke's theory, it is precisely because *each person's particular will* is equal that the majority rules. Rousseau argues that this majority of private wills is not identical to a universal will, or what he calls a *generalized* will, but instead is a mere aggregation of particularly self-interested wills.

Particular interest is characteristic of the "natural individual," not of the citizen. As a citizen, I relate to each person *generally*, which means I abstract from my own private self-interest and look at each person's interest equally. Locke's individual, by contrast, has not truly become a *citizen*, because the primary concern is still private interest. This is why he thinks we can reserve rights against the political community for ourselves. For Locke (and for Hobbes, as well), each individual has the right to judge whether liberty, or property, or life is being threatened. This distinction between particular and general interest, combined with the individual's tendency to judge in a self-interested manner, reduces to a private self-interest that thus holds a right against the political community. By contrast, for Rousseau's citizen, such a reservation of rights is contradictory, because the legitimate political community just *is* the preservation of liberty, *precisely in the alienation of private right*. Rousseau famously says that a citizen who refuses to recognize this, and who acts from their private or particular interest against the common interest, must be "forced to be free." Since the common interest, the general will, protects each citizen from personal dependence on others (this dependence is the necessary consequence of following our particular will in opposition to the general), we are not fully free in opposing the general will, but only in obedience to it. This requires further explanation.

When entering the contract that constitutes political society, what I desire is to avoid constraints to my liberty. The greatest constraint to my liberty is my consideration of myself as a private individual, that is, in my competition with others for particular goods and rights. Rousseau seems to reason in this manner: from my individual standpoint, what is opposed to my freedom is my dependence on the will or judgment of other individuals. This is the result of my constant striving *against* and comparison with them. If I forsake this concern with striving against them, giving them equally what I take for myself, then I can be free from this limitation. This is what it means to treat others, not as objects of a "particular" or "natural" will, but as the object of a "general" or "social" will. This is actually in the interest of my liberty, since now my right is truly "unopposed" by others, because no other enjoys a right that I do not enjoy. Therefore, the general will is not opposed to my natural desire for liberty, but in fact is the *completion of it.* Liberty requires an indifference to another's opposition to my concern , and such indifference comes from equality of rights, which destroys the comparative basis of dependence. Recall that for Rousseau the primary sense of social dependence comes from our comparison of ourselves with others.

In Rousseau's thinking, this substituting of the general interest for self-interest in political activity is the main content of the legitimate social contract. Each person equally alienates his or her rights to the community. In such equality, no right is given to another that one does not already possess, because the law of the land is to be applied generally. For this reason, each citizen's liberty is now given the sanction of the entire state; each member is now an "indivisible part of the whole." In this "alienation" of my will to the general will, crucially, I am given over to *no one in particular*, but to the state (which mimics the original condition, but now with the conscious intent of the state). Since all are given equal rights, there is no individual to whom I am beholden.

From the point of view of individual liberty it looks like this: in entering the social contract, I am no longer *particularly* dependent on others, but *generally* dependent on the community as the guarantor of the conditions for my liberty in equal rights. But since this community is constructed to be the condition for my liberty from oppression by particular others, it is not opposed to my independence, but is what I most wish. It therefore is a "dependence" in accord with the content of my desire, or liberty. If I were to act against the community, I would only do harm to my own liberty; thus, if I threaten to act against it, I need to be "forced to be free."

An example where this can be clearly seen is with regard to Rousseau's doctrine of property. Rousseau consistently maintains that private property, in legitimate political community, is absolutely subject to the community's rights; an individual alienates all goods to the community in entering into the contract. Private property is not a right prior to community as in Locke, but instead is a right conditional on the purposes of the community. Insofar as it facilitates the liberty of each person, private ownership is allowable; however, if it violates the purposes of the contract, the community has a right to regulate it, and if necessary sometimes even to possess it. Rousseau says that the general rule regarding property is to avoid drastic inequality, for drastic inequality creates a condition where one or few have certain liberties or opportunities at the expense of many; it becomes a constraint on the liberty of *all*. The poor are constrained by the deprivation of opportunities that come with property; the rich also are constrained by always having to fight off the advances of the poor, for example through the threat of crime. A practical example of a policy that would reflect Rousseau's thinking here is in modern states where progressive taxation is used to redistribute wealth. In so doing, there is an attempt to equalize the opportunities that come with property.

Another example that seems to be in the spirit of Rousseau's thought is the prevailing interpretation of the **equal protection clause** of the Fourteenth Amendment to the U.S. Constitution. This amendment, which was passed in the aftermath of the liberation of African-American Slaves at the end of the American Civil War, has been interpreted to say that the rights that are granted to some people must be granted to all. Any law or social institution that prevents some minority or individual from access to rights that the majority possesses must be seen as opposed to the Constitution (the social contract, Rousseau might say, of the United States), and therefore illegal.

Many of the crucial legal decisions of the second half of the twentieth century that involved the civil rights of African Americans, women, and other minorities have used this Amendment to strike down laws or practices that promoted inequality. In so doing, these decisions guaranteed certain rights to all citizens equally. The rights of one person or group of persons is not to be bought at the expense of the rights of another. In light of Rousseau's theory, this means that the function of the social contract is closer to fulfillment than when minorities or individuals were denied equal access to these rights. Once again, it is crucial to see that, in Rousseau's view, this does not merely benefit the denied minority; rather, from his point of view, the white male majority would be benefitted as well, since they no longer would have to defend a "private" right against those who would destroy it, but instead share a right in common with all, and with the backing of all.

Law, the legislator, and the general will. What we have discussed thus far has been the general character of legitimate rule. To summarize the argument:

the obstacle to liberty in political society as it exists in modern states is our subjection to the particular will of another. This is a result of an interpretation of liberty that necessarily puts us into competition with others over goods that are necessarily scarce; ultimately, as Hobbes pointed out, this comes from a concern with self-preservation. The solution is to eliminate, as much as possible, the competition over scarce goods. This is done by "generalizing" our will; this we do when we alienate private rights to a community that guarantees our freedom from the obstacle of others' wills. It does so by guaranteeing that all are subject to an equal social condition, in which no one's liberty is deprived so that another may have it, because the other's right is not excluded by my own liberty.

This requires equality of rights and at least relative equality of property. The individual therefore alienates private rights to the community, but only on the condition that we receive back from society a greater guarantee and perfection of liberty than we could have in nature or unequal society. This is not so different from the arguments of Hobbes and Locke; ultimately, they too argue for a form of political community that guarantees greater (and more equal) liberty than could be guaranteed without political community. What distinguishes Rousseau is that Rousseau sees that *social equality* must be more radically interpreted than in the views of Locke or Hobbes.

Rousseau's understanding involves a transformation of the individual's primary concern in taking political action. Citizens must no longer take as the primary concern in political action our *private* good to the exclusion of others; down this road lies, in fact, a restriction of liberty by social competition with others. If we thinks about the experience of competition over scarce goods or honors, it always involves a *lack* of liberty; we must always concern ourselves with our own *relative* position against others. The political actor must avoid competition, and hence, when engaging in political decision making, look at the good of each equally and disinterestedly. This notion of disinterested consideration of others for the sake of our own liberty prefigures in some ways the more recent political thinking of philosophers like Rawls, whose reasoning hinges on the perspective of an "original position" withing a "veil of ignorance."

At this point, however, a difficulty arises. It might be charged that to require people to make political choices in such a non-self-interested way is somewhat naive. Rousseau seems to imply that all persons, when entering political community, implicitly agree to the conditions of the social contract. However, it is difficult to argue that in *actual* political communities, the political actors act in the impartial manner required by the general will; it seems that they act according to *particular* self-interest, or according to what Rousseau calls *faction*. A faction is a part of a political community that acts as a group according to that group's private interest; this private interest is not essentially in accord with the "general will." For example, a particular economic group could persuade the populace that its particular economic interests are beneficial to the community, when really they are beneficial only for that particular group, and actually do harm to the community as a whole or to the equality of property that Rousseau argues for. But if the populace is so persuaded, do they not act against the "general will"? Rousseau answers that they do.

This raises a difficulty. How is the general will to be put into action? After all, the general will does not, *of itself*, act; rather, it is individuals who act; and who is to say, when they act in the name of the community, that what really comes out is not these individuals' or some faction's *particular* will? Locke and Hobbes, it seems, do not have to solve this problem, since the political will is what the majority (for Locke) or the sovereign government (for Hobbes) say that it is. But for Rousseau, this cannot be a final solution, since then we leave the general will open to abuse by a private will; we must find a solution that is not subject either to a tyranny of a majority (Locke) or to the tyranny of a minority (Hobbes).

Rousseau's ultimate solution to this difficulty is ingenious: he borrows from both of his predecessors. From Hobbes, he borrows the idea that the ultimate judge of these matters must be someone who is not a party to the contract; from Locke, he borrows the idea that the ultimate judge cannot be a particular person.

Rousseau acknowledges the difficulty, and at first appears to preserve it. He does this by his insistence that the voting of individuals determines the general will. This institution would seem to have no guarantee, however, against the "tyranny of the majority." The people could vote to treat a minority unequally, or even be persuaded to treat themselves unequally. We cannot avoid, simply by majority vote, the difficulty of a private will masquerading as the general will of the community. Rousseau himself famously says: "There is often a great deal of difference between the will of all and the general will. The latter considers only the general interest, whereas the former considers private interest and is merely the sum of private wills" (Cress 1987, 155).

Here we run into the difficulty that we saw in discussion of Locke's notion of property: the difference between procedural and substantive liberty. Let us grant that the general will preserves the ideal conditions for liberty; but if the voters *freely* choose a different set of institutions than are ideal, can we really say that liberty has not been actualized? The way Rousseau handles this problem outside of the context of voting is that the individual who acts against the general will of the community must be "forced to be free." This seems to make sense in cases of law enforcement, for example. If law encodes the necessary conditions for liberty, and if I break the law, then *I am actually acting unfreely*; by being punished (or recognizing the law's deterrent effect) I am "forced" to act as a free individual. But the same reasoning also would seem to apply to the situation of voting: if the majority decides to act in a way that harms their liberty, should they not be constrained from doing so?

A practical example might be in order. Let us say that, in the wake of terrorist attacks, the U.S. Congress decides to create legislation that gives police the breadth of discretion to, in certain cases, search and seize property without obtaining a judicial warrant. Let us say that this legislation is even supported by the majority of citizens, and becomes law. In the next few months, the Supreme Court responds by striking down this legislation as an unconstitutional violation of the Fourth Amendment as a result of a private individual bringing a suit against the United States. It would seem that, against the will of the majority of individuals, the Court has acted to preserve certain liberties; it has "forced" these individuals to be more free than they themselves wanted to be. With the mention of the Constitution, we begin to see the spirit of Rousseau's solution to this difficulty. The Constitution is, to some extent, the fundamental will of the people of the United States; however, it is not necessarily the will of particular individuals and may be opposed to the majority will.

Even so, we might still think that there is an unresolved difficulty in this example. Is a free society more government "by the people," or is it "for the people"? From Rousseau's point of view, the question is this: how do we ensure that what the individual citizens *actually* vote for is in the best interest of their liberty?

Rousseau seems to answer this first by his instruction to the voter, which is to vote impersonally and objectively, and by his argument that such generalization is in the interest of the voter's liberty. This, however, merely forces the same question on another level: who is to judge that the voters have been persuaded, and have voted so as to preserve their general liberty? Is it the majority who decides this? Or the individual? Or is some "sovereign," as Hobbes would have it, needed to interpret the general will authoritatively beyond the easily corruptible judgments of individuals following their particular interests?

Rousseau addresses this question by first casting doubt on simple majoritarianism. The will of all, as particular individuals or factions of private interest, is not identical with the "general will." Furthermore, the people are easily corrupted or factionalized; so the framers of a political society should take care to arrange the society so that factions become ineffective, and should take care that issues of central import should be decided slowly and perhaps with near unanimity.

This advice by Rousseau is often overlooked, and clearly is of a similar mind to that of the framers of the United States Constitution. James Madison, in particular, was extremely concerned with the problem of factions, and we can see in the notions of the balance of power between the branches of the federal government, as well as the institutions of federalism, the attempt to minimize the distorting action of factions. Furthermore, the difficulty of emending the Constitution takes into account Rousseau's concerns about quick and thoughtless change, and has been quite effective (with the exception, perhaps of Prohibition) at keeping frivolous changes from becoming ones that are constitutive of the political community.

The minute that we begin to speak of framers of society, we no longer simply have decisive political power in the hands of the people, conceived of in Locke's terms—a collection of natural individuals. *"The people,"* in Rousseau's usage, does not simply mean the action or opinion that most or an overwhelming majority of individuals favor. The will of "the people," rather, is the general will, which must be distinguished from the will of all. Rousseau summarizes the difficulty by stating that the public will, even if desired, is not properly understood by the "blind multitude." What is necessary to give this blind multitude appropriate sight, says Rousseau, is a legislator who will embody the general will in a fundamental code of law.

Rousseau thus introduces the legislator as the one who can guarantee the coincidence of the will of all and the general will. This is the comprehensive manifestation of the need to "force" individuals to be free. The regime that liberty requires is not ultimately founded on rational persuasion of the people based on what they do want, but on what *ought* to be done for the sake of their liberty, sometimes against their own immediate opinion of their good. The legislator is the one who bridges the gap between what is desired and what ought to be, thereby shaping society.

Legislators cannot merely do whatever they want; they are constrained by the concerns for which the general will is formed—equality understood primarily as "liberty from particular dependence." For legislators simply to use the political community for their own private profit would contradict their purpose. Legislators are constrained by the nature of Law, which is to treat people generally, not according with particular interest. What Rousseau means by this can be seen in the common saying that "no person is above the law." This means that law treats all equally in regard to a particular class of action. The law does not distinguish between particular individuals; it proscribes certain penalties for certain actions, no matter who the actor is. No law says "John Smith shall be penalized if he steals a pencil, but no one else shall"; it does not mention people by name. All are "equal before the law"; it treats people generally—as members of a society that may or may not perform certain kinds of actions.

The question of the Legislator's role, then, is not merely, what can he do, but rather what *lawful* thing can he do? This said, Rousseau grants great discretion to his framing of institutions that are applicable to particular circumstances. A legislator in France may choose different institutions from those appropriate to South Africa, but they must both tend toward the same lawful end. For some governments, this may require aristocratic forms; for some, democratic. This is left to the prudence of legislator. This power over constitution is not insignificant, especially given that the multitude is easily deceived regarding their true interest, and Rousseau uses august language in describing the legislative task; the legislator, he says, must change the nature of human beings from self-interested to socially interested in shaping them for social liberty.

Legislator, for Rousseau, would have to be extraordinary, since they would have to, unlike most people, shape society *in a disinterested manner*. Rousseau describes them, in fact, as a gods among men. They would somehow be both interested in determining the course of a society, and yet be unconcerned with particular power or interest—they are not interested in being princes or assembly-men. Rousseau compares them to the engineer who creates the political machine that will give birth to princes and gives a voice to the mute sovereign that is the general will. The comparison to an engineer is useful; an engineer uses natural forces to transform nature in accordance with a purpose not given in nature. Rousseau describes his political engineer in similar ways: it is within the legislator's capacity to transform human nature. It is not an arbitrary transforma-tion however; humanity is made over, one might say, in the transition from individual to citizen, in the image of the desire for secure liberty.

This talk of engineering and transformation reveals that there will be a conflict between the legislator's aim and the goals of the natural individuals who are to become citizens. The legislator cannot persuade the people by argument to see the legislator's aims as their own. The legislator, Rousseau says, must have recourse to a rhetoric that can "win without violence and persuade without convincing" This rhetoric is that of religion; legislators must attribute their plans for society to the divine. Rousseau says that this is not quite unjust, for the character of the legislator *is* somewhat divine. Religion, as the public cult, becomes the means by which the legislator persuades the people. Before we think this completely absurd, it bears some reminder that the preamble of the Constitu-tion of the United States has this phrase in it: "we believe that all men have been created equal *in being endowed by their Creator* with certain inalienable rights: life, liberty, and the pursuit of happiness." The italicized part makes it clear that the founders of the United States appealed to religion to persuade individuals of the justice and wisdom of the Constitution.

Rousseau, in contrast against Locke and in agreement with Hobbes, is acutely aware of the difficulty of maintaining a proper public opinion among a commu-nity's individuals. Hobbes had been concerned with this, particularly in the area of religion; Rousseau, as well, takes this to be of central concern to the effective-ness of the original framers' activity. Religion, he says, must be a civic religion, or one in service of the constitution of the state according to the general will. Further, the sovereign has a right to censor public opinion in accordance with the general will, since it is opinion that is the true source of action.

Rousseau, despite this seemingly illiberal tendency in the name of liberty, is quick to point out that when the law and general will are disregarded, censorship will do little good. Yet it is clear that by this doctrine public opinion is the ground of the acceptance of general will, and hence must be maintained. In fact, given that censorship has to do with judgment and opinion by which law can be effective, providing for it may be the legislative work that is most crucial. Rousseau speaks of the customs and opinions of the people as the most important aspect of the legislator's lawmaking; it is the great secret concern of the legislator.

Rousseau is ultimately closer in many ways to Hobbes' position regarding the relation between the sovereign (the general will), and the governed, but he is closer to Locke as regards the government. The legislator, as the person who embodies the general will in the fundamental law of the community, is prior to the government, and like Hobbes' sovereign, the legislator constitutes the unity of the people. But unlike Hobbes' sovereign, the sovereign is in "the people" (understood as the general will), not in the government. Like Locke, "the people" is sovereign and prior to the government. However, the people are not simply the majority of a collection of individuals; rather, "the people" is constituted by the act of the legislator, who creates a people out of previously private individuals and transforms them into citizens. In this constitutive function, Rousseau's legislator resembles Hobbes' sovereign, but without the desire to be a member of government, and hence susceptible to the corruption that Locke argues an absolute sovereign would be subject to.

This does not yet give a determinate picture as to what the legitimate institutions of government will look like. Rousseau leaves this to the prudence of the legislator. Thus the answer to this question cannot be fully determined ahead of time; rather it depends on the pre-political character of the group of people in question. The aims or ends of political society must always be what Rousseau calls "republican"—that is, the aim of relative equality so as to eliminate dependence on particular individuals. The appropriate form of government and constitution will vary based on factors such as the age of the community, climate, size of territory, custom, the character of the people, and economic conditions. In some circumstances, this will mean that the institutions will be those of liberal democracy; in others, monarchical or aristocratic institutions may be appropriate. The political machine, as it were, must be adjusted to take advantage of the raw materials that are present; but its aim is ultimately the same.

Conclusion and difficulties. With Rousseau's doctrine of the legislator, religion, and censorship, we are forced to confront a paradox. How can Rousseau claim that the end or aim of his political philosophy is *liberty*, and yet advocate a civil religion, censorship, and moreover a theory of government where the legislator "molds" or "shapes" the people? These all are ordinarily considered *restrictions* on liberty. Liberty, that is, seems to require, in some sense, *force*; a people must be "forced to be free," not only in extraordinary or criminal cases, but as the *essence of political constitution*. The "general will" is described by Rousseau as absolute, authoritative, sacred, and inviolable as much as is Hobbes' sovereign—perhaps even more so. But is such absolute sovereignty not, in principle, opposed to liberty?

Rousseau's argument is that the general will embodies the principles of the most complete liberty available, but such complete liberty is not strictly individual, but rather social. Thus society, in the interest of the liberty of all, may restrict the actions of those individuals who would seek to take more than their share. As we have seen, this is in their own interest, for such restriction seeks to eliminate their particular dependence on other individuals, and hence approximate the condition of the original state. This is undoubtedly the most persuasive part of Rousseau's argument; however, it is also the most troubling, especially when it comes to the question of what we might call individual consent. Rousseau seems to appeal beyond the people's actual opinions to what those opinions *ought* to be, if they knew what was *really* in the interest of their liberty. What this seems to imply is that the people *are not yet free*. This is why someone who is from outside the people must come in and reshape their opinion—the legislator. However, if the people would have to be re-made in order to be satisfied with Rousseau's political state, then why would we think that it would be a good idea for human beings to strive for this political state? If humans, as they are, find Rousseau's theory unattractive because it restricts their liberty, why would we think that Rousseau's idea of legitimate government to be worthy of choice? This difficulty can be re-stated in terms of Rousseau's theory of social development. If people as they currently are differ significantly from natural or original man, then why should a political theory that tries to approximate the natural state of liberty be seen as attractive to current people? For Rousseau the extreme difference between the general will and the will of all forces us to these questions.

This difficulty is related to the difficulty of "procedural" versus "substantive" liberty that we have spoken of in previous chapters. If we use free or liberal "procedures" for making decisions (like voting, in which each person's free choice is given equal weight), this does not guarantee that the results of such procedures will be what is required for a "free" society, in Rousseau's terms. The easiest way to see this difficulty is with regard to Rousseau's doctrine of property. Rousseau says that the social regulation of property should tend toward making sure that the distribution of property is relatively equal. However, in countries like the United States, it can happen that the majority of the citizenry might support policies that lead to wide discrepancies between the wealthy and the poor. Now, since the majority has voted freely, can we really say that such a country is not a free society? Or is it not free because it has not appropriately embodied the require-ments of the "general will"?

We will see that these same issues arise in the moral and political philosophy of Kant. Kant says that it is from Rousseau that he learned the central lessons for moral philosophy. For Kant, there is a radical opposition between the moral law that is appropriate for free or autonomous beings, and the particular desires of actual human beings. This corresponds roughly to the opposition of the general will to the particular wills of individuals in Rousseau. Kant, likewise, has to address in his moral and political works the question of how or why individuals as naturally constituted should align themselves with a moral law that is irreducible to their natural understanding of their good. We shall see how Kant handles this question in our next section.

There is one further difficulty in Rousseau that we shall also see in Kant. Rousseau argues that liberty, in society, in order to become actual, requires equality of right. Liberty requires freedom from particular dependence in opposition to other men, and if I have all the rights another person has, I do not experience any loss by his gain. What is crucial for Rousseau is not some absolute notion of right, but that no one individual is deprived of rights by the granting another person those rights; relative equality of right is what is important. This does not, however, give us much guidance as to *what sort of right* and how far such rights are to go, for each and every person.

For example, in a communist dictatorship of the type that used to exist in the former Soviet Union, all people were (in principle) to be treated equally; but they were all equally deprived of the right to publicly criticize the government. Would we want to call this society as free as one where people are all equally free to criticize the government? There seems to be a substantial difference between the two, and yet on the basis of relative equality of rights, we cannot distinguish between the two, because *both grant to one citizen the same right that it grants to another.* Thus, from Rousseau's theory, can we say that both are equally legitimate? The objection here is that Rousseau's doctrine of liberal equality is without substantive content. A similar question can be raised about the basis of Kant's moral philosophy, what he calls the "categorical imperative."

These objections should not make us lose sight of the significant contributions that Rousseau makes. Rousseau radicalizes and completes the ideas of Hobbes and Locke in his notion of a sovereign that is essentially irreducible to the will of particular individuals. This notion has had a great influence on liberal thought up to our own day. Secondly, the idea that liberty, if it is to be social, requires at least relative equality of rights is an idea that has had not only great theoretical influence, but great practical influence on the politics of Western democracy. Implied in this idea have been the great movements toward equal rights for women, civil rights for ethnic and racial minorities, and the rise of the welfare state and democratic socialism in several nations. Furthermore, the theories of Rousseau and Locke, and the conflicts apparent between them, have set the stage for much of contemporary debate in both politics and political economy.

2. Kant's Philosophy of Right

Immanuel Kant (1724-1804) is regarded as one of the great philosophers who have worked out, in impressive detail and argument, a systematic and comprehensive way of understanding the entirety of human experience. Kant's political philosophy is a subdivision of his moral philosophy. Kant admitted that he owed much to his study of Rousseau when developing his own political and moral thought. What seems to be of crucial importance is Rousseau's distinction between general and particular wills that was discussed in the previous section. Kant is impressed both by Rousseau's notion that the general will is irreducible to a function of particular wills, and that it is yet the result of the interest of the particular will's liberty taken to its logical conclusion.

This grounds the nature of Kant's moral and political system. Kant argues formally for the irreducibility of the general will to the particular will in the basic concepts of his moral thought. We shall demonstrate this by looking primarily at his *Grounding for the Metaphysics of Morals*. Kant's political system is the part of his moral thought that deals with the "external aspect" of our actions, i.e. our actions looked at without concern for the *motive* from which they are undertaken. This is described in *The Metaphysics of Morals*, as well as in *Perpetual Peace*. In both of these works, we find a further contribution of Kant's: the extension of social contract theory to international relations. These developments will be the focus of the first two sections of our discussion below.

Rousseau's argument that the interest of the particular will is ultimately fulfilled by institutions that are demanded by general will is also taken up by Kant. This signals a founding contribution of Kant to political thought. Kant speculates and argues that it is not only morally necessary, but also *historically inevitable,* that the interests of particular will must lead to institutions in accordance with the morally right. Kant argues that nature has a plan by which the institutions that are morally justified according to the philosophy of right will inevitably come to pass, or at least be approximated. Kant argues for this in *Perpetual Peace*; but it is explicitly the subject of *The Idea of a Universal History with a Cosmopolitan Purpose*. This will be the focus of the third section below.

The morality of autonomy. As we noted in the discussion of Rousseau's idea of the general will, what makes the general will *general* is that it is irreducible to any particular person's interest. The general will is neutral or impartial with regard to the content of any particular desire. An example can clarify what this means. If we hold that "each individual has a right to the freedom of speech," the right we advocate is *indifferent to* what any particular person may happen to speak about. This indifference or impartiality means that we treat the act of speaking *generally*, without regard to the particular content or interest expressed or advocated in the speech.

Furthermore, if we *ought* to act so that each individual has the right to the freedom of speech, this means we should act in this way whether the speech of the individual in question serves our particular interest or not. From the standpoint of our own interest, what an individual says may be judged boring, distasteful, stupid, or even evil; however, in granting the *right* of all persons to free speech, we act so that our particular interests do not determine our action.

But if it is not our particular interest or inclination that motivates our actions in such cases, what does motivate us? We would ordinarily say that we might not agree with what a person says, but we do *respect the right* of the person to say it. The question that Kant sets to answer in his political and moral thought is why we should have this "respect for a right" that opposes our particular judgments and interests. For Kant, all moral laws (and political rights that follow from it) have the function of a respect for what is right that cannot be reduced to and is superior to our particular inclinations or interests.

Kant grounds his answer to this question in the concept of the *autonomy of the will*. The autonomy of the will means the capacity of the will to set its own laws, of "being a law unto itself." An autonomous being, for Kant, is one that acts by a law that is it gives itself; this is the full positive meaning of what we usually call freedom or liberty. It would be easy, and mistaken, to take this notion to mean that a person could do anything that he or she wishes. Kant explains that the will's freedom requires that we act "independently of any property of the objects of volition"(Kant 1981, 44). The freedom of the will requires an indifference to the *objects* of volition—to what we might call the purposes or goals to be achieved by the action that we will. This idea incorporates something we noted in our example regarding free speech; we respect a person's right to free speech even if we find the particular object of their act (the content or purpose of their speech) to be contrary to our particular inclinations.

If, by contrast, our actions were *not* governed by a respect for right, our allowing a person to speak or not would be wholly determined by its agreement or disagreement with our inclinations and desires. In this case, Kant would say that our wills were *not free or autonomous* in acting against our respect for another's right. In so acting, we make the value of *right* dependent on some inclination or desire that is external to what right itself requires. My motive, in the case of preventing the speech of a distasteful speaker, is not determined by right, but by a particular interest. If a motive is to be *autonomos*, it must be free or impartial toward all actions by which we might satisfy our particular desires. An act that is motivated solely by particular desire or inclination is not truly free, because for Kant our particular inclinations are the result of natural causes and conditions that are not the result of our independent wills. When we act according to our natural desires, that is, we do not act freely, but according to what is given by nature. Autonomy of the will requires a basis that is not given simply by nature. Kant says:

> A good will is good not because of what it effects or accomplishes, nor because of its fitness to obtain some proposed end; it is good only through its will, i.e. it is good in itself. When it is considered in itself, then it is to be esteemed very much higher than anything which it might ever bring about merely in order to favor some inclination, or even the sum total of all inclinations (Kant 1981, 7).

Since the precepts for autonomous action cannot be given in natural inclination, their ground must be elsewhere. For Kant, this is given in the *concept itself* of self-legislative freedom (the *autonomy*) of any rational being. The will is not valued only insofar as it brings about the results in accordance with some given inclination, but is to be valued *in itself*, since what gives dignity to persons is their capacity to legislate for themselves. Coming from the idea of liberty itself,

Kant says that moral action is determined entirely by "reason alone," that is, independent of any content given by interest or inclination. What causes an act to be of moral worth is its being consistent with the *idea* of autonomy, regardless of its usefulness in obtaining the satisfaction of particular inclinations or even their sum total. Kant argues that this idea is present in our ordinary understanding of *duty*. When choose to "do our duty," we are acting *against* our immediate inclinations or desires, in favor of an act that is supposed good even if it is painful. The example Kant uses is the fair treatment of a customer by a shopkeeper. Kant argues that this action does not have moral worth unless the shopkeeper chooses to treat the customer fairly when it would be in his particular interest to cheat the customer. In this, the shopkeeper acts against his interest from a motive of "fair play" or "duty" to his fellow human being. Any shopkeeper can act fairly when it is in his interest; but moral worth is truly tested in the case where right and interest diverge.

Kant's example can be supplemented by contemporary examples. For instance, in the late 1990s and early 2000s, it was found that several executives at Enron (a large energy services company) had falsified crucial bookkeeping records that were made public and misrepresented the well-being of the company to investors. In so doing, they were able to give themselves massive bonuses and salary increases, as well as sell stock that they owned that was of inflated value. When the company failed and this became public, there was a public outcry against these executives. Kant's reasoning can be followed in seeing why what they did was wrong, *even if we do not regard the consequences that followed for the thousands of investors who were left holding worthless stock when the company folded.* If you are an executive of such a company, it is usually in your interest to be honest about bookkeeping; the consequences of not doing so can include jail time and the loss of business to your company. However, imagine what these executives at Enron must have thought: that they could get away with dishonest business dealings without doing themselves *any* serious harm. They turned out, in this case, to be incorrect. But imagine if *they were correct* in this assumption, and that they *could* get away with it. Should they have done it? If we are to answer "No" to this question, the justification cannot be in terms of interest or inclination, but only in terms of a duty to be honest in business dealings, *no matter how it contradicts self- interest.*

What motivates such duty is not desire or interest, but what Kant calls a reverence or respect for the law implicit in duty. When we obey the law despite our self-interest or inclination, we do so not from inclination, but out of respect or reverence for some higher motive than our own desires. The motive of duty differs from the motive of inclination in the place it gives to the autonomy of the will. In the case of acting from inclination or interest, my will is merely a *means* by which the satisfaction of my inclination is achieved; my will's value is not in this case *self-determining* (or autonomous), but its value is determined by some given circumstance and inclination. Being determined by something other than itself, Kant calls this the *heteronomy* of the will.

In acting out of **duty**, my motive clearly denies that the value of my will is determined by my particular *desires or inclinations*, which are concerned with the *consequences or results* of action. My will's value is not "conditioned" by its usefulness in achieving these results or satisfying these desires, but has an *unconditioned* and independent value. I am moved by a will that manifests its independence by opposing my natural inclination or concern with consequences. This is why Kant says that the object of my inclination cannot be given respect; it is "merely an effect and *not the activity* of the will" (Kant, 1981, 13). In the case of following inclination or desire, the will is not valued for its own sake, independently or autonomously, absolutely or without conditions. Rather it is valued only as a means, and no means is valued absolutely.

Once inclination or desire is disregarded, however, it might be thought that there can be no law at all. Where does the command that the will must follow come from, if it is entirely independent from desire or inclination? Kant answers, "since I have deprived the will of every impulse that might arise for it from obeying any particular law, there is nothing left to serve the will as principle except the universal conformity of its actions to law as such; i.e. *I should never act except in such a way that I can also will that my maxim should become a universal law*" (Kant 1981, 14).

The italicized portion of this quotation is called the **categorical imperative.** It is categorical because it applies absolutely, not merely *if* certain inclinations are to be fulfilled or *if* certain goals or ends are to be achieved as results. Kant contrasts the categorical imperative with imperatives (commands) that do have such an "if" nature; he calls these latter "hypothetical" imperatives. For example, "*if* you want to succeed, you should work hard." By contrast such to hypothetical imperatives, the categorical nature of the moral law reflects its independence from particular interests or objectives; it leaves the will autonomous by saying that it should respect only those laws compatible with autonomy.

What this imperative means in ordinary language is not so easy to say. We might ask initially: what maxim can I *not* wish to be made a universal law? Exactly what does Kant mean that one *cannot* wish that a principle of action become a universal law? Kant gives an example of something that is forbidden by this imperative in the un-truthful making of promises. Kant reminds us that our motive in keeping our promises cannot be based on interest if the action is to have moral worth.

In his explanation of this, Kant seems to incorporate something that many thinkers had noticed before: the evidence for the universality of the law against theft is that no thief likes to be a victim of theft. Yet, for Kant, the ground cannot be in empirical evidence of what people do and do not like, since the moral law cannot be based on interest or inclination. Even if every person were to like to break promises when it was to their advantage, and were to accept the consequence that others would likely "pay them back in like coin," the action would be wrong in being self-destructive. What this means is not entirely clear, unless it means this very concern with consequences that Kant seems to deny as significant for determining moral action. If I am honest merely because to be otherwise is (in principle) to be subject to others' dishonesty, am I not merely concerned with the consequences? Being concerned that my promises would become ineffective or that others would pay me back in being dishonest seems to be concerned with the consequences of universalizing my principle. If we take promise-keeping to be a maxim because it accords with my self-interest, it is difficult to see how Kant's theory differs from that of Hobbes, who argues that the keeping of contracts or promises is necessitated strictly by self-interest.

Perhaps taking another example will clarify the issue. One might think it justified to murder a Hitler or a Stalin in order to prevent the atrocities these men committed. Is such a murder morally permitted? The "categorical" rule that such an act would follow is that I may kill another person if the consequences for doing so are beneficial. From Kant's point of view, the question becomes: can I will that all persons may kill others at their discretion (whenever there are desirable consequences for themselves or others)? If we were to answer yes to this, Kant may argue that a "contradiction" would result, for I would be granting the right of all men to kill me, and all others. Once again, it is difficult to see what Kant means that willing such a possibility would be self-contradictory. Perhaps we can ask the question this way; is it consistent for me to wish that, through my action, I bring about a condition whereby my own existence at the mercy of another's discretion?

It becomes easier to see what Kant means if we look at his second major formulation of the moral law. The second formulation of the law is explicit with regard to the moral law's relation to the autonomy of each person. Since each person is self-legislating, this means that each person's will has value, not as merely a means to satisfying some inclination or set of inclinations, but in-itself. The value of each person is not, then, as a means, but as an end in herself, as a value that is not dependent upon another value. This if formulated by Kant as the *"practical imperative"*: *so act as to treat humanity, whether in your own person, or in another, in every case as an end, never as a means only.*

Now we can get a better handle on exactly what is self-contradictory about principles such as the false promise or killing for the sake of some desirable consequence. In both of these cases, we use another person, who is valuable as an end in herself, as self-legislating or autonomous, as if the other person were merely a means to some end that we may happen to desire. We treat the other as if he or she had no independent value, but were to be given value only by being a means to some interest or desire. This is even true in the case of morally repugnant individuals who have themselves violated the moral law in horrifying fashion such as Hitler or Stalin.

To take the example of a false promise: if I make a promise to another, with the intent to break it if it becomes convenient to me, then their capacity to legislate or choose for themselves is seen merely as a means to get what I want, meaning that if I can get what I want in some dishonest manner, I can discard my respect for their freedom. In keeping a contract, by contrast, I respect the other person's autonomy in that I respect their choice to promise themselves to me. Likewise, if I kill another person because of some beneficial consequence that comes of it to myself or others, I violate the right of another to legislate for himself as he pleases; dead people cannot legislate for themselves at all.

In both of these cases, the free agency or autonomy of another is violated. It is for this reason that my making these maxims universal is self-contradictory. If I were to make discretionary killing universal, I would be making it possible for another to kill me when it suited his or her interest. In so doing, I would be advocating the violation of *my* freedom, or I would contradict that which in myself is worthy of being called truly *my self*. Thus, the concern for consequences is not entirely without merit, but it is precisely the consequences for *autonomy*, that makes the concern *moral*. It is true that any or every individual could in reality say that they are unconcerned with such consequences, that their inclinations move them to deny their own autonomy; but this does not make such a concern morally worthy.

The self-contradictory nature of immoral maxims can perhaps be best seen in Kant's prohibition of suicide. Kant says that one might commit suicide to relieve the painful or suffering nature of one's existence. When contemplating the *moral* worth of suicide our concern is whether, in killing ourselves, we contradict the essential autonomy of our will, or we treat our existence as merely a means to some purpose. It should be clear that in suicide, we do not look at our person as *itself* valuable, but only as valuable if it is useful toward the satisfaction of certain inclinations. The suicide reasons that if someone's existence does not achieve certain *outcomes,* it is disposable. But this denies the inherent value of the person's humanity. Killing, whether of oneself, or of others, is inherently self-contradictory in that both suppose a principle that violates a person's independent value.

We see in Kant's moral law, not only a respect for liberty or autonomy, but an inherent equality. It is in *any* person that we are to respect the value of their autonomous will. In practice, this would seem to outlaw certain kinds of acts or institutions. For example, chattel slavery, as practiced in America before the Civil War, would seem to be immoral. In chattel slavery, the main aim is to deny the enslaved person's autonomy or liberty for the sake of using this person as an instrument for the slaveholders' interests. It seems, also, that theft would be prohibited, since in stealing, I violate the ability of another to dispose of his property according to his own will or choice; I disregard their liberty for my own interest.

In morality, we are not only obligated to recognize the autonomy of ourselves and others, but to "advance" this autonomy or make it more effective in the world. So far, we have only discussed those duties of the moral law that preserve a person's fundamental autonomy; these duties Kant calls *"perfect" duties*, since they are to be done without exception, because to refrain from them would be an absolute denial of autonomy. Those that advance autonomy, by contrast, are called *"imperfect" duties.* If we ignore them, autonomy is not denied, but it is not advanced; performing these are dependent, therefore, on our *capacity* to do so. Kant gives as examples (a) of an imperfect duty to oneself, the development of natural abilities, and (b) of an imperfect duty to others, generosity that helps others develop their abilities. Kant's reasoning for such duties is that *any* end for a being which sets its own end is to be valued (as long as it does not conflict with our autonomy), simply because it is the end of an autonomous being. Thus I should seek to promote those ends in both others and myself, by developing the capacities to achieve those ends. This distinction between imperfect and perfect duties is crucial for Kant when we turn to what he calls the realm of "Right," of which politics is a division. The concern of Right is with perfect duties we have to others. Before turning to Kant's theory of political right, however, we should note Kant's third major formulation of the moral law, since it explicitly uses the political language of sovereignty and kingship.

This formulation is that one should act *"so as to be a sovereign member of the kingdom of ends"* (Kant, 1981, 39). This formulation looks at the moral law that we give to ourselves in terms of what it should result in—a community where all are ends and respect each other as ends. What is crucial about this conception is that each member of such a "kingdom" is both sovereign and subject. As a kingdom, each member is subject to certain laws; however, as the kingdom is one in which each person is treated as having autonomous value or what Kant calls *dignity,* the law we obey accords with our own autonomy. In according with our autonomy, it is the law that should be chosen for ourselves as autonomous beings. A law we choose for ourselves is not a law that we are merely subject to, as given by another; rather, it is the one that we author freely. So, even as we are subject to the law of a kingdom of ends, we are at once the author of such a law and are therefore the sovereigns of such a kingdom. This logic should remind us clearly of Rousseau's theory, in which we become perfectly free in submitting to the law that prevents us from having any right that others do not have, hence preventing us from being used by others as a means to their ends.

Right and republican government. For Kant, political philosophy is a division of moral philosophy. Morality concerns itself with both actions and motives. An act, to be morally good, must be both a correct act and motivated by a concern for autonomy. In the *Metaphysics of Morals*, he divides this subject into the Metaphysic of Virtue (which has to do with motive) and the Metaphysic of Right (which has to do with the external action itself). Political thought falls into the latter division, since for Kant, as for Rousseau, politics has to do primarily with law, and law is primarily concerned with conformity of external action, and only secondarily with motive. Like all moral action, however, the concern of politics is still with autonomy or freedom of the individual. Law and political community are to be understood in their relationship to personal liberty. The primary concern of *right* has to do with the actions between people that preserve their mutual autonomy or freedom. Thus the universal principle of right is that *"every action which by itself or by its maxim enables the freedom of each individual's will to co-exist with the freedom of everyone else in accordance with universal law is right"* (Reiss, 1970, 133).

Kant emphasizes the difference of the realm of right from that of morals as a whole. Morality has to do with the reform of motive as well as action; right has only to do with action itself. A person who acts according to right does not have to do so because he desires another's freedom.

We can both know and enforce what is right without demanding that everyone be motivated in a purely moral manner. In fact, it is *because* all people are not motivated by pure morality that politics and the state becomes necessary. If all were motivated by pure morality, there would be no need of public authority; but since they are not, right demands that there be an authority to enforce right. If the state exists to provide the laws that make mutual freedom possible, then it becomes necessary that the community coerce any individual who threatens to destroy mutual freedom by breaking the law. Kant therefore argues that coercion or force is necessarily part of right.

This notion of right implies reciprocal coercion (since it does not have to do with a moral *motive*, or virtue), and thus prepares the ground for political right. As in Rousseau, the state comes to be for making this reciprocal coercion actual in a just manner, one that preserves the liberty of all equally. And as in Locke and Hobbes, the state is a necessity because of the possibility that people will not respect the conditions for reciprocal right, or lack a common judge in any dispute over right. The state is defined, as in Rousseau, by both a complete quitting of the state of nature and by its purpose in guaranteeing reciprocal right. This notion of reciprocal right, is, for Kant, implicit as an ideal for any actual political community. The true law of the state, then, is not merely whatever laws happen to be enacted, but the idea of reciprocal right.

As with Rousseau, also, for Kant the sovereign people cannot err in law-making action, since the sovereign people (singular) is constituted by the idea of reciprocal right manifested in its general will. The difficulty that we have seen in previous chapters between "procedural" and "substantive" right still lingers in Kant's theory; we can see this in his account of the rights of the citizen:

> The three rightful attributes which are inseparable from the nature of a citizen as such are as follows: firstly, lawful freedom to obey no law other than that to which he has given his consent; secondly civil equality in recognizing no one among the people as superior to himself….and thirdly, the attribute of civil independence which allows him to owe his existence and sustenance not to the

arbitrary will of anyone else among the people, but purely to his own rights and powers as a member of the commonwealth (Reiss 1970, 139).

The difficulty arises in Kant's stressing *consent* as the condition of lawful freedom. What if the people consent to a law that promotes civil inequality or harms civil independence? If this law were enacted, would the legislature not be committing an injustice? If consent is the way we understand the general will, does this not cause a conflict between what the people *do* freely enact and what they *ought* to? This difficulty is critical, since the principle of right is not based in any way on the actual inclinations of human beings, but is based only on the "idea" of right. It can therefore never be reduced to what people actually consent to, even if such consent is unanimous. What we *do* happen to agree to can never be a substitute for what we *should* agree to. This difficulty, for Kant, is not resolved by conscious human action, but by the action of nature or fate working through human choices. This we shall turn to in more detail in the section on Kant's philosophy of history below. For now, it is important to see that his notion of history answers to a difficulty present in Kant's philosophy of right.

This difficulty is also implicit in Kant's argument that prohibits revolution. On the one hand, it is the people who set the fundamental law of society; on the other, the people as an aggregate or a majority cannot revolt against "the most intolerable misuse of supreme power" (Reiss, 1970, 145). For Kant, unlike for Hobbes, this is right not because of the consequences of disunion in civil war, but because of the very idea of a legal constitution. As in Rousseau, we forfeits entirely our "natural freedom" to the state, which guarantees a more perfect social freedom. To claim a reservation against the state would be to say at the same time that we are forfeiting our natural freedom and at the same time that we are keeping it. Such an act is "self-contradictory."

International right. One of Kant's singular contributions to political thought comes in the realm of international politics. When Kant turns to the international situation, he uses the same reasoning used in the national situation, but with certain modifications. What had made a political state necessary was the necessity to enforce right in a situation in which there was no common judge, or where there was what Hobbes and Locke had called a "state of war." Kant simply notices that this is the condition that in fact exists in the international situation; states have no common judge between them, and so neither do persons within these states. Being in a condition similar to that of pre-political individuals, individual nations should seek to escape the state of constant war, much as individuals do when forming a state.

It is here that domestic and international situations do differ slightly. Individual nation-states, already having a sort of sovereignty, do not give over their sovereignty to an international state, as individual persons do to a state. Rather, they aim to form a "confederation" or alliance for peaceful interaction.

International right seeks to preserve the autonomy of individual states, much like political right seeks to preserve the autonomy of individual persons. Given that nations do not respect the sovereignty of foreign states, however, international law must regulate first war and then peace. Peace being the goal, all the rules of war (its declaration, practice, and cessation) are meant to ensure that the long-term goal of a peaceful confederation is not obstructed. Kant argues, based on this aim, that no war may be *punitive*, that is, thought of as a punishment of a subject by a sovereign. According to international right, no individual nation can be thought to be sovereign over another, so therefore a nation acting as if it were would violate international right. Furthermore, since the aim of war is eventual peace between autonomous states, wars of conquest or extermination are wrong, since these seek to destroy an individual state's autonomy. The only sorts of wars that are legitimate are those by which a nation seeks to maintain its autonomy. Wars of defense or of a "first strike" to prevent an imminent attack are therefore legitimate.

Furthermore, the *way* of fighting wars can be limited by the aim of a future peace. For Kant, this precludes the use of spies, assassins and poisoners, because a state that uses such treacherous methods would destroy the trust that is required for the establishment of a lasting peace. The concern for future peace also governs post war activity in the composing of treaties. Kant emphasizes the prohibition of a punitive peace, for the same reasons as forbidding punitive wars. The victor, if demanding reparations from the loser, would act against the goal of lasting peace, since in doing so one undermines the right of the losing state to liberty.

A historical example that would make Kant's point here would be the peace that followed the First World War. The victorious powers of France and Britain set punitive conditions for the peace against Germany by making the Germans responsible for compensating the victors for damages suffered during the war, against the recommendations of American President Woodrow Wilson. A persuasive historical case can be made that these actions caused, in part, the economic difficulties and political resentment that made possible the rise of Adolf Hitler and set the stage for the Second World War. A punitive peace undermines the demands of international right for a more lasting peace.

In *Perpetual Peace*, Kant sets forth several preliminary conditions for a lasting peace, the conditions under which war may be waged and the methods that may be used, as well as conditions regarding international finance (which can threaten the independence of states) or a standing army (which can be seen as creating an atmosphere opposed to peace). He then proposes what he calls the definitive articles of peace. These argue, in line with what we have discussed, that statesmen should aim at the sort of confederation proposed above. In addition, however, Kant argues that the confederacy of states should be among states that are *republics*, that is, states which aim at the principles of political right within each nation. Republican governments are set up to guarantee individual liberty and meant to represent the will of the people. Kant contrasts such governments which those which are non-representative, such as absolute monarchy. Kant argues here from the perspective of international right, not political right. That is, he says that *republican* forms of government are more likely to be in favor of peaceful than war-like behavior. In a republic, those who govern lose their own property, freedom, and even life in war, so there is less likelihood they will enter into war hastily and foolishly. Only the immediate external threat to these things would cause them to take the risks of war. By contrast, non-republican governments do not themselves bear the primary costs of war, so they are more likely to enter into unnecessary or punitive conflicts. This is why republican government makes possible a perpetual peace.

History. The previous two sections have focused on Kant's theory of political and international right, which are derived from Kant's morality of autonomy. We have seen that there is for Kant a radical difference between respect for autonomy and the natural inclinations of human beings. In this, Kant develops and refines the distinction found in Rousseau between natural freedom (or self-interest) and social freedom (or right). Kant appears to agree with Rousseau against the more self-interested justifications of political community found in Hobbes, and to some degree in Locke. He is fond of saying that the principles of right would still hold, even if men were angels; actual human inclination makes no difference to what is right.

Kant inherits the difficulty to which Rousseau's answer is the extraordinary person of the Legislator: what is the difference between the general will (what Kant would call the principles of Right) and the will of all (what Kant would call the collection of particular inclinations)? Since Right is not necessarily the collective inclination of all, how is it to become law for the collection of humans that make up a political community? And how can we reconcile this Right with the sort of freedom implicit in the vote, whereby individuals can vote their self-interest as well as the "general will"? Kant's government may be "for the people," but is it really "by" the people, if its design is not chosen freely by the people?

In Kant, this difficulty is heightened by the opposition between the moral law and natural human inclination. Kant consistently emphasizes that the moral law is not the object of natural desire or inclination, nor is it derivative from some ordering or summation of such desires. This gives the moral law (and the political right derived from it) an independence from the uncertainty and changing pattern of natural desire. This independence, however, seems to come at a price; if it is opposed to human desire, how are we to be convinced that we should find it good, or itself desirable? Furthermore, can Kant have any reasonable expectation that humans ever *will* desire to follow it?

In the realm of political right, at least, Kant attempts a reconciliation of desire and morality. Since politics does not have primarily to do with motive, but instead with external actions, it may be possible that right can be actualized without the proper motivation that is crucial to the realm of morality as a whole. In other words, the institutions of political and international right may be desired, eventually, by most or all human beings, but *not* out of a purely ethical motive. In fact, morality may come as a result of right, not right from morality. It is this suggestion that guides Kant's historical speculation in *Perpetual Peace* and *The Idea for a Universal History with a Cosmopolitan Purpose*.

In the First Supplement of *Perpetual Peace*, Kant sets forth the basic idea: "Perpetual peace is guaranteed by no less an authority than the great artist Nature herself *(natura daedala rerum)*. The mechanical process of nature visibly exhibits the purposive plan of producing concord among men, even against her will and indeed by means of their very discord." (Reiss 1970,108).

What Kant means by this becomes clearer in the first few propositions of *Universal History*. He argues that since nature has made no species without the intent to fulfill its specific purpose, and nature seems to have equipped humanity for autonomous self-rule, nature must propose that humankind should eventually fulfill that purpose. In humans, as opposed to other species, this purpose is not fulfilled in the first generation of individuals, but requires a longer period of time—this opens the door for humans to have a *history*. The presence of reason makes it necessary that this goal take historical time, since reason's freedom from what is merely given opens us what Kant calls an "unlimited range" of projects, that cannot be fully achieved in one generation alone. The goal of this historical development is the free exercise of reason in action that is encoded in Kant's moral and political thought.

Having established the idea of purposive nature in historical time, Kant turns to the means by which the goal is reached. Kant says that nature places in human beings an "asocial sociality"; they do not live merely in peace with their fellows, but live competitively. Yet needing our fellows *precisely for such competition* (competition is necessarily social), we are dependent on our fellows. This competitive sociality forces human beings to develop talents and capacities that would have remained unused if they had been simply peaceful by nature.

Ultimately, the drive to fully develop human capacities can only be fulfilled in a republic based on the principles of political right and international right. The choice of such institutions is not *morally* motivated, however, but is forced upon humans by the necessities of competitive self-interest. The very desire that they have to get the better of another eventually forces them into such institutions. The essence of Kant's reasoning here is like that of Hobbes. Humans, out of their self-interested nature, seek peace as a means for creating a state where they can pursue their self-interest and develop their capacities more securely. The institutions for doing so ultimately accord with the principles of right, although they are not sought out for moral reasons. This is why Kant dramatically emphasizes that a nation of devils could act according to right if they possessed understanding. Nature, that is, works by means of the self-interest of individuals to bring about institutions whose ultimate justification is not self-interest, but in the moral idea of rational autonomy that is the root of Kant's moral system. Ultimately, this resembles Rousseau's reasoning that the desire for liberty necessarily leads to the cessation of the demand of a right *against* others.

Nature seems determined to accomplish this purpose regardless of whether individual persons are motivated to bring it about, and yet Kant suggests that it is the duty of philosophers and other intellectuals to encourage and hasten the coming of this goal, precisely by means of the propagation of the doctrine of right itself. In writing such a history of the future, Kant says, we can rescue the contemplation of history from the notion that it has neither hope nor purpose. When we look at the history, we are tempted to see in it a gruesome spectacle, in which empires and peoples rise and fall, without any purpose; it becomes merely "one damn thing after another." Many good persons fail, while the evil seem to have their day in the sun. Our hopes for the future would seem to despair, since our own political actions, too, would seem to be doomed to be looked at this way from the perspective of the future. But if we see a plan of nature present in it, history is no longer a mere account of the past, but the subject of philosophical speculation concerning the purpose and nature of human being. The philosophy of history can therefore be a hope for, and a means to, future progress.

Influence and difficulties. Kant's political thought is not often given the credit that his moral and theoretical work is. However, it would be hard to discount his contributions in several major areas:

First, his theory of republican government clarifies and formalizes what had been either unsaid or said less clearly in Rousseau. The notion that right involves the maximization of freedom compatible with the freedom of others might be considered to be the ultimate principle of liberal thought. In addition, his justification of the coercive power of the state as implicit in the very notion of right is extremely important for how we conceive of the justice of the great force and power we find in contemporary government. The notions of liberty and equality in these notions have had great influence on such contemporary thinkers as Rawls and Dworkin.

Second, his notion of international law is the dominant paradigm for thought about it today. The extension of the principles of republican government to the notion of an international federation has been felt in contemporary politics in both the ideals and the practices of the United Nations. The U.N. is an international federation that tries to regulate, albeit with the great difficulty the task involves, the practice of war, peace and other conflict between nations. It also provides a forum for communication between nations so as to begin to sort out conflicts before they begin. Furthermore, Kant's notion that the prosecution and conduct of war should be in the interest of future peace lies behind the accords reached at such agreements as the Geneva Convention.

Finally, Kant's notion of an inevitable historical progress working through, yet against, the aims of particular human beings, has had by now a great influence and history of its own. Furthermore, his understanding of *how* the aim of history is attained and what the role of the philosopher is in its attainment had great influence on the thought of Hegel and Marx. Also, the notion of historical progress is not the exclusive preserve of Marxists, but has been ingrained in the very culture of the modern world.

In previous sections of this chapter, we have indicated some of the standard difficulties that have been found with Kant's moral and political thought, along with some Kantian replies to these objections. Here we shill take up his notion of historical progress to indicate the major difficulty. Kant assumes that nature has a plan for the human species that must inevitably come to fruition. But it seems that two sorts of objections can be given to the argument that Kant gives for this inevitable history.

First, does a plan of nature *inevitably* come to fruition? Kant bases his assumption upon autonomous self-rule being the essence of human nature; but does the nature of all species inevitably result in the full development of the species' potential? Could not accidental factors, factors of "environment" (either natural or social) inhibit this development (as it does in other species)? For example, under ideal conditions, an acorn planted in the ground becomes a healthy oak; but in nature, ideal conditions only rarely present themselves. If the soil is less than healthy, or there is a lack of sunlight, or an overabundance of other trees, one will not have a healthy oak, but, at best, a sickly dwarf. Why can we not conceive of the human species as subject to analogous natural accidents?

Even if we grant a negative answer to this question, is not the notion of inevitable progress opposed to the very radical nature of autonomy that Kant supposes throughout his work? If human reason grants autonomy, this would seem to grant the ability to refuse what nature plans for humanity, even if what nature plans would be the fulfillment of autonomy. This radical break from other natural species is, in fact, that which Kant acknowledges in saying that human beings are capable of "endless projects." As *without end*, can we assume an inevitable progress, or is it more reasonable to look at history as an endless account of coming closer to Right and then falling away?

When we ask this question, we assume that the actual choices of individuals or nations can be ultimately at odds with what they "ought" to choose. Thus the difficulties with history ultimately reflect a difficulty that we spoke of in the section on political right above. This is the issue of substantive and procedural liberty. For Kant, the moral law and the theory of right are "substantive" liberty. But Kant grants in his historical thought, and as the foundation for his political thought, that such right is not necessarily to be the intent of *individuals*. The coercive action of the state is grounded in this, as is Kant's rejection of the right to revolution. So, we might ask, what can we say of a political community that, through voting or some other way of representing the popular will, chooses to reject what right requires? Or, to take Locke's view, what if even *individuals* choose to do so? Can they be thought to have chosen "freely," even if against their own substantive liberty? Kant's moral theory may give us a good way of beginning to respond to such a difficulty; such a choice would be self-contradictory. Even so, it does not seem necessary for a choice to be consistent in order to be "free."

This difficulty is related to another one: Kant's divorcing of Right (the objective recognition of autonomy in action) from Virtue (the subjective motivation to recognize autonomy). That is, although the principles of morals are the source of the idea of political right, Kant does not demand that political actors be morally motivated. If it were, coercion and the state itself would not be necessary. Thus a nation of *devils* could be just as good citizens as morally good individuals. This claim has been present since Hobbes, who claims that the laws of nature are derived from the right of nature, which persuades us toward acquiring all we can, at the expense of others and indifferently to the commands of God or virtue. Law is merely selfishness enlightened by reason.

It seems highly questionable, however, that this is the case; furthermore, it is dubious whether such a community could be called a political community rather than an economic or strategic alliance. To make this point, we should recall the thought experiment proposed by Glaucon in Plato's *Republic*. Glaucon argues that the perfectly unjust person would have the appearance of justice while practicing injustice. If such a "devil" is possible, then it seems that any person/devil would be motivated to except himself from the institutions and laws of right whenever it was possible to do so for his own self-interest. If there were in this way a whole nation of such devils, it seems that public right would not hold for long. And even if it were not a whole nation, but merely a minority, would the state be a state of right if certain individuals excepted themselves from its laws?

The reply to this could be Hobbes': if *everyone* did this, the degeneration of the state would lead to the state of war, which is against everyone's interest. Kant, however, cannot leave it at this. The principles of right are correct whether people believe them or not. This seems only to heighten the tension between what is to be done and what ought to be done, and a political community would be constituted primarily as a police state to "force us to be free." We can still therefore accept the force of the Glauconian argument; the truly great would manipulate appearances, while the weak would ally to enforce justice. In the case of the nation of devils, the only recourse that the state has against the law-breaker is coercion or force; we can try to catch the clever law-breaker and convict him publicly. In the case of both the law-abiding devil and Glaucon's deceptive devil, what causes the person to abide by right is not right itself, but external necessity or force. *It is precisely this that makes one wonder if such a community is a community of freedom.* It seems, rather, that a true *community* of politics requires that the law be chosen for its own sake, precisely as good or noble. Both for a community of *right*, and for a *community* of right, it seems that a concern for virtue must be a concern of politics. It seems that it is virtue alone that could reconcile right and interest. This is a primary contention of thinkers such as Aristotle.

It could be further argued that these difficulties stem from problems internal to Kant's moral philosophy itself. As we have seen in the first section, Kant encodes in his moral philosophy a rigid distinction between moral action and action according to inclination, which Kant says is subject, like the rest of the natural world, to mechanical causation. This gives us a radical distinction between what we "ought" to do and what we actually desire. This makes two things difficult to determine: (1) whether anyone can ever act morally, and (2) what acts are in accordance with autonomy or self-rule. This second problem is more crucial for political thought. The difficulty is this: how does respect for another's freedom determine anything *necessarily* without a consideration of the desires or consequences present in the particular situation?

To restate this problem somewhat: the notion of liberty seems to be in some way indeterminate. This does not necessarily make it useless as a political principle; on the contrary, its indeterminacy is precisely its value. We recall that all contract theory begins with the rejection of an authoritative natural end or ordering of desires that we see in the thought of ancient philosophy. What this seems to imply, however, is that people have a right to desire whatever they in fact do desire—this was Hobbes' postulate. Will, as autonomous or separate from desire, is an empty concept for thinkers such as Hobbes and Locke. It would seem to follow that whatever we do is by nature right. This does not exclude the possibility of political community, but it does seem to mean that political community does not guide desire, but on the contrary is the *result* of what people happen to desire.

Rousseau and Kant see that something has been lost with the rejection of the Aristotelean position, and thus they return to the notion of an "end" or "goal" for humanity that is irreducible to what people happen to desire. However, their notion of an end is *not* Aristotelean, since they accept from Hobbes that there is no *natural* order of right; natural inclination for Kant is entirely a-moral. Therefore, the end cannot be contained in inclination, but must be found "outside" nature. It is found in the liberty of reason, and so the end is "self-determination" as such. But self-determination does not tell us much about the end for which the self is to be determined. Thus it seems it can be filled in by looking at what people (or most people) are inclined to do. But if this is the case, there is no substantial difference between what is done and what ought to be done.

This has generally been the major criticism of Kant's notion of moral law—that it is ultimately without content, since self-determination is an empty or merely formal concept. To go any further along this line of argument would take us beyond our purpose here. In Kant's defense, however, we might wonder what the concept of liberty *does* imply substantively. Could it not be argued, for example, that chattel slavery is opposed to self-rule? This seems fairly clear. However, in other cases (such as lying or free speech), drawing the line seems less clear, since the consequences of lying or infringing a person's speech seem to depend on a consideration of the particulars of the situation. The question is whether we can talk reasonably about a substantive content for autonomy that is prior to what people actually desire in concrete circumstances. What does respect for individual liberty actually require?

In conclusion, let us say this: Kant's theory of moral and political right remains to this day a serious contribution to and development of the attempt to ground moral and political right in the idea of autonomy or self-determination. Thus it is a necessary beginning point, to which most serious contemporary liberal thinkers return, for a discussion of modern liberal morals and politics. Whether we find Kant's principles ultimately persuasive depends on an answer to the final question that we have just raised: does the concept of self-determination provide us a standard for how we ought to act, both for ourselves and towards others in community? And if so, does the freedom or autonomy of each person without exception constitutes the greatest moral and political value?

Chapter Seven
The Normative Basis of Marxism

Anyone who has ever written a philosophy paper knows that an idea develops and evolves as we write about it. Similarly, if a philosopher writes many articles and books to develop an idea, we often can find many different expressions of the idea, depending on whether we read the earlier or later works. This is nowhere more true than in the writings of Karl Marx (1818-1883). The early Marx, for example as found in the *1844 Manuscripts* (see Bottomore 1963), is clearly a self-actualizationist in his value assumptions. He decries capitalism for its destruction of the ability of workers to actualize their potential as human beings, and there is a great deal of emphasis on "dehumanization" in the workplace and "alienation" of workers from their own labor and from themselves. Marx's later work—for example his *Capital* (1848/1906)—contrasts in both style and substance. In the later work, there is much less mention of the self-actualization dimension, and more discussion of scientific and economic issues. In these later works, the purpose is to show, scientifically and logically, that capitalism would inevitably destroy itself because of the increasing concentration of wealth, and thus would be replaced with socialism.

This evolution of Marx's ideas about capitalism and socialism leads to divergent interpretations of what Marx was actually saying, and even disagreement as to what basic philosophical assumptions he was using to ground his ideas. Those who focus more on the early work see him as exhibiting a strong kinship to Aristotle in his normative assumptions, because the emphasis is on the value of self-actualization, and the way the capitalist mode of production thwarts this value (Schaff 1970; Tucker 1971). But many scholars who focus on Marx's later work interpret his normative assumptions very differently. Some read him as an ethical relativist or an ethical nihilist (for example, Kamenka 1969), while others think he believes in a theory of justice in which distributive justice has intrinsic value and the injustices of capitalism are among its most objectionable features (Cannon 1978; Schweickart 1978). Some try to synthesize all these views into a theory of human freedom not unlike that of Locke, in which the value of freedom is infringed when the product of workers' labor is alienated from them and then used against them as form of enslavement (Maschner 1969; Ring 1977). Still others think he essentially make no normative assumptions, but rather is simply describing, from a scientific point of view, the principles of social development, and predicting where history is likely to lead in the future, based on these scientific principles (Mandel 1971).

Just as when a student writes a philosophy paper, there are different ways to see the relationship between the initial position the author takes and the final expression that is the culmination of the thought process. Did Marx reject his earlier self-actualizationist value assumptions? Did he simply shift from that theme and decide to focus on economic issues instead? Or were the later economic writings actually *based on* what he said in the earlier works? There seems to be little consensus among scholars, nor among political leaders who have used Marx's ideas. The communist governments of Cuba, China, and the former Soviet Union are substantially different from each other, although each purports to be based on the teachings of Marx. Moderately socialistic governments such as those in Israel and Western Europe also reflect some of Marx's ideas, although they do not publicly identify themselves as "Marxist."

Despite the varying interpretations of the evolution of Marx's philosophy from earlier to later works, there is definitely a continuity, and there is little formal evidence to suggest that Marx ever rejected his earlier views. It is more likely that he thought the entirety of his work constituted at least a logically consistent body of work. In this chapter, we shall discuss both the earlier and later work.

1. Marx's Early Works: Capitalism Creates Alienation and Dehumanization

In his early work, it is clear that Marx stresses psychological and social determinism. Marx goes even further than Aristotle in holding the society as a whole responsible for the moral character of its individuals. Capitalism is a system that encourages the society as a whole to refuse to take this responsibility seriously. In Marx's view, capitalist society refuses this responsibility essentially because extensive government social programs and humane, worker-friendly working environments would run contrary to the interests of capitalists to exploit workers as they see fit. The capitalist society then develops an entire ideology enshrining "free enterprise" and the "freedom and responsibility of the individual" as the highest values. By disseminating this ideology among the workers themselves by whatever means are available, the capitalist ideology forestalls the resistance of the workers against policies that further their own oppression. And, according to Marx, this very oppression creates such fear in workers—in concrete terms, fear of job loss and possibly failure even to survive in the economy—that workers are prone to deceive themselves that an alliance with the ideology of the oppressor is their best hope.

Notice that the primary problem with capitalism, in Marx's view, is that it thwarts human development—the thriving of the social individual as a whole human being, and the ability to form human relationships not dominated by competitiveness and mutual opposition. This in turn assumes that human attitudes, beliefs, and other personality dimensions are determined by social and economic forces. Marx's determinism can be stated in this way: The individual's character, including his or her moral character, is determined by a combination of heredity and social environment. The social environment in turn is controlled by economic forces. Thus, if we want to eliminate such social problems as crime and emotional neuroses such as anxiety and depression (with their attendant social consequences), we must eliminate the socio-economic factors that cause our society to produce criminals and emotionally disturbed individuals.

Why does Marx believe that people's socio-economic situation is responsible for making people into the kinds of people they are? There are two reasons:

(i) The first reason is that empirical evidence seems to point in this direction, at least to a considerable extent. For example, if there were no cause-and-effect relationship between socio-economic factors and subsequent criminal behavior, then we should expect to find a correlation of zero between people's socio-economic background and whether or not they choose a life of crime. Instead, as the famous Marxist criminologist Enrico Ferri and others were pointing out during Marx's own lifetime, we find significant correlations between criminal behavior and these other factors.

To move to more recent data, the criminologist James Short (1980) points out that, when the stock market crashed in 1929, U.S. crime rates approximately doubled; when Roosevelt instituted his work-relief programs, crime rates fell about halfway to the previous levels. Short reviews an impressive array of such correlations between crime rates and economic problems, including unemployment rates, stagnant wages, and swings of the stock market. Others have pointed to social factors that are only indirectly related to poverty and working-class living conditions. Clifford Shaw, in a book called *Delinquency Areas* (1929) shows correlations between geographical areas of cities and crime rates. Moreover, crime rates for specific ghettos tend to remain constant even though different racial and ethnic groups may occupy the same ghetto at different times throughout its history. According to Walter Miller (1978), psychological factors must be involved as well, since only one-fifth of all lower-class juvenile delinquents were found to be "emotionally disturbed," whereas two thirds of all middle-and upper-class juvenile delinquents were "emotionally disturbed," using the same standard of measurement—a significant difference between the two groups. This finding seems to imply that impoverished conditions associated with social class can be causal factors in the development of criminal behavior even without the "emotional disturbance" needed to make an upper-class juvenile into a delinquent. The lower-class juveniles may turn to crime even without the "emotional disturbance" factor—presumably because of poverty, gang-ridden neighborhoods, and other socioeconomic factors that have nothing to do with their mental condition. The psychological factors that determine the behavior of the upper-class juveniles are also important from the Marxist perspective, because the alienation that capitalism fosters affects the mental well being of the ruling class as well. Further support for a generally deterministic view of crime is suggested by Sutherland and Cressey (1974) who argue that a subculture in which deviant behavior is widespread and approved will tend to foster further deviant behavior on the part of its members. Later, we shall discuss more evidence for this social-determinist thesis.

Like the Marxist criminologist Ferri, and consistently with the more recent sociologists and criminologists just mentioned, Marx argues that it is meaningless to blame individual criminals for the way they have turned out, or to admonish poor people that they should "pull themselves up by their bootstraps." What we need to do is to eradicate the *causes* of such problems. In his early work, Marx thought that nothing short of eliminating the economic system of capitalism, and substituting socialism for it, could make possible a society in which people are not prevented from fully actualizing their human potential and developing into truly constructive and creative contributors to the social life of the community.

(ii) In order to understand Marx's second and more philosophical reason for believing that economic forces determine human development, we must look at his basic theory of human nature in some detail. Only years after Marx's death were his early manuscripts of 1844 rediscovered in the 1930s (yet even then they continued to be suppressed by the Nazi German government until the late 1940s). At that point, scholars began to realize that Marx's economic theory is only one implication that Marx intended to draw from a basic philosophic viewpoint. This basic viewpoint contrasts against the usual image of Marx as an "empirical scientist," and instead is almost an "existentialist" philosophy in its emphasis on people's *alienation* from themselves, as the result of their alienation from each other (through class divisions and competition), as well as their alienation from their own life-activity, or labor (through the separation between labor and the *ownership* of the means and outputs of production). As Marx sees it, workers are alienated from their working life and from control over the way it is conducted on a daily basis.

As Marx scholar T.B. Bottomore (1963) interprets Marx's early work, we are alienated in two senses: First, the vast majority of people (and perhaps all people) have lost control of the products of their own activity, because these products, in the capitalist system, now confront them as inhuman ruling powers. Secondly, in the process of work itself most people are not productive in the sense of freely exercising their natural powers, but instead are constrained to perform uninteresting and degrading tasks.

Similarly, Marx, in his *1844 Manuscripts*, speaks of the relationship of the worker to the product of his labor as "an alien object which dominates him"

(Bottomore 1963, 125). At the same time, the relationship of labor to the act of working is a relationship between the worker and *his own activity* in which the latter appears as

> . . . alien and not belonging to him, activity as suffering (passivity), strength as powerlessness, creation as emasculation, the *personal* physical and mental energy of the worker, his personal life . . . directed against himself. . . . This is *self-alienation* as against the above-mentioned alienation of the [product of labor] (Bottomore 1963,125-126).

This self-alienation leads to **dehumanization**, in which workers are no longer able to develop their human potential either intellectually or creatively. As the Socialist Workers Party activist Harry Ring puts it, "An auto worker has the freedom to stand on an assembly line eight hours a day, turning the same screw, or maybe two screws, on every car that comes by, five or six days a week, until the company grants the worker the freedom to be unemployed." (Ring 1977, 10). The worker is then likely to become emotionally repressed, sometimes even emotionally disturbed, self-deceptive or irrational, and will tend to adopt unrealistic or ill-informed political interpretations of the situation, in response to the well-orchestrated rhetoric of politicians out to influence opinion. For example, devious politicians convince workers that immigrants are responsible for their problems, and stir up racial and ethnic strife which are then manipulated to win elections. Once the situation reaches this point, people are incapable of even identifying the source of their problems, which is the capitalist system of exploitation itself. The fact that the capitalist-dominated media are constantly bombarding people with manipulative propaganda also contributes to this outcome. Thus Marx writes in the "Critique of Hegel's Philosophy of Right" that "The call to abandon their illusions is a call to abandon a condition which requires illusions" (Bottomore 1963, 44).

The psychologist Erich Fromm summarizes Marx's thinking on this point as follows: "Man has become alienated from his work, from his fellow man, and from himself; he transforms himself into a thing, occupied with production and consumption. Unconsciously he feels anxious, lonely, and confused, because he has lost . . . the conviction of who he is and what he lives for" (in Schaff 1970, x). Also, according to Fromm, Marx emphasizes in his value theory that human beings have intrinsic value. i.e., that we are ends in ourselves, and not merely means "for institutions or purposes outside of [ourselves]" (in Schaff 1970, x).

What is the ethical presupposition on the basis of which Marx regards the capitalist organization of society as *undesirable*? Notice that Marx is advocating a normative position here. It is true that Marx deems the eventual revolution *inevitable* (because a system that increasingly destroys the ability of workers to consume their own products is not sustainable); yet it can hardly be denied that Marx wants to enlighten the masses as to what will be required to ensure that this revolution will be a genuine socialist revolution (and not, for example, a fascist one)—and that he does place a moral value judgment on the process.

It seems to many recent scholars that Marx's ethical goal was to overcome human self-alienation, thus allowing the complete actualization and development of each individual's consciousness and personality. According to Adam Schaff, a well-known Polish expositor of this "humanist" interpretation of Marx,

> Marx's point of departure is an individual who not only thinks and reasons but also *acts* consciously and rationally. *Labor* is the fundamental form of this transforming activity —because man, unlike mythological forces, creates everything from something, not from nothing. Human labor *transforms* the objective reality and thereby turns it into *human* reality, that is, a result of human labor. And in transforming the objective reality—nature and society—man transforms the conditions of his own existence, and consequently himself, too, as a species. In this way, the human process of *creation* is, from man's point of view, a process of *self-creation*. It was in this way—through labor—that *Homo sapiens* was born, and it is through labor that he continues to change and transform himself (Schaff 1970, 70).

In his emphasis on the development of the human consciousness and character, Marx is again in agreement with Aristotle. "That which is the best," Marx approvingly quotes from Aristotle in his doctoral thesis, "has no need of action but is itself an end" (Kamenka 1969, 12). Thus, according to Kamenka, "The process [through which man became a slave to things or institutions that he had himself created] Marx, following Hegel, called (self-) alienation and estrangement, or later, *fetishism* and *dehumanization*. . . . Man's nature consisted of a set of potentialities; freedom allowed him to go about the task of realizing them to the full" (Kamenka 1969, 12). Or as Marx says, "Money is the essence of man's . . . work and existence, alienated from man, and this alien essence dominates him and he prays to it" (Botomore 1963, 37).

2. The Working Out of the Theory

Why does Marx choose the system of *capitalism* as the villain on which all this exploitation, self-alienation and dehumanization is to be blamed? Here again, Marx the philosopher is more prominent than his "empirical scientist" persona, because his reasoning is based more on logic than on empirical data. Ernest Mandel (1971), a reliable interpreter of the economic side of Marx's thinking, sees the law of the *"ever-increasing rate of profit"* under capitalism as the backbone of Marx's economic system. The way this law works is as follows: Suppose the average rate of profit for all investments in a given year is 20%. There will be some fluctuation around this figure: some companies will earn more than 20% for their investors, some less. As a result, investors will tend to withdraw their capital from those that earn less than 20% (which therefore will tend to go out of business) and re-invest the money in the companies that earn more than 20%. It follows that the average rate of profit has increased in the process. Let's suppose it has increase to, say, 21%. The same thing happens again the next year, thus increasing the average rate of profit again, and so forth. The average rate of profit therefore tends continually to increase, and the law of survival is that each company is under severe pressure to earn more each year than the average for that year. Thus more and more capital is concentrated in fewer and fewer hands, resulting in monopolization and the power on the part of large corporations to hold down wages while increasing prices.

Eventually, it will become necessary for companies to hold down wages while increasing prices in order to continue increasing their profits. Meanwhile, the companies that go out of business each year lay off their workers, thus swelling the ranks of a constant *"industrial reserve army"*—a mass of unemployed proletarians who are so desperate for work that they effectually compete with those who do have jobs, which tends to hold down wages.

Since the only responsibility of a company in the capitalist system is to make money, the company will work against all other values that might interfere with this goal, including wherever necessary the well-being of workers, consumers, and the environment. And the increasing concentration of wealth will lead to an increasing concentration of *power* on the part of wealthy companies to thwart all other values not consistent with maximizing profits. If capitalism is left unchecked by an opposing power, workers will have less and less bargaining power, unions will be crushed, and workers in effect will be enslaved.

According to Marx, there are only four extraneous factors that tend to hold in check this process of increasing concentration of capital in fewer and fewer hands, which increases the rate of profit, and thus increases misery for the worker—and these four factors are all only temporary:

(1) *Increasing technology* allows companies to increase their rate of profit by increasing workers' productivity without increasing the degree of exploitation.

(2) *The discovery of new natural resources* has the same effect.

(3) *Imperialist exploitation of the Third World* provides a new source of cheap labor and raw materials so that domestic laborers can continue earning the same wage while the company increases its profit. Wars also result from these imperialist activities, and the wars themselves temporarily delay the process of "amiseration"—increasing economic misery—of the worker, by providing new markets and also by killing off part of the industrial reserve army.

(4) *Liberal governmental policies*, by means of peaceful measures such as anti-trust laws, hold the power of the corporations in check to some extent. But ultimately, these liberal policies become powerless, according to Marx, because eventually either the profits of corporations or the welfare of the workers will have to be sacrificed in order to keep the system of ever-increasing profit going.

The reason capitalism has worked so well and lasted so long in America, according to Marxists, is that all four of these inherently temporary factors have tended to work to the advantage of both the American worker and the American capitalist. Increasing technology, new natural resources, imperialism, war, and liberal government policies have all been exceptionally prominent features of American history. But when America runs out of its wealth of raw materials, when exploitation of the Third World (including both cheap labor and cheap raw materials) has reached its limit, etc., then, according to Marxists, American workers too will feel the crunch, because they will have to compete with the wages of workers in "economically undeveloped" countries.

While the above account is somewhat oversimplified, it should suffice for our purposes here to summarize Marx's reasons for pinning the blame for human self-alienation, thwarted self-actualization, and dehumanization on the capitalist economic system. The important point, as far as philosophical assumptions are concerned, is not whether capitalism, or some other force, or a combination of capitalism and other forces, is the ultimate cause of the problem. This may well be an empirical question. The more philosophical question is whether Marx's general system of socio-political thought, including both his value theory and his theory of social determinism as it affects human nature, is valid to begin with.

3. Criticisms and Marxist Responses

Among the many criticisms of Marx's theory, we shall concentrate on those which are relevant to an assessment of his normative and ontological claims about why capitalism is counterproductive. Marx claims that (a) the proper goal of society should be to allow the maximum development of human freedom, interpreted as the ability to actualize our human potential; (b) conversely, if individuals do not develop their potential, society is to blame; (c) it is primarily through work that human beings actualize themselves; (d) if political revolution is required in order to ensure the attainment of self-actualization by means of reorganization of the means of production, then such revolution is desirable.

Marx's theory as a whole is a "policy position," which means that it contains both an ethical claim about what kinds of things are valuable and a social-scientific claim about the best means of achieving this value. In Marx's case, there is also an ontological claim about what kind of beings humans are. Because of the politically controversial nature of Marxism, there is a tendency to run together criticisms of Marx's social-scientific claims with his normative (i.e., ethical) and ontological claims. To do so is to confuse the issue and therefore to treat Marx's ethical theory unfairly. It is possible that his ethical theory could be valid while some of his social-scientific claims are not. At the same time, Marx's ethical claims are based partly on his ontological theory of human nature, which in turn is difficult to separate from his social-scientific claims. Thus it is difficult to consider the ethical aspects of the theory in complete isolation from the social-scientific aspects.

Bearing in mind this interrelatedness of the theory, especially in its ethical and ontological aspects, let's look at some criticisms of each of the four above-mentioned theses.

(a) The thesis that the proper goal of society should be to allow the maximum development of human potential. Against this position, it is obvious that utilitarians will hold that the development of human potential is not as important as is human happiness. From a utilitarian viewpoint, if the capitalist organization of society is materially productive, its members will be happy because in this case their needs—both biological and recreational—will be met. Of course, if socialism makes people happier than capitalism, then utilitarians will gladly support socialism; but they will not support socialism for the sake of self-actualization or the realization of the greatest possible human potential, as if this were an intrinsic value independent of human *happiness.* Whenever Marx mentions Mill, he does so in a scoffing tone, emphasizing that "happiness" is too flimsy and frivolous a value on which to base a social or political doctrine. Nonetheless, a utilitarian can argue that, as a matter of fact, human beings do not feel the need or desire to actualize themselves even to the extent that is already available to them in our present society; instead, they prefer to read pulp literature, watch sex and violence in movies and on television, and read magazines about the personal lives of movie stars and other celebrities. It is clear, the utilitarian may argue, that what people value is happiness, pleasure and contentment—not the "full actualization of their human potential" about which Marx is so concerned. And if that is what they want, then society should provide it for them.

Marx's response to this criticism is that people may *think* they value the insignificant little pleasures that capitalism offers them, in the same way that heroin addicts think they want a fix. If capitalism had never addicted people to beer, baseball on T.V., and a boat in the carport, if it had not made them into the kinds of creatures who know no greater values than these, if it had not undermined our self-esteem so severely that we have given up the ideal of self-development—then our true values could be felt. Utilitarianism places the cart before the horse, according to Marx: it asks people what they want *in their present condition* rather than asking what we *would* want in our *ideal* condition. Social philosophy, for Marx, must begin with a vision of what humans *can* be, not merely what they *are.* Here Marx's reasoning is quite parallel to Aristotle's. Since it is society that makes people what they are, it is misleading to ask people *as they are* whether they would prefer for society (and therefore "human nature" itself) to be different. If society were different, then human nature would be different.

Many justice theorists, working from a concept of either distributive or retributive justice, also would argue against Marx's thesis that self-actualization as the ultimate value, for two reasons:

(i) If a society gives "unto each according to his need" and takes "from each according to his ability"—as Marx thinks would be required for seif-actualization—then these supposedly necessary conditions for self-actualization themselves are unjust, and therefore should be superceded in favor of the greater value of *justice:* To each according to his *deserts*, some might say. Moreover:

(ii) Self-realization is subject to the same criticisms as utilitarianism in this regard. If the choice is between 100 units of self-realization distributed among 100 people, or 101 units to be distributed among only 10 people, then Marx, to be consistent, should prefer the 101 units, since this option would produce the greater total quantity of self-realization. But such an unequal distribution of the self-realization obviously would be unfair.

Marx would reply against argument (ii) that equal or at least equitable distribution of *all* the opportunities and benefits of society is necessary to everyone's self-realization; therefore the situation hypothesized could never arise. Unlike in other self-realizationist theories, Marx's theory requires justice in the distribution of all opportunities and resources. Without justice, there can be no self-realization.

Against argument (i), Marx would argue that since social determinism is true, the word "desert" is meaningless. People do not "deserve" to be punished for being unproductive or criminal, because they were made into what they are by forces that the society itself exerted on them during their social development. Capitalism, as described by Marx, is a cut-throat and dehumanizing system. It will always find ways to thwart the human development of many its individuals, so that they turn out to be criminals, drug addicts, or "slackers" on the job. The real blame for such personality outcomes is the society itself. The easy availability of guns, the lack of adequate job security and other safeguards against the impoverishment of discarded segments of the working class, and the cult of consumerism encouraged by capitalism—all of these factors contribute to these outcomes. In countries where guns are not so available, and where there is a more effective safety net for workers who lose their jobs or cannot find jobs that pay a living wage, crime rates are much lower than in the U.S.

This response leads naturally to the Marxist position with regard to the second criticism of Marx:

(b) The thesis that, if individuals do not develop their potential, society is to blame. A belief that the lives and fortunes of humans—including their personality development—are the product of social conditions was increasingly prevalent at the time of Marx, for two main reasons. First, there was increasing empirical evidence that criminal behavior is influenced by educational and economic factors in a person's environment. We saw earlier that this kind of evidence was emphasized by Enrico Ferri, the creator of the "rehabilitation" school of criminal justice. But the economic and educational causes of crime were also stressed by Cesare Beccaria (1963), who developed the "deterrence" theory of criminal justice. Beccaria's idea was that, if criminal behavior is determine by social causes such as poverty, then the only purpose of punishment should be to deter future crimes, not to take retribution for past ones. Also, the utilitarian philosopher Jeremy Bentham (1948) argued that beneficial outcomes can be achieved if we understand the causes of the types of behavior we wish to change.

The second influence on Marx's determinism came from a very different direction. Hegel had already popularized the notion that there is a natural unfolding of philosophical attitudes through history—from the earliest Biblical times when any war automatically resulted either in genocide or at best enslavement of those who lost the war (for example, the Hebrews' genocide against the Canaanites and many other peoples as reported in the Book of Joshua), through various stages of Medieval property relations in which serfs were required to work the land at the mercy of the landowner, to the development of industrial capitalism, in which workers must sell their time and labor to the owner of capital. Hegel had argued that the unfolding of philosophical ideas governing how humans should behave toward each other—like all other philosophical ideas—follows an orderly logic, which Hegel called a *"dialectic."* Each new philosophical viewpoint is confronted with undesirable and illogical consequences (Marx calls them "contradictions"), and as a result, an opposing viewpoint develops. Hegel called this opposing viewpoint an *"antithesis"* to the *"thesis"* against which it is opposed. But the antithesis itself entails undesirable and illogical consequences, until finally people think of a way to incorporate the desirable elements of both the thesis and the antithesis into a new viewpoint: a *"synthesis."* An example would be the way modern democracy tries to incorporate both majority rule and the rights of minorities against a "tyranny of the majority." But the synthesis itself also entails contradictions, so the historical process of developing ideas continues.

Why did this Hegelian concept of a historical dialectic lead to *social determinism* in Marx's thinking? Because if the way people think is determined by an unfolding historical thought process, this in turn presupposes that human psychology is constructed in such a way as to be determined by what is going on in the social and physical environment. For example, in the U.S., most political conservatives of the 1950s espoused ideas about race relations that now would be considered unacceptably racist by even the most conservative politicians and voters. As the times change, so do people's philosophical and psychological attitudes—in response to social-environmental influences.

But because Marx, unlike Hegel, is a *materialist,* he emphasizes the *physical* and especially *economic* conditions that determine psychological outcomes. For example, although empirical studies of criminal behavior were primitive in Marx's time, he would have smiled approvingly at much of the later criminological work that shows the influence of economic factors on crime rates—for instance, James

Short's finding that crime rates in all major U.S. cities more than doubled immediately following the stock market crash of 1929, and the correlations between poverty and crime documented by DeFronzo (1983) and others. Marx would also be pleased to know of DeFronzo's finding that more liberal welfare payments to mothers with dependent children tend to decrease crime rates in a city.

Now let's talk about the objections against Marx's assumption of psychological and social determinism. Many people reject determinism prematurely, because they think that if criminal behavior is completely predetermined, for example, then the society would not be justified in punishing people fro committing crimes, and the result would be chaos. Of course, it is true that punishment for purely *retributive* reasons would not be legitimate if determinism were true: this is why deterministic criminologists like Ferri and Beccaria reject pure retribution as a justification for punishment, and insist instead that only deterrence or rehabilitation can be legitimate reasons to punish offenders.

This shows that a belief in determinism is not such a serious impediment to accepting the type of ethical theory that defines right actions in terms of good consequences. In these theories' sense of the word "should," to say that someone "should do X" may mean nothing more than that "It would be good if the person did X." Thus, it would be equally true to say "It would be good if John Smith did X" (i.e ., "John Smith should do X")—regardless of whether Smith's character and actions are completely predetermined or not. But then if Smith does the wrong thing, the purpose of punishing him would only be to deter future prospective criminals from making similar bad choices.

As an example of the importance of this issue in influencing ethical beliefs, let's consider a little further the impact it has had in the theory of criminal justice over the past hundred years. Rehabilitation theory, as we have seen, is based on a body of evidence collected by criminologists suggesting that criminal personality and behavior have causes, a sampling of which we have already discussed. According to Ferri and the other criminologists of the "positive" school (as Ferri called it in his time), if crime has causes, then it can also have preventions and cures. But the greater the extent to which crime is caused by factors beyond the control of the potential offender (who is in a sense "victimized" by these causal factors), the less sense it makes to morally blame the criminal for having ended up with his unfortunately objectionable attitudes and behavior patterns. On the other hand, it would still make sense in this case to try to change his character, to remove him from society in order to protect potential victims, and even to punish him in order to show him and others who are tempted by crime that the society will not tolerate such behavior, thus deterring future offenses as much as possible. In this way, the law-enforcement institutions of the society make themselves into one of the determining factors that cause people to be prone to choose a law-abiding way of life.

At the other extreme of criminal justice theories, a trend now exists in the U.S. away from deterrence and rehabilitation, and toward a *retributive* theory of punishment. It is illuminating to contrast modern retribution theory against the rehabilitation model of justice, for here we encounter two theories that are almost perfectly opposite each other. Whereas Ferri and other rehabilitationists assume that all human actions and personality traits are predetermined by necessary and sufficient causal factors—so that it makes sense to try to rearrange the determinants in such a way as to cause the criminal or potential criminal to change his behavior patterns—the retributivist must assume just the opposite, i.e. , that people have a free, non-predetermined choice between right and wrong, and therefore deserve punishment if they purposely choose the wrong, knowing it to be wrong. This free will is necessary to retributive theory because of the traditional ethical principle that "ought implies can." If determinism is true, then it is never the case that anyone *could* have acted in any other way than the way they did act.

It should be noted, however, that, while retribution and rehabilitation are utterly opposite in this respect, the issue becomes more complex when we consider that behavior may be determined to a great extent but not completely. In this case, it would seem unfair to blame someone who has all the disadvantages in life to the same extent that we blame someone who has all the advantages. This issue becomes a messy one for retribution theory: Should excuses be allowed to a certain extent? Many retributivists say no, because of the basic retributive principle that the crime must precisely correspond to the punishment and that judicial discretion in the sentencing of individual offenders is the most prominent of all sources of unfairness. Moreover, if retributivists were to grant that determinism is even partially true, then they would be faced with a dilemma: It would then seem that both rehabilitation and retributive punishment should be administered with regard to the same offender at the same time. But this would be impossible, or at best impractical, because rehabilitation requires indeterminate sentences: a prisoner must be released when and only when he has been rehabilitated. This, however, would be unfair by retributive standards, because it would lead to situations in which the person who has committed the greater offense might end up with the lesser punishment. Also, rehabilitation, when seriously practiced, might well prevent the prison experience from being a very *punishing* one, thus violating the primary purpose of imprisonment from the retributive point of view. However, to measure precisely the unpleasantness of sanctions for various individuals is problem enough for the retributivist even without the added difficulty of deciding how much determinism and how much free will is present in the personality development of each individual offender.

In this regard, Marx's deterministic viewpoint has an advantage. There is no need to worry about what an offender "morally deserves," in Marx's view, because if any of us had had literally *all* of the same social-deterministic influences as the offender, we would have been exactly like him, so there is no need for a judgment of what the person "deserves" in purely *retributive* terms. It is only necessary to decide what the most effective way to handle criminals would be from the standpoint of protecting law-abiding citizens *from* such offenders in the future, and discouraging future prospective offenders from adopting a life of crime. And this would require either imprisoning or rehabilitating them, for as long as needed to accomplish the purposes of deterrence and/or rehabilitation.

As a scientific hypothesis, the verification procedure for the strictly causal type of determinism runs as follows: If the choice to engage in a given behavior (for example, crime) were a free choice, we should find a zero correlation between the person's behavior and any antecedent factor beyond the person's control (for example, whether or not he was a victim of child abuse). But in fact, we find a significantly greater correlation between criminal behavior and such antecedent factors than would be explainable by chance alone. Therefore, there must be a causal explanation of some sort for the correlation. While it is true that a correlation between antecedent A and consequent B does not show that A necessarily causes B, it does show that either A at least partially causes B, or that both A and B are caused (at least in part) by some third factor or complex of factors. But in either case, B has a cause—either it is caused by A, or it is caused by the third factor which causes both A and B (thus also causing them to correlate with each other). The determinist argues that, the more antecedent factors we can show to correlate with the consequent behavior, the greater the degree of causal determination has been proven, and the greater the probability of complete determinism.

We should note that the determinist picture of the causation of behavior does not entail that some particular antecedent A is the *complete* cause of some particular behavior E, but rather that B is caused by a *large number* of antecedents interacting with each other. Thus the common objection so often raised by prosecuting attorneys—that if determinism were true, then we should expect to find a perfect correlation between A and B—rests upon a serious fallacy. Obviously, not every victim of child abuse grows up to be a criminal. But according to determinism, whether he does or not will depend *partly* on this factor and partly on a great number of other factors.

The main problem with this defense of determinism is the difficulty, if not impossibility, of demonstrating that *all* (rather than some or most) actions have causes, and that these actions are completely caused by their antecedents rather than only *partly caused*, or caused to a great *extent*. No matter how many instances the determinist can point to in which someone's action is largely the result of antecedent factors, it cannot be proven that *all* actions in *all* instances are completely determined by such factors. But the supporter of free will does not deny that some or even most actions and choices are largely predetermined; free will needs to affirm only that *some few* actions and choices involve some degree of free choice. It may even be conceded that a person who is pressured by causal factors to commit wrongdoings is quantitatively *less* deserving of blame than his non-pressured counterpart who commits the same crimes with no provocation or excuse; however, this would not mean that he is not to be blamed—only that he is *less* to be blamed than the non-pressured counterpart.

But, against this argument that no amount of empirical evidence is enough to prove determinism, Marxists have a strong response available to them: either a person's character, at any given time, is caused by some previous actions and choices on the part of the person; or it is caused by some external factor(s); or it is not caused at all. If it is *not caused at all,* then it is not caused by the person in question, and therefore cannot be the result of his or her choice. If it is caused by an *external factor,* then obviously no free choice is involved in this case either. And if it is caused by the person him- or herself, i.e., by some *previous actions and decisions* on his/her part, then we can again ask with regard to each of these previous actions and decisions: why was the person's character at *that* time constituted so that he or she decided to act in that particular way. In answering this question, we are again confronted with the same dilemma. We can ask at this point whether the person's character at *this* time has already been determined by external factors, or by random chance, or by still earlier choices the person had already made. It is clear that we could continue this line of reasoning indefinitely. In doing so, we would notice that, at each point in time, the only control the person could have exerted over his or her character or actions at that time would have to have been the result of choices and actions that had been committed at *earlier* times; these in turn would be attributable to external factors, to chance, or to choices and actions that had been committed at *still earlier* times. Once we have traced this process all the way back to the time of birth, we have accounted for all the causal as well as chance factors that cause the person to have a particular character structure at any given time. Thus the agent's character, actions and choices are ultimately completely attributable to causal and/or chance factors beyond the person's control.

It is sometimes argued that determinists merely *select* facts from an individual's background which appear as though they could have caused him to turn out as the kind of person he happens to be; if the same person, given the same background, had nonetheless turned out in some different way, then the determinist would merely have chosen different facts about the person's background that might look congruent with this other outcome, and would have focused exclusively on these, pretending that this shows that the person's character was predetermined. No matter how the person turns out, the determinist can always find something in the person's background that appears to be a likely cause for the outcome. Thus, according to this argument, it is always possible to look *backward* from the facts, once we already know them, and construe some past event as the cause of someone's character, but the crucial test would be to insist that the determinist *predict in advance* how someone is going to behave or what kind of character the person is going to have.

But this argument is a classic "straw-man" argument; it accuses determinists like Marx of having said something they did not really say, then proceeds to tear down this "straw man." It sets up the determinist position as though the proponents of determinism had argued from someone's present character to infer what the past causes of it might have been. But it is not necessary for Marx to prove what the specific cause of each specific behavior might be—only to prove that the thesis of determinism is true in general. Besides the argument just mentioned, there are also statistical correlations that do not seem explainable except in cause-effect terms. So, in general, both these arguments point to a deterministic view of character development.

This line of objection to determinism therefore seems to assume unfairly that if someone cannot explain the causation of every single behavior, then the deterministic thesis must be false. In the same way, many opponents of the theory of evolution argue that, since evolutionary theory cannot explain all the facts about biology, then evolution must be false.

On the other hand, it is true that simply to cite statistical correlations, by itself, would not establish the truth of determinism. We simply would still not know, on the basis of such reasoning, whether a complete social determinism is true or not. This is why determinism is a philosophical position rather than merely a social-scientific one.

But if the social determinist thesis is granted to Marx, then it might well be that the society itself is responsible for the character it caused its less fortunate members to have. From this viewpoint, it might seem that criminals should not be punished, since it would be odd for the society to punish the victims of its own ultimate corruption. But as we have seen, Marx's response to this is consistent with the deterrence and rehabilitation approaches to criminology, which do not rule out punishment where needed. There is no contradiction or incompatibility between punishing wrongdoers and at the same time reforming the society in such a way as to produce fewer wrongdoers. Without punishment, laws would be ineffectual.

An old Islamic legend has it that a rich king once went on a journey, entrusting his wealth to one of his servants. When the king returned to find that the servant had stolen some of his money, he took the servant before a famous Imam for judgment. The Imam sentenced the servant to be severely punished because, in Islamic legal theory, the purpose of punishment is to help those who are weak in character to avoid wrongdoing by making the punishment severe enough and certain enough to put fear into the heart of even the weakest character. But the wise Imam also sentenced the king himself to be punished, because the king should have known that, by leaving a servant so weak in character with such a great temptation, he was causing the servant to sin. This legend shows that the roots of social-determinist thinking are very old, and are not confined to Western culture.

(c) The thesis that it is primarily through work that people actualize themselves. This may well be a more vulnerable point of Marx's system than the mere claim that self-actualization should be the goal of social life. Marx seems to equate the "life" of workers with their "activity" and this "activity" in turn is equated with the worker's "labor"—thus equating the worker's "life" with his or her "labor." We see this clearly in Marx's rhetorical question, "For what is life but activity?" (Bottomore 1963, 125), and he is clearly referring here to the activity of labor. To a greater or lesser extent, this equation of life with work could well be viewed as an overgeneralization. The equation may have held as a literal truth for the many unfortunate proletarians of the nineteenth century who labored sixteen hours a day. These workers' lives were almost entirely equivalent with their labor time; it could therefore be argued at that time, with Marx, that if their work was demeaning, dehumanizing, etc., this fact would prevent them from developing their human potential. But is the same thing true of modern workers, who work only eight or ten hours a day? Why can these workers not "develop themselves" during the other six to eight waking hours per day?

Those who raise this objection against Marx might go on to insist, as do many contemporary "self-actualization" psychologists such as Abraham Maslow and Carl Rogers, that work is not even the most important way in which people develop themselves intellectually and emotionally, though Maslow and Rogers do grant that work is *one* important way. More important, they argue, are human relationships. Honest, communicative relationships help people to get in touch with their own thoughts and feelings so that they develop into mature, intellectually self-honest people who will then honestly seek the truth regarding both factual and value issues—thus avoiding fetishism, dehumanization and self-alienation, all the things Marx wanted to avoid, without the necessity for a violent political revolution.

Many Marxists will respond here that these "honest, communicative relationships" and this "mature self-honesty" are fine, but they do nothing to put food on the table, win decent working conditions, overthrow an inherently unjust and inhuman system, or promote social change. But those Marxists who respond in this way sound as if they are relying on an interpretation of Marx as a justice theorist or a utilitarian, not a self-actualizationist. Such responses may not bew consistent with what Marx himself actually thought, at least if we judge from his earlier work— that self-alienation is the problem to be overcome, and self-actualization the value to be promoted. Moreover, the attempt to interpret Marx as either a justice theorist or a utilitarian in his basic value assumptions would then face the problem of answering all the objections against Marx that would be raised from the utilitarian standpoint. Particularly problematic would be the utilitarian objection that people in their present condition are happier watching television than working for social change. Moreover, those who opt for a deontic or justice-theory interpretation of Marx are faced with the problem that many theories of justice tend to entail a belief in free will, which has no place in Marx's system. Strict determinism is an integral and foundational aspect of Marx's thinking; it is for this reason that the social system must be blamed for the individual's failures.

In fact, the ethical relativists of the Marxist camp are fond of dismissing theories of justice on the basis that its "moral intuitions" are merely sedimented solidification, in the form of prejudices, of the attitudes and values of the current ruling class. Consider, for example, Sir David Ross's absolute demand for respect for private property as a deontic and supposedly "intuitively-self-evident" principle (Ross 1965, 22). Why should the intuition on the part of Marxists, that property should be equally distributed (or equitably redistributed), not also be just as subjective and arbitrary, especially since this intuition does not even seem to be shared by most of those who would benefit from such a redistribution?

Deontic and utilitarian "Marxists" may also be completely mistaken in their claim that the kind of self-actualization the contemporary self-actualization psychologists are interested in does nothing to further social change. Perhaps people would not be taken in by the rhetoric and logical fallacies of a Nixon, for example, and perhaps they would not support his policies or elect and re-elect such politicians, if they were mature, intellectually honest and self-actualized to begin with. Perhaps psychological development must precede political maturity, rather than following as a consequence of it. After all, the German people might not have *elected* Hitler if they had been thinking clearly to begin with. The problem this poses for Marxism is that Marx assumes that political events determine psychological development, and this assumption may reverse cause and effect. It may be our psychological problems that cause us to elect the wrong politicians.

But here the Marxist has a come-back. It is true that the German people elected Hitler, but it is also true that the rise of Naziism in Germany had an ultimate *economic* cause, not just a psychological one. The war reparations and the worldwide depression, which hit especially hard in Germany, caused the German people to become so desperate as to support Naziism. Not only the dehumanizing nature of labor under capitalism, but the totality of economic conditions causes people to become irrational and inhuman, and to make illogical political decisions.

Still another Marxist response to this objection might be that, although it is true that the contemporary proletarian (in the northern-hemisphere, affluent nations) does not work sixteen hours a day as in Marx's time, it is still true that our attitudes are molded primarily as the result of the work we do and our interrelations with our working environment. An underling who is oppressed at work is likely to take out his pent-up hostilities on his wife at home, or to develop drinking or drug problems. A popular musician who stays constantly on the road is more likely than others to develop a promiscuous sexual adjustment, with attitudes and ways of relating that harmonize with this economic given of the profession. In the capitalist system, people "becomes what they do." Thus, when someone asks a new acquaintance, "What do you do?" there is no doubt that they are referring to the single most important element of what a person is in the capitalist system—our work. It should also be borne in mind that not only a person's work, but also the work our parents did as we were growing up will indirectly influence our attitudes and thought-structures.

Finally, the Marxists might also respond, with Karl Kautsky (1936), that the proletarian in the Northern industrialized nations has it easy today because we live off the benefits derived from the complex exploitation of the Third World, where tenant farmers have been forced off the land they had worked for centuries to make room for tea and coffee plantations, and where the economies of the countries have been made dependent on Western markets and thus "decapitalized" (i.e., Third World investors have withdrawn their investments from their own countries in order to invest in Western companies). It is in the Third World that the "amiseration" of the proletariat is proceeding full-scale.

In fact, Marxists of this international, Kautkyist bent often argue that the proof that we in the advanced nations are still self-alienated and distorted in our attitudes and beliefs is that we enjoy the benefits resulting from Third World misery, while at the same time we still pat ourselves on the back in smug self-admiration, thinking that we are to be commended for our accomplishments, and that "free enterprise capitalism" (backed up by military threat) is a good thing (except when the Arabs raise oil prices).

What about the objection that self-alienation itself may be what causes our political confusion rather than the socioeconomic system being the cause of our poor psychological development? Perhaps this can only be resolved empirically. But the question may well become a quantitative one at this point: *How* important are economic and working conditions, as compared with human relationships, in helping or hindering a person in his progress toward self-actualization? It also becomes a question of the direction of causation. Do psychological problems cause people to become so distorted in their thinking that they support capitalism, which further alienates them from themselves; or, on the contrary, does capitalism alienate people from themselves to such an extent that they become distorted in their thinking, thus supporting capitalism? Correlatively, must social revolution (in the sense that people will become clearer in their political thinking) precede political revolution, or *vice versa*?

(d) The thesis that, if political revolution is required in order to ensure the attainment of self-actualization of the human individual by means of reorganization of the means of production, then such revolution is desirable. This thesis is only marginally related to our philosophical concerns here, and it involves many empirical-scientific questions. Some questions about it are, briefly, as follows:

(i) Why not liberal-democratic "evolution" toward socialism rather than revolution?

(ii) Would complete socialism not limit people's freedom, as in China and the former Soviet Union? Here Marxists are quick to point out that to equate the Soviet Union with socialism is like equating the doctrines of Christianity with the practices of the Spanish Inquisition. Certainly, socialism would limit the freedom of the rich to get richer at the expense of the poor; but in Marx's ethical system, this would not be an undesirable thing, either for the rich or for the poor. (The rich also are self-alienated as a result of the distortion of their thinking to support capitalism, and also a result of their alienation from their fellow-humans.) Perhaps more important, socialists emphasize that in a socialist system, it must be the people who control the government and its decisions, so that it is the people who decide in what ways to limit each others' freedom. In this regard, Marx is reminiscent of Rousseau on the question of freedom.

(iii) An argument given by St. Thomas Aquinas, whose ethical system is similar to Aristotle's, is that any good done by a violent revolution is outweighed by the harm done by the violence of the revolution itself, at least as a general rule. Obviously, Marx could respond simply that this empirical claim on Aquinas's part is just untrue. If it were true, hardly any wars could ever be justified for any reason whatever, because it could equally well be argued that wars in general inflict more harm in terms of actual human suffering than the amount of difference they make to the benefits of the people involved. Not even a war of self-defense could be justified on this reasoning—and this would contradict Aquinas's own theory that there *can* be "just wars." This is an important issue among Marxists, because many Catholic priests in exploited underdeveloped countries are now engaging in revolutionary activities.

(iv) Is it not realistic to acknowledge that Utopia cannot be completely achieved, that we can only come more or less close to achieving it, that some injustice will continually crop up and we will continue to have to fight it in ways peculiar to the particular situation at hand? If so, then perhaps people must always live in a continuing tension between capitalist exploitation and social progress. This does not mean that we should not strive toward as much social change as possible, but simply that all human development and enjoyment of life should not be postponed until "after the revolution."

(v) Is there not a vicious circle between the claims that (a) people cannot develop their rational and creative potential until after the revolution, and (b) the revolution cannot take place, or at least cannot be a true socialist revolution, until people become rational enough to embrace socialism? As the recent philosopher Maurice Merleau-Ponty says, the ruling class before and after a revolution usually tend to have more in common with each other than either of them does with the people.

Chapter Eight
Contemporary Thinking About Justice

Questions about justice are central to social and political philosophy. In fact, the idea of justice is probably the most basic idea of social and political philosophy, because every view of what society is or what political institutions and arrangements are best or desirable has an implicit view of what is fair, just, or equitable. For example, Plato believed that justice was the rule of reason in the individual and the state. John Stuart Mill argued that justice existed in the society *Utilitarian* that achieved the greatest good for the greatest number of people. Marx argued that a just society was one where each person contributed to society according to the best of her ability, and received from society according to her need. Each of these positions about the relationship of society and the individual yield a different idea of what is just.

However, saying that ideas about society contain explicit or implicit ideas about justice does not go very far in defining what justice *is*. Consider what comes to mind when you hear the word "justice." Is it some idea of fairness or equality? Think again: what constitutes fairness or equality? Every society and economy produces goods and services that people desire. But how are such goods to be distributed? Should they be distributed according to merit, talent, or power? How should society deal with those whose social position means that they do not receive a "fair" share? Moreover, what constitutes a fair share? Some people say a fair share is an equal share. But this is a very questionable assumption. Don't young children in a family often get more of their parents' time than older children who are better able to take care of themselves? Should workers in a company be paid equal amounts for performing various specialized tasks requiring different kinds and amounts of training, experience and responsibility? Should those who work hard or acquire additional training receive higher salaries?

Moreover, there are senses of the word "justice" that concern other issues than mere equality. Does justice permit or require the imposition of the death penalty and, if so, for what offenses? Is it just to permit legalized abortions? When is it just to go to war? Questions about justice are not as simple as they seem at first glance.

While each person would have an opinion about each of these questions, what reasons might be offered to support the positions?

A concern for fairness starts very early in our development as humans. On the one hand, we have intuitions or feelings about what we think is just or fair in particular situations. On the other hand, closer examination often shows that such feelings often are vague, ambiguous, and difficult to express in way that transcends particular situations or interests. Yet most people feel that justice concerns "receiving what is one's own" and historically justice has always been closely associated with the ideas of desert, equality and fairness. Thus people typically affirm that rewards and punishments are justly distributed if they go to those who deserve them. However, sometimes "the just thing" is not getting what one deserves but what exhibits care and compassion for concrete persons caught in circumstances not of their own making. Sometimes we affirm that justice demands strict impartiality, but often a strictly impartial decision appears to lead to consequences that seem unfair, unmerited, or demeaning. For example, few parents aim at strict impartiality when seeking to do the best thing for their children. Even judges recognize from time to time that the strict application of the law as written does not address the heart of the legal problem before them. In spite of the ambiguity in our ideas and feelings about justice, most of us are sure that we want others to treat us justly, so we expect some measure of equity from institutions such as work and government. We expect justice from others and usually aim to be just ourselves.

While people often disagree about what justice *is*, there are some things that we agree it *is not*. Justice is not the imposition of might over right or, as we might more accurately say, a just society is not one that serves the interests of the powerful or the officials of the state. Justice is not a matter of mere self-interest or adherence to social rules to avoid punishment. Most people have been in a situation where sacrificing an individual interest to a social or common good seemed to be the "right" thing to do. And, while every society has views about what is just, society's views about justice expressed in principles, rules, or laws do not mean they *are* just. If that were true, then justice would only be a matter of what a society believes is just. So figuring out what is just would mean merely reading off the correct answer from society's rules, laws, conventions, and principles. However, examples abound of laws or social practices that people have later judged to be unjust, as for example, slavery, the oppression of women, the exclusion of minorities or the socially disadvantaged from participating in some or all of society's institutions.

One way of understanding justice is that it is a social virtue or excellence. It is a necessary virtue of individuals in their interactions with others, and the principal virtue of social institutions. Just as individuals can show desirable qualities such as integrity, charity and loyalty, so a society can also be more or less economically prosperous, efficient, charitable, humanly cultivated, free, and so on. Still, what qualities do or should characterize a just state or social institution? How are such qualities assured or cultivated? Is justice universal–independent of–actual contexts? Or do contexts determine what justice is?

1. What Are Justice Theories?

(Justice theories ask and try to answer questions such as the ones just discussed about justice and the relationship of individuals to the institutions of society) In this sense, they are explanations of what justice is and how people might achieve the qualities of justice in society. (Every theory of justice holds that society should enhance our efficiency, permit our talents to flourish, and make us more secure.) Every theory of justice seeks to explain how to do this and why certain actions, policies, or laws are just and others are not. Thus, where theories differ, or even contradict each other, is in the terms and relations each regards as essential to defining and explaining what justice is.

For example, some theories start with the individual and the relationship of individuals to the institutions of society to argue that individuals have basic, universal *rights,* the preservation of which is essential to just institutions. Others begin with the view that persons are embedded in particular societies and cultures with particular views of *the good* and a *good life,* and then argue that justice consists of the habits (or virtues) that sustain the conditions of social living that are necessary for individuals to pursue their vision of a good life. Yet other arguments by-pass the issues of rights or the good and argue that justice means the efficient operations of fundamental social functions such as the economy or the mechanisms of "public choice" or some similar institution.

There are certain expectations of adequate justice theories. As explanations, they must be consistent, comprehensive and systematic. Such explanations should offer principles or standards to guide decision-making in concrete contexts; that is, they should be workable—some would say "realist," practical and achievable. Finally, they should be rationally defensible, which includes not only offering reasons to support their conclusions, but also addressing objections that might be offered that cast doubt on their conclusions.

According to John Rawls, perhaps one of the most influential recent theorists, "Justice is the first virtue of social institutions, as truth is of systems of thought" (Rawls 1971, 3). Some late twentieth century thinkers will contest the claim that "truth" or "justice" are epistemologically or morally meaningful. Still. in so far as any "talking about justice" is meaningful and not nonsense, it is rational; and rational discourse, even if it denies the possibility of certain kinds of rationality, must be defensible, based on adequate reason. Thus, justice theories are a kind of conversation about fundamental issues of social living. They are not merely opinions or contending perspectives.

Language for thinking about justice. There is no agreed upon definition of what justice is. However, talk about justice over the last 2,000 years has yielded some useful language for talking about justice. First, justice talk involves issues of *fairness, equality, merit, desert, interest,* and *equity.* These terms, while related, do not mean the same thing. For example, suppose your are a member of a student group assigned to complete a project. One student works hard and does most of the work. Two students do very little. They watch television. When the presentation is made, all three students receive the same (i.e., "equal") grade. Is it fair? If you are like most students, you will say "no," because all students receiving the same grade does not seem *equitable.* Each should be treated the same (evaluated according to their contribution) and not just receive an equal outcome (the same grade). Thus, the student doing the work, we might reason, "deserves" or "merits" a higher grade. The students who watched television deserve or merit a lower grade compared to the student who did the work. This outcome, it might be argued, would be "fair" or equitable to all students even if it is not equal or the same for every student.

What this example shows us is that terms like *merit, desert, fairness, equality* and *equity* are *normative* terms. This means that there are judgments made according to some standard. Using them correctly requires making value judgments. All justice theories will agree that thinking about justice requires making value judgments. Where they differ, however, is what the standard or criterion of such judgments is. So "justice-thinking" involves our reasoning about what is good, valuable, worthwhile, or what should or should not be done or, we might say, about the basic *principles* that should direct social living.

The distinction between rules and principles can be drawn in this way: *Rules* are specific norms (standards) that either guide or constrain behavior or thought. For example, "Do not steal" is a rule, as is "One ought not to steal," or "Stealing is [morally] wrong." *Principles,* on the other hand, might be regarded as generalizations that ground the specific rules. Thus, the principle "One ought to respect the property of people" grounds, so to speak, many different rules like "Do not steal," "One should not destroy what belongs to others," "Employers should not withhold an employee's wages without legal cause," and many others besides. The line between rules and principles is often very fine and often may be unimportant for our purposes. What is important to note is that rules and principles express in language the idea (or sense) of *obligation,* necessity, duty, responsibility, or a strong form of "oughtness" with regard to actions.

Duties and obligations are considered to be more binding than other kinds of "ought" statements. For example, we may say that someone ought to be more polite or ought to give more money to charitable organizations, but these statements by themselves do not necessarily imply that these people have a *duty* or *obligation* to behave in these ways. By contrast, when we say that people are obligated not to murder other people, we are making a stronger statement than other "ought" statements entail, and we assume that the obligation not to murder people outweighs or "trumps" other kinds of ought claims.

While it is easy to recognize the sense of obligation expressed by rules and principles, one can legitimately wonder whether the obligation expressed is justified or warranted and on what grounds it is, if it is. To consider the legitimacy of obligation, we often refer to *values*. Thus it might be argued that one ought to respect the property of others *because* people have an absolute dignity. This claim expresses the value of persons as persons. Many thinkers regard the dignity of persons is an intrinsic value. An *intrinsic value*, as noted earlier, is something that is desired or valued for its own sake or as an end in itself. On the other hand, an *extrinsic* or *instrumental value* is something that is desired or valued because it leads to realizing another value—a means toward an end. Thus, money, on most accounts, is an extrinsic value, a means to higher values such as survival, a comfortable life, and the like. The idea of value expresses what is desirable or what "should be." So rules, principles and obligation are related to values, and values are the ultimate justification for rules, principles, and obligation. We might express this as follows: rules and principles express the sense of obligation (to act or to refrain from acting in certain ways) imposed on us by the values we choose and enact.

One way of thinking about justice theory is that it seeks to explain what obligations are required by certain fundamental values—like freedom or equality—and the ways in which these obligations are best expressed as principles and rules to guide conduct or behavior. While this process is not as simple as it appears in this description, all justice theories use the language of rules, principles, obligation and value.

Some thinkers, however, do not use the term "value," but instead use "the *good*" or "the good life." This tradition goes back to Aristotle. "The good" on this account means whatever is valued. Superficially, there is little difference between the terms "value" and "the good." Both mean "worth" or "that which is desirable." So is there any real difference? The word "value" appeared first in the seventeenth century to refer to monetary worth. In the eighteenth century, when economics was assuming more and more importance in thinking about society and politics, the word "value" gradually replaced "the good" to refer to what was worthwhile, esteemed, prized, desired, or highly regarded, though "the good" retained more of a moral connotation than "value." (Thus, a "good person" is one who is morally admirable, while a "valuable person" emphasizes a person's practical usefulness.) In most cases, "value" and "the good" are synonyms. But it is still important to be careful, in that "value" often emphasizes the subjective quality of something being valued by someone. Many writers, especially those who build on Aristotle, intentionally use the term "the good" to emphasize the objective qualities of the good as something that is good or valuable whether or not many people actually value it.

This difference is at the heart of the "rights-good" debate that separates liberal justice theorist from the "communitarian" justice theories that will be discussed below. Communitarians often argue that notions of "the good" or "the good life" precede rights. Liberal theorists often argue that "rights" trump "the good." More on that later.

"Rights" in the strongest sense are *warranted* or *justified* claims to another person's consideration, protection, or action. "Rights" language generally means that others "owe" one acknowledgment and respect of the right for its own sake. Consequently, rights imply a corresponding *duty*. If one person claims a right that another must or ought to respect, it makes sense to say that the other person has a duty to acknowledge and respect that right. For example, if you have a right to your property, as some justice theorists claim, then I have a duty (or obligation) not to steal, damage, or use the property without permission, or in any other way fail to respect that right. Obviously, rights-talk starts to blend with other normative terms such as rule, principle, law, and value.

One of the major controversies about rights is whether rights are *natural* or *conventional*. John Locke, for example, believed that rights such as life, liberty, and property were natural or innate. David Hume, on the other hand, believed that rights were conventions conceded by society through government. The term "human rights" usually refers to natural rather than conventional rights.

"Entitlement" is another word often associated with rights-talk, especially where rights are regarded as social conventions. Obviously, if a person has a right, then he or she is justified or entitled to claim the benefits of that right. So, for example, a worker is entitled to his or her wages. An employer is not entitled to withhold or use for another purpose workers' wages or benefits. The idea of entitlement incorporates the idea of what people are owed by virtue of their relationship to institutions, organizations, and social processes. How these basic terms are used and related is a large part of what distinguishes justice theories from each other. It also frames the disagreements among them.

A common distinction is made in "justice-thinking" among retributive (or desert-based) justice, distributive justice (equitable allocation of benefits and burdens), and commutative (exchange) justice. *Retributive justice* covers that which is due to a person as punishment for bad behavior or reward for good behavior, not for purposes of achieving some outcome such as deterrence of crime, but simply because of what a person morally "deserves." *Distributive justice* concerns what is due to ourselves and others by way of equitable spreading of benefits and costs of social living—fair distribution of all types opportunities, resources, and burdens in a society. *Commutative justice* deals with what constitutes a fair exchange of goods. More recently, distributive and commutative justice have collapsed into a concern for *social justice*. Social justice concerns questions about the allocation of goods, power, opportunities, access to decision-making, fundamental respect among people, and the basic structures of society. In other words, social justice tends to provide an explanation of who gets how much of what good(s) and how often. This chapter and the next one will focus on contemporary conversations about justice in this enlarged sense of social justice, although these conversations about justice also have implications for the more classical categories.

Mapping the contemporary conversations about justice Contemporary debates about justice are complex and often contradictory; however, we can organize the different views into two basic sets of positions. One set, typified by John Rawls and Jürgen Habermas, can be described as *universalist, impartialist,* or *tradition-independent.* This set of theories argues that the principles of justice are independent of particular contexts, and would remain valid regardless of whether many people believe they are valid. They are universal in the sense that they are meant to apply to any and all contexts. A justice theory, these theorists believe, offers systematic procedures—consistently applied rules—for achieving "just" states or ends. As the product of universal reason, such principles transcend particular questions about what is just in particular contexts or situations in which justice is at issue, and instead they offer an *impartial set of rules* or procedures for determining what is just.

For example, if there are reasons why denial of basic rights to women is unjust, then those same reasons will imply that this denial of rights is equally unjust in all contexts, even those where women's basic rights traditionally have been denied. In this sense, a justice theory is said to offer the criteria or standards to judge the justice or injustice in particular cases. This position is often called the "rights tradition" because its thinking about justice aims at securing basic, fundamental rights and along with that, of course, justifying when and how social institutions may use their coercive power to command obedience or compliance to law, policies, and the like.

We have spoken so far of the "impartial" or "universalist" position, represented by Rawls and Habermas. But there is also another tradition within the field of justice theory. This alternative position, typified by Alasdair MacIntyre and Michael Sandel, affirms that thinking about justice is always tradition- or context-dependent. According to these "contextualist" thinkers, the liberal or rights-based ideal of a set of universal, impartial procedures for adjudicating particular policies, programs, social institutions, or political associations is an unrealistic ideal because our notions of what is good or valuable, and thus what is to be desired, are shaped by the particular communities and societies—or traditions—in which people live. Such thinkers criticize *tradition-independent* positions, such as Rawls' theory, for being too abstract and insensitive to the way traditions contain specific concepts of the good; they already presuppose an idea of a good life that enters into the understanding of what kind of life and goods are to be desired, and already contains traditional ways of dealing with questions of justice. Traditions—meanings and values that inform concrete ways of life—affect the way people think about what is good and bad, valuable and worthless, or just and unjust.

On this account, questions about justice arise in concrete contexts, and the standards or criteria for a just resolution of the question are likewise concrete and particular. So, on this view, thinking about justice is always *tradition-dependent,* meaning that every notion of the good is embedded in a tradition that is "self-informing"; thus these theorists hold that no notion of the good exists independently of particular traditions. In a way, the tradition supplies the basic rules for thinking about justice—or even, as MacIntyre claims, rationality itself.

Many positions in this tradition can also be classified as *"communitarian"* positions, because of their emphasis on the central significance of concrete human communities for our ideals of justice. This group of thinkers generally regards justice as aiming at a common or shared good rather than at universal rights. While the community's idea of the good will usually contain some respect for certain kinds of rights, the rights are valid only because the overall idea of the good life in that community calls for them to be respected. They are not valid independent of the community's judgments, but rather depend on its judgments for their foundation.

This renewed conversation about the foundation of justice that started in the twentieth century is built on the heritage of the eighteenth century, when Western political institutions were freeing themselves from political absolutism and ecclesiastical authoritarianism; this was a time when the idea of "rights"—what institutions (especially governments) owe to their citizens—was first clearly articulated. Addressing the balance between freedom and coercion, or between liberty and institutional intrusion into the life of citizens, remains a prominent feature of contemporary debates about justice.

A more recent set of contributions to contemporary thinking about justice comes from feminist theorists. These new theories do not fit neatly onto the map of positions just outlined. Feminist theorists have criticized liberal justice theories like Rawls' as arguing for a rational impartiality that is impossible to achieve. Susan Okin, for example, argues that Rawls systematically overlooks the importance of "gendered social relations" to the formation of our feeling of self-esteem, which is one of Rawls' primary social goods. Others, like Carol Gilligan (1982), Nel Noddings (1989), Virginia Held (1989), Margaret Walker (1992), and Sarah Hoagland (1988, 1992), argue that the rights language of liberal justice theories systematically excludes the moral voice of women, and is biased in favor of masculine "justice-reasoning." For this reason, they also criticize tradition-dependent positions because many "traditions" are sexist, gender-biased, or patriarchical. So feminist philosophy, while a new voice in the conversation, is a serious challenge to both liberal and communitarian theories.

Obviously, a brief overview of these positions cannot go very far toward settling the issues. We need to take a closer look at the justifying arguments for the alternative positions. Moreover, a grasp of the basic landscape of contemporary theories can serve as a reminder that conceptions of justice carry us back to basic questions about the nature of human beings, the self, and our relationship to others in common cooperative projects.

2. Setting the Scene: Justice as Fairness Secured by Rational Consent

John Rawls (1921 - 2002) wrote two important and influential books which reflect the evolution of his thinking about justice: *A Theory of Justice* (1971/1999) and *Political Liberalism* (1993). The first of these two books is already recognized as one of the most significant philosophical books of the twentieth century. It has influenced the thinking of philosophers, political scientists, economists and lawyers. Rawls' justice theory is a contemporary version of *social contract* theory and so is sometimes called modern *contractarianism*. It is the baseline for contemporary discussions about justice. We shall see later, however, that Rawls later modified many aspects of his position in response to criticisms and changing times.

In *A Theory of Justice*, as we briefly summarized in an earlier chapter, Rawls argues that in the *"original position,"* a group of rational and impartial people can establish a mutually beneficial principle of justice as the foundation for regulating all rights, duties, power, and wealth. As we explained earlier, the "original position" can be defined as the position that a set of initial social-contract bargainers would be in if none of them had any knowledge as to which position they personally might occupy in the resulting social structure. This idea that people in such a position would bargain in a rational way in their attempts to work out the most mutually advantageous contract that they possibly could is an assumption about human nature—that is, about how people will act because of what they are like. Given this assumption about human nature, Rawls attempts to show that basic rights and liberties are founded on mutually beneficial agreements that members of society make among themselves. Thus, the fundamental principles of justice are those to which "free and rational" persons *would* agree *if* they were in an "original position" of perfect equality. Rawls characterizes his project as being one that "generalizes and carries to a higher level of abstractions the familiar theory of the social contract as found, say, in Locke, Rousseau, and Kant" (Rawls 1971, 11)—a conception of justice to which people in a hypothetical equal bargaining position would agree to. "The choice which all rational men would make in this hypothetical situation of equal liberty . . . determines the principles of justice" (Rawls 1971, 12).

However, people are not in and cannot create a situation of perfect equality. To overcome the problem of bias and a lack of objectivity, Rawls uses a *thought-experiment*. A thought-experiment is a philosophical tool to test a hypothesis that we cannot test experimentally the way a scientist might in a laboratory. Rawls' hypothesis is that, if people could choose the principles to direct social decisions, they would rationally favor a decision principle that would distribute goods with the minimum degree of inequality necessary for social cooperation and the maximum degree of freedom for individual action.

Imagine, he says, the origin of human society as if it were a game. The first thing people (the players) have to do is to choose what kind of society to live in and the rules that they will live by. In making these basic choices, no "player" in the game knows in what position he or she will start the game. This includes not knowing what advantages or disadvantages he or she might have or what the outcome of the game will be. This original starting point where one is choosing how one will start occurs, on Rawls' account, behind a *veil of ignorance*. Behind this veil of ignorance, no one knows anything about him or herself, nothing of his or her natural abilities, or position in society. This includes no knowledge about the player's sex, race, nationality, culture, education, or individual tastes. All individuals are simply rational, free, and morally equal beings.

The idea of the original position is to set up a fair procedure so that any principles agreed to will be just. The aim is to use the notion of pure *procedural justice* as a basis of theory. Somehow we must nullify the effects of specific contingencies which put people at odds and tempt them to exploit social and natural circumstances to their own advantage. In order to do this, Rawls assumes that the parties are situated behind a veil of ignorance. They do not know how the various alternatives will affect their own particular case, and they are obliged to evaluate principles solely on the basis of general considerations.

> It is assumed, then, that . . . no one knows his place in society, his class position or social status; nor . . . his fortune in the distribution of natural assets and abilities, his intelligence and strength, and the like. Nor, again, does anyone know his conception of the good, the particulars of his rational plan of life, or even the special features of his psychology such as his aversion to risk or liability to optimism or pessimism. . . . The persons in the original position have no information as to which generation they belong to in part because questions of social justice arise between generations as well as within them, for example, the question of the appropriate rate of capital saving and of the conversation of natural resources and the environment. . . . They must choose principles the consequences of which they are prepared to live with whatever generation they turn out to belong to. . . . No one knows his situation in society nor his natural assets, and therefore no one is in a position to tailor principles to his advantage (Rawls 1971, 136-140).

From this condition of ignorance, what each player is trying to do is to choose the "best conditions" for maximizing the possibility of a good (positive, favorable) outcome for him or herself. All we can take for granted is that each person wants to achieve the best outcome possible for him or herself and that no player has any particular interest in the outcome of others. Rawls calls this *"disinterest,"* meaning that the interests of others do not enter our calculations of what kind of society would be best. The effect of these restrictions on knowledge is to render Rawls' parties (the players) strictly equal.

This position *is not to be confused with egoism*. The players are not "selfish," because the original position does not offer any opportunity for others to fare worse than themselves, and when all else is equal, they might very well prefer to see everyone happy, insofar as possible. However, this motivation does not enter into their calculation of what the best way to distribute opportunities, resources, and burdens will turn out to be; for that purpose, each bargainer, with equal bargaining power, must work for the best outcome for him or herself within the context of reaching an agreement about the ultimate shape of the social contract. In this situation, then, the principles of justice favored by one player will be the same as the principles of justice favored by any other player.

One feature of justice as fairness is to think of the parties in the initial situation as rational and mutually disinterested. This does not mean that the parties are egoists; that is, individuals with only certain kinds of interests, say wealth, prestige, and domination. But they are conceived as not taking an interest in one another's interests.

There are other things of a general nature that we know in a "real world," too. First, there will be competition as well as cooperation, and this cooperation is beneficial because it will increase the goods to be distributed. Second, competition and the moderate scarcity of desirable *primary social goods*—such as rights and liberties, powers and opportunities, income and wealth, and the basis of self-respect—means that questions about justice (fairness) in the distribution of goods and benefits will be an issue. Third, every player in the game will try to maximize his or her share of the primary goods of life as much as possible. Moreover, each person will try to fit together the best means to reach desired ends in a rational and coherent way. In other words, on Rawls' account, each person is a *rational self-interest maximizer* who attempts to acquire goods in a situation where there is a wide variety in the natural distribution of natural assets and abilities and significant differences of sex, race, and culture that will distinguish groups of people from each other. Each person expects everyone else to act the same way to maximize his or her interests in the same situation. "This condition is to ensure the integrity of the agreement made in the original position . . . [It] does not mean . . . the parties apply some particular conception of justice. . . . it means that the parties can rely on each other to understand and to act in accordance with whatever principles are finally agreed to" (Rawls 1971, 145).

Given this hypothetical situation, Rawls argues that each person as a rational agent would choose two things: maximum liberty, and the greatest possible amount of desirable primary goods *that can be equitably divided.* He formulates these choices as two principles that direct any subsequent social relationship and arrangements expressed as rights, rules, laws, social policies, or entitlements. The first principle is formulated as follows:

> **The Principle of Liberty:** Each person is to have an equal right to the most extensive basic liberty compatible with similar liberty for others.

The second is

> **The Principle of Difference:** Social and economic inequalities are to be arranged so that they are both: (a) reasonably expected to be to everyone's advantage and (b) attached to positions and offices open to all.

Further, when the two principles conflict, reason directs us to defer to a third principle governing the relationship of the two. That is, the principles are in a serial (or lexical) order. Liberty can be restricted only for the sake of liberty, and not for the sake of economic or other social gains (Rawls 1971, 132).

The principle of liberty affirms that each person would want conditions of maximum liberty or freedom because a rational person would want the maximum sphere of action to realize his or her life plan or valuable goals. The principle also affirms that everyone must have an equal share of such freedom.

However, even if every person is morally equal, in the "real world" significant differences among individuals (ability, skills, cultural and intellectual gifts, race, gender, or basic situational advantages) lead to social and economic inequalities under conditions of liberty. Thus, no rational person would want a system of rules that could not be *changed* if it is advantageous to everyone to do so.

The difference principle allows certain kinds of inequalities, as long as such inequalities meet the two conditions: (1) equal opportunity or access to position or office, and (2) the inequality is to everyone's advantage. What the principle of difference affirms is that a rational person operating without bias would want a system in which there is the greatest equal division of goods because we want to "start" the game with as good a position as possible. However, a rational personal would not want a completely equal distribution of goods and opportunities, because then there would be no incentive to work hard or improve.

To maximize our chances, we will always agree to an equal-share starting point. So, to chose less than perfect equality would not be rational. However, since we all want as much of the desirable goods as possible (and not simply an equal share), we may agree to some inequality, if the effect of the unequal division of goods means that there will be *more goods for all,* especially for those who might be the most disadvantaged once the veil of ignorance is lifted. Rawls affirms: "Social and economic inequalities, for example inequalities of wealth and authority, are just only if they result in compensating benefits for everyone, and in particular for the least advantaged members of society" (Rawls 1971, 132). So, on Rawls' account, choosing a *somewhat* unequal division of goods is still a rational choice, because competition tends to *increase the total amount of goods to be distributed.* But at the same time, any rational reflector must take account of the possibility that we might find ourselves among the disadvantaged; we will therefore prefer a rule insisting that any inequalities must be *to the advantage of all,* particularly the disadvantaged.

Rawls calls this strategy the **maximin rule.** This rule is borrowed from theories about how to make business decisions under conditions of risk. The maximin rule is one among many rules that investors follow in trying to balance risks against possible gains that go with those risks; it stipulates that people in the original position would choose in such a way as to "maximize the minimum outcome," that is, to make the *worst possible* outcome (the outcome for the lowest position in society) as painless as possible.

The choice of the maximin strategy is simple to understand. Suppose I am the original bargaining position. I do not know who I will be in society, nor what kind of society I may be in when the veil of ignorance is lifted. With no way of calculating my chances of being among the least advantaged, it is reasonable to avoid the worst possible situation by protecting the position of the least advantaged person. Thus, a rational agent will accept inequalities of distributions of desirable goods as long as such inequalities not only increase the total amount of benefits, but also work to the advantage of the least advantaged members of society. But an inequality that benefits the already well-to-do at the expense of the least advantaged would not be chosen from the standpoint of the original position. In other words, a rational agent will try to avoid the worst possible result by maximizing the minimum.

Still, how might *inequality* actually *improve everyone's* outcomes? This is easy to understand. Suppose there were five pin-makers, each earning $ 5000 from their labor. Suppose further that one worker has a special ability to do a particularly difficult job quickly. By paying this worker an extra $1000, the workers can accelerate the process and make all the workers more productive. In this way, the workers could produce more pins and so increase the total income to be distributed among them. Consider the following schemes:

	Scheme 1	Scheme 2	Scheme 2 six months later
Worker #1	5000.00	6000.00	6500.00
Worker #2	5000.00	4750.00	5500.00
Worker #3	5000.00	4750.00	5500.00
Worker #4	5000.00	4750.00	5500.00
Worker #5	5000.00	4750.00	5500.00
Total	25,000.00	25,000.00	27500.00

In the scheme represented in the first column, payments are equally distributed and so are just, since no one has any more than the others and all share the labor. In the second scheme, payments are no longer equal because each worker's income is reduced to pay the skilled worker more, in order to accelerate the production of pins. By producing more pins for sale, income increases, so after a period of six months there are more "goods" to distribute. Allowing the *inequality* of the initial payments is still a *fair* agreement, on Rawls' account, because production increases and everyone benefits from the increased production by receiving increased benefits as shown in the final scheme in the third column. Everyone benefits, and no one is less well off than before. It is fair or just because it meets the demands of the principle of difference under the maximin strategy.

One criticism of Rawls' justice theory occurs precisely at this point. In a "real" world, does increased production translate into equally shared benefits based on the idea that benefits of inequality must benefit those who are the least advantaged? Empirically, this does not seem to be true. Generally, benefits of increased production are distributed *unequally* because those with power are able to demand a greater share of valuable social goods. For example, the skilled worker might ask for a greater share and threaten to stop working unless he receives it. Since the other workers' increased income depends on the skilled worker's contribution, they may be willing to give him the greater share, reasoning that they are still better off than they were before. However, the skilled worker's percentage of income relative to the other workers continues to grow, and to grow at a rate faster than the income of the unskilled workers.

In a later work, *Political Liberalism* (1993), Rawls tries further to clarify some of these questions. He sees his theory not so much as trying to prove what justice really is, but rather to show that rational bargainers in an original position *would agree* to see justice in a certain way. This means that there is no need to defend the thesis (as he seemed to do in *A Theory of Justice*) that a certain distribution system is the most fair one possible, and that it is possible to compute mathematically what this distribution system would be like by using game theory. What the game theory should be applied to, he now says, is merely the question as to what kinds of political institutions and procedures are the best ones to decide such questions. Thus he emphasizes that the requirements of justice tend to center primarily around *procedural justice*. The person in the original position would not want to set in stone specific policies on specific political issues, if instead it is possible merely to set up political procedures for resolving all such issues when the occasion should arise.

In our earlier example about whether U.S. citizens "tacitly consented" to fight in the Viet Nam War when they were drafted for service, Rawls believes that the rational bargainer would not need to agree with the war in order for the war to be legitimate. The rational bargainer in the original position would only need to agree that certain *procedures* are the best ones by which to arrive at decisions about going to war in general—for example, that only the legislature has the power to declare war, and that certain legal rules will restrain the way they go about waging the war. If those procedures were then the ones used to decide to make war in Viet

Nam, or anywhere else, then indirectly, citizens have "tacitly consented" to serve as stipulated in the procedural arrangements.

To understand how Rawls gets to his basic position about justice, as well as the criticism of it, we have to take a detour to understand something about power and social relationships which anticipates issues that will loom large later. "Power" has several overlapping meanings: influence, authority, control, domination. These meanings are not completely interchangeable. To say that the President of the United States has influence on the making of laws does not mean the same thing as to say that he dominates the making of laws. The first is a true claim. The second is usually false. Yet each claim implies that the one who has influence or one who has dominance has *power*.

What seems common to both notions of power is that power rests in a concrete relationship. This relationship might be a relationship to others, as in domination, or over some process or a state of affairs, as in influence. However, what is common to both ideas is that "power" is the capacity to act. So, every person possesses some measure of power insofar as we are self-directed and able to act on decisions that we make. When that capacity to decide and act is restricted or curtailed in some way, we are most apt to say of ourselves that we do not have or have lost power. So the meaning of power seems to be the capacity to make and act on decisions—especially those decisions that affect ourselves. However, our capacity to make decisions about things that affect ourselves can be limited by others making decisions *for* us, or by circumstances limiting the *range* of choices, or by the limited *resources* that affect an individual's ability to change such circumstances. Each of these factors limits our autonomy or ability to direct our own lives in the direction we desire.

Another aspect of power is the capacity to join with others to act. So, even though our power may be limited as individuals, membership in a group often increases our power. Consequently, groups are often able to act in way to adjust the rules or expectations to the benefit of the members of the group. This is generally what we mean when we speak of "social power."

People, either as individuals or as collectives that have power, are able intentionally and unintentionally to shape the "rules" of the game to their benefit, even if only by arguing to preserve the status quo. As long as the status quo disfavors certain individuals or groups relative to other individuals or groups, then those less favored are always "playing the game" under a handicap—not unlike someone on crutches trying to run a race. We might argue that everyone has an equal chance to run as long as we do not restrict anyone from running, but our capacity to run is not identical.

The same thing is true about our relative social positions. No matter how we arrange the rules of the game, some people are better players than others, often for reasons not within their own control, and consequently some are always playing under a handicap. What Rawls' theory of justice is trying to do is to find an impartial *procedure* or set of *rules for making rules* to adjust the rules of the social-economic game so that there are no unfair advantages at the starting line, particularly when such advantages continue to grow with each turn in the game (for example, with each generation's accumulation of wealth in a family).

Rawls recognizes that "outcomes" in the social game are never equal and will never be. The problem is to justify such inequalities when they do occur and to redress those that cannot be justified, thus ruling them out of play. What Rawls does is remove certain kinds of inequalities based on an unequal distribution of power (economic, gender, social class, etc.) from the table.

However, Rawls may not be completely successful in this strategy, because it depends on an agent's willingness to minimize the risk of things turning out to his or her disadvantage. Minimizing risk, Rawls says, is the rational thing to do. However, why should it be rational to minimize risk rather than to maximize the chance of gain? It is as reasonable to imagine that a person might be willing to take a risk on an unequal distribution of benefits—that is, to gamble his future—in exchange for a so-so possibility of a greater advantage later. For example, a person in the original position *may prefer* to try her chance with a society of four wealthy capitalists and one poor idler to a society of five middle class clerks.

Another criticism of the theory concerns the veil of ignorance. No one ever makes any choices in complete ignorance—as Rawls' own thought-experiment acknowledges—yet Rawls' conditions of knowledge under the veil of ignorance constitute the basic equipment of a rational agent, and these conditions seem somewhat arbitrary. Could a person, even if he were willing, think away his wealth, talent, skills, or social advantages, and at the same time retain the notion of competition and better or worse positions? "Better" and "worse" are evaluative terms and so require some standard or notion of comparison. So critics charge that, in order to make *any* decisions, even within the original position, a person must already have contextualized ideas about what constitutes a good life, what activities have value, etc.—all items of knowledge that Rawls would need to deny to the person in the original position, in order to ensure impartiality. Moreover, even if the choice in the original position could be a completely impartial one, there is no way to get from an actual society to the concept of society that Rawls represents as the ideal. This criticism argues that Rawls' theory fails on the basis of practicality and workability.

Finally, other critics argue that Rawls' theory runs contrary to our moral intuition that a notion of merit or *moral desert* does play a key role in our understanding of what is fair or just. Go back to the example in which two students profit or benefit from the work of a third. This "free-rider" effect is often a result of the rational choice for self-interest maximization, where time and leisure are as much values or desirable goods as are such goods as grades or money.

In spite of the criticism that has been leveled at Rawls' theory of justice, it has several strengths. First, it removes justice from a recognition of one's own particular self-interest. While our desire for goods is self-interested, Rawls' theory does not require an ability to spell out specifically what those interests are. While it is true that we know that we have an interest in outcomes, Rawls' argument assumes only that our fundamental or basic interest is in producing the best outcome possible, and it does not depend on specific knowledge of what our particular interests are. Second, the theory includes an explicit concern for the procedures (rules, norms, social practices) by which benefit and advantage is determined in any society. The principles of justice are impartial. Third, Rawls provides support for the advocacy of the "rights" of the least advantaged to be treated fairly. And fourth, it provides a basis on which the disadvantaged can demand recognition of their rights.

That said, we also have to recognize that Rawls' theory has some very specific weaknesses. First, the difference principle assumes that we can easily identify who the least advantaged are. This usually means using economic criteria—power and wealth. But are power and wealth the only measures of disadvantage? One form of disadvantage is being excluded from full social participation. For example, the Jewish community, one of the richest communities in the United States, has often been victimized by subtle exclusion from full social participation. While Rawls would argue that "social participation" is a "primary social good," participation is not as measurable as economic criteria are.

Second, the anthropology underwriting Rawls' "rational agent" assumes a "flat" or one-dimensional view of human being and society. He assumes, for example, that humans always rationally calculate what is to their advantage or disadvantage in economic—or at least material—terms. However, human motivation is more complex, and addressing some inequities may require a greater altruism and human concern than an appeal to individual rights based on social duties. Don't those who claim rights have corresponding duties too? That is, do we have a social obligation (as individuals) to participate and contribute to the good that our cooperative efforts have created? Correlatively, many argue that Rawlsian rights create a disadvantage to those who are inventive, industrious, enterprising, and motivated to succeed. If their innovation and creativity disadvantage others by comparison, then what they create must be, according to the Rawlsian principle, redistributed to at least the partial advantage of others.

Third, Rawls' position assumes a radical individualism in which "goods" are determined by desire, and thus any good is truly good as long as its acquisition and use is procedurally "fair." But if "the good" is individually determined, how do we have a basis for distinguishing real from apparent goods—for example, distinguishing a "drug" economy from one with real productive capacity in terms of the human good?

Rawls' rights theory is a significant improvement over a merely utilitarian notion of justice in the distribution of the benefits of social living. It provides a means of redressing imbalances, especially when these occur over relatively long periods of time. It provides an impartial standard of judgment that seems to be associated with our basic intuition of what is fair. However, the objections to

Rawls' theory have led to other ways of viewing what justice requires. One of the earliest to appear and which continues with wide acceptance, particularly in practical politics, is Robert Nozick's notion of justice as entitlement or merit.

3. Justice as Receiving What I Am Entitled To

The first objection to Rawls' justice theory was from Robert Nozick (1938 - 2001), who was a colleague of Rawls at Harvard University. In *Anarchy, State and Utopia* (1974), Nozick questions the primacy of Rawls' basic principle of arranging social inequalities so that they are to the greatest benefit of the least advantaged.

For Rawls, justice arises out of the basic structure of society that assures that social schemes are fair—especially to those who are least advantaged. As we have noted, this view is not without its problems, especially in practice. Rawls' theory requires that the state through its administrative and judicial institutions redress imbalances of fairness. In other words, the State is morally required to intervene in the lives of institutions and citizens to insure the conditions of justice. However, one might argue, as did Adam Smith and others in the eighteenth and nineteenth centuries, that the best governed are the least governed. Nozick takes this position by arguing for the notion of a "minimal state" whose moral duty is to ensure only "entitlement" rights, not to guarantee any purported right to distributive justice.

By *"entitlement,"* Nozick means the protection of goods and rights that people possess, and have not acquired by illegitimate means—i.e., means that are determined to be illegitimate by a reasonable set of criteria for legitimate acquisition and transfer of goods, which will be spelled out later. With regard to rights, people do not need to acquire them, and cannot transfer them, since they are possessed simply because these rights ought to be enjoyed by every human being regardless of circumstances. For example, we all have the right to expect others not to steal our legitimate property—property that we obtained by reputable means; thus the State has an obligation to protect that right. But if the basic rights are all negative rights—that is, the expectation that others will *not* violate our life, liberty and property—then the government cannot violate any of those rights either. It follows that the state cannot violate legitimate property rights in order to provide less important benefits to others. And this leads to Nozick's claim that the State should be minimal.

> The minimal state is the most extensive state that can be justified. Any state more extensive violates people's rights. Yet many persons have put forth reasons purporting to justify a more extensive state. . . . I shall focus upon those generally acknowledged to be most weighty and influential . . . [such as] the claim that a more extensive state is justified, because necessary (or the best instrument) to achieve distributive justice (Nozick 1974, 149).

Nozick offers the following assertion based on his view of the relationship of the individual to the State.

Individuals have rights, and there are things that no person or group may do to them (without violating their rights). So strong and far reaching are these rights that they raise the question of what, if anything, the state and its officials may do. How much room do individual rights leave for the state?.

. . . A minimal state, limited to the narrow functions of protection against force, theft, fraud, enforcement of contracts, and so on, is justified; . . . any more extensive state will violate persons' rights not to be forced to do certain things, and is unjustified; . . . the minimal state may not use its coercive apparatus for the purpose of getting some citizens to aid others, or in order to prohibit activities to people for their own good or protection (Nozick 1974, ix).

For Nozick, the sole purpose of the state is to assure "peace and security of person." This means that the function of the state is negative—to keep its members from harming one another, with harm being understood not merely in physical terms but also in terms of interference with people's choices about their own lives.

Nozick's version of this libertarian thesis can be framed as an argument: every person has natural negative rights to life, liberty, and property. The possession of rights does not depend upon the consent of others. They are essential moral constituents of personhood. Thus, no one (including the State) can justifiably harm, restrict the freedom of, or take legitimate property away from another without that person's consent. Such rights are general rights that apply universally.

1. Rights have correlative duties; therefore, everyone has the duty not to interfere with a right holder's life, liberty, and property.

2. Each person possesses these rights simply in virtue of his humanity. She does not have to do anything to obtain this moral protection. That is, every person is entitled to the protection of his/her right from injury by others.

So social living consists of *negative rights* and *positive entitlements*. No person has the right to harm another. Likewise, every person is entitled to protection and security of person and property. So, no one has the right to harm us or to take what rightfully belongs to us. That is, we are *entitled to* freedom from the harm that would result if what is ours were taken from us by anyone—including, and especially, by the State. Nozick's theory of justice is based on two central concepts: personal freedom and property.

The key to this view that justice means receiving and disposing of what "rightfully belongs to us" is understanding what "rightfully belongs to us" means.

For Nozick, society is composed of individuals whose lives are made up of many exchanges and transactions that they are free to pursue or not to pursue. The important idea underlying Nozick's view of the State and what is fair is his emphasis on "free choice"—the capacity of each adult human being to enter into agreements and transactions with others without coercion. But along with choice goes responsibility for both the gains and the losses.

> What each person gets, he gets from others who give to him in exchange for something, or as a gift. In a free society, diverse persons control different resources, and new holdings arise out of the voluntary exchanges and actions of persons. . . . The total result is the product of many individual decisions which the different individuals involved are entitled to make (Nozick 1974, 149).

On this view, any exchange is "fair" as long as it meets two conditions.

a. The original acquisitions of holdings are legitimate *(the Principle of Justice in Acquisition)*, and

b. the exchange is legitimate (the *Principle of Justice in Transfer*).

If the world were wholly just, the following inductive definition would exhaustively cover the subject of justice in holdings: a person who acquires a holding in accordance with the principles of justice in acquisition is entitled to that holding.

1. A person who acquires a holding in accordance with the principles of justice in transfer, from someone else entitled to the holding, is entitled to the holding.

2. No one is entitled to a holding except by (repeated) applications of 1.

Thus, according to Nozick, the complete principles of distributive justice would say simply that a distribution is just if everyone is entitled to the holdings they possess under the distribution.

> A distribution is just if it arises from another just distribution by legitimate means. The legitimate means of moving from one distribution to another are specified by the principles of justice in transfer. The legitimate "first moves" are specified by the principle of justice in acquisition. Whatever arises from a just situation by just steps is itself just. . . .
> . . . The existence of past injustices (previous violations of the first two principles of justice in holdings) raises the third major topic under justice holdings: the rectification of injustice in holdings. If past injustice has shaped present holdings in various ways . . . then what now, if anything, ought to be

done to rectify these injustices? . . . How far back must one go in wiping clean the historical slate of injustices? . . . The principle of rectification presumably will make use of its best estimate of . . . information about what would have occurred . . . if the injustice had not taken place (Nozick, 1974, 151-153).

Thus Nozick understands justice within a context of exchange of valued goods among people. Usually this is understood as economic exchanges, but such exchanges may also include non-material goods such as friendship, trust, freedom, and the like. However, economic exchanges are the easiest to understand.

Obviously, if people are involved in economic exchanges, there are going to be unequal outcomes. Some people will, in the end, have more than others. However, "having more," along with all the benefits that accrue to having more, is not unjust if the exchange that led to the gain meets the two conditions of just holdings and just exchange.

It works this way: Imagine that you are a member a society of thirty people. Suppose each member of the society had $5.00 that they gave to David Robinson to watch him play basketball. As a result, twenty-nine people now have nothing, and David Robinson now has $150.00. On Nozick's account, there is nothing unjust about this arrangement, because we could have chosen to save our $ 5.00, spend part of it and save some, or spend it elsewhere. Robinson, Nozick would say, *merits* or *is entitled to* his reward for being able to play basketball in a culture that "values" basketball.

Of course, if there were only this one transaction in our society, we would have nothing and Robinson everything. But a society is made up of thousands of routine daily transactions. For example, to have the energy to play basketball, David Robinson must eat. So he pays Jones for dinner ($10.00). To prepare the dinner, Jones pays Rodriguez for beef and vegetables from his farm ($6.00), and Rodriguez needs help to plant, harvest and transport his goods, so he hires Cortez ($1.50). Thus the initial $150.00 is further distributed as follows.

Robinson	$140.00
Jones	4.00
Rodriguez	4.50
Cortez	1.50

Again, these exchanges are fair on Nozick's account because they meet the two conditions of just exchange. Granted, Jones, Rodriguez, and Cortez receive less than Robinson. But they could have chosen not to work for him, or could have worked for others.

Continuing, let us also suppose that Robinson can only play basketball once a week, but he has to eat every day. Then we get the following distribution of exchanges:

Robinson $70.00
Jones   28.00
Rodriguez   31.50
Cortez   10.50

What this fanciful story shows is that the flow of goods in the transactions is constantly readjusting. What each person has of social goods readjusts with each transaction. People retain their entitlement to what they have, to use as they decide or choose. What a person has depends on the choices each person makes. Moreover, according to Nozick, there ought not to be any effort to provide special benefits to the "least" advantaged. In Nozick's scheme, no one is "disadvantaged" if he or she retains the power to choose. In fact any effort to equalize the holdings of each person is actually a "disadvantage" to those who make "good" choices and increase their holdings relative to the holdings of others. Nozick offers this maxim to summarize his view: "From each according to what he chooses to do, to each according to what he makes for himself (perhaps with the contracted aid of others) . . ." (Nozick 1974, 153).

Many people find Nozick's libertarian argument plausible. However, it is not without significant weaknesses. First, it assumes that all transactions are fair as long as they are entered into freely. However, the empirical data of the market operation suggest that they are not. For example, suppose that Robinson, instead of playing basketball, actually has a corner on the salt market, salt being necessary for human survival. Everyone does not need to watch basketball, but everyone needs to have salt in their diet. Robinson can use his advantage to benefit more from every transaction in the cycle of exchange.

Second, the market model that underwrites the theory of just exchange assumes that every dollar is the same as every other dollar. This is a common-sense position—$ 5.00 = $ 5.00 whether we spend the five dollars on food or basketball. But the meaning of a dollar spent for food (when one is hungry) is greater (more important, imperative) than a dollar spent to watch basketball. In economic terms there is less *"elasticity"* in the demand for essential goods than nonessential goods. Those who are economically disadvantaged are likely to endure disadvantaged, if endurable, conditions in order to provide for essential goods—more likely than those who are economially better off. Arguing in the face of economic necessity that a person has a choice about whether to work or not under a particular set of conditions is disingenuous. The quantified value of economic exchanges under certain conditions varies according to a person's relative economic vulnerability (see Ellis 1998).

Third, Nozick's entitlements break the connections between economics and other spheres of human living—social, political, and cultural relations. Applying his model of justice to questions of economic justice is relatively easy because economic values are easily quantifiable. However, social, political and cultural values are easily distorted and systematically undervalued when quantified.

Fourth, there is a problem analogous to one of the problems of Rawls' theory: Nozick's theory requires a strong sense of the individual as a bundle of self-interested desires. That is, it assumes that the person already comes equipped with a conception of the good, and that the questions of justice only concern themselves with how to distribute these pre-established goods for people. The criticism, then, as with Rawls' theory, is that what justice consists of may be derivative *from* a person's overall conception of the good life, rather than independent of it.

That said, it must also be acknowledged that Nozick's theory has strengths. First, Nozick has an important insight. Goods are not simply distributed. They are also produced, and those who produce goods have a stake or entitlement to benefit from their production. Justice is not simply a matter of the "greatest good for the most" or concern for the most disadvantaged. It also concerns what we are entitled to because our labor and effort adds to the stock of the social good.

Second, Nozick's position is "inserted" into history. Rawls' contract theory begins with an "ideal," *a-historical* original position. Nozick short-cuts by insisting that consideration of justice must begin with "what is held" at a particular time in history (not some ideal time). Many of our justice issues concern the "injustice" of present holdings whose origin lies in the past, and whose "choices" are not *our* choices or the choices we would have made (because we recognize the injustice)—for example, wealth that results from past slavery or from theft committed by our ancestors.

But is it realistic (or just) to require present generations to bear the penalty for past injustice? We can trace African-American poverty to slavery and to the disadvantages of emancipation, which were not conditions that any contemporary individuals imposed. So the justice discussion is not the justice or fairness of the "present" historical system, but of past injustice. Can the present "correct" the past? And if the present is used to correct the past, to what extent does the correction represent an injustice toward the present? And how long (especially if we are all self-interested actors) does the correction have to continue in order to redress the past?

4. An Interlude: The Idea of Liberals and Conservatives

The conversation between Rawls and Nozick may sound familiar because it resonates with political positions that we typify as "liberal" and "conservative." Political liberals promote public policies that intervene to address perceived problems. Political conservatives, on the other hand, believe that government's role in addressing problems is minimal. They argue that the normal operation of institutions, especially economic institutions, is the best way to address problems.

A good example is the Congressional debate in late 2001 about how to stimulate the economy. One problem of unemployment is the loss of health care benefits. President Bush proposed to address the problem with legislation that would require employers to make health care benefits available to laid-off workers. Laid-off workers who buy health care benefits would receive tax credits. Senate Democrats, on the other hand, proposed legislation for the government to provide health care benefits directly. The Bush proposal was regarded as the conservative option because it minimized government's intrusion into the economy. The democratic proposal was regarded as the liberal option because it supported direct government involvement via taxes in the provision of benefits, in order to allow for a more just distribution of an essentially Rawlsian type.

Most of our thinking about politics and justice is not through the careful critical focus of philosophy. People think little about fundamental questions about the nature of society and political associations. The discourse is a practical discourse of "common sense" or "everyday" politics. In this common sense discourse, we are prone to use labels to identify the political commitments of parties and individuals. The labels "liberal" and "conservative" are two of the most common. Thus many people label Bill Clinton as a political liberal, meaning that he favors policies and programs of government intervention to assure the conditions of justice and fairness. People identify George W. Bush as a political conservative, meaning that he tends to favor policies and programs that reduce the intervention of the State. Likewise, there is some temptation to identify Rawls' position as justifying liberal policies and programs, and Nozick's position as providing justification for conservative policies and programs. However, it is useful to straighten out this language, because "labels," while they simplify thinking about complex issues, often mask important distinctions.

"Classical liberalism," associated with thinkers like John Locke, Adam Smith, and John Stuart Mill, emphasized the idea that *liberty* is a very important value, and should not be limited unless there is some justifiable and important reason to do so. In its early versions, it therefore held that the best government is the one that governs the least—that is, the one whose intrusion into the private lives of citizens is minimal. This was grounded on a commitment to maximize the range of individual freedom and autonomy, particularly regarding the individual's relationship to the State and public institutions. Thus the commitment to securing rights to free speech, assembly, association, press, religion, and the like was paramount. These fundamental rights were, on Locke's account, "inalienable," both in the sense that they are intrinsic to moral personality and in the sense that they are unforfeitable. The role of government was to secure these rights from unjustified interference by others, including intrusion by the State and by public institutions.

After the mid-nineteenth century, however, subtle changes in political practices started to accrue as liberals came to see the necessity to pass laws to aid those who could not provide for themselves—the old, the sick, the unemployed, the unprotected young. They did not abandon the principle that government should not infringe liberty without important justifications, but they came to believe that there *are* many important justifications for infringing liberty. This "Great Shift" from "liberal to liberality' started slowly, but moved rapidly from the 1880s onward.

Along with the shift in citizens' expectations of government was a change in the vocabulary of political identification. In the United States, "liberals" are those who favor regulation and government intervention into "social problems" through State-mandated policies and programs. "Conservatives," who ironically are also heirs of "classical liberalism," support policies that minimize government action in favor of economic and market solutions to social problems. So, when George W. Bush invaded Iraq, he stated that his purpose was to establish a "liberal democracy" in Iraq, even though in the liberal-versus-conservative spectrum Bush is very conservative. The word "liberal" has come to have two different meanings. All Western democracies are "liberal democracies," because they all believe that no one should agree to give up their liberty to the government unless for a very important reason. But "liberals" (in the more partisan political sense) are those who recognize more legitimate justifications for state intervention than conservatives do.

In Europe, however, the word "liberal" is usually applied to those who retain a commitment to free markets. Generally, Europeans use the labels "right" and "left" to distinguish the difference between those who favor a minimalist state from those who favor an activist political state—the political positions that Americans would classify as "liberal" and "conservative."

Both Rawls and Nozick are "classical liberals." Both affirm the primary value of freedom. Both assume that human beings rationally fit means to ends to secure whatever on their own view is "good" or "better" among many possible social goods. Thus individuals are self-determining and autonomous, and respect for their self-determination and autonomy is the basis of the moral justification of every form of social association, including the State. Rational consent grounds all legitimate political association and all institutions, including the State; to this extent, consent is voluntary.

The differences between Rawls and Nozick are conceptual ones, having to do with what the rationale is for a just political system, and with differing concepts of justice. There may well be more on which they agree than on which they disagree. It is in this light that the political nomenclature of "liberal" and "conservative," "left" and "right" is best interpreted. Certainly, there is a danger failing to understand the members of one's own political family if one makes this language the basis of ideology. This has often happened in recent American political rhetoric. There is not so much that separates the political programs of liberals and conservatives, compared with other programs that would ground government power in religion, or loyalty to a warlord, or belief in a specific conception of the good life to the exclusion of other conceptions.

This is not to say that the differences between Rawls and Nozick do not matter. They certainly do, because each leads to a different set of consequences for the nature of the State. However, unless we understand what unites them, it becomes more difficult to understand other positions whose criticism of the "classical liberal" position which they both share is far more radical than Nozick's criticism of Rawls.

Insofar as Rawls provided a renewal of philosophical thinking about political association and justice, his work remains a baseline or touchstone for contemporary justice theories. As we have seen, his position was almost immediately challenged by Nozick, whom some regard as providing a conservative-friendly response. However, Nozick's was not the only voice raised. There are the voices of feminism, critical theory or discourse ethics, communitarianism, and personalism. Our next chapter will begin to consider these more substantially dissenting voices by discussing Susan Okin's "liberal-friendly" criticisms of Rawls.

Chapter Nine
Contemporary Thinking About Justice—
The Feminist Critique

Since most forms of feminist philosophy view feminism as essentially political, it is not surprising that feminist thinking about justice has likewise been extensive, and has in some measure reshaped traditional thinking about justice. Broadly, feminists start from the view that social and political structures in society discriminate against women. In light of this point, feminist political philosophy aims to show how traditional political philosophy is implicated in this discrimination.

However, from this basic core of agreement, feminist thinking covers a wide diversity of arguments and positions. Some direct their work to showing how the resources of political philosophy may be employed in the service of women; this type of feminist thinking proposes ways in which traditional views of justice might be employed to remove the injustice of discrimination. Other feminists argue that traditional theories are so implicated in the structures of power and domination that they must be discarded completely. Correlatively, we can divide feminist discussions of contemporary justice theory into two camps: some feminists argue for the consistent application of concepts like justice to women, in the way these concepts have traditionally been employed. Others argue for extensive revision of those concepts, or even a radical replacement of them.

1. Opening a Conversation on Gender and Justice

Susan Moller Okin, in an important book in the feminist canon, *Justice, Gender and the Family* (1989), illustrates the position of feminists who affirm the basic value of traditional theory while offering a corrective critique of it. She starts by taking up one of the central facets of Rawls' theory—the knowledge that must be included in the *"original position"*—to argue that liberal theory provides a tool to deal with unjust social relations. However, this liberal theory of justice systematically discriminates against women by virtue of its silence on women, gender, and forms of gender-based injustice. That is, the person in the original position must not know his or her gender, and therefore may lack real understanding of what it is like to be of a particular gender. For this reason, liberal theory must be modified in order to count women into its framework of thinking about justice. Thus Okin is not arguing that traditional liberal theory should be abandoned, only modified. The modifications she proposes are substantial and substantive, particularly in terms of implications for deriving principles of justice from Rawls' original position.

Okin's argument starts with a broad, close analysis of the place of women, family, and family relationships in existing social institutions. These institutions systematically discriminate against women and in turn legitimate their bias as being due to natural differences between men and women. Consequently, these institutions are inherently unjust. This injustice contradicts the liberal commitment to maximizing the liberty and equality of all parties to the implicit social contract. Describing and addressing this inherent self-contradiction of liberal theory is the substance of Okin's critique of liberalism.

> We as a society . . . don't believe people should be constrained by innate differences from being able to achieve desired positions of influence or to improve their well-being. . . . Yet substantial inequalities between sexes still exist. . . In economic terms, full-time working women (after some very recent improvement) earn on average 71 percent of the earnings of full-time working men. One-half of poor and three-fifths of chronically poor households with dependent children are maintained by a single female parent. The poverty rate for elderly women is nearly twice that for elderly men. . . . Underlying and intertwining with all these inequalities is the unequal distribution of unpaid labor in the family (Okin 1989, 3-4).

Okin's opening position is easy to concede because of the large number of inequalities based on gender in American society. They constitute blatant examples of injustice. However, this is not Okin's point. She uses this fact to support a simple claim. If gender-based inequality is a significant feature of actual social relations, then gender is relevant to any discussion of justice.

If Okin merely meant that inequalities based on gender are unjust or unfair, there would be no problem with incorporating this claim into a traditional liberal account of justice such as Rawls' theory; such inequalities can be addressed wholly adequately within a traditional liberal account. However, Okin means more than this. She is arguing that a failure to consider the significance of gender and gender-structured social relationships for deliberation in the Rawlsian "original position" means a perpetuation of gender-based discrimination that fundamentally distorts the deliberative process of the Rawls type of social contract. "There is strikingly little indication, throughout most of *A Theory of Justice*, that the modern liberal society to which the principles of justices are to be applied is deeply and pervasively gender-structured" (Okin 1989, 89).

Okin's problem with Rawls' original position is this: Rawls believes that gender is one of the characteristics—like skills, talent, or social position—that are morally relevant contingencies hidden behind the *"veil of ignorance."* Accordingly, anything that is hidden by the veil of ignorance must be passed over in silence. Yet knowledge that society is gender-structured by custom and law, and the consequence of that fact, would be part of the body of general knowledge about society possessed by each party in the original position. In other words, a person in Rawls' original position would have no knowledge of what our gender will be when the veil is lifted, even though we know that we will be gendered and that gender will matter. What Okin wonders is: given the significance of the fact that societies are gender-structured and that gender matters, how can Rawls remain silent about the issue of gender? Okin traces the problem to the impartialist, universalist moral and political tradition that grounds Rawls' liberal tradition. The choices of the person in the original position are tacitly meant to refer to a choice someone would make as a "head of household"; and traditionally, the person in this position has been male. Thus the original position, despite its attempt at impartiality, is gender-biased after all.

Okin insists that gender is not a generalization about human beings, like talent, skills, or social position, but has a specific social and cultural location: the family or household that shapes the moral motivation and attitudes toward gender and social positioning based on gender. Gender is not a natural endowment distributed more or less randomly. It is a social construction that carries with it specific roles, duties, and social benefits and disadvantages. This view draws Okin to the substance of her critique of Rawls. The "parties" in the original position are choosing "as heads of households." This seemingly gender-neutral term is, Okin argues, ambiguous because "heads of households" are usually presumed to be male (Okin 1989, 91-92). This assumption is not in itself sexist, according to Okin, because "the head of a family need not necessarily, of course, be a man." Yet, " the very fact that . . . the term 'female-headed household' is used *only* in reference to households without resident adult males implies the assumption that any present male takes precedence over a female as the household or family head" (Okin 1989, 92). The problem, then, is that Rawls and other hypothetical social contract theorists assume a "public/domestic dichotomy" and therefore assent to the conventional view that "life within the family and relations between the sexes are not properly regarded as part of the subject matter of a theory of social justice" (Okin 1989, 92).

Okin's critique of the implicit sexism of impartialist positions must be taken seriously for two reasons. First, family relationships are partial, not impartial. Indeed, *"partiality"*—responding to the member whose need is nearest—is part of the family's strength. However, the very partiality of role relations within families sets up a social differentiation of care-givers and care-receivers that is by its very nature asymmetrical and which cannot therefore be regulated by impartial rules.

Second, what goes on in the family is often insulated from criticism because it is regarded as being in the *private sphere,* which enjoys special privilege from pubic scrutiny—yet family dynamics have public consequences. This is the key part of several feminist critiques of Rawls. For example, until recently, cases of domestic violence were not regarded as criminal assault, but domestic disputes, and hence treated with less seriousness than assaults. While this perspective has changed somewhat, familial institutions are not generally regarded as open to public scrutiny or criticism because family relations are private. Yet, on any account, the family is the primary formative factor of personality and basic attitudes that people bring to their public activity. Family shapes the values of self-respect, self-worth, and personal identity through which people manage—or fail to manage—the demands social living.

It follows that justice in the family and for each member of the family is an issue that requires redress *prior to* the original position. If the moral habits of family relationships shape the moral thinking of individuals and lead to the view that gender matters, then the rationality of rational agents is, in effect, gendered. Gender cannot be treated as a feature of human existence, like a talent or skills. It is fundamentally part of the way people think. Since rationality is what parties carry behind the veil of ignorance, the quality of moral thinking will affect agreement on the principles of justice. How people think about justice cannot be separated from the family experience. Thus, family experience cannot be separated from justice. "Yet, remarkably, major contemporary theorists of justice have almost without exception . . . bypassed the fact that the society to which their theories are supposed to pertain is heavily and deeply affected by gender, and faces difficult issues of justice stemming from its gendered past and present assumptions" (Okin 1989, 8).

Okin criticizes Rawls and other liberal theorists on the ground that these theories are not realistic representations of the terms and relations constitutive of society, and therefore they distort the principles of justice as derived from the original position. This does not mean that Okin disagrees with liberal theorists like Rawls that we ought to seek the conditions of liberty and equality. What she does contest are practices that ignore the family as the ground of moral relations. She challenges whether Rawls has adequately discerned the role of family, and perhaps other sub-political social institutions, as a condition for the achieving a perfectly "neutral" standpoint. Thus rather than minimizing the potential distorting influence of injustice perpetuated by family as an institution prior to the formulation of the principles of justice, liberal theories treat injustice against women and children as occasions of injustice to be addressed according to the principles of justice. It is as if a physician were to permit a disease to continue in order to demonstrate the efficacy of the cure for the disease.

Okin's strategy for theoretical correction is to press on what she views as the internal inconsistency of Rawls' theory. Families nurture the basic moral sensitivity that makes reflection from the original position possible. Yet the injustice of family institutions makes nurturing the reciprocity and role-reversal required for an undistorted rationality in the original position difficult, if not impossible. Without the virtues learned within the family, and by observing gender relations in the family, children would not develop enough empathic skills to imagine what it is like to be in a position other than one's own—skills that are presupposed in the "original position." Moreover,

> If gendered families are *not* just, but are, rather, a relic of caste or feudal societies in which roles, responsibilities, and resources are distributed not in accordance with the two principles of justice but in accordance with innate differences that are imbued with enormous social significance, then Rawls' whole structure would seem to be built on shaky ground. . . .How, in hierarchal families in which sex roles are rigidly assigned, are we to learn, as Rawls' theory of moral development requires us, to "put ourselves in another's place and find out what we would do in his position"? . . . How will children of both sexes come to develop a sufficiently similar and well-rounded moral psychology to enable them to engage in the kind of deliberation about justice that is exemplified in the original position? (Okin 1989, 99-100)

Okin's position has weight. The family is a *basic institution* in which justice must be rendered within the Rawlsian scheme, because it is a foundational social institution. This claim is grounded on two justifications. First, most people live in families, so their opportunities in life are affected by how families are structured. Second, families are where equality or inequality between men and women is learned, and thus they are a training ground of citizenship. Since opportunities for individuals are affected by one's place in the family, Okin proposes that these positions be equalized through social reforms such as day care, family leave, and an equal division of income so as to avoid economic dependence of either partner in a marriage.

What Okin offers in her account are correctives to Rawls' oversights that led him to fail to consider the standpoint of women in gendered society on our understanding of justice.

> Rawls says that self-respect or self-esteem is "perhaps the most important primary good," and that "the parties in the original position would wish to avoid at almost any cost the social conditions that undermine [it]." Good early physical and especially psychological nurturance in a favorable setting is essential for a child to develop self-respect or self-esteem. . . . and high-quality, subsidized child care facilities to supplement [good parenting] would surely be fundamental requirements of a just society (Okin 1989, 107).

Although Okin argues that women make a specific and identifiable contribution to one of Rawls' *primary social goods*, we should also remember that such contributions can be shared by both men and women. Thus, the principles of justice that Rawls arrives at are, she says, inconsistent with gender-structured society and with traditional family roles. If Rawls' principle of just distribution is assumed to include gender issues, then "Gender, with its ascriptive designation of positions and expectations of behavior in accordance with the inborn characteristics of sex, could no longer form a legitimate part of the social structure, whether inside or outside the family" (Okin 1989, 103).

In other words, not only are women systematically ignored by the theory, but basic family relationships and structures are incompatible with the theory. The contributions of the family, usually maintained by women, and women's direct contributions to self-respect or self-esteem, are undervalued and ignored. Rawls affirms that these are the important primary goods that parties in the original position would avoid undermining, at all cost. Studies show that self-worth is nurtured within the family in the early years of a child's life. If self-worth is in fact among the most important primary goods, failure to consider justice and the family does seem to be a significant oversight. Further, such a failure is inconsistent with the crucial import of the family—and female caring in the family—that nurtures one of the basic social goods, if not the most important one of all. Thus Okin is correct that silence regarding gender and relationships in gendered societies is not just problematic, but it crucially distorts the society in which justice is sought and the frameworks in which rational choices are made.

While a Rawlsian account could take into account the standpoint of women, this is not sufficient. What needs to be recognized is that the gendered relations of actual existing society are barriers to genuinely impartial justice. What is needed is knowledge of the real effect of gender on human relationships and institutions and acknowledgment that gender is a central justice issue. A start is to insist that the veil of ignorance hides from participants their sex as well as their other particular characteristics, talents, and circumstances. If we choose principles to guide the development of just institutions, policies and programs in society without being aware of our sex (in the original position), we would be careful to assure complete social and economic equality between the sexes. Also we would protect both sexes from the need to serve or provide for the pleasure of the other. More important, perhaps, we would emphasize the importance of boys and girls growing up with equal respect for themselves and equal expectations for their personal development. In the end, Okin concludes that our current gender structure is incompatible with the attainment of social justice. The complete development of a nonsexist, fully human theory of society requires the disappearance, or at least the minimization, of gender. "The family is the lynchpin of gender, reproducing it from one generation to the next. . . . Family life as typically practiced in our society is not just, either to women or to children. Moreover, it is not conducive to the rearing of citizens with a strong sense of justice" (Okin 1989, 170).

Okin argues for complete, real *equality* between genders. This value is prioritized in her proposals for social reform. Such reform is directed to changing ways of thinking about gender and gender-structured relationships. Since gender is a *social construction*, we can change ways of thinking about gender by changing social relations. If a society promotes full equality between sexes, then the principles of justice will privilege real equality in relationships rather than merely redressing inequality as it happens to occur.

However, it must be remembered that traditional liberal theory privileges two values, not one: equality *and* freedom. Some critics of Okin, like Drucilla Cornell, argue that her proposals for social reform are an unwarranted limitation on the freedom of the individual in favor of State interference in family structures in an attempt to assure equality. Okin's answer is that justice is not always achieved by the maximization of freedom, if the individuals involved are in unequal positions to start with. In the end, what is required is absolute equality. With regard to Rawls' "veil of ignorance" that must be assumed in the original position, Okin points out:

> We may, once the veil of ignorance is lifted, find ourselves feminist men or feminist women whose conception of the good life includes the minimization of social differentiation between the sexes. Or we may find ourselves traditionalist men or women, whose conception of the good life, for religious or other reasons, is bound up in an adherence to the conventional division of labor between the sexes. The challenge is to arrive at and apply principles of justice having to do with the family and the division of labor between the sexes that can satisfy these vastly disparate points of view and the many that fall between (Okin 1989, 174).

Thus Okin believes that equality will promote a pluralism of values that will extend freedom. Also, we must keep in mind that Okin does not intend to produce a complete theory of justice. Okin's argument that gender plays a significant role in our notions of justice provides a substantial point of critique of "impartialist" theories of justice. Yet one wonders what a feminist theory of justice *would* be. Okin does not offer one. She believes we can reconfigure a liberal theory of justice to incorporate the factor of gender. What is needed is to acknowledge that social relations are gendered and so are essential, not incidental, to the formulation of the principles of justice.

Other feminist writers are not so charitable to impartialist approaches such as Rawls'. The problem is not reconfiguring liberal theory to incorporate issues of gender to address problems with gender-structured relations. What is needed is a more radical critique and a particularly feminist point of view.

2. Justice, Freedom, and the Development of Person

Drucilla Cornell, in a way similar to Susan Okin, considers one particular aspect of liberal theory—in this case, the way it takes for granted the concept of what is a "person"— in order to exploit what she sees as internal tensions and contradictions that need to be addressed in a chastened and corrected liberal theory. However, unlike Okin, Cornell comes closer to a complete theory of justice. She argues that the point of justice *is* the development of persons. This in turn requires freedom of the person.

> [W]ithout minimum conditions of individuation, we cannot effectively get the project of becoming a person off the ground. I am using the word "person " in a particular way. *Per-sona,* in Latin, means . . . what shines through a mask. . . . For a person to be able to shine through she must be able to imagine herself as a whole even if she knows that she can never truly succeed in becoming whole or in conceptually differentiating between the "mask" and the "self." The equal worth of personhood of each one of us must be legally guaranteed, at least in part, in the name of the equivalent chance to take on that project.
> A person is not something "there" on this understanding, but a possibility, an aspiration. . . . We must protect, as a legal matter of equality, the equivalent bases for this chance to transform ourselves into the individuated beings we think of as persons. . . . We cannot assume as a given that a human creature is by definition a free person. . . . The equal protection of minimum conditions of individuation can only insure that none of us is cut off from that chance of freedom (Cornell 1995, 4-5).

Cornell regards Rawlsian liberal theory as an ally in securing the three conditions of the minimum individuation to permit a human creature to become a person.

> There are three conditions that insure a minimum degree of individuation that I defend as necessary for the equivalent chance to transform ourselves into individuated beings who can participate in public and political life as equal citizens. They are as follows: 1) bodily integrity, 2) access to symbolic forms of oneself from others, and 3) the protection of the imaginary domain itself. . . . My defense of minimum conditions of individuation is in alliance with Rawls' egalitarianism as opposed to Kant's more conservative conclusions (Cornell 1995, 4-13).

Cornell's criticism of Rawls and similar liberal theorists is that they fail to consider these conditions which precede, on her account, deliberation in the original position.

> Rawls does not address the question of what conditions are necessary for us to be able to symbolically pull ourselves together to the degree that would give us an equivalent chance of becoming persons. . . . That question is "prior" to the

beginning point of a *Theory of Justice*, which postulates each one of us as a person with the two capacities [a sense of justice and a capacity for the good] needed to engage in practical reason Sex takes us back in time because it is foundational to human being. . . . The care involved in reproducing a human creature as a rudimentary self is an overwhelming task. That effort and that care performed by the primary care-giver is often "disappeared" in starting political philosophy with the assumption that we are persons from the beginning, rather than creatures whose equal worth is postulated as personhood. Asking this question facilitates the reappearance of the material not just as a function, but as a labor which actively brings us to the point of sufficient individuation after which we may undertake the struggle to become a person (Cornell 1995, 17-18).

Again, this position is similar to Okin's view. However, Cornell criticizes Okin's program of social reform as invasive of freedom. It does not secure the imaginary domain that allows individuals to grasp and understand themselves as situated and gendered beings whose life project will necessarily be gendered and for whom sex will figure into the vision of the good life. Indeed, Cornell perceptively grasps that Okin's position, which de facto defines women's condition as comparatively disadvantaged, in fact falls into the trap of devaluing the feminine. Cornell's appeal is for a psychic space, not a social space, that exists prior to the deliberation of the original position.

Feminism has at its heart the demand that women be treated as free human beings. We claim the right to be included in the moral community of persons as an initial matter. Inevitably, persons are involved in integrating, struggling with or against, reimagining or accepting their "nature" as they draw themselves together to represent who they are. Coming to terms with the meaning of our "sex" is part of this undertaking. Further, the equivalent evaluation of our sexual differences cannot be used to deny us political and legal recognition, which provides a source of meaning to us as to how we wish to live out our lives. Negative constructions that preclude this recognition stamp us as unequal and must be disallowed at the level of abstraction . . . . I am not arguing that we should cease to address issues of gender discrimination as matter of social inequality. I am arguing that if we are not equivalently evaluated as free persons as an initial matter, we will be unable to fairly correct that definite inequality; our life chances and prospects will be limited by the very definition of our inequality (Cornell 1998, 20).

It is sexual situatedness that needs to be included in and protected by the principles of justice. A community of free and equal persons, on Cornell's account, are sexual beings, whose sex and sexual expression are part of the person—the *"persona"*—which each party to the social contract envisions and struggles to achieve.

3. Feminist Theory: A Deeper Critique of Justice as Rational Consent

Both Okin and Cornell affirm the critical usefulness of a rights-based theory of justice. Accordingly, both direct their criticism to what each believes, for different reasons, is a lack of realism in theories that do not take into account the role of gender in creating just social, institutional, and political relations. In other words, traditional rights-based justice theory only needs to be corrected, not abandoned.

A deeper feminist critique rejects right-based justice theories as relevant from a woman's standpoint. All social and political structures discriminate against women. Likewise, traditional justice theory, on this account, is implicated in that discrimination because its notion of rationality is gendered. If this is so, then one must abandon traditional theories. No theory can simply be reconfigured. The fault line is too deep for that. What is required is a new start with women's ways of thinking.

This critique starts with the view that talk about justice moves in two gender-specific directions or types of thinking. One is "justice reasoning" that stresses rules, rights and universal principles based on *detached disinterest* or disinterested *rationality*. This mode of reasoning, feminists argue, is particularly a male mode or masculine voice of ethical thinking that stresses principles, rules, disinterested-ness, impartiality, and logical consistency. The second direction is *"care reasoning,"* which stresses responsibilities and relationships that depend on a sense of connected and remembered acts of caring for and being cared for by others. It is not impartial, detached, disinterested, or abstractly objective. Rather it is intersubjectively engaged, partial, and sensitive to the way particular contexts and circumstances affect what is morally appropriate.

This distinction between two ways of moral thinking can be traced to Carol Gilligan's (1936-) work in moral psychology. Gilligan and others were puzzled by a curious finding based on Lawrence Kohlberg's (1927-1987) studies in moral development. Drawing on extensive empirical studies, Kohlberg argued that ethical development occurs in three stages, moving from self-centered thinking to abstract principles:

1. In preconventional morality, people are guided in their moral decisions either by what those in power say is good or by what will satisfy some immediate need. Values are based on pleasure and pain.

2. In conventional morality, people act to please others. Moral decisions are guided by obedience, often strict, to rules, or by following traditions because people expect others to respect authority and law and order.

3. At the postconventional level, people adopt moral principles not because we are told to do so, but rather because we recognize how they promote a rational, objective, and impartial respect for human beings by emphasizing individual rights, fairness, and a sensitivity to the common good.

Other researchers using Kohlberg's protocols and methods found that most women did not develop beyond the conventional stage of moral thinking. This result held across social, class, educational, and cultural differences. On this basis, researchers concluded that women in general have a lower degree of moral development than men. This result, however, is counterintuitive, since in most cultures, including American society, women are regarded as a civilizing or "moralizing" influence as the primary moral teacher, particularly providing the earliest moral education for both boys and girls.

Gilligan, taking up this problem, hit on an obvious but overlooked fact. Kohlberg restricted his study to only males. In other words, his data set was limited to male experience. Thus, his theory of moral development was based on male moral experience. Specifically, Kohlberg's description of moral development was limited to the moral development of males reared to be independent, autonomous, and *principle-directed* moral agents. Others adopted Kohlberg's protocols and used them with other groups, including women. But these protocols were based on a specific population and yet applied to different populations—thus imposing on different populations a foreign model of moral thinking. Hosts of subsequent research projects based on Kohlberg's studies, repeated and replicated the same mistake. In other words, Gilligan believed that Kohlberg's method caused a biased opinion against women. In his "stage theory" of moral development, the male view of individual rights and rules was considered a higher stage than female point of view of morality in terms of its caring effect on human relationships.

Gilligan argued that the failure to include women in the original studies overlooked the possibility that males and females think differently about moral relationships. Gilligan aimed to correct this oversight. In her book *In A Different Voice: Psychological Theory and Women's Development* (1982), Gillian argues that in fact there are two distinct moral voices or "themes" rather than one voice being comparatively under-developed when compared to another. "[T]he failure of women to fit existing models of human growth may point to a problem with the representation, a limitation in the conception of the human condition, an omission of certain truths (Gilligan 1982, 1-2). What Gilligan means is that men and women's development, particularly their *moral development*, is different. Society teaches females to be sensitive caretakers of others, especially those in their web of relationship, even if it means violating abstract moral principals. For women, moral development consists not in becoming more abstract and less caring, but rather more sensitive to how care and compassion can be extended to more people and refined to accommodate different circumstances. Instead of thinking of ethics in terms of impersonal, abstract moral principles with right and wrong answers, women think of ethics in terms of personal moral responsibilities and conflicts that need to be resolved to maintain stable interpersonal relationships.

> Women's place in man's life cycle has been that of nurturer, caretaker, and helpmate. . . . . But while women have taken care of men, men have in their theories of psychological development, as in their economic arrangements, tended to assume or devaluate that care. When the focus on individuation and individual achievement extends into adulthood and maturity is equated with personal autonomy, concern with relationships appears as a weakness of women rather than a human strength (Gilligan 1982, 17).

Consequently, "The moral imperative that emerges repeatedly in interviews with women is an injunction to care, a responsibility to discern and alleviate the 'real and recognizable trouble' of this world. For men the moral imperative appears rather as an injunction to respect the rights of others and thus to protect from interference the rights to life and self-fulfillment" (Gilligan 1982, 100).

This position allows Gilligan to return to a central problem that critiques of liberal justice theories raise: that such theories prescind from the real contextual realities of justice issues. They abstract moral actors from the concrete exigencies that drive decision-making.

> Hypothetical dilemmas . . . are useful for the distillation and refinement of objective principles of justice and for measuring the formal logic of equality and reciprocity. However, the reconstruction of the dilemma in its contextual particularity allows the understanding of cause and consequences which engages the compassion and tolerance repeatedly noted [in women] to distinguish the moral judgments of women. Only when substance is given to the skeletal lives of hypothetical people is it possible to consider the social injustice that their moral problems may reflect and to imagine the individual suffering their occurrence (Gilligan 1982, 100).

Gilligan does not deny the usefulness of such exercises, only their completeness. A complete account of the moral landscape must also include an *ethics of responsible care* as well as an *ethics of rights and justice*.

> The morality of rights is predicated on equality and centered on the understanding of fairness, while the ethics of responsibility relies on the concept of equity, the recognition of differences in need. While the ethics of rights is a manifestation of equal respect, balancing the claims of other and self, the ethic of responsibility rests on an understanding that gives rise to compassion and care. Thus the counterpoint of identity and intimacy that marks the time between childhood and adulthood is articulated through two different moralities whose complementarity is the discovery of maturity (Gilligan 1982, 164-165).

In Gilligan's reconfigured map of the moral domain, moral development has three stages:

1. a person cares only about and for himself or herself;

2. he or she recognizes a responsibility to care for others;

3. he or she accepts the principle of care as a universal ethical criterion and acknowledges that this requires sensitivity to the different needs of individuals in different situations.

What Gilligan posits is a trajectory of moral development based on relationships that moves from an ethics of self to an ethics of care for others. On this account, the foundation of moral decision-making is context sensitive. Thus justice theories that draw on the prior moral development of participants need to be more context sensitive and less rule or principle directed. This flies in the face of the liberal commitment to impartiality as the work of universal reason. If Gilligan is correct, then moral thinking has different voices; impartial procedures reflecting a male voice would, in spite of intentions to the contrary, result in unjust results by excluding those voices tuned to a different moral vision.

Gilligan's work has been very influential and provided a basis for the deep feminist critique of justice theories. However, her work is not without its feminist critics. Christina Hoff Sommers (*The War Against Boys: How Misguided Feminism Is Harming Our Young Men,* 2001), for example, hotly contests the reliability of Gilligan's research base and thus also her conclusions. She argues that Gilligan has drawn her conclusions on insufficient data. She condemns Gilligan's use of anecdotal evidence. According to Sommers, researchers have not been able to replicate Gilligan's work, and the samples used were too small. Sommers thinks the field of gender studies needs to be put to the test of people from fields such as neuroscience and evolutionary psychology rather than education. She feels strongly that promoting an anti-male agenda hurts both males and females, nor is it helpful, she argues, for girls and women to be told that they are diminished or voiceless.

While acknowledging that this critique and debate are unsettled, we can recognize that Gilligan's contribution to the contemporary debate about justice lies precisely in showing that an abstract notion of justice distorts the meaning of justice and leads to unjust results. For example, positive law recognizes a principle of mercy and mitigating circumstances that are context dependent rather than rule dependent. We have a stronger responsibility to our own children than to children in the Third World, although to a lesser degree we have a responsibility there as well. It is also true that distorted notions of justice can lead people to lose their humanity. This is a common story in literature. It is also a common theme of feminist political theory. "The blind willingness of sacrifice of people to truth, however, has always been the danger of an ethics abstracted from life . . . It is the ethics of an adulthood that has become principled at the expense of care" (Gilligan 1982, 104-5). Later Gilligan says,

> While an ethics of justice proceeds from the premise of equality—that everyone should be treated the same—an ethics of care rests on the premise of nonviolence—that no one should be hurt. In the representation of maturity, both perspectives converge in the realization that just as inequality adversely affects both parties in an unequal relationship, so too violence is destructive for everyone involved. This dialogue between fairness and care not only provides a better understanding of the relations between the sexes but also gives rise to a more comprehensive portrayal of adult work and family relationship (Gilligan 1982,104-174).

Virginia Held, among many others, makes a similar point by saying that traditional ethical positions, like utilitarianism and rights-theory, are concerned with social organization, control, and domination. The Kantian emphasis on duty sees ethics as a matter of sorting out competing claims, in which our choices are considered matters of sacrifice and compromise rather than creations of new values, and our care for one another is legitimated only if it is authorized through the authority of reason as our duty. Consequently, they do not provide moral guidance in a real world.

> Most moral theories . . . are ideal theories, theories that attempt to construct a view of what justice or moral rights or the public good could mean in an ideal society. The foremost example in recent years is . . . Rawls. . . . The difficulty with ideal theory is that it suggests only what we ought to do in an ideal society, not what we ought to do here and now, given the very unideal societies in which we live. . . . Actual societies are the result of war, imperialism, exploitation, racism, patriarchy—the imposition of the will of the strong on those who have been overcome. Nowhere do we have a society that remotely resembles the community of free persons evoked by various ideal theories (Held 1989, 2).

By contrast, in feminist ethics, caring in the real world, not rights or duty in an ideal world, is central to morality. Doing one's moral duty, for example treating someone fairly or justly, does not mean that we should ignore the circumstances, people, or future interpersonal impact of our judgments. Instead, we must consider such things if we are to avoid the mistakes of the ethics of justice based on principles and rules.

Thus a feminist theory of justice focuses on the social structures that impede human development. Contemporary society is, on many feminists' accounts, set up to encourage competition among individuals who are self-interested. In an environment in which competition and independent self-interest are basic assumptions, masculine preferences for fairness, equality, and impartiality seem to be more appropriate. But in an environment that cultivates relationships with other people, an ethics of care and responsibility is more important than one of justice. So to foster such an ethics, promoting a social environment based not on marketplace competition or contracts between rational, self-interested economic agents, but on family relations such as those between a caretaker and a child, is important. Rita Manning provocatively puts it this way:

> I have often wondered if taking a class in moral philosophy was the best way for students to become sensitive to moral concerns. It seemed to me that a better way would be to have students work in soup kitchens or shelters for the homeless. I am convinced that taking care of my children has made me more open to moral concerns. In taking care of the hungry, homeless, and helpless, we are engaged in caring for (Manning 1992, 46).

Care theorists stress the importance of sensitivity to the entire context of choice. Such choices are not made behind a hypothetical veil of ignorance, but in full knowledge of parties, problems and particular needs. Indeed, care theorists argue that each party in the Rawlsian theory is a self-contained individual who has no relations, except as a possible head of household. Consequently, they are sharply critical of any attempt to reduce ethical choices to following rules that admit no exception. Moral rules express, or should express, the responsibility that arises from the relational roles that one takes on in society.

> My roles as mother, as teacher, as volunteer, put me in particular relationships to others. These roles require and sustain caring. My obligations to my infant children and my animals is to meet their basic needs for physical sustenance (food, shelter, clothing, health care) and for companionship and love. My obligation to my students is grounded in my roles as teacher and philosopher and their psychological needs to discover who they are and how they can live with integrity. Here I feel a connection with my students but also with teaching and philosophy. But if one of my students comes to me needing another kind of care, I may be obligated to provide it, though I may not be obligated to do it single-handedly. My response depends on my ability to care, my obligation to care for myself, and my sense of appropriateness of the need and the best way to handle it (Manning 1992, 47).

Thus, Manning's *care ethics* de-emphasizes the idea of the independent individual and instead stresses that persons exist in a web of relationships. Care ethics tries to be sensitive to the indefinitely complex system of relationships that build up in a community over time. On this account, justice is caring for the constitutive relationships of social living.

However, one can offer several cogent criticisms of an ethics of care as a justice theory. First, the implicit partialism of an ethics of care can conflict with the demands of justice. Some concrete relationships in which people, particularly women and minorities, exist are oppressive or exploitative. Should those be nurtured and preserved? Obviously, care ethics require modification to incorporate a theory of rights to guard against this possible problem that was the point of Okin's work discussed above.

Second, an ethics of care can blur the distinction between the care-giver and the persons or things cared for; that is, an ethics of care can demand self-sacrifice and invite a lack of attention to the care-giver's own needs. An exclusive identification of care and justice can lead a person to a degree of self-sacrifice that is inappropriate and ineffective. One may argue that a care-giver has a right to a personal space that puts some distance between the care-giver and the one cared for.

Third, translating caring as an attitude and value into public policy that is coherent and meaningful is difficult. As Manning and others point out "we do not live in a caring world." Indeed, many institutions and relationship systematically discourage caring. For example, in bureaucracies, the rules encourage uniformity and impartiality of decisions and limit the discretionary authority required by decision-makers to bend the rules when they are tempted to care too much for employees or clients.

Still another approach to an ethics that draws on women's experience can be found in the "maternal ethics" discussed in the work of Virginia Held and also of Sara Ruddick. They argue that a good mother-child relationship is a promising paradigm for any relationship. On their account, the self-interested, maximizing, rational agent model of Rawls' contractarianism or Nozick's libertarianism is inadequate. If the basis of social relations are human relations, then one should notice that most human connection and interaction does not take place between equally autonomous, powerful and informed adults. Rather, it occurs between unequals, such as parent-child, student-professor, professional-client, doctor-patient, and employer-worker. Therefore, a caring, although unequal, mother-child relationship provides a normative standard for the assessment of relationships that are inevitably imbalanced. Presumably, mothers have their children's best interests at heart. They try to protect and teach them, and make them socially acceptable and successful. In the process, they teach both themselves and their children to be sensitive, responsible people, aware of others' needs, and develop mutual respect.

Held goes a bit further. She argues that the family freed of its patriarchal past provides a potential model for modern political associations rather than models for managing the competition of "self-interest maximizers."

> Societies are composed of persons in relation to one another. "Personal relations are among the most effective relationships. Western liberal democratic thought has been built on the concept of the individual, seen as a theoretically isolatable entity. This entity can assert interests, have rights, and enter into contracts with other entities. But this individual is not seen as related to other individuals in inextricable or unseverable ways. This individual is assumed to be motivated

primarily by a desire to pursue his or her own interests, though he or she can recognize the need to agree to contractual restraints on the ways all persons may pursue their interests.

. . . The difficulties in building trust and cooperation and society itself on the shifting sands of self-interested individuals are extreme. Perhaps we need people to be tied together by relations of mutual concerns and caring as well as by contracts it may be in their interests to break. The relationship of mothering parent and child, hardly understandable in contractual terms, may be a more fundamental one than the relation between consenting contractors (Held 1989, 206).

Such relations, she argues, characterized by mutual concern and respect, acting as a counterpoise to self-interest and atomistic individualism, would promote socially cooperative rather than individualistically competitive values. Mutual concern and respect requires respect for the autonomy of the other that renounces the right to decide for that other what is best for him or her. This would entail an unwillingness to impose one's will on the other or even attempt to coerce another at any level.

Feminist theory has not developed a systematic justice theory. Indeed, according to some, to do so would run counter to basic feminist thinking. However, feminist theory does provide a significant critique of the implicit sexism of existing theories, and it lays the groundwork for recognizing the importance of a basically different type of alternative to traditional justice theories: the communitarian approach. In this type of theory, we can see the emphasis on the community's responsibility to nurture its members that is emphasized by the feminists, and also the idea that the *development of the person* is a project and an intrinsic value independent of and prior to distributive justice, as emphasized by Drucilla Cornell in the above discussion. Our next chapter will consider communitarian theory *per se* in some detail.

Chapter Ten
Justice As if Context Mattered:
Communitarian Theories of Justice

We saw in the last chapter that one contribution of feminist theory to justice thinking is a reminder that justice is context-sensitive. Liberal theorists do not deny this when it comes to applying the "rules" of justice. However, they appear to deny it in formulating the rules for justice. Femininists, on the other hand, argue that unless all the contexts that give rise to questions of justice are taken into account, we risk misconstruing the meaning of justice. Thus context influences the formulation of the rules. Rawls recognized this and tried to reduce the number of contextual factors that could bias a decision about the principles and procedures of justice by eliminating the influence of contextual factors in the "original position." Factors like, sex, class, talents, skills and any conception of the "good life" are hidden behind the veil of ignorance. In this way, he hoped to achieve the liberal ideals of impartiality and universality.

There is another stream of theorists who emphasize contexts because, they argue, all justice is context or *tradition-dependent.* If justice theories are explanations of the "rules" for understanding and interacting with others in particular communities, societies, and groups, then the idea of justice cannot abstract from concrete contexts. The "idea" of justice is what "rules" objectify. Therefore, we cannot separate context from talk about justice.

On this account, community is basic to context, and so *contextualists* are also known as *communitarians.* "Strong" contextualists or communitarians argue that contexts are decisive for decision-rules. Justification of normative judgments lies in the context of moral dialogue about substantive norms or values in or between traditions, not in impartial procedures. Thus, one must take context into account in the explanation of what justice *is* and in formulating decision-making rules.

To understand this group of positions, which is more varied than traditional liberal theory, you might think of a conversation. We have already been talking about justice as a kind of conversation. It is a very complex conversation concerning values and goods, rights and rules, and how people might best order their lives with others. For example, the discussion of "equal outcomes" between utilitarians and contractarians is a conversation about the meaning of equality and how to achieve it. Utilitarians, in general, emphasize that "equal" means "same" or "identical." Contractarians, on the other hand, take the view that "equal" means "equitable," "fair," or "similar." How we understand the meaning of equality shapes significantly what constitutes an "equal outcome" in any distribution of goods.

Every conversation is a transaction of meaning. The meaning of any particular conversation is dependent on its context or horizon of interpretation. For example, suppose we say "The Vikings are coming to town." The meaning of this claim would be very different were it said in tenth century Britain when invading Vikings were the scourge of everyday life than when it is uttered in twenty-first century Texas during football season. Knowing what was meant or intended by the claim requires knowing the context in which it was uttered. Or suppose you receive a letter in the mail on which the symbol "A-" appears. How you interpret the "A-," and more importantly its significance for your life plan, would be very different depending on whether the letter comes from your doctor's blood lab or your school's registrar. To understand the meaning requires knowing the context or horizon in which the meaning appears.

In a similar way, contextualists argue that the meaning of justice is always fitted into an interpretive context. This context of meaning is not about the meaning of words, but rather the meaning of values, goods and ideals of the good life. The context is quite particular and concrete. It is not *universal*, the same for everyone, nor is it *abstract*, an idea dissociated from particular examples. If this is true, then a theory of justice, as an explanation, must start from the context, not abstract from it.

1. MacIntyre's Communitarianism

One important communitarian, Alasdair MacIntyre, argues that ideas about the good, the good life, and value have their meaning only in relation to concrete contexts, and positions that abstract from these concrete contexts inevitably distort the meaning of justice. A tradition is a bit like a language that not only fixes meanings, it shapes what we can express and talk about. According to MacIntyre, thinking or reasoning about what is desirable, worthwhile, or valuable is always dependent on the tradition in which it is situated.

> I am never able to seek for the good or exercise the virtues only *qua* individual.
> . . . What the good life is for a fifth-century Athenian will not be the same as
> what it was for a medieval nun or a seventeenth-century farmer. But it is not just
> that different individuals live in different social circumstances; it is also that we

all approach our own circumstances as bearers of a particular social identity. I am someone's son or daughter. . . a citizen of this or that city, a member of this or that guild or profession. . . . Hence what is good for me has to be the good life for one who inhabits these roles. As such, I inherit from the past of my family, my city, my tribe, my nation a variety of debts, inheritances, rightful expectations, and obligations. These constitute . . . my moral starting point.

. . . This thought is likely to appear alien and even surprising from the standpoint of modern individualism. From the standpoint of individualism I am what I myself chose to be. I can always, if I wish to, put in question what are to be taken as the merely contingent social features of my existence. I may biologically be my father's son; but I cannot be held responsible for what he did unless I chose implicitly or explicitly to assume such responsibility. I may legally be a citizen of a certain country; but I cannot be held responsible for what my country does or has done unless I choose implicitly or explicitly to assume such responsibility. Such individualism is expressed by those modern Americans who deny any responsibility for the effects of slavery upon black Americans. . . . The story of my life is always embedded in the story of those communities from which I derive my identity. . . . What I am, therefore, is in key part of what I inherit, a specific past that is present o some degree in my present. I find myself part of a history and that is generally to say, whether I like it or not, whether I recognize it or not, one of the bearers of tradition (MacIntyre 1981, 220).

Just as an individual's intentions, values, frameworks of meaning, and identity are embedded in a particular history, so too is a culture or tradition. A *tradition,* the set of meanings and values that inform a concrete way of life, is a framework in which the "conversation" or "story" of particular lives take their meaning. A tradition, according to MacIntyre, is a way of thinking that provides the framework and rules of rationality, not some abstract notion of reason. Tradition attaches individuals to particular times, places, webs of relationships, values, ideas, and relations of ideas.

This concept is very different from the detached, disembodied individual of liberal theory. Remember that in Rawls' original position, the individual is separated from particular features of the self such as kinship, sex, talents, skills, and particular views of what the good life is. This is a feature of liberal theory of which communitarians are critical. Indeed, communitarians like MacIntyre argue that the liberal ideal of reason is only one tradition among several possible traditions.

On a communitarian account, values, meanings and commitments exist in shared traditions before any moral conversation about legitimacy, power, justice, or the "rules" of social association. The community frames notions of the good that form the kind of person one is becoming.

. . . What *I* particularly enjoy will of course depend upon what sort of person I am, and what sort of person I am is of course a matter of my vices and virtues .
. . . What we find generally pleasant or useful will depend on what virtues are

generally possessed and cultivated in our community . . . . Man without a culture is a myth. Our biological nature certainly places constraints on all cultural possibilities; but a man who has noting but a biological nature is a creature of whom we know nothing (MacIntyre 1981, 160-161).

MacIntyre's point is that "justice as fairness" or "impartiality" is a tradition of justice thinking that is historically and culturally located. Historically, MacIntyre has a good case on this point. The traditionally liberal view of the individual, the individual's relationship to society, and values such as freedom and autonomy took their rise in the eighteenth century. Furthermore, these views are not universal; there are historically and factually other views. What is more controversial is MacIntyre's conclusion that there is *no reason* to privilege the liberal notion of rationality over other alternatives.

> How are we do decide among the claims of rival and incompatible accounts of justice competing for our moral, social, and political allegiance? . . . It would be natural enough to attempt to reply to this question by asking which systematic account of justice we would accept if the standards by which our actions were guided were the standard of rationality. . . . Yet someone who tries to learn this at once encounters the fact that disputes about the nature of rationality in general and about practical rationality in particular are apparently as manifold and as intractable as disputes about justice (MacIntyre 1989, 2).

However, MacIntyre also uses his position to affirm that liberal rationality, including its "thin" anthropological assumptions about human nature and community, distorts the idea of justice by disembodying the individual from communities that frame the criteria of a good life. Before evaluating this conclusion, we need to understand the steps in the argument.

On the communitarian argument, society, for the most part, determines the personalities of its members and so determines, in large measure, what they want in life. If society determines what people want, then people cannot *already* know what they want in order to *enter into* a contact to help them get what they want (as if they already knew what they wanted *prior* to entering the contract). Therefore, the social contact cannot be justified on the grounds that it helps people get what they would have wanted *before entering into* the social contract. Instead, it *causes* them to want the things that they end up wanting. It is their wants, or the formation of those wants, that causes their wants to conflict. So, if what people want is determined by the community (or tradition of rationality), then the community should not just distribute what people want. It should take responsibility to produce individuals whose wants will be socially constructive rather than destructive. If a society does not take this responsibility, then it has not distributed opportunities and benefits as justly as it could have.

This argument makes two important and critical assumptions. First, the personality—the complex of wants, desires, goals, values, character, and states of mind and feeling—is socially determined. Second, personality is realized or actualized through social relationships. It is not merely mechanistically determined through the satisfaction of biologically generated desire. For example, hunger is a biological response. A steak or a bowl of oatmeal will satisfy a person's hunger and need for protein. However, whether an individual desires a steak or oatmeal is not. Preferences for steak or oatmeal are largely socially determined. Likewise, a snug hut or a mansion will provide shelter against a cold northern winter. Protection from the cold is a biological need. Preference for a hut or a mansion is determined by a host of social factors.

For communitarians, social relationships and communities have normative legitimacy because they define the "moral starting-point" of each individual life. In this sense, the traditions, practices, and conventions of communities have a moral claim on each person because the context of one's community is both "a good" *and* informative of what is good ("value-informing"). Thus every notion of justice, or the good, is framed by its particular and concrete historical location in which the idea is meaningful or intelligible. Without a concrete rather than ideal context, the just, good, or right thing to do loses its meaning.

In other words, prior to questions about which *principles* are just lies the context of a *political community* in which such questions are meaningful. The existence of a political community depends on a prior consensus of what *is* just or what constitutes the good life. So, on MacIntyre's account, bargainers in the original position can only meaningfully bargain if they enter the "original position" with the community formed values (the tradition) that have formed *them*. If this is true, then Rawls' effort to derive principles of justice prior to entry into the political community is hopelessly redundant or logically self-justifying.

On MacIntyre's account, *"practices"* ground moral reflection and action. A practice is

> any coherent and complex form of socially established cooperative human activity through which goods internal to that form of activity are realized in the course of trying to achieve the standards of excellent which are appropriate to and partially definitive of that form of activity, with the result that human powers to achieve excellence and human conceptions of the ends and goods involved are systematically extended (MacIntyre 1981, 187).

In other words, if a form of activity serves the purpose of defining standards of excellence for those who participate in that activity, then MacIntyre calls such an activity a "practice." Practices define what counts as a good outcome for those who participate in the practice. Examples of practices are farming; the arts; sciences; games; and "sustaining human community" (that is, politics). Such "practices" are a unity of practical reasoning and consist of two kinds of goods: goods that are external to the practice and goods that are internal to the practice. *External goods* are the goods of the practice for the practitioner. For example, a farmer by farming achieves economic independence, supports his family, and occupies a certain position in the community. These are all "external" goods—goods external to the practice itself, but achieved by it. External goods, especially power, fame, and wealth, when they are acquired through a practice, typically "belong to" the one who exercises the practice. Usually, external goods are such that some people have more than others. Thus, they are objects of competition. To some degree, these external goods are "earned," "merited," or deserved.

Internal goods, by contrast, are goods required in order for the practice to *be* a practice at all, and these can be acquired only by practicing the practice. For example, the idea that a competent sense of rhythm is a good thing is an idea internal to the practice of jazz. Without good rhythm, we would not be practicing jazz, but some completely different activity. Similarly, honesty is a good which is internal to the practice of accounting.

Further, internal goods, unlike external goods, are those goods whose achievement contributes to the good of the community of practice, and thus they are socially cooperative and enrich the community. For example, playing with a competent sense of rhythm contributes to a situation in which the community of jazz musicians can practice their skills; it helps to maintain the practice in general. Since accounting is a practice, accountants must compete for business, prestige, power, and reputation. Such competition, however, is *external* to the practice of accounting. Honesty, on the other hand, which is a fundamental value of accounting, is the *condition for the possibility* of the practice itself, in the same way that jazz musicians' respect for a good sense of rhythm is a condition for the possibility of the practice of jazz. An accountant with excellent accounting skills would find it difficult to "be an accountant" if her or his reputation was one of dishonesty rather than honesty. Likewise, accounting as a practice depends on each accountant to be honest as well as accurate, precise, skillful, knowledgeable and so on. The "rules or norms" or "authority" of a practice rest on its internal, not its external goods.

MacIntyre argues that the rules and principles of justice are an expression of the practices that sustain a concrete way of life or tradition, along with the virtues and habits corresponding to these principles. If this is true, then it makes sense to define "excellence" or "virtue" *in relation to* concrete communities of practice.

> A virtue, like courage, justice, or honesty, is an acquired human quality the possession and exercise of which tends to enable us to achieve those goods which are internal to the practices. . . . [The goods of a practice] can only be achieved by subordinating ourselves within the practice in our relationship to other practitioners. We have to learn to recognize what is due to whom; we have to be prepared to take whatever self-endangering risks are demanded along the way. . . . In other words we have to accept as necessary components of any practice with internal good and standards of excellence the virtues of justice, courage, and honesty. For not to accept these, to be willing to cheat . . . so far bars us from achieving the standards of excellence or the goods internal to the practice that it

renders the practice pointless except as a device for achieving external goods (MacIntyre 1981, 101).

For example, if we continuously and indiscriminately foul while playing basketball, then we are no longer playing basketball, but instead have transformed the game into something other than basketball. In order to play the game, we have to obey the rules of the game. In a similar way, what we might call the "social virtues"—justice, courage, equity, fairness, giving people their due, willingness to act at personal cost, and honesty—are not definable according to an abstract, ideal principle or set of principles, but instead are integrally tied to particular contexts related to particular kinds of social relationships. They are dependent on context.

One criticism of MacIntyre is that his position falls into ethical relativism—the position that affirms that the morally right thing to do depends on an individual or groups of individuals. However, this may be an unfair criticism. He is not arguing that morality depends on the subjective preferences of individuals or groups of individuals, but rather that moral judgments depend on the concrete contexts of existing practices. Take justice (giving what each person is due) as an example. What one owes the other in concrete contexts differs whether one is a mother correcting a child's dishonesty or a business manager correcting a dishonest employee, because the excellence intended by raising a child or managing a business differ. General principles of justice cannot encompass the difference because universalism that transcends the particular cannot accommodate the good intended by different socially embedded practices.

The notion that the "right thing to do" might vary according to the good embodied in a practice as practice by those of "good character" allows MacIntyre to recover an older notion of justice as *desert* or *merit*. Justice as desert is grounded by on the assumption that one is responsible for the outcomes or consequences because of one's effort. For example: Mark "deserved" to win the race because he trained harder than anyone else (intention). Sally "deserved" her raise because of her hard work and self-sacrifice (good will); Katy "deserved" every kindness shown her because of her humanitarian efforts.

The notion that desert forms a basis for justice is categorically rejected by Rawls, because in Rawls' view a social contract should not have the authority to regulate anyone's outcomes (for example, by "giving people what they deserve") except in ways that benefit all the parties to the contract. For the government to punish an immoral person simply because he "deserves" to be punished does not benefit the parties to the contract, whereas punishment purely for deterrence purposes does benefit them (by protecting them from crime). So, in Rawls' view, the government should have the authority to punish criminal for deterrence purposes, but not merely for purposes of moral "desert." But MacIntyre's view is different, since MacIntyre does make room for a concept of "desert" to be an integral part of the social contract. Ideas of desert are needed to constitute the practice of the community, and with not community, there is no contract.

As an example of Rawls' view on this point:

> It seems to be one of the fixed points of our considered judgments that no one deserves his place in the distribution of native endowments, any more than one deserves one's initial starting place in society. The assertion that a man deserves the superior character that enables him to make the effort to cultivate his abilities is equally problematic; for his character depends in large part upon fortunate family and social circumstances for which he can claim no credit (Rawls 1971, 104).

This judgment is one widely shared by contemporary justice theories. Yet the fact that procedural liberalism makes no room for desert is a major criticism that MacIntyre aims at Rawls and Nozick.

> The notion of desert is at home only in the context of a community whose primary bond is a shared understanding both of the good for man and of the good of that community and where individuals identify their primary interests with reference to those goods. Rawls explicitly makes it a presupposition of his view that we must therefore exclude any understanding of it that we may have from our formulation of the principles of justice. Only those goods in which everyone, whatever their view of the good life, takes an interest are to be admitted to consideration. In Nozick's argument too, the concept of community required for the notion of desert to have application is simply absent. . . .It is, from both standpoints, as though we had been shipwrecked on an uninhabited island with a group of other individuals, each of whom is a stranger to me and to all the others. . . . Not surprisingly . . . their views exclude any account of human community in which the notion of desert is in relation to contributions to the common tasks of that community in pursuing shared goals could provide a basis for judgments about virtue and injustice (MacIntyre 1981, 251).

MacIntyre thinks the contrtactarian rejection of desert is inevitable because a notion of desert is at home only in the context of a community whose primary bond is a shared understanding of what is "good for" a person and "of the good of" that community. Consequently, in a contract approach, the interests of the individual are promoted over the community that makes possible the cooperation and collaboration that produce the social goods that sustain individual projects and life plans. Desert makes sense only when people realize they are all in their situation together.

This is easier to understand through an example, such as students cooperating on a project. The class project represents a common or shared good. It s not simply the means by which each individual student realized his or her own good—a grade on an assignment. There are goods "*internal*" to the project, such as cooperation, solidarity, working with others toward a common goal, and the like. When one student does all of the work with others "going along" for the ride, then the shared good is not realized. The "free riders" use it for their individual interests in a grade. When each student receives the same (or equal grade), our sense of justice is disturbed. It is not "fair" for one student to do the work and others to receive exactly the same share of the good. The student who does the work *merits* or *deserves* more than the students who do not contribute to the common project.

Liberal theories of justice, such as Rawls' and Nozick's, systematically exclude the notion of the community or social interest from the meaning of justice, in favor of the plurality and diversity of interests of individuals who share no common bond *except* the desire to maximize their share of desirable goods, and whose appeal for redress when their interests are frustrated is either an appeal to entitlement, or an appeal to social need. By contrast, on Macintyre's account, justice in the modern state is framed by particular judgments, not rules, however derived. There is no universal legitimation of social or political orders.

> The tradition of virtues is at variance with central features of the modern economic order and more especially with individualism, its acquisitiveness and its elevation of the values of the market to a central social place. It now becomes clear that it also involves a rejection of the modern political order. This does not mean that there are many tasks to be performed in and through government which still require performing: the rule of law, so far as it is possible in a modern state, has to be vindicated, injustice and unwarranted suffering have to be dealt with, generosity has to be exercised, and liberty has to be defended, in ways that are sometimes only possible through the use of governmental institutions. But each particular task, each particular responsibility has to be evaluated on its own merits (MacIntyre 1981, 254).

MacIntyre's position is based on the claims to loyalty, duty, obligation and the good that precede choices about what *is* good. This view in one way or another underlies all communitarian positions. But communitarians are less a single tradition of justice talk than a multiplicity of traditions. Thus, Michael Waltzer's views about justice are similar to but not identical with MacIntyre's.

2. Waltzer's Version of Communitarian Thought

Michael Waltzer, in *Spheres of Justice, Thick and Thin* (1994), argues that there are no singular universal principles or definitions of justice, even if a minimalist content of morality can be identified. The liberal universal ideal of liberal impartialism is only ideal, not real.

> It is popular these days to think of the minimum in procedural terms–a thin morality of discourse an decision that governs every particular creation of a substantive and thick morality. Minimalism, on this view, supplies the general

rules of the different moral maxims. A small number of ideas that we share or should share with everyone in the world guides us in producing the complex cultures that we don't and needn't share–and so they explain and justify the production. . . . This ingenious doctrine faces two serious difficulties. First of all, the procedural minimum turns out to be more than minimal. . . the thin morality is already very thick–with decent liberal or social democratic thickness. The rules of engagement constitute in fact a way of life. . . . They are creatures of history; and they inhabit a society that "fits" their qualities and so supports, reinforces, and reproduces people very much like themselves. . . . The second difficulty perhaps only restates the first. Rules of engagement assume, obviously, that in the beginning there are rules and the there are engagements. Minimalism precedes maximalism . . . . The minimal morality prescribed by these theories is simply abstracted from, and not very far from, contemporary democratic culture. If no such culture existed, this particular version of minimal morality would not even be plausible (Waltzer 1994, 12-13).

Implicitly, Waltzer criticizes Rawls' theory as too one-dimensional, what he calls a "thin morality," because it insists that goods are distributed according to rules based on a unique or singular principle such as autonomy, self-interest, or equality.

Simple and straight-forward equality is a very thin idea, reiterated in one form or another in (almost) every distributive system, and useful in the criticism of certain gross injustices, but quite incapable of governing the full range of distributions. It serves more as a constraint, a kind of critical minimalist–as when we say that someone is not being treated "like a human being" or when we condemn racial discrimination. Any effort to enforce equality across the board iis immediately self-contradictory, for the enforcement would require a concentration, and therefore a radicilly unequal distribution, of power (Waltzer 1994, 33).

In a democracy, justice is worked out as it grapples with the inevitably messy claims and counter-claims, points of view, and pressures of a pluralistic society. Such working out of the claims of justice occurs at different levels of generality. For example, in multi-layered levels of American government, justice takes into account, at its best, the complex, "thick" interweaving of people, communities, institutions, ideals, laws, values, associations and circumstances in which real people live and act. Thus the idea that there is an ideal of universal equality, or egalitarianism, is a mistake.

Goods that are normally distributed in any society are too different to be distributed according to only one general criterion. To almost every one of these various kinds of goods we should apply a criterion that is characteristic for it. Thus, we have diverse spheres of justice in which there are different criteria that tell us which distributions are morally right. If the result is to be just, a criterion which holds in one sphere should not be applied in another one. Rather than a singular principle of justice, what we in fact have, according to Waltzer, are multiple claims to justice. We must respond to each sphere with appropriate context-sensitive principles. There are two reasons for this: first, equality is appropriate in some social realms but inappropriate in others. And second, the kind of equality that is appropriate varies from sphere to sphere. The equality of opportunity and access that one expects in the economy does not have the same meaning as equality in the family. The relationship between employers and employees is not the same relationship between parents and children even if legitimate subordination characterizes both.

> The basic idea (of spheres of justice) is that distributive justice must stand in some relation to the goods that are being distributed. And since these goods have no essential nature, this mean that it must stand in some relation to the place the these goods hold in the (mental and material) lives of the people among whom they are distributed. Hence my own maxim: distributive justice is relative to social meanings (Waltzer 1994, 26).

"Sphere corruption," or injustice, occurs if the distribution appropriate to one area is affected by the kind of distribution appropriate in another. For example, there are some goods, such as judicial impartiality, which we should not sell. There are activities that are appropriate to the economic sphere where justice provides the norms for economic transactions which would be totally inappropriate to the court system. Judicial impartiality should be available equally to all. When someone uses economic advantage to buy a reward or avoid punishment, then justice is offended. There are other goods, such as internet domain names or caviar, that should be sold and need not be available equally to rich and poor. However, if control of tradeable goods results in command over judicial impartiality, this is "tyranny." On Waltzer's account, "tyranny" invariably involves a failure to maintain a proper separation of spheres of justice. Waltzer's alternative is to respect sphere sovereignty or, we might say, to give each sphere its "due."

Granted, if the independence of distributive spheres is not breached, some individuals will always do better than others in any of the spheres, but it is highly unlikely that these will be the very same persons in all of the spheres. Thus, *"sphere sovereignty"* is the means to render individuals their due. Following this scheme, pluralism allows many small inequalities but not any uniquely, great one which has an impact on all kinds of goods. Thus, everyone has a much greater chance to be "winner" in some respect. At the same time, the negative aspects of trying to equalize everyone in every respect, as in an impartialist or egalitarian model, are avoided.

> If we attend to the goods being distributed, and to their social meaning, and to the principles and procedures that follow from their meaning, then we will be able to recognize scandalous and tyrannical boundary crossings. These are not the only form of injustice, but they are the most common forms in any society that

has achieved some significant degree of differentiation. The theory of complex equality provides an account of what is wrong with plutocracy, theocracy, meritocracy, gerontocracy, technocracy, and every other effort to make one good, and the qualities associated with its possession, dominant over all other goods and qualities. This is the critical force of the theory. I want to stress that this criticism, directed against aggressive boundary crossings, is also a *defense of boundaries* (Waltzer 1994, 35).

Walzer, like Rawls, is trying to describe a society where no social good can serve as a means for some people dominating others. To that degree, Waltzer probably strikes to the heart of the "liberal-communitarian" debate. On Waltzer's account, the "justice problem" is not that there are rich and poor, but that the rich subjugate the poor through deference or privilege. Crucial to demands for equality is what people with wealth have the power to do to those without it. Wealth not only allows people to buy better cars, television sets and houses, it also gives them greater esteem in the eyes of others, makes them more attractive to others, allows them to give their children more advantages, manipulate the system of justice, and so on. So the "justice problem" becomes one of providing a means to sort out competing claims for justice.

Waltzer therefore rejects rights-theory theory as too broad, abstract, and a-historical. Abstract principles of justice are meant to apply to any and all spheres of human activity. This only undercuts what is appropriate to each sphere. The rights-based view leads inevitably to injustice as it induces sphere confusion. For example, a large organization like an army division or company can survive *only* because rules regulate the interactions of relative strangers. In a family, however, people meet, quite literally, as familiar. They know one another's needs, aspirations, strengths and weakness. The application of impartial rules—for example, that each member ought to be treat in exactly the same way—would undermine the purpose of family and eventually destroy it. Thinking about each person's particular needs in a large institution would render it in effective and likewise destroy it.

For Walzer, distributions of desirable goods are just or unjust *relative to* the *social meanings* of the goods at stake. Social meanings are historical, and the just and unjust distributions change over time. For example, take goods that confer social status to the holder. In the 1920s, owning a car was an American status symbol. Today, owning a car does not confer status, but owning a certain kind of car does. As social meanings vary through time, they also vary in the same time between cultures and nations. In the West, access to credit, particularly credit cards, confers status. To be denied access to credit without sufficient reason—for example because of a false or incorrect credit report—would be regarded as "unjust." In Muslim countries, this issue could not arise because lending and borrowing at interest is considered morally wrong is forbidden. The different cultures have developed different ways to "trade" in money but the social meanings of these economic exchanges vary considerably.

Goods have meanings that are internal to the practices that constitute groups, communities and institutions, and are socially constructed. They develop through interactions and practice. Let us use the comparison to language again. The word "bad" originally meant "evil," "wicked," "unsound," "inoperative," or "dysfunctional." However, through its particular use in some speech communities, it could acquire the meaning of "good," "exceptional," "the best of a kind," "desirable," or "admirable." Both the original and the acquired meaning were built up through use in particular language-using communities. Their meanings are *socially constructed,* that is, determined not by abstract or *a priori* "rules," but by use.

According to Waltzer, all ideas (meanings) of justice are constructed meanings. This means, in part, that they contain their own principles of distribution. For example, in religious communities, ecclesiastical office is distributed according to piety and devotion, not efficiency or productivity. On the other hand, piety counts for nothing and efficiency for everything among managers in large corporations. The meaning of love and marriage in American society requires that marriage should be distributed according to individual inclinations rather than by the family, state, or market. In Islamic societies, however, marriages are arranged by family with little input by the parties affected. Thus, "fair" distribution is not conformity to an abstract principle, but instead it means acting fairly according to the meaning of socially determined possibilities.

3. Sorting Out the Arguments

If we consider the communitarian position as a whole, recognizing that there are distinct differences among individual communitarians, we can summarize its criticism of liberalism in three modes of argument:

First, liberalism rests on an *individualism* that is both ontologically and psychologically false. Ontologically, liberal theories assert that only individuals exist. Consequently, all presumed properties of groups are reducible to properties of individuals viewed collectively. Psychologically, liberal theory seems to assume that individuals are motivated solely by preferences for private goods. This is the base meaning of "rational agent" and "maximizing self-interest." Consequently, individuals participate in groups only as a means to achieving such goods.

Liberal theory can easily deal with this problem on its own terms. The normative political thesis of liberalism does not require an individualistic premise. Moreover, the premise is neither the ontological individualism nor the motivational individualism which communitarians have attacked. Liberalism is individualistic only in a moral sense. Liberals hold that what matters ultimately, morally speaking, is the self-determination and well-being of individuals. Moral individualism does not commit anyone to ontological individualism. Similarly, affirming that individuals are morally primary does not commit one to denying that groups exist or that they are reducible without remainder to the properties of individuals viewed collectively.

Liberalism can readily admit that in order to describe the interest that individuals have in participating in groups it is necessary to make reference to institutions and practices. They simply deny that this is required prior to any decision about principles of *distribution*. Concrete institutions and practices are the *consequence* of starting points, not the condition for the possibility of *determining* the starting points.

Liberals can also agree that the institutional or social concepts used to describe the interests that individuals have in belonging to groups and pursuing shared ends are not reducible to pre-institutional or pre-social concepts such as that of the "atomistic" individual existing in a state of nature. Liberalism, as a normative political thesis about the priority of the basic civil and political rights (and the proper role of the state and the limits of its authority), does not entail ontological or psychological individualism. Liberals simply affirm that a political order that protects the basic civil and political rights of individuals is preferable to political orders that do not, or to those which submerge the interests of individuals to the authority of the majority. This gives government or the state a limited role protecting a large private sphere in which diverse individuals and groups can flourish. In the long run and in most cases, this state of affairs best serves the autonomy and welfare of individuals.

A second communitarian criticism of liberalism is that it undervalues political life, viewing **participation in political community** as only an *instrumental good.* As an instrumental good, political participation is valuable as a means toward the attainment of the varied range of private ends that individuals have; however, it is not valuable in itself.

To some degree this is an appropriate criticism, since in liberal theory all goods are instrumental to each individual's life plans and goals. However, it is necessary to be careful to understand what participation in political life means. On the one hand, it may mean that political participation is an *intrinsic value*—a good to be pursued for its own sake. There seems no reason to assume a liberal theorist would have to deny this. Liberal theory allows for any number of intrinsic goods in the framework of distributable goods. Moreover, liberal theorists also value distributive justice *intrinsically,* and not merely extrinsically or instrumentally.

Another view of the *intrinsic good* of political participation is the Aristotelian idea that it is required for a complete or good life. This claim, however, is problematic for both liberals *and* communitarians. Liberals would deny that we can define in advance what is required for a "good life." Each individual makes the decision of what "basket of goods" are worthwhile pursuing. What liberal theory tries to do is to protect a sphere of freedom where such choices can be made. Thus, political participation may be an intrinsic good that one may choose.

However, one cannot insist, without imposition on the self-determining choices of others, that political participation is essential to a good life. Rather, it is a feature of some individual lives. To affirm that political participation is essential is to prejudge the good in favor an *a priori* determination of what *is* good. In that sense, then, communitarians would be correct that liberal theories undervalue political participation. As long as the value of political participation is one choice among many that individuals ought to be free to make, then it is a possible value, not a necessary one. This does not offer any substantive criticism of the liberal position. However, if a communitarian insists that political participation is a requirement for a complete or good life, then political participation becomes instrumental to a complete or good life. If political participation is an instrumental value, then the claim undercuts the communitarian position. In either case, it appears that this communitarian criticism of liberal theory cannot get off the ground.

The third communitarian criticism is that liberalism conceives of *"the self"* as being given prior to its ends. The communitarian thesis here is that an individual's identity is to a significant degree constituted by allegiance to the ends to which they are committed *by virtue of their membership in the community,* and the roles they occupy in it. MacIntyre and Waltzer both assert that individuals are embedded in their particular, historic communities.

Liberals need not and should not deny that when human beings become aware of themselves as moral agents and thus deliberate and decide what they ought to do, they already recognize themselves as having a moral-personal identity. Nor is there any reason, on a liberal theory account, to concede that this identity is constituted to a large extent by the various roles in which people find themselves in the practices of their community (or communities). Liberals can freely grant this point. That these roles carry along with them obligations and commitment also follows.

However, it would seem that liberal theory does underestimate the meaning of "embeddedness" as a particular location in history and in particular communities that are in fact value-informative. For example, the liberal values of "universality" and "abstract impartiality" arises in the eighteenth century. Through education, formal and informal, these values have become part of the "general view" of what justice is. Thus MacIntyre and Waltzer are correct in claiming that liberal universalism and impartiality are themselves culturally and historically located. Communitarians do get a critical purchase on this account, though perhaps they extend this criticism too far in assuming that what has a historical origin is *relative* to the context that gives rise to it.

Imagine just how odd it would sound if someone were to claim that the truth of Darwin's theory of evolution was relative to the nineteenth century "tradition" that gave rise to it. Likewise, the fact that universalism and impartiality were Enlightenment ideals does not necessarily mean that they are solely dependent on the culture that gave rise to them. The fact that ideas have dates is not reason to reject the ideas or to assume that there is no further transformation of the idea as it goes forward in history. To a high degree, communitarians reify and freeze traditions in time, and to that degree they are just as a-historical as the liberals whom they criticize. Communitarian thinkers are critical of the decline of moral and political communities in contemporary societies. They argue that the formalist, a-historical, and individualistic legacies of Enlightenment thinking are historically implicated in developments that have led to the decline of community as a way of life. Particularly today, they argue, this Enlightenment legacy so constricts our imagination and impoverishes our moral vocabulary that we cannot even conceptualize solutions to the current crisis, which could transcend the "rights-entitlement-distributive justice" trinity of political liberalism. However, as we have argued above, this assumes that traditions are static rather than dynamic. This criticism of liberal tradition, then, may be unfair.

A central feature of contemporary liberalism is its assertion of the priority of the right over the good. The principal motivation behind this claim is the belief that questions of right or justice should outweigh or trump considerations of social utility or the common good. In this way, we secure for individuals a domain of thought and action free from intrusion by others. Individuals are guaranteed a right to develop freely their own identities and, in turn, to participate in the democratic process as autonomous citizens. Thus, many liberal rights impose limits or constraints on the pursuit of private and public interests. Other rights aim to secure or render more effective the participation of individual citizens in shaping or defining the common good or democratic will. In either case, the net effect of such rights is to remove certain items from the agenda of collective decision making or majority rule.

At a deeper level, however, the prioritization of rights over the good is based on the affirmation that the concept of rights is to be defined *prior to* and *independent of* a conception of the good. The well-ordered state is to place a priority on the enforcement of the basic individual and civil rights—rights such as the ones found in U.S. Constitution's Bill of Rights. According to this view, individual concepts of the good are invariably particular and diverse. Thus, they cannot provide a suitable basis for justifying principles that define the basic terms of social cooperation. Questions of justice are supposed to be neutral with respect to alternative conceptions of the good.

This argument goes back to Immanuel Kant, whom we discussed in an earlier chapter. Kant defined rights not with a view to the objects that are willed, but in relation to the universal features of practical reasoning or moral agency. While contemporary liberals have abandoned Kant's idealist metaphysics, they have generally followed him in defining the right independently of the objects that individuals want or the ends that they pursue.

What constitutes the self is not any specific set of ends or attachments, but simply its capacity to choose. This is a *"thin" view of the self* in which the self relates to its ends as a "system of desires." These desires can perhaps be rationally ordered according to their relative intensity, but they do not essentially determine the self's identity. Communitarians argue that this notion of the self undermines the notion of moral agency itself. A self that exists prior to its ends must be a self without character or moral depth. If this is true, then this "thin" self is incapable of self-knowledge in any morally serious sense. (Sandel 1982/1998, 180). If all justice does is protect the capacity of an agent to make arbitrary choices, it becomes unclear why it should even be valued as the first virtue of societies.

Charles Taylor argues that we cannot resolve questions of right or justice by adopting a neutral stance toward the goods that humans value. We must, he says, enter "the thicket of the languages of qualitative contrasts: in order to make unavoidable, if difficult, choices from among the diversity of goods" (Taylor 1982, 32). In pluralistic societies, like those that characterize the modern international community, it would seem that consideration of the diversity of possible goods is in order. Particularly once we concede that community and the traditions of communities are crucial in the constructions of a diversity of notions of what constitutes "the good life," it would appear that this communitarian criticism does score a critical point against the liberal position. An adequate theory of justice must find a way to deal with value pluralism in the world without falling into *relativism*, which is untenable, and *majoritarianism*, which imposes the values of dominant majorities on minorities, often in an unjust way.

Waltzer's position, like the positions of feminists and MacIntryre's communitarian, have done much to promote a lively conversation about justice. While one admires the effort of traditional liberalism to secure a "level field" of impartiality for justice, contextualist positions are a reminder that the real world is a bit messier than the ideal world of a Rawlsian thought-experiment. Contexts do seem to matter and require a place in our thinking about justice.

However, the liberal-communitarian debate is not the end of the conversations about justice. This conversation has been principally a debate in English-speaking countries, especially the United States. A similar conversation characterizes European thinking about justice too. To that we can now turn.

Chapter Eleven
Back to Impartiality and Beyond: European Voices in the Justice Conversation

Some people think that the liberal-communitarian debate is intractable. There is just no way to resolve the impasse between procedures and contexts. The solution is to choose a side and reason accordingly. This view is partially justified, especially if we keep the terms of the debate as they are. However, a promising direction leading to a potential resolution of the debate comes from a set of lively conversations in Europe.

Continental European political thinking, for a variety of reasons, flows in different directions from those of American thinking. First, rationalism and Hegelian idealism influenced European thinking more than American political thought. Second, the legacy of the French Revolution (1789) and the several European Revolutions of 1848 deeply influenced European political thinking about public order and stability. Third, Europeans, especially continental Europeans, had to deal with the brutal totalitarianism of National Socialism and fascism.. The turmoil of national economic reconstruction, Stalinism, the Hungarian Revolution, the Czechoslovakian uprising, the Berlin Wall, the ideological battles and fall of Communism after World War II, and the student "revolts" in 1968 are part of that heritage. And fourth, Europe has been more *ethnocentric* than the United States. This ethnocentrism slowed the process of nation building in a way that America never faced because of its "melting pot" ideal. Thus Europeans were conscious earlier and more deeply than Americans of *cultural pluralism*. Nevertheless, forms of the liberal-communitarian debate are part of European political thought, but with a different inflection.

1. Critical Theory—Unmasking "Hidden Persuaders"

Critical theory as a philosophical school is descended from Hegel (1770-1831) and Marx (1818-1883). In Hegel's view, philosophy is locked into unresolvable dichotomies like "being" and "nothingness" or freedom and determinism, and these dichotomies are only expressions of a deeper rift within cultural life, such as masters and slaves, rich and poor. The purpose of philosophy is to overcome these rifts and to restore unity to the human project. Marx followed a similar line of thinking. For him, philosophy is the discipline that raises to consciousness the operative horizon of everyday life and subjects it to rational criticism. He argued that, because Hegel could not conceive of really radical changes in modern culture, he tended to rationalize temporary historical conditions as though they were eternal necessities. Analysis of the historical and social location of these realities yields a new consciousness, and liberates human beings from alienation. On this view, social critique is a kind of "brush clearing" of human consciousness that sets in motion a process of inevitable change.

The object of a critical theory of society is to understand human beings as producers of their own historical way of life in its totality. The existing relations that are the starting point of science are not regarded simply as givens to be verified and to be predicted according to laws of probability. An essential element in the historical efforts and powers of humans is the goal of emancipation from the relationships that enslave people. Further, critical theory sees itself as an essential element in the historical effort to create a world that satisfies the needs and powers of human beings, beyond merely "being free." The critical analysis of the social world is not an end in itself, but a necessary step in the process of transforming the world into one that satisfies human needs.

Of the critical theories to appear in philosophy, the most enduring is the Neo-Marxism associated with the "Frankfurt School." The Frankfurt School was a collaboration of philosophers and social scientists who tried to adapt Marxism to the social and political realities of their time after world War I. Their project included the explicit intention to include the social sciences in a critical theory of society. Max Horkheimer (1895-1973) particularly was committed to using economics, psychology and cultural theory to analyze how we might achieve a rational organization of society. Theodor Adorno (1903-1969), working after World War II and the experience of German totalitarianism, adapted the original project to try to understand how fascism and Stalinism emerged as political philosophies and programs in the modern world.

Critical theorists feared that modern Western societies were turning into closed, totalitarian systems that destroyed individual autonomy. Events before and after the Second World War seemed to provide ample confirmation of this possibility. Critical theorists believed that totalitarianism developed in part because of the expanding role of science and technology in modern society. One consequence of this expanded role was an emphasis on *instrumental rationality* as the dominant, if not only, form of reason.

"Instrumental reason," according to critical theorists, denies that there are any inherently rational ends or goals of human action. Instrumental rationality focuses exclusively on the choice of effective, efficient means for attaining arbitrary ends.

For example, a business person uses instrumental rationality in deciding how best to schedule her employees to meet production deadlines or sales targets. Students use it to decide what to study and how hard to study in relation to other demands on their time and energy. Within its proper domain, instrumental rationality is not problematic. Problems do occur, however, if instrumental reasoning becomes the *dominant or only* form of reasoning people use. This is obvious once we realize that instrumental reasoning is only connecting means to ends. This begs the question as to what ends ought to be pursued in the first place. Prior to a decision about the best means to reach an end is deciding which ends to pursue.

For example, suppose a person wants to get rich. There are several ways to do this; one can steal, kill a relative who is already rich, work hard, or win a lottery. All four ways lead to the same end; however, most people would argue that there is a qualitative and moral difference between the four means. If we think only in terms of efficiency, it is hard to explain what the precise difference is, except in terms of which is more efficient. Explaining why one means is qualitatively or morally "better" than another requires a reflective consideration of the final ends or goals.

Consideration of final end or goals is not a matter of fitting means to ends. A decision about final ends implies some standard for choosing among ends. If "getting rich" is the final end, then any of the four means are acceptable since they are efficient and reach the goal. Indeed, theft or fraud may be much more efficient than winning a lottery. But why should one choose to get rich over the respect of others, or one's own well-being? If one's goal is the respect and admiration of one's fellow citizens, it is unlikely that a person who steals or kills to achieve the goal will be admired and respected unless one lives in a community that values theft and murder. Within this view of ends, getting rich is instrumental to the respect of others, and thus *how* one gets rich would matter—not just efficiency in doing so. Consequently, we would judge the means according to how each means contributes or does not contribute to the goal we have chosen. If instrumental reason excludes deliberating about ends, then critical theorists point out that the ends become merely arbitrary. There is no necessary reason for preferring one set of ends over another. Affirming that there is no basis to prefer one set of ends to another is, of course, a variation of *relativism*, discussed in the first chapter.

Critical theorists argue that instrumental reasoning started to dominate our modes of thinking as modern science grew in importance and authority, since modern science tends to abstract from the question of ends. This process of seeing every problem and question as yielding to scientific answers started in the seventeenth century and continues today. As science came to dominate social decision-making, it distorted the meaning of society. The result was that final ends were unimportant. What mattered was efficiency in achieving ends—upon which there was insufficient reflection.

The debate about cloning provides a good example of what critical theorists draw our attention to. On a radio program discussing the 'pros' and 'cons' of cloning humans, a British scientist asserted that the fact that humans *could* clone another human being meant that another human *would* be cloned. There were no meaningful scientific, political or moral barriers to doing so. However, the fact that something *can be done* does not mean that it *ought to be done*. Any discussion about whether people should clone humans is not a scientific discussion. It is a discussion about desirable ends. It is this moral conversation about ends that critical theorists argued instrumental rationality has displaced from the public sphere of political conversation.

The critical theory world view is "pessimistic" about society and the human prospect if it continues in the same direction. What we need, they argue, is a corrective to the scientific, instrumental way of thinking. Horkheimer and his colleagues conceived of critical theory as way to resist the implications and consequences of purely instrumental thinking in contemporary society by taking a critical stance regarding the fundamental commitments and consequences of contemporary society. By "critical," they meant making discerning judgments about humans, our modes of thinking and organizing the products of our thinking in groups, institutions, and society. By "theory," they meant an explanation of the human phenomena in all of its aspects, especially their social aspects. The critical theorist seeks to unmask the "hidden," and often irrational, factors that motivate our actions as individuals and groups.

The basic method of critical theory is *"internal"* or *"immanent" criticism*—or, we might say, criticism "from the inside" of existing societies. Like contextualists, critical theorists argue that every society has certain fundamental, central values that implicitly guide its members on how to realize a good life. People internalize these values as social practices. The practices socialize the goals as values. Thus, they become part of the way the world "is" to members of that community or society.

This set of tacit claims about what constitutes a good life precedes the effort of any particular individual to realize the good life. For example, many students choose to pursue higher education as serving the goal of social success. But the link between education and social success is one that precedes any student's choice of attending university. Indeed, so closely has society linked success and education as a set of institutionalized practices that many students do not feel that they are free to make any choice except to attend college. Now, increasingly we hear that people must continue their education as a life-long project. Thus, for many students, attending university is less about acquiring knowledge than about making grades and acquiring credentials in a race for success. Many universities are less institutions of learning than they are *credentialing* bodies. However, the fact that Americans equate education and success does not mean that there is a necessary link between the two, or that education *ought* to be in service of success. To a great extent, there is a conflict or tension between the purpose of the university as an institution for education and an institution for credentialing.

This exemplifies the point of critical theory. If we take the key operative values in the way people actually act or organize their lives, we have a testable, "internal" standard for making judgments about actions and ways of organizing actions in institutions. Thus, while most students pursue their degrees assuming that higher education is a key to success, we can convert the practices and goal into a testable hypothesis. Critical theorists think all groups, institutions, and societies betray or fail to live to up their basic or fundamental values—largely because the ends have been chosen in an irrational way to begin with. So all groups, institutions, and societies are open to criticism, or better, critique.

It is important to grasp that critical theorists do not impose a standard on a way of life. There is no *a priori* good or moral ideal to which all people of societies ought to subscribe. What is good are the concrete values operative in existing groups, institutions, and societies. In this sense, critical theorists affirm *value pluralism*. However, they use a society's own terms and relations to judge or test the degree to which groups, institutions, or a society *actually realize* the values to which people claim to be committed. The United States provides a good example. One of our fundamental value affirmations, expressed in the *Declaration of Independence* and the *Constitution*, is the equal value or worth of all people. However, one does not have to study American history long to know that "all people" at various times has included only some people. We created many institutions, like poll taxes, and practices, like the rhetoric of "separate but equal," to reinforce and legitimize inequality among races. On a critical theoretic account, this process continues. Analysis of institutions and practices as human constructions—especially those concerned with justice, fairness, equality and equity— enables us to see the ways people fail to realize the very values they affirm. The strategy of the Civil Rights Movement, in the thinking of Martin Luthar King, was to force people to confront the self-contradiction between the values they espoused and the reality of segregation and inequality.

Critical theory provides a complete program of social criticism. This program has many implications for understanding society and politics. However, now we are only interested in one important aspect, of a critique of justice.

2. Jürgen Habermas: Another Voice of Impartiality

Jürgen Habermas (1929-) was for a time Adorno's research assistant. Some of Adorno's concerns, such as the problem of totalitarianism and human freedom, are questions that Habermas continues to address. However, he has developed a significant original voice in philosophy. Habermas takes MacIntrtyre and Rawls as poles to pilot a way between communitarianism and liberalism to develop his theory of justice. With liberalism, he affirms the central importance—indeed urgency—of an *impartialist* position for adjudicating value conflicts. Like

MacIntrye, however, he wants to incorporate a "thicker" view of human beings' embeddedness in history and society. Like liberals, he recognizes the critical importance of impartiality that makes relations among relative strangers possible. But like the communitarians, he argues that impartiality cannot be grounded in abstract, a-historical principles.

> Against liberalism in the abstract sense, I would maintain that the legal order of any community is "ethically impregnated." Citizens share a political culture shaped by a particular history. The constitutional principles are, without any harm to their universalist meaning, interpreted from the perspective of this political culture, which provides at the same time the base for a constitutional patriotism.
>
> Against communitarianism, I would insist on the requirement that the constitutional state carefully keep both the shared political culture and common civic identity separated from the subcultures and collective identities which are, as a consequence of equal rights to cultural membership, entitled to equal coexistence within the polity. The national legal order, although ethically impregnated in terms of the political culture shared equally by all citizens, must remain neutral with respect to these prepolitical forms of life and traditions. Remaining "neutral" means—and this is the critical edge of neutrality—decoupling the majority culture from the political culture with which it was originally fused, and in most instances still is.
>
> . . . I am defending liberals against the communitarian critique with regard to the concept of the "self." The individualistic approach to a theory of rights does not necessarily imply an atomistic, disembodied, and desocialized concept of the person. The legal person is, of course, an artificial construct. . . . But legal persons, too, should and can be constructed as socialized individuals. They are members of a community of legal consociates who are supposed to recognize each other as free and equal. The equal respect required from legal persons pertains, however, also to the context of those intersubjective relationships which are constitutive for their identities as natural persons.
>
> Together with the communitarians I am, on the other hand, critical of the liberal assumption that human rights are prior to popular sovereignty. The addressees of law must be in a position to see themselves at the same time as authors of those laws to which they are subject. Human rights may not just be imposed on popular sovereignty as an external constraint. Of course, popular sovereignty must not be able to arbitrarily dispose of human rights either. . . .
> The solution to this seeming paradox is that human rights must be conceived in such a way that they are enabling rather than constraining conditions for democratic self-legislation (Habermas 1995).

Habermas has not offered a systematic theory of justice, and perhaps never will. However, his work on *communication theory* and *discourse* or *communicative ethics* frame a substantial outline of one that Habermas himself has used to join several different conversations about justice, law, and government. His tries to tease out a set of procedures that, if followed, would yield a principle for legitimating or justifying social practices and institutions. The key for understanding Habermas' position is his ideal of a moral community as one whose norms and practices are fully acceptable to those who are a party to them. Such a society would be one of consensus among free and equal persons rather than subjects bound by obligation or an imposed agreement.

Communicative action—towards consensual discourse. Habermas situates the moral point of view within the discourse of a community of selves. Human beings are "linguistic animals"—and the interesting thing about language is that it is rule-governed. One must obey rules recognized by all speakers to communicate anything to anyone. The rules do not have to be negotiated for every conversation. They are a practice that transcends particularity to achieve a kind of pragmatic universality constituted by all competent speakers. Another interesting thing about language as a normative system is that the "rules" do not constrain speakers, but actually increase the range of a speaker's freedom to understand the communicative acts of oneself and others. The rules of language increase our power to communicate, but only if we follow the rules.

On Habermas' view, language is the foundation of social and political association. He sometimes represents the social-political sphere as an extended conversation where people "talk about" what is right and wrong. The moral point of view, on this account, is carried by language. In "talking about" our interests, agenda, life plans and goals, we come to understand one another. The process of communication is one of achieving common understanding. Habermas calls this process *communicative action*—to be distinguished from *instrumental action,* which connects means to ends, and also from *strategic action,* the effort to persuade others of some fact or idea.

The goal of communicative action is not to persuade or *influence others to* a point of view. Rather it aims to reach an agreement or *mutual understanding about* something in the world. Take a simple example. Suppose I believe the world is flat and want to persuade you to believe likewise. The effort to persuade you to believe or affirm that the world is flat is strategic action. However, strategic action is preceded by having some idea of what you and I "count" as persuasive which you may well demand to understand what I am saying. Suppose I offer as evidence "My uncle told me the world is flat"—a mere appeal to authority. You might respond that is not acceptable evidence. Who is your uncle? Why is he a respectable authority? Why should I accept your authority? I can muster authorities who affirm the earth is not flat. Why should I accept your authorities over my authorities? This difference here is not about the "fact of the earth" but rather about what "counts" as persuasive evidence. Resolving it requires not strategic action but communicative action which concerns the grounds of understanding one another. We cannot resolve our disagreement about the "fact of the earth" until we resolve the prior set of questions about the framework of our conversation.

On Habermas' account, to engage in communicative action, any substantive ends a person may have are subordinated to the goal of achieving a mutually shared definition of the agent's lifeworld through a cooperative process of interpretation. For example, when people reach an impasse in a conversation because they do not understand each other, the conversation moves into a different mode of questioning until understanding is reached. This mode is not one of trying to persuade another to agree with a position, accept a point of view, or do something. Rather, it is a mutual exchange of "understanding"—did you mean this, that, or the other? Habermas argues that this communicational process is (1) *rational*, because it appeals to reasons acceptable to all in the conversation; and (2) assumed to be *universal*, because speakers assume that the "rules" of rationality are binding on all, including themselves.

Habermas admits that these assumptions do not show that communicational procedures *are* rational or universal; however, to get communication off the ground, one must assume they are. In other words, when we act communicatively, we tacitly accept the validity of certain claims raised without objection, because each person supposes that the other is prepared to provide reasons for them if their validity were questioned. However, misunderstanding, conflict, and lack of agreement are moments when the conversation shifts from one about the topic at hand to one about the nature of the misunderstanding, disagreement or conflict. What reasons can we accept to resolve our misunderstanding, disagreement, or conflict to move the conversation on?

Communicative action, morality and justice. Habermas is making a distinctly Kantian set of moves here. As in Kant's thinking, morality concerns human actions. Practical reasoning forms a distinct arena of discourse. This practical discourse, when joined with the conversation of others, is social and political as individuals coordinate their actions, especially using complex symbol systems such as language with others. What we seek is agreement on what is right or "rightness"—which is similar to but not the same as "truth" in the realm of theory. "Rightness" intends knowing what ought to be done just as "truth" intends knowing what is the case. Just as we offer reasons to validate or justify truth claims, such as "There is a rabbit in the quad," so we offer reasons to support normative claims, such as "Capital punishment is morally wrong."

Also like Kant, Habermas insists that moral reasons are universal and impartial. However, unlike Rawls and other impartialists, he shifts the ground away from a single reason or set of reasons that autonomous rationality could derive for itself by reflecting on its own operations. Instead, Habermas insists that we take into consideration the viewpoints of all who would be affected by the adoption of any moral action or normative claim. He "lifts" Rawls' veil of ignorance and demands that we participate in a discourse where all are fully aware of the other's perspectives and interpretations. Thus, from the start consideration of the principles of social organization are dialogical—a conversation from particular, known points of view.

For example, if Native Americans object to use of the word "Braves" to describe a baseball team, Habermas will not say "A rational person would not raise that object: calling the team 'braves' is actually a compliment to the Native Americans' bravery." Instead, he will try to understand what the Native Americans count as good or bad reasons for arguing that something is insulting or complimentary.

This move toward a "dialogical form of practical reason" is required of "post-modern societies," according to Habermas, where an irreducible plurality of "goods" conditions and limits the horizon of moral conversations. Ethical ideas represent duties and obligations within a just society—a society in which "rights" trump competing "goods" in circumstances of conflict.

> If we want to decide normative questions having to do with the elements of living together not by . . . the power of the stronger, but rather by nonviolent conviction based on rationally motivated agreement, then we have to concentrate on the circle of questions accessible to an impartial evaluation. We should not expect a generally binding answer if we ask, what is the good for me or for us or good for her, for that we must ask, what is *equally good for all*. This "moral point of view" projects a sharp but narrow circle of light which throws into relief, against the mass of all evaluative questions, those action conflicts that can be *resolved* in relation to a universalizable interest: the question of justice (Habermas 1990c, 118).

Thus the starting point of justice is the "givenness" of a social order. From this point of view, all norms, social and moral, are internally related to a social order as the means of adjudicating among conflicting interests. Interests are partial; the interest of justice, however, is impartial. It takes into its reach all those conflicts that can be adjudicated.

Communicative ethics and the procedures of discourse. Habermas's *discourse ethics* is part of his larger project to sustain, in a reconstructed form, the Enlightenment project of political emancipation and democracy. It is an attempt to define the formal rules and communicative presuppositions that make it possible for participants in a practical discourse to arrive at a valid, rational consensus on social norms. In particular, Habermas seeks to ground discourse ethics on what he takes to be a fundamental assumption of conversation or discourse—especially when people make statements such as "You ought not to be a racist," "It is only fair to reward people according to their labor," and the like. The "ought" in such claims signifies that the moral norms (avoiding racism, providing just rewards) are not valid solely for the individual who happens to accept them. Value conflicts are extended conversations to bring others to accept our point of view. The "argument" assumes that these norms are valid for all people. Validating these norms is the work of communicative action. Communicative action precedes substantive discussion about values, norms of action, plans, or policies. In essence, if one can get one's opponents to agree to certain "rules of discourse," then one has them in a position to accept arguments, if they make sense, and thus to accept the conclusions of the arguments, even the conclusions in question are ethical or valuational. Thus communicative action is a process of giving and criticizing reasons for holding or rejecting particular claims.

This process is most obvious in the natural sciences and law. When scientists claims that the motion of subatomic particles are unpredictable, they do not mean that these motions are unpredictable here and now but that later in a another time or place they will be predictable. The scientists assumes that the claim is "true" regardless of time, place, or person. They are quite prepared to offer evidence to this effect. The kind of evidence that is acceptable, according to the normative requirements of standard science, are "set" by the community of scientists who adjudicate the acceptability or unacceptability of the claim. The claim to be accepted or rejected is substantive. The evidentiary standards are procedural. The process of accepting or rejecting the claim is an argument. To the extent to which we grant that such argumentation leads to universally valid claims—an admission we are likely to make in the sciences—we concede Habermas' central point. Communicative action describes and explains a rationality capable, through discourse, of arriving at universal norms.

According to Habermas, both theoretical (scientific) and practical (ethics and politics) discourses are argumentative enterprises. They test and contest claims of truth or rightness by invoking validating or legitimizing reasons. A practical discourse aims at a rationally motivated consensus on norms. The goal of discourse ethics is to articulate the formal, objective, and universal criteria that guide practical discourses. These universal criteria are the standards that distinguish between legitimate and illegitimate normative claims.

> Philosophers of diverse backgrounds always come up with principles whose basic idea is the same. *All* variants of cognitivist ethics take their bearings from the basic intuition contained in Kant's categorical imperative. What I am concerned with here is not the diversity of Kantian formulations but their underlying idea, which is designed to take into account the impersonal general character of valid universal commands. The moral principle is so conceived as to exclude as invalid any norm that could not meet with the qualified assent of all who are or might be affected by it (Habermas 1990a, 63-64).

The process of consensus grounded on universal principles, Habermas argues, is not an abstraction limited to personal morality. It serves the social or public purpose of prescribing impartiality and general reciprocity that characterize all valid norms. The emphasis on universal inclusion and consensual validity is directed to the problem of value pluralism and cooperative social action. Every point of view has a place in the public discourse aiming at consensus. For Rawls, however, particular points of view are hidden behind the veil of ignorance. Habermas claims no such ideal possibility. Multiple points of view constitute the public sphere. What we need is not suspending points of view but bringing every point of view to the table.

Defining the criteria that guide practical discourses, discourse ethics depends on two core values: *freedom from coercion* and *dialogical consensus.* The first value, freedom from coercion, pins down the conditions necessary to achieve rational agreement. All agreements must be open to all. No agreement can be forced or coerced, even by majoritarian rule. No agreement is consensual if any point of view is omitted from the conversation. This affirms the original freedom of all members of a community. Freedom implies equality. Equality means, in part, that all participants have an equal voice in the discussion regarding proposed norms and procedures. In particular, consensus emerges here as a requirement for agreement or consent. Consensus or agreement on procedures is the goal of the dialogical process.

The second condition, dialogical consensus, affirms that procedures have a higher priority than substantive content, because it is through the procedural rules that we establish a legitimate consensus. The relation of language to what is spoken about provides a rough analogy to what Habermas means. Before people can speak about anything, there must be a vehicle for speaking. A rule-guided symbol system like language mediates any particular content, and therefore precedes it. Likewise, a norm of action is legitimate only if all those possibly affected would agree to the rule by which it is decided.

What one ought to accept as a rationally motivated agreement, however, has two very demanding conditions, designed to assure that all affected have an effective equality of opportunity to assume dialogical roles—that is, to speak or have a voice. It must be (1) a fully public process *free of political or economic power;* and (2) it must be public as to *access.* Anyone capable of speech and action who potentially will be affected by the norms under dispute must be able to participate in the discussion on equal terms. These conditions are more demanding than they appear, and are rarely fulfilled in actual democracies.

Suppose a small community—a town or village—must decide whether to damn a small creek to produce hydroelectric power for the town. The immediate question is whether to build the damn. This is the substantive issue. The project will affect everyone. The hydroelectric plant will provide a reliable and inexpensive source of power. New jobs will expand the tax base. More public services will be potentially available to everyone. The expected surplus of electrical production will reduce local taxes, affecting all property owners and most permanent residents. However, some will be more affected than others. Some farms will be flooded by the lake created. This will require the removal of some farmer, and perhaps a major lifestyle change. Local citizens able to invest in the project will receive a reliable return on their investment. Thus, while everyone has an interest in the outcome, not everyone's interest is the same. A simple majoritarian process would assure that everyone affected regardless of interest have a chance to speak or vote for or against the proposal. It would be efficient and on most accounts effective. But is it fair? Perhaps not.

On Habermas account, discussion of the project, the substantive value question, requires public access to all conversations. Access would include not only conversation about the substantive issue, but also the procedures proposed to frame the discussion of the substantive issue. These procedures are usually determined not by public consultation, but by committees, councils, or administrative bodies, in the hidden "backroom" of politics. Habermas' position implies more than merely having open meetings that everyone can attend. Public attention to the procedures and rules of the conversation precede any discussion of the issue. Thus, discussion of these procedures must be open to all. Attention must be given to facilitate public participation and accessibility, not merely making an invitation to participate. Moreover, no single interest, especially the economic interests or the interests of the political elite, can dominate the conversation. Hidden or invisible interests, like the environment, the historical, sentimental, or cultural value of the flooded lands could be obscured. Moreover, access may require "giving" voice to these interests that might be without an actual voice, such as past or future generations. Thus, before the substantive conversation can get off the ground, on Habermas' account, attention must be directed to the procedures to secure agreement on the procedural rules of the process.

Besides these procedural rules regulating communicative interaction, participants must also be able to shift, alter or change the agenda. For example, imagine what would happen if one of the participants tried to switch the public debate from the economic benefits of the project to a question about the "best lifestyle" for the community. Or suppose someone argued that garbage removal had to be addressed before discussing the hydroelectric project. In all likelihood, objections would be offered to the effect that such questions were not relevant, or that they "clouded" the issue. In a practical discourse, nothing can be out of bounds or taboo, regardless of the opinions of the powerful, wealthy, or traditionally authoritative on what might be "relevant." The principles of procedural validity permit everyone a fair hearing and an open discussion. On these grounds, it becomes possible to discern whether a common interest *can become* the basis of a consensus. The point of communicative ethics is not to resolve substantive value conflicts, only to assure the fairness of argumentation once the terms and relations of community are fixed. This is to affirm that fundamental values are not objects of communicative discussion.

While conflicts involving fundamental values often cannot be resolved, such resolution is not necessary in a model of communicative ethics. What is required is that the compromises be considered fair. They are fair if the rules regulating such discourse are themselves open to debate and in principle capable of general agreement at a deeper level of justification. Methodological procedures of discourse are meant to institutionalize the rules governing fairness and impartiality. If the procedures are fair, then the outcome is just.

Habermas, somewhat in the style of Rawls, offers three standards or principles to justify this conclusion:

Principle 1: a principle of universalization, one that intends to set the conditions for impartial judgment insofar as it "constrains all affected to adopt the perspectives of all others in the balancing of interests" (Habermas 1990a, 65). The principle of universalization itself states: "All affected can accept the consequences and the side effects [that the proposed moral norm's] general observance can be anticipated to have for the satisfaction of everyone's interests (and these consequences are preferred to those of known alternative possibilities for regulation" (Habermas 1990a, 65) .

Principle 2: Only those [moral] norms can claim to be valid that meet (or could meet) with the approval of all affected in their capacity as participants in a practical discourse (Habermas 1990a, 66). In short, the conditions for the practical discourse out of which universally valid norms may emerge include the participation and acceptance of all who are affected by such norms, as such norms meet their interests.

Principle 3: Consensus can be achieved only if all participants participate freely: we cannot expect the consent of all participants to follow "unless all affected can freely accept the consequences and the side effects that the general observance of a controversial norm can be expected to have for the satisfaction of the interests of each individual" (Habermas 1990a, 93).

The principle of universalization explains what our everyday intuition would outline for us as a strategy for solving moral conflicts: the principle of impartiality. If procedures are impartial, then agreements are just and free of coercion or hidden persuaders. Thus, universalization and impartiality emerge from concrete contexts of value discourse. As in tradition-dependent positions, Habermas affirms that the rules of justice cannot rescind from traditions. All conversation starts in them. But unlike contextualists, he affirms that the normative requirements for open discourse transcend particular traditions to make universal claims and achieve impartiality. This, however, does not "imperialize" or "subjugate" the particular in the name of a transcending reason. "The principle of universalization (U) is formally stated as follows: A norm is valid only if all affected can accept the consequences and the side affects its general observance can be anticipated to have for the satisfaction of everyone's interests (and these consequences are preferred to those of known alternative possibilities)" (Habermas 1990a , 65).

Thus, on Habermas' account, the principle of universalization formally determines those conditions that we must meet if the claim of legitimacy supposed by moral commands and norms is really justified. This principle is at the same time a principle for *argumentation,* because it summarizes the normative implications bound up with the situation of "entering into an argument." In other words, if one can get one's opponents to agree to certain "rules of discourse," then one has them in a position to accept arguments, if they make sense. In so far as the arguments are acceptable to all parties to the discourse, the conclusions of the arguments are acceptable, even if the values driving the conflict are still contested.

Habermas' position is not a pure proceduralism. He acknowledges that a sense of solidarity must further complement these procedural rules between participants. Such solidarity involves concern for the well-being of both one's fellow human beings and of the community at large. As Habermas has put it,

> Under the pragmatic presuppositions of an inclusive and noncoercive rational discourse among free and equal participants, everyone is required to take the perspective of everyone else, and thus project herself into the understandings of self and world of all others; from this interlocking of perspectives there emerges an ideally extended we-perspective from which all can test in common whether they wish to make a controversial norm the basis of their shared practice (Habermas 1995, 117-8).

For Habermas, the general conditions of the ideal speech situation and the rules of reason, especially as coupled with this sense of solidarity, describe the necessary conditions of democratic polity. In this way, Habermas reaches his goal of justifying democratic polity over alternative forms—especially as those forms are supported by relativism or majoritarianism.

At the same time, these conditions and rules establish the legitimacy of pluralism. That is, a diversity of communities and participants, while following the same set of rules regarding discourse, may establish diverse sets of norms as legitimate for a given, but not all, communities. This pluralism offsets especially postmodern critiques of modern rationality and technology as "totalizing," and thus totalitarian, in spite of their intentions not to be.

Since moral conflicts, such as pornography, the limits of free speech, abortion, internet privacy, or labor justice, are extended public arguments, the rules of argument offer specific guidelines for a discourse community as it seeks to resolve such difficult ethical issues. The rules of argumentation entail the requirement that norms affecting everyone should be acceptable and accepted by everyone. Insofar as they are, fairness is assured and justice served.

Counter-points to Habermas' theory of procedural justice. Criticisms aimed at liberal theory by communitarians and feminists are also relevant to Habermas. As a "proceduralist" theory, only the norms of the "justice game" are validated. There is no addressing of the substantive issue of the good or the good life. When we take the value claims of justice conflicts concretely rather than abstractly, it is the substantive value disagreements that drive them. Rules and norms help adjudicate conflict only where there is a prior commitment to the value of resolving them. In other words, rules and norms rest on a prior value consensus. Thus Habermas is vulnerable to a similar kind of criticism as feminists aim at Rawlsian impartialism. Even a critic as sympathetic to Habermas' project as Seyla Benhabib argues that the distinction between normative (justice) and evaluative (questions about the good life) discourse needs to be jettisoned in favor of bringing questions about the good life forward to the center of the discussion. "There is no privileged subject matter of moral disputation . . . the language of rights can be . . . challenged in light of our need interpretations, and that the object of moral theory (needs to be) enlarged that not only issues of justice but questions of the good life as well are move to the center of discourse" (Benhabib 2000, 169).

While a procedural justification may validate some norms, it is not obvious that they would be sufficient to settle the conflicts that arise in a pluralist world, which are conflicts of substance, not process. We can return to the example of a small town deciding whether to build a hydroelectronic plant. The "rules" of discourse could perhaps get issues and participants to the table. Basic rules of civility and process might be assured, and the requirements of publicity and contribution met. Even agreement about the meaning of agreement could be secured. But none of these provide any way through the thorny substantive issue of what kind of life is worth living in a particular community at a particular time. Thus, Habermasian justice theory lacks a workable decision principle.

As another example, think about the intractable disagreement between the 9/11 terrorists destroying what they believed to be major symbols of a decadent way of life that, on their account, threatened not only to their way of life, but the only acceptable way of life. Would discussion of what counted as rationally motivated argument in fact resolve the underlying conflict? Proceduralists like Habermas are correct that "courts" cannot ultimately "rule" on substantive value disagreements—only on the procedures used to reach decisions. This is not to minimize the importance of "rules" for adjudicating conflicts. However, the "rule" of law" seems to require something more than procedures and rules.

3. Iris Marion Young: Justice as Self-development

Real political discourses are not discourses in "ideal speech communities." Habermas admits as much. Ideals must situate themselves eventually in real communities. Iris Marion Young (1949 -) is sympathetic to the idea of a political ethic based on communicative practices, but argues that Habermas' universalist ideal of rational discourse and consensus is politically problematic because it is not possible. Also, as a goal, it excludes some voices from the political conversation of real communities.

The goal of rational consensus through dialogue assumes that all members of society who are affected by actions and programs can recognize and agree on certain general interests. Young argues that this view assumes a preexisting consensus or shared understanding of the "society game." In the West, the value of cooperation, self-determination, independence, and non-interference would be examples of such a prior consensus. Others values like strength, corporate solidarity, and kinship obligations that one finds in African cultures represent another kind of consensus that is not commensurate with the first. The Islamic view of just society as directly ruled by God through the *Qu'ran* and *sharia* provides an example of a third kind of consensus that is incommensurate with the other two. In a context of global cultural pluralism that characterizes contemporary, multicultural societies, we cannot assume that sufficient shared understandings exist to appeal to all parties in most situations of conflict. Consequently, Young affirms that genuine consensus among different normative positions is impossible.

Not only is consensus amid difference implausible, the goal of universal agreement actually privileges dominant voices who have the social position, time, or resources to master the discourse rules. The search for generalizable interests is biased toward the positions of politically dominant groups which are portrayed as universal and rational when they are actually the interests of ruling elites. Thus, Young attacks the notion of rationality at its root. Like everything else, social rationality is a *constructed* reality. Claims to universality are only pretensions. The voices of the marginalized and oppressed are unlikely to be heard and recognized precisely because they will be discounted as irrational on a universalist model. Those who have the economic capacity to participate in discussions, who have special or technical knowledge, or who speak standard idioms can present their own views as compatible with general interests. Compatibility with general interests is the standard for deciding what and who is rational. "The less privileged are asked to put aside the expression of their experience, which may require a different idiom, or their claims of entitlement or interest must be put aside for the sake of a common good whose definition is biased against them" (Young 1997, 65-66).

Moreover, economic and social factors set up conditions unfavorable to full political participation by many potential players. Since they are marginalized, their voices are not heard, and silence is taken as agreement or acquiescence. Consequently, the conditions that work against full political participation are not likely to be addressed because they are part of the "rules" of play. To keep the analogy of the game, they are part of the field of play, recognition of which constitutes "rationality." Policy proposals must be "realistic," "practical," or "workable" to be part of the conversation. Finally, the goal of consensus may encourage people to interpret others' claims in terms most immediately understandable to themselves, without giving due accord to the differences of others. According to Young, discourse ethicists like Habermas write as if parties to political debate need only put themselves in the place of others in order to affirm consensusal agreement. However, Young argues that putting oneself in the place of others is usually impossible, especially for those who are socially and politically privileged. They lack the relevant experience, especially the experience of marginalization and exclusion. On Young's account, it is ontologically impossible for people in one social position to adopt the perspective of those in the social position with which they are related in social structures and interaction. In particular, people who are at different positions within societies stratified by power, or who occupy groups with different histories in a multicultural society, cannot fully exchange their perspectives with one another. Furthermore, as the oppressed may better understand issues such as disability access, sexual harassment, or cultural protection, it appears to be unfair to insist on a relationship of symmetrical understanding with each side trying to reverse perspectives with the other.

The goal of consensus, by suggesting that understanding through overcoming differences can be attained, is more likely unjust than just, even if it is politically workable at all. A more adequate normative ground for politics lies in recognizing the importance of others on their own terms. Thus, she moves towards a "politics of recognition," not abandoning the quest for justice, but asserting that it lies in a different direction. Communicative ethics ought to be one in which difference is taken as a resource, not something to overcome. She argues that justice means that people have to engage each other with an attitude of "wonder" or "enlarged thought," that recognizes the other as other, as different and non-symmetrical, deserving of respect but not necessarily similar to or susceptible to being understood from one's own position. Young suggests a politics in which different voices are recognized as involving irreducible views, but in which each pne's thinking is enlarged by connecting people, ideas and interests without collapsing differences into shared interests. This in the end is the work of an enlarged public sphere—or civil society—not a theory of justice or principles of legitimation.

Activities of self-organization in civil society are the means for breaking through the silencing Leotard calls the *differend*. . . . when a group's suffering or grievance cannot be expressed, or cannot fully be expressed, in hegemonic discourses, associational activity can support the development among those silenced new ways of seeing social relationships or labeling situations as wrong. In these self-organizing activities disadvantaged or marginalized sectors and groups sometimes articulate affirmative self-conceptions in response to denigrating or devaluing fostering and nurturing substantive ends of mutual aid and shared symbols and practices. . . .Social justice involves not only self-determination [as in classical political theories] but also self-development.

... Just social institutions provide conditions for all persons to learn and use satisfying and expansive skills in socially recognized settings. . . . Self-development in this sense . . . entails the use of resources for education and training. . . . While self-development is not reducible to the distribution of resources, market- and profit-oriented economic processes particularly impinge on the ability of many to develop and exercise capacities. Because this is so justice as self-development cannot rely on the communicative and organizational activities of civil society alone, but requires positive state intervention to regulate and direct economic activity (Young 2000).

The justice at which Young aims is not limited to distributive justice. Goods are not products for self-development, but a condition of the possibility of human development. This enlarged sense of justice as self-development includes the development of each person's capacities for full participation in the range of social life.

Justice as self-development requires the interaction of civil society and state in a healthy public sphere. State institutions limit economic power and coordinate action across large scale activities. Their virtues are centralized power, rules and procedures, and bureaucracy to apply and adjudicate rules in systems. Their legitimacy is the degree to which they address public problems. Legitimacy is based on the extent that they address problems identified through broad public discussion with remedies that respond to reasonably reflective and undominated public opinion in the public sphere. The associations of civic society identify problems, interests and needs in society. Their legitimacy is a provision for participation, developing new ideas, applying alternative practices and organizing criticism of state and economic power. The public sphere connects people and power via communicational processes.

Justice-Talk: What are the issues? (Again!) This sketch of the positions about theories of justice allows us to draw the central issues together. Drawn together as a single discourse rather than a mere diversity of opinions, several important issues emerge.

First, critical theory, communitarianism, and feminism have the same antipathy to the idea that the individual is constituted before all social interaction that is implicit in liberal contract theories of society. Justifying norms for communities is difficult when the community is viewed as only a collection of individuals.

The "thin" anthropology of liberalism assumes that human development is a simple determinism of desires and instrumental rationality. Liberal theories do not seem to require the "thin" view of self insofar as all conversation about any particular view of the good life is bracketed by neutrality. However, a "thin" anthropology might be the result of such bracketing. Socially embedded practices—good and bad—do shape the expectations of persons and institutions.

Frustrated expectations are often a prime sources for characterization of policies, programs or actions as unjust or unfair. Not to incorporate a means of bringing a "thicker" view of persons and communities to the conversation seems to distort the conversation.

However, as Young shows, affirming a "thicker" view of persons and commitments makes conversations about "the good" infinitely more complex. Procedures, when they become part of the playing field, can exclude voices from the conversation. Commitment to rationality is commitment to the value of reason, not just to the "fact" of reasonableness. Civic associations which cultivate a greater degree of participation from individuals may cultivate self-development, but they are not sufficient for adjudicating potential injustice due to unfair playing fields.

Habermas, like the liberal theorists, tries to ground social norms without prejudging questions of values. To this extent he is a proceduralist who is confident that rules can clear a space of impartiality. Unlike the liberals, he does not ground this on natural rights theory or contractarianism. He favors a communicative theory based on the notion of rational consent. His approach transposes into the realm of theory the "art of separation" that liberals practice in the sphere of public praxis.

Communitarians, conversely, want to bridge or reduce the gap between descriptive and evaluative expressions between the right and the good, between the grounding of norms and their application. They are unwilling to pay the price Habermas pays for universality. Their attacks are directed against the formalistic bias that characterizes liberal theories. They regard procedural formalism as a pretension, if not a mistake. One cannot, they argue, generate norms, rules, institutions, and principles that are neutral regarding value, culture, or concrete historical contexts that frame the problem. They reject the belief that there is any core of procedures that any actor, no matter how situated, must accept as valid and universal.

The proceduralist view of society is that social interaction is held together by the "shared rules of the game" upon which individuals and groups who hold diverse ideas of what the game is can agree. Feminists criticize this position. Explicit and implicit gender rules systematically distort "the game" to exclude some players from full social roles freely chosen. Likewise, communitarians affirm the context-specific nature of the validity of norms: principles of justice are drawn from a reservoir of value-consensus that exists before any public discourse. For the proceduralist, "talk about justice" establishes the rules on which all conversation partners can agree. For contextualists, dialogue mediates what modern thought has differentiated—facts and values, rules and application, the right and the good, the individual and the community, form and content, methodological and substantive problems.

Given these differences, it is not surprising then that there are different notions of what "justice talk" validates. For contextualists, validity is the social binding force of values, imperatives, rules, and laws. A norm is valid when it is socially enacted and socially accepted. For proceduralists, validity is the rational legitimacy of the procedures that guarantee fairness of process and universal participation in public dialogue. Where liberals and critical theorists disagree is over the degree of institutional control required to assure impartiality and fairness.

This brings us to the heart of this debate that is about the relationship of "private" and "public" worlds. For contextualists, the private and public intersect as tradition—shared commitments about values, interests, and meanings. Culture forms the individual even as individuals contribute to cultural patterns and understanding. Culture provides the form and content of personal identity and is a point of personal identification. Private values are drawn from the public context of tradition and culture. Liberal and critical proceduralists, on the other hand, separate the private from the public, seeking to find a balance to assure the greatest range of personal liberty free from the constraint of public coercion.

For liberals, this means the least public sphere possible in favor of an enlarged private sphere. By taking issues off the "public table," one reduces potential conflict and maximizes personal freedom to choose one's life plan. For critical theorists, this means the desire to institutionalize the processes of critical reflection in a way that assures optimal personal freedom within a public sphere. In each case, however, the public sphere is a means to an end that yields to an instrumental rationality of procedures that govern the public sphere.

For communitarians and feminists, the public and private spheres are not so easily distinguished and disengaged. Feminists argue that the private-public dichotomy is a tool of patriarchy to keep from public view essential justice issues regarding the family and gendered relationships. Both communitarians and feminists insist that the *public persona* is formed from the reservoir of the meanings and values informing concrete ways of life. These "ways of life" deserve respect, autonomy, and affirmation. Yet, as we have seen, affirming value pluralism poses some critical problems for making judgments about the potentially problematic meanings and values in those ways of life. Genital mutilation of young girls may be "just" in terms of the values affirmed by certain cultures. However, it is difficult to deny the moral intuition that it is fundamentally and universally "wrong" in any culture.

This debate about justice, as it stands, highlights the issues that make moral affirmations difficult. No position can overcome the basic context-dependent/context-independent dichotomy that has led to the debate and which continues to drive it forward. The context-dependent position fails to develop an adequate notion of critical judgment that permits one to judge rightness or wrongness within or among traditions. The context-independent position has a notion of judgment, but its notion of normative justification has difficulty rising above a circular argument about the justification of foundational normative claims.

Context-dependent positions, like MacIntyre's, account for the sedimentation of normative experience in traditions, institutions, language, and history. However, they fail to account adequately for the sense of human freedom with regard to traditions and their values. Formalist positions, like those of Habermas, Rawls, and Nozick, by starting with the problem of freedom, demonstrate the malleability of norms regarding their human content. However, they fail to account adequately for the sense of givenness of social roles and social institutions as value sedimentations within human experience. So what we are left with is a two-headed notion that dialogue is a structure (norm) and yet transformative (malleable). Nevertheless, the question that no one has answered is: What is dialogue such that it is both normative and transformative and provides a link between private and public worlds? An important additional issue is that neither position develops a notion of value sufficiently objective to found a distinction between social progress and decline.

Some theorists would dispute that this idea is in play. "Progress" and "decline" have no purchase in the meaning of justice. However, following Aristotle, we may assume that our intentions as social and political actors aim at some good. To be sure people will disagree about which human actions and which futures will constitute movement toward "the good" in real life situations. However, there will be little disagreement among the parties whether the intention of the actions is to leave us better or worse off than when we started. It is this direction of movement from a present toward a "better" or "worse" future that is the concern of moral inquiry and so of our claims about justice and injustice in concrete situations.

4. A Personalist Theory of Justice: Paul Ricoeur and the Conversation of Ethics

Paul Ricoeur (1913-) is a philosopher in the hermeneutic tradition widely regarded as the greatest living phenomenologist who has written extensively on politics and justice. Ricoeur regards himself as a personalist philosopher. Continental *personalism* is a philosophical movement that originated with many, mostly Catholic, thinkers after World War II. In France, it was closely identified with Emmanuel Mounier (1905-1950). His journal *Esprit*, to which Ricoeur has been a notable contributor. As envisioned by Mounier, personalism pilots a course between the collectivism of Marxism and the radical individualism of existential-ism that dominated philosophy in France after World War II. Like Marxism and existentialism, personalist philosophers believe that philosophy should be socially active, seeking to realize the social and political structures that foster the complete development of the person. A person, on a personalist account, is both social and individual and cannot be reduced to one or the other without loss.

Ricoeur subscribes to the personalist commitment to person as the focal ontological reality. A person is not just an existent in the world, but an existent who is conscious. Ricoeur is also committed to the view that theory cannot replace practice. While often neglected as a political thinker, many recognize his philosophical project for its practical political sophistication and intellectual rigor. Ricoeur affirms the significance of the central requirement for impartiality in liberal justice theories. With Rawls and others, Ricoeur affirms that justice is a *regulative idea*—like truth—that guides the actors in social practices, the operative routine of social living. Justice consists of the "rules" that make life among relative strangers possible. Thus, it is a virtue of political rather than individual action. The political on this account is the sphere of impersonal relations.

> We have come to the point where politics appears as the setting par excellent for the achievement of human potentialities. The means by which it exercises this function are first set in place by what Hannah Arendt called the "public space of appearance." This expression extends a theme originating in the Enlightenment—that of "publicity" in the sense of coming to light of day, without constraint or dissimulation, of the whole network of alliance within which each human life unfolds its brief history. This notion of a *public space* first expresses the condition of the plurality resulting from the extension of interhuman relations to all those that the face-to-face relations of "I" and "you" leaves out as a third party. In turn, this condition of plurality characterizes the will to live together of a historical community—people, nation, region, class, and so forth—itself irreducible to interpersonal relations. . . . As the word ["power"] indicates, political power is, across all the levels of power already considered, in its continuity with the power by which I have characterized the capable human being. In return, it confers a perspective of endurance over time and of stability on this edifice of powers; more fundamentally, it projects the horizon of public peace understood as the tranquility of the order.
>
> It is now possible to pose the question concerning what specific ethical values arise from this properly political level of the institution. We can answer without hesitation: justice. "Justice," John Rawls, writes at the beginning of his *Theory of Justice*, "is the first virtue of social institutions as truth is to systems of thought." But to what does justice stand in relation? Not to "you" identifiable by your face, but rather to the "everyone." . . . The application to human interactions of the rule of justice presupposes that we can take society as a vast system of distribution, that is, of sharing roles, burdens, tasks, well beyond the distribution that takes place on the economic plane of market values (Ricoeur 2003, 8-9).

On Ricoeur's account, justice does not exist *independently* of social practices. It emerges from conventions, rules, and tradition as a critical or dialectical self-reflection between what is affirmed as good (as in a good life) and what is accepted as legal (as socially permitted or forbidden). As such justice cannot be fully comprehended by principles and rules. However, it must be expressed by them.

The American practice of slavery provides a good example of what Ricoeur means. The social practice of slavery in the United States was legal from 1619 to 1863. This did not make it good. Slaves were excluded from the civic community. The Constitutional principle of "the equality of all men" did not extend to slaves because they were excluded from the meaning of "all men." However, slaves were persons in the sense affirmed by "all men." There thus ensued an extended, sometimes violent, conversation about slavery as a practice that resulted in a reframing of the principle of equality. The concrete dialectic between the meaning of equality and what the law forbids and commands found expression in changed law. Change in the law, however, did not end the dialectical relation, which continues into the present.

By defining justice in terms of a dialectic between proceduralism and contextualism, Riceour tries to reconcile the proceduralism of Rawls or Habermas and the context-sensitivity of MacIntyre, Walzer, and Young. He does this by maintaining the dialectical tension between "rules" and "contexts" without a premature resolution in favor of rules *or* contexts.

Ricoeur's starting point for understanding justice is the nature of *the person*, because politics presupposes persons and a reflection upon persons endowed with the capacity to choose and act. This reflection is a necessary preface to political philosophy in which the legitimate state is the realization of ethical intentionality in the political arena.

> Politics draws alongside ethical intentionality in giving it a sphere of action. It also draws us towards the second condition of ethical intention—mutual recognition. This recognition causes me to affirm: "Your freedom is as valuable as my freedom.". . . Thus, as a communal organization, the State, gives legal form to what seems to constitute the neutral third term of ethical intentionality: knowledge of the rule. . . . What this means is that the civil law defines, orders, and regulates social roles (debtor, spouse, property owner, etc.) in such a manner that the holders of such roles are treated equally under the law. Equal treatment under the law is not the same thing as equality of opportunity or equality of outcomes (Ricoeur 1997, 403).

This "anthropological preface" affirms that *the person*, as distinguished from the human, is a unique actor (an individual) who is morally responsible for his or her individual actions. However, individuality does not exhaust the meaning of a person. A person is also constitutively related to others persons and institutions that also have moral responsibility. This intersubjective moral responsibility is not exhausted by the sum of individual moral responsibility. Community transcends individuals. It cannot be regarded merely as the aggregate of individuals comprising it at a given moment. Thus, "community," like persons, can be said to act and have intentions.

Ethical intentionality, the moral commitment of the self to others, precedes ethics as law, principle, norm or imperative. The ethical self can be adequately appropriated only insofar as the self understands himself or herself through relationships with the other, especially as mediated by institutions, that constitute complete personal being. This ethical intentionality consists of three interrelated experiences that move from the personal self to impersonal institutions. Thus, Ricoeur affirms:

> the "ethical intention" is *aiming at the "good life" with and for others, in just institutions* . . . . The major advantage of entering into the ethical problematic by way of the notion of the "good life" is that it does not refer directly to selfhood in the figure of self-esteem. If self-esteem does not indeed draw its initial meaning from the reflective movement through which the evaluation of certain actions judged to be good are carried back to the author of those actions, this meaning remains abstract as long as it lack the dialogic structure which is introduced in the reference to others. This dialogic structure, in its turn, remains incomplete outside of the reference to just institutions. In this sense, self-esteem assumes its complete sense only at the end of the itinerary of meaning traced out by the three components of the ethical aim (Ricoeur 1995, 172).

The key elements in this definition are (1) a *good life,* (b) *with and for others,* (3) *just/fair institutions*—corresponding to the three forms of the person pronouns *"I," "you,"* and *"he/she."* Clarifying the structure of personal relationships is the concern of an ethical perspective according to the moral experience of the self.

The first ethical experience is the experience of the self as free. Indeed, the self is realized in the effort to secure its liberty. This fundamental notion yields an ethics of action. Freedom only reveals itself in action—what Ricoeur calls, the "work" of freedom. Action renders freedom objective from mere subjective possibilities. By acting, one testifies to one's presence in the world. Attestation distinguishes oneself from a world of things as one expresses oneself as a person-in-the-world who moves from "I am able to do" to "I have done." The regulative idea at this level is not principle or law, but deeds. Ethical failure is the difference between the personal freedom that one aspires to bring into being by doing something, and the freedom one realizes by so doing. The ethical intention is to bring one's freedom into being. It controls the second movement of ethical experience.

The second ethical dimension is the self's relation to others. The acting self is not an atomistic, free individual. The self also encounters, is contested by, the other who is also seeking to realize its freedom. What Ricoeur means is that the self as "I" encounters the opposition of the liberty of the "second person," the other ("you"), in the sphere of personal action. It is in the encounter with the "personal others" that one encounters the demands and imperatives of interaction. This relationship is a dialogical interaction of "willing the liberty of the second person." This is the dialogue of intimate relationship, of family, home, and friendship. It is the dimension of "love" that spontaneously seeks the good of the other, and that has no need of rules or normative justification. The ethic of the second person is the dimension of personal and interpersonal action that yields an ethics of interaction.

The ethics of intimate relation is "willing that the freedom of the personal other be." This means acting to enlarge the freedom of the personal other. Ethical failure here is to objectify the other by denying the other's presence as a free subject—denying the other's freedom by making him or her an instrument of one's own needs and desires. In this way, one denies the other's demand for recognition as person. In so doing, what I do is to deny my own freedom; I objectify my own being, because I am a self like the other and so my action toward the other reflects the self I am becoming. While the ethical can be expressed as a principle ("Thou shalt not kill another"), principles are not regulative, given the immediacy and intimacy of this second movement of ethical intentionality.

The third movement of ethical intentionality, and the proper dimension of public or political dialogue, is the experience of the impersonal "third-person." These are the institutional relationships of socially cooperative living that are not bound by intimate relations, but impersonal relations guided by imperatives, rules, and norms. These relationships are not mediated by direct (face-to-face) interaction, but by the rules and normative expectations of impersonal social intercourse.

> The fact that the aim of living well in a way that encompasses the sense of justice is implied in the very notion of the other. . . . Correlatively, justice extends further than face-to-face encounters.
>
> Two assertions are involved here: according to the first, living well is not limited to interpersonal relations but extends to the life of *institutions*. Following the second, justice presents ethical features that are not contained in solicitude, essentially a requirement of *equality*. The institution at the point of application of justice and equality as the ethical content of the sense of justice are the two investigations into the third component of the ethical aim. . . .
>
> By "institution" we are to understand here the structure of *living together* as this belongs to the historical community—people, nation, region, and so forth—a structure irreducible to interpersonal relations and yet bound up with these. . . . What fundamentally characterizes the idea of institutions is the bond of common mores and not that of constraining rules (Ricoeur 1995, 194).

The full public sphere of institutional life regulates impersonal relations. While personal desire and care for the other next to me can regulate personal and intimate relations, they are not sufficient to order the impersonal relations of life with strangers. It is to the domain of regulative institutions that justice fully and properly applies.

My desire to get home this afternoon provides a simple example of the difference between the private and public spheres of action. In driving home I have neither the desire nor interest in personally negotiating the rules of the road to get from work to home. The driving code consists of the rules and the skills to perform the complex transactions implicit in the code. The code formalizes a set of mutual, impartial and impersonal expectations that do have to be negotiated every time I drive. The norms expressed by the code 'normalize' a framework of being in the world. The impersonal scheme is driven originally by personal desire. However, the scheme functions independently of my desire. It does not require my personal approval or disapproval. In short, the scheme is the condition of the possibility of being able to drive safely. The scheme, not my desires, provides the normative structure, as articulated in imperative, rules, laws, and principles. Admittedly, the code constrains my actions. I cannot drive in any old way. However, the existence of the code gives me the liberty to drive as it gives others the same liberty. The constraint is actually necessary to the freedom to drive.

Ricoeur characterizes the dimension of the socially impersonal as an on-going conversation. The intimate self through the sociality of the impersonal human being enters into a conversation that precedes me, to which I contribute for a certain period of time, and that continues after me. The conversation that precedes me is the meanings and values informing a concrete way of life. In this conversation, the ethical life is a perpetual transaction between the project of freedom and its ethical situation outlined by the given world of institutions.

The ethical movement for Ricoeur is a move from self to institutions, through value, to imperative and law or formal principles. This movement is one from the sphere of the intimately personal to the objectively impersonal, from the intimately known to the anonymous. This movement from intimate relations to impersonal other requires a greater and greater specification of the acceptable reasons for actions, a greater formalism, and a more rigorous normative justification. Ricoeur's threefold movement of ethical experience brings three significant clarifications to the relationship of the private and public spheres of value as they move from the informal to the formal.

First, there is a reciprocal relationship between morality as social practice and ethics as a critical justification of acts according to law, principles, or theory. Political action is a moral enterprise that is continuously constructed as a shared public discourse. The discourse justifies impersonal social institutions in relation to some notion of "the good life" that realizes the ethical perspective. The "ethical perspective" of relationship is the organizing principle of all human action, a *telos*, a horizon or limit toward which all action is concentrated—of persons and communities of persons. In light of this, other patterns of human action (for example, daily routines, life plans, my life story) assume a certain order and hierarchy, the connectedness of a whole life as persons achieve an ethical identity—moral selfhood.

Ethical identity concerns not just the being of the self, but being with and for others. Self-esteem includes the value of others in whom the self recognizes itself. To value others, however, is not just an intimate relational connection to others. It also thrusts one into the pursuit of equitable social institutions. The achievement of an ethical identity—the full emergence of moral being—transcends social conventionalism or ethical relativism to find its full expression only in the desire for the truly good, the authentically valuable, expressed in interpersonal relations as solicitude and in institutional relations as equality. Justice, on Ricoeur's account, is a "regulative idea" whose *telos* or end is "a good life." This "good life" is not merely an individual good or a good of intimate friends. It is also a common or shared good of virtual strangers.

Ricoeur's three dimensional model shows precisely what is different between the private and public spheres, but also it shows why the private sphere necessarily moves to the public. The architecture of the self includes a public dimension. Liberal-critical proceduralism tries to preserve a critical and real distinction between the private and the public that is essential to human freedom. However, the distinction may be purchased at the price of misunderstanding what is at stake in the private-public differentiation. It may isolate the private from the public with the concomitant necessity of trying to bridge artificially what is really immanent in human experience. Communitarians, on the other hand, will not tolerate a private-public distinction. They so preserve the private sphere of the self, but at the price of undervaluing the necessary formalism of rules and procedures to guide public action and to avoid action being imposed by the strong on the weak or to protect the privileges of the powerful.

Second, there is a difference between dialogue among intimates and discourse as a public process of offering adequate reasons for normative action. One can reasonably assume that intimate dialogue, the ethic of intimate interaction, does resolve value conflicts and disagreements about values, principles and norms of action. There is no reason to assume that public dialogue as a process of argumentation and justification ought to be able to accomplish the same thing when we recognize that the intelligibility of procedures is the facilitation of the value of social relationships. Indeed, rules of discourse are required in order to assure reasonable disagreement about norms and values in a public forum.

Children playing a game can illustrate this point. The action of the game embodies characteristics of both intimate interaction and public formalism. The game is an intimate action—a relation of the face-to-face. Conflicts are resolved by reference to rules, not relations. The rules are the game distributing the roles of players and the limits of action. Resolving disagreements about the rules permits greater freedom of intimate action. Such rules permanently contest an imperial self that tries to impose its liberty on the other. "The rules are not what you say but what we agree." Such contestation yields the "true self" that is known in its relations. That is, the structural requirements that sustain schemes of public discourse operate to shift and transform the values motivating the intimate self as the self interacts through such schemes.

Take the example of "changing one's mind" as the result of interaction. Most people have had the experience of going into a meeting "knowing" exactly what she wanted (needed, would demand, ask for, beg for) to realize after the meeting that while one got exactly what one wanted (needed, demanded, asked for, begged), during the interaction, what one wanted (needed, demanded, asked for, begged) had changed in response to a variety of factors ranging from new information to a new understanding of the other(s) with whom one was in interaction. This is not an uncommon intersubjective experience as human beings collaborate in a wide range of ways to meet personal and corporate goods.

This insight drives to the heart of the liberal idea of value. Liberals argue that one cannot have a public discussion about values because values represent some nonnegotiable architecture of the self. So values permitted into the public sphere are minimal to reduce conflict. Communitarians understand that values drive social interaction forward and so conflicts about values are not pathological, but creative. What communitarians fail to appreciate adequately, however, is how public values can become systematically distorted and require the critical judgment of reason.

Third, an ethics of personal relationship is more intimately related to the realm of desire, that is, personal value, than public discourse that is related to the impersonal dimension of social institutions and justice. The normative dynamism that governs institutions is related directly to the realm of social, public order and its legitimation. Legitimation of social order is ultimately historically conditioned. On Ricoeur's account, it is turned toward a consensus which precedes us, and therefore which exists.

However, there is also another critical moment that anticipates a future freedom in the form of a regulative idea which is not a reality, but an ideal. Thus, Ricoeur argues, the fact that the law legitimates a public order, giving personal desires, values, and norms the "stamp" of universal accord, does not mean that the order is free of criticism. What is required is that one return to reconsider the concrete actions that fulfill the criterion of the law and justice. This is to acknowledge that discourse has a normative structure which makes specific demands on anyone who joins the conversation. Likewise, any sphere of human living has a structure of norms, rules, principles and operative routines that imposes requirements whose procedures makes normative demands on contexts. Justice mediates between the two to approximate the conditions required to live a good life with and for others in just institutions.

Chapter Twelve
The Postmodern Riposte—
Contesting Universalism

One way of looking at contemporary justice theories is that they are an extension of a conversation that started in the seventeenth century with the breakdown of the Christian religious-cultural synthesis. Popular challenges to absolute monarchies and classical versions of the natural law began to step into the vacuum. This period—perhaps as yet incomplete—was a transition from "classicism" to "modernism." To a significant degree, this transition set the terms and relations of the conversation. But what happens to the idea of justice if the traditional terms and relations of the conversation are challenged at their root? Is it possible to reconfigure the debate entirely? This is the challenge of postmodernism.

1. What Is Postmodernism?

The nature of postmodernism makes it difficult to define. In one sense, it is a descriptive term used for forms of architecture, art, philosophy and literature. In another sense, it is an epistemological position used across disciplinary boundaries in philosophy, literature, and social sciences. Moreover, those who call themselves "postmodern" not only express conflicting views, but they are also interested in barely overlapping subject matters: art, communications media, history, economics, politics, ethics, cosmology, theology, methodology, literature, and education. So in a real sense "postmodernism" is defined by its negation of the "modern." The lack of a definition in a real sense represents postmodernism well.

In philosophy, "postmodern" refers to a movement that developed in France in the 1960s as younger French intellectuals rejected the standard philosophical models of Marxism, phenomenology, and existentialism. Postmodernists, for the most part, deny the possibility of objective knowledge of the real world. Language is not transparent, they say. Consequently, words do not have "univocal" (a single or primary) meaning. Words and texts do not have singular meaning, but rather multiple interpretations none of which completely grasp the meaning of the word or text.

Virtually in every kind of intellectual endeavor, postmodernism tries to show that what others have regarded as a unity, a single, integral existence or concept, is plural. The human self is not a simply unity, hierarchically composed, solid, self-controlled. It is, rather, a multiplicity of forces or elements. It would be more true to say that a person has selves rather than a self. There is no unity of the human self—no unambiguous presence of the self to the self. There is no meaningful distinction between rational inquiry and political action.

Moreover, postmodernists deny the transcendence of norms. Norms such as truth, goodness, beauty, rationality, are no longer regarded as independent of the processes they serve to govern or judge, but are rather products of an immanent reason in those processes. For example, where most philosophers might use the idea of justice to judge a social order, postmodernism regards the idea of justice itself as the product of the social relations that it serves to judge. That is, the idea was created at a certain time and place, to serve certain interests, and is dependent on a certain intellectual and social context. This obviously complicates any claims about the justice of social relations.

This idea is easier to grasp if we understand the postmodernist rejection of the modern. On most postmodernist accounts, the meaning of "modern" is a quest for order, rationality and rationalization, and creating order out of disorder. The assumption is that creating more rationality is conducive to creating more order, and that the more ordered a society is, the better—the more rationally—it will · function. Because modernity is about the pursuit of ever-increasing levels of order, modern societies constantly are on guard against anything that might disrupt order. Thus modern societies rely on continually establishing a binary opposition between "order" and "disorder," so that they can assert the superiority of "order." But to do this, they have to have things that represent "disorder"—modern societies thus continually have to create/construct "disorder." In western culture, this disorder becomes "the other"—defined in relation to other binary oppositions such as right/wrong, good/bad, normal/abnormal, well/sick, black/white, rational/irrational, etc. Thus anything non-white, non-male, non-heterosexual, non-hygienic, non-rational (etc.) becomes part of "disorder," and has to be eliminated from the ordered, rational modern society. Michel Foucault (1926 - 1984) in his study of the appearance of the asylums for the insane in Western societies expresses it this way:

> The asylum is a religious domain without religion, a domain of pure morality, of ethical uniformity. Everything that might retain the signs of the old differences was eliminated . . . . Now the asylum must represent the great continuity of social morality. The values of family and world, all the acknowledged virtues, now

reign in the asylum. But their reign is a double one. First, they prevail, in fact, at the heart of madness itself, beneath the violence and disorder of insanity, the old solid nature of the essential virtues is not disrupted. There is a primitive morality which is ordinarily not affected even by the worst dementia; it is morality which both appears and functions in the cure . . . . This inalienable virtue is both the truth and the resolution of madness. Which is why, if it reigns, it *must* reign as well. The asylum reduces difference, represses vices, eliminate irregularities. . . . In one and the same movement, the asylum becomes . . . an instrument of moral uniformity and of social denunciation. The problem is to impose, in a universal form, a morality that will prevail from within upon those who are strangers to it and in whom insanity is already present before it has made itself manifest (Foucault 1965, xx).

The ways that modern societies go about creating categories labeled as "order" or "disorder" have to do with the effort to achieve stability. Foucault argues that stabilization requires "normalizing" human desires, actions, and performances around a statistical center. Normalizing judgments (the Normal) impose a standard or reference on actions that is experienced as a power that constrains and coerces conformity to accepted forms of order. Thus a basic idea like "equality" (treating similars similarly) is a statistical fiction because any notion of similarity or sameness among individuals is pure construct. On Foucault's account,

The power of the Norm appears through the disciplines. Is this the new law of modern society? Let us say rather that, since the eighteenth century, it has joined other powers—the Law, the Word (*Paroles*), and the Text, Tradition—imposing new delimitations on them. The Normal is established as a principle of coercion in teaching with the introduction of a standardized education and the establishment of the *ecoles normals* (teachers' training colleges); it is established in the effort to organize a national medical profession and a hospital system capable of operating general norms of health; it is established in the standardization of the industrial processes and produces. Like surveillance and with it, normalization becomes one of the great instruments of power at the end of the classical age. For the marks that once indicated status, privilege, and affiliation were increasingly replaced—or at least supplanted—by a whole range of degrees of normality indicating membership of a homogeneous social body, but also playing a part in classification, hierarchization, and the distribution of rank. In a sense, the power of normalization imposes homogeneity; but it individualizes by making it possible to measure gaps, to determine levels, to fix specialities, and to render difference useful by fitting them one to another. It is easy to understand how the power of the norm functions within a system of formal equality, since within a homogeneity that is the rule, the norm introduces, as a useful imperative and as a result of measurement, all the shading of individual differences (Foucault 1977, xx).

Jean-Francois Lyotard takes this postmodernist line a step further. He equates normative stability with the idea of "totality," or a "totalized system." Totality, stability and order, Lyotard argues, are maintained in modern societies through the means of *"grand narratives"* or *"master narratives"* that are stories a culture tells itself about its practices and beliefs to legitimate or justify the existing forms of order. A "grand narrative" in American culture might be the story that democracy is the most enlightened, rational form of government, and that democracy can and will lead to universal human happiness. But these master narratives are only constructions to legitimate forms of oppression, domination, exclusion, and violence serving the purpose of order. For example, the idea of the American "melting pot" that homogenized cultural differences in favor of a uniform public sphere leveled cultural uniqueness and particularity. This narrative, like all grand narratives, glosses over difference. The difference that is glossed over, silenced, that does not have a voice in the narrative, Lyotard calls *"the differend."*

> The differend is the unstable state and instant of language wherein something which must be able to be put into phrases cannot yet be. . . . This state is signaled by what one ordinarily calls feeling: "One cannot find the words," etc. A lot of searching mus be done to find new rules for forming and linking phrases that are able to express the differend disclosed by the feeling, unless one wants this differend to be smothered right away in a litigation and for the alarm sounded by the feeling to have been useless. What is at stake in a literature, in a philosophy, in a politics perhaps, is to bear witness to differends by finding idioms for them (Lyotard 1983, 13).

Every belief system or ideology has its grand narratives, according to Lyotard. For Marxism, for example, the "grand narrative" is the idea that capitalism will collapse in on itself and a utopian socialist world will evolve. For liberal democracy, it is the idea of freedom from constraints in the pursuit of personal life projects and goals. In this sense, grand narratives are a kind of meta-theory, or meta-ideology, that is, an ideology that explains an ideology, such as Marxism or liberalism—a story that is told to explain the belief systems that exist.

> [Against] the "philosophies of history" that inspired the nineteenth and twentieth centuries' claim to assure passage over the abyss of heterogeneity . . . [we can oppose in every case] counter-examples to their claim. —Everything real is rational, everything rational is real: "Auschwitz" refutes speculative doctrine. This crime, which is real . . . is not rational. —Everything proletarian is communist, everything communist is proletarian: "Berlin 1953, Budapest 1956, Czechoslovakia 1968, Poland 1981" (I could mention others to refute the doctrine of historical materialism: the workers rose up against the party). . . . —Everything that is the free play of supply and demand is favorable for the general enrichment and vice-versa: the "crises of 1911 and 1929" refute the doctrine of economic liberalism. And the "crises of 1974-1979" refute the post-Keynesian revision of the doctrine. The passages promised by the great doctrinal synthesis end in bloody impasses. Whence the sorrow of the spectators in this the end of the twentieth century (Lyotard 1983, 180-181).

Lyotard compares the creation of narratives to games, a favorite postmodern metaphor, in which "rules" of the game create the game. Applied to the idea of justice, justice would be one social game among many whose rules create the game and so set the rules.

> [L]anguage games are the minimum relation required for society to exist: even before he is born . . . the human child is already positioned as the referent in the story recounted by those around him, in relation to which he will inevitably chart his course. Or more simply still, the question of the social bond, insofar as it is a question, is itself a language game, the game of inquiry (Lyotard 1984, 16).

Lyotard argues that all aspects of modern societies, including the natural sciences viewed as the primary form of knowledge, depend on such "grand narratives" to legitimate or justify their activity—but the legitimation is a self-legitimation. Thus postmodernism sets as its primary task a critique of grand narratives, to raise awareness that such narratives serve to mask the contradictions and instabilities that are inherent in any social organization or practice. In other words, every attempt to create "order" always demands the creation of an equal amount of "disorder," but a "grand narrative" masks the "constructedness" of all these categories by explaining that "disorder" *is* chaotic and bad, and that "order" *is* rational and good. Postmodernism, in rejecting grand narratives, favors *"mini-narratives"*—local histories or stories that explain small practices, local events, rather than large-scale universal or global concepts. Postmodern "mini-narratives" are always situational, provisional, contingent, and temporary, making no claim to universality, truth, reason, or stability.

> . . . [N]o self is an island; each exists in a fabric of relations that is now more complex and mobile than ever before. . . . A person is always located at "nodal points" of specific communication circuits, however tiny these may be. . . . [N]ot even the least privileged among us is ever entirely powerless over the messages that traverse and position him at the post of sender, addressee, or referent. One's mobility in relation to these language games . . . is even solicited by . . . the self-adjustments the system undertakes in order to . . . [combat] its own entropy; the novelty of an unexpected "move," with its correlative displacement of a partner or group of partners, can supply the system with that increased performativity it forever demands and consumes (Lyotard 1984, 15).

2. Postmodernist Theory of the State

Foucault argues that knowledge merges with power to enforce conformity to artificial discursive consensuses that subjugate the individual to the forms of order.

Knowledge and power shape a network of control that encompasses every aspect of everyday life managed by "normative rationality." The "totalizing system" is not a grand narrative, but a set of procedures.

Postmodern politics. The heading of this subsection—"politics" rather than "political theory"—was quite intentionally chosen to emphasizes that postmodernist thinkers offer less a political theory than a political program or praxis. This does not mean they do not theorize about politics in the sense of offering descriptions and explanations of political phenomena and institutions. They do. However, their theory is more a problematizing of the political than a systematic, coherent presentation of the nature and function of politics. This is due to the nature of postmodernist objections to meta-narratives that have, on their account, lost their meaning and only serve to oppress and exclude. Separating "politics"—relations of authority—from the other spheres of human living is artificial, creating an order where there is none. Consequently, politics is everywhere in the family, the workplace, the school, clubs, and even in academic philosophy. Formal political structures are only one narrative among many possible narratives. Political experience is fragmented. It cannot be bound by principles or rules. It is often the prime location of self-legitimating structures of domination.

Postmodernist theory affirms that justice theories are often only disguised rationalization for distorted power relationships. For example, Foucault claims that political ideas like "rights," "principles," and "justice" have legitimated power relationships in society. Only by exposing how such ideas serve as instruments of political domination or exclusion is "justice served"; paradoxically, justice as an idea is itself an instrument of domination or exclusion. This, coupled with the postmodernist suspicion of theories as meta-narratives and the postmodernist critique of Habermasian universalism, will carry us somewhat away from justice theory toward a more general discussion of postmodernist political thinking.

Foucault: Justice as invention and control. Foucault rejects the view, implicit in Habermas, that there is a normative human nature. He also rejects the view that science provides universal truths (knowledge). Human beings produce their own historical way of life in its totality. Thus, *truth, verification, model, theory, reason, rationality, argument, knowledge, nature, essence* and the like have meaning only within the historically limited and cultural bounded community that produce them. These concepts are social constructions that have the social function of "normalizing relations" to make certain kinds of intersubjective action possible. Their meaning is their function in society, not their representation of reality.

For example, the existing relations that are the starting point of science are not regarded simply as givens to be verified and to be predicted according to laws of probability. They are a particular mode of discourse in which "truth" is determined by the structures of authority to "rule" certain claims "in" and certain claims "out" of bounds. This is similar to the "rules" of chess that authorize certain moves and forbids others. The "rules" normalize or standardize play. Thus the "game" is constituted by the rules. Mastery of the rules allows strong players to dominate weaker ones. Also, one cannot play "checkers" according to "chess rules," and so "chess players" can exclude checker players from the board.

Foucault takes this position because he is a *social constructivist*. Constructivists affirm that scientific, and other beliefs are largely or entirely determined by social forces, that scientific and other facts are constituted by social interactions, that scientific rationality has no trans-cultural epistemic warrant, and that the empirical content of scientific and other statements is perpetually open to re-negotiation. Thus, constructivism is the view that all ideas and concepts are fabricated and radically contextualized. Reality is created by social reality. Since concepts and categories are based on the social reality, more important than "what questions" we ask are questions about how views of human nature and science have functioned in society historically and actually.

It is thus obvious that Foucault rejects any form of universalism and aligns himself epistemologically with relativism. This fundamental commitment carries through consistently. He denies that there is any external position of certainty. There is no universal understanding that is beyond history and society.

On Foucault's account, one of the hallmarks of Western political philosophy is a fascination with theory generated from abstractions, first principles, and utopian idealism. Understood this way, Western thinkers have approached the problem of political order by building models of the just social order or affirming general principles to deduce and evaluate existing social and political conditions which we then *reify* or *hypostatize*, taking representations as existing concretizations of the "real world." You may have been aware of this method in reading this text. The hiding commitments, values, and position behind the "veil of ignorance" in Rawls' "original position" is a particularly good example. So are the concepts of a "social contract," "natural law," and even an "ethics of care." For Foucault, this taking an abstraction as a real existent is an archetypical example of the "will to knowledge" that has left Western societies in the dark about the real functioning of institutions and power.

Foucault's "archeology of knowledge" is an effort to unmask the problematic of reification and to reveal the *social function* of knowledge and conceptualization. On this view, the real political task in a society is to criticize the workings of institutions that appear to be both neutral and independent but are not, and instead are instruments of domination and political violence whose reality is hidden in an obscurity that must be revealed so they may be opposed.

Now one might think that on this account "justice" might be the vehicle in such a struggle. But it is precisely at this point in his thinking that Foucault takes a turn that startles the imagination. Justice is another conceptualization that masks a will to knowledge and subtle forms of social control. "The idea of justice in itself is an idea which in effect has been invented and put to work in different types of societies as an instrument of a certain political and economic power or as a weapon against that power. . . . One can't, however regrettable it may be, put these notions forward to justify a fight which should . . . overthrow the very fundaments of our society" (Foucault 1974a, 187).

On this account, justice becomes political action as a critique of power and domination. The following text is not atypical. "One shouldn't start with the court as a particular form, and then go on to ask how and on what conditions there could be a people's court; one should start wit popular justice . . . and go on to ask what place a court could have within this. . . . Now my hypothesis is not so much that the court is the natural expression of popular justice, but rather that its historical function is to ensnare it, to control it and to strangle it, by re-inscribing it within institutions which are typical of a state apparatus" (Foucault 1974b, 1).

Foucault provides a methodological program for doing so. First, examine systems of power and right as they reveal themselves in their concrete institutional forms such as prisons, schools, and asylums. Second, examine how systems of power and right, whatever the professed intentions of their practitioners, succeed in constituting their projects. Third, recognize how systems of power and right diffuse power throughout a society so that many individuals both exercise power and are subject to it. Fourth, recognize that systems of power and right inevitably bring into existence forms of knowledge that are no more than ideologies that help maintain those systems in place. This program is the *sine qua non* of political philosophy.

Schematically, we can formulate the traditional question of political philosophy in the following terms: how is the discourse of truth, or quite simply, philosophy as that discourse which *par excellence* is concerned with truth, able to fix the limits of power? The [question] I would prefer to pose is . . . this: what rules of right are implemented by the relations of power in the production of the discourses of truth? . . . In a society such as ours, but basically in any society, there are manifold relations of power which permeate, characterize and constitute the social body, and these relations of power cannot themselves be established, consolidated nor implemented without the production, accumulation, circulation and functioning of a discourse. . . . We are subjected to the production of truth through power and we cannot exercise power except through the production of truth. . . . Power never ceases its interrogation, its inquisition, its registration of truth: it institutionalizes, professionalizes and rewards its pursuit. . . . It is truth that makes laws, that produces the true discourse which, at least partially, decides, transmits and itself extends upon the effects of power. In the end we are judged, condemned, classified, determined in our undertakings, destined to a certain mode of living or dying, as a function of the true discourses which are the bearers of the specific effects of power. (Foucault 1974b, 93-94).

Thus truth is a local production. Truth can make no universal claim. It only describes regional exercises of power relevant to and dependent on specific social and historical conditions.

> Truth is a thing of this world: it is produced only by virtue of multiple forms of constraint. And it induces regular effects of power. Each society has its regime of truth, its "general politics" of truth: that is, the types of discourses which it accepts and makes function as true; the mechanisms and instances which enable one to distinguish true from false statements, the means by which each is sanctioned; the techniques and procedures accorded value in the acquisition of truth; the status of those who are charged with saying what counts as truth (Foucault 1974b, 131).

Consensual discourse on the Habermasian model is local. It cannot claim universality. As local it is partial. It serves a community of interest. Moreover, it only instantiates a new power relation because all discourse servers a speaker's interests even if "speaker " and "interest" are taken in the largest possible sense of a community that transcends an individual. Thus the domination of power must be exposed again to reveal the forms of social subjugation. Foucault's *archeology*, meant to uncover origins from the bottom up, tends toward *an-archy*, revealing that which has no origin or beginning, but which exists only as a defused presence in intersubjective relations.

> My general project over the last few years has been, in essence, to reverse the mode of analysis followed by the entire discourse of right from the time of the Middle . . . to give due weight . . . to the fact of domination . . . to show not only how right is, in a general way, the instrument of this domination—which scarcely needs saying—but also to show the extent to which, and the forms in which right (not simple the laws but the whole complex of apparatuses, institutions and regulations responsible for their application) transmits and puts into motion relations that are not relations of sovereignty, but of domination. Moreover, in speaking of domination I do not have in mind that solid and global kind of domination that one person exercises over others, or one group over another, but the manifold forms of domination that can be exercised within society, not the domination of the King in his central position, therefore, but that of his subjects in their mutual relations; not the uniform edifice of sovereignty, but the multiple forms of subjugation that have a place and function with the social organism.
>   The system of right, the domain of the law, are permanent agents of these relations of domination, these polymorphous techniques of subjugation. Right should be viewed . . . not in terms of a legitimacy to be established, but in terms of the methods of subjugation (Foucault 1974b, 95-96).

Thus, political theory becomes an anti-politics, the despairing rejection of the belief in emancipatory social transformation, as well as a variety of efforts to create a new or reconstructed politics. There can be no large scale transformations, only piecemeal reforms and local strategies designed to enhance individual freedom and progressive change. Foucault rejects utopian thought and the category of "totality" as terroristic, violent and cruel, while searching for new "styles" of life as different as possible from each other.

Lyotard: Discourse and domination. Lyotard's *The Postmodern Condition: A Report on Knowledge* (1979) is often said to represent the beginning of Postmodern thought. Later, with the publication of his essay "Answering the Question: What is Postmodernism?" in 1982, Lyotard addresses the debate about the Enlightenment and specifically Jurgen Habermas' take on the Enlightenment project.

Lyotard, as we saw earlier, argues that all aspects of modern societies rely on "grand narratives," a sort of *meta-theory* that searches to explain the belief system that exists. These "grand narratives," in other words, represent totalizing explanations of things. Christianity, Marxism, libertarianism, Enlightenment, and contractarianism represent prominent examples of metanarratives. They are organizing schemes and dominant modes of thought. All political thought falls into the category of metanarrative on Leotard's account. For Lyotard, the Enlightenment project as promoted by Habermas is an effort at authoritative explanation.

Lyotard argues that the role of postmodernist thought is to question, critique, and deconstruct these grand narratives by observing that the move to create order or unity always creates disorder as well. Instead of "grand narratives" that explain all totalizing thought, Lyotard argues for a series of mini-narratives that are provisional, contingent, temporary, and relative and which provide a basis for the actions of specific groups in particular local circumstances.

In *The Differend: Phrases in Dispute* (1983), Lyotard argues that the concept of power-free consensus implicit in Rawls and explicit in Habermas is incoherent, and cannot serve as a basis for normative validity. He draws on Wittgenstein's philosophy of language to argue that language use can be viewed as various games or genres in which speech is given meaning only in relation to the other aspects of that particular game. It follows from this theory of meaning that one genre of discourse cannot be translated into another. "Phrases obeying different regimens are untranslatable into one another" (Lyotard 1983, 48). From this, Lyotard infers that when political dialogue occurs between people who speak different idioms, any decision that is reached will occur in one idiom at the expense of the other. "Damages result from an injury which is inflicted upon the rules of a genre of discourse but which is reparable according tot hose rules. A wrong results from the fact that the rules of the genre of discourse by which one judges are not those of the judged genre or genres of discourse" (Lyotard 1983, xi).

Thus judgment, on Leotard's account, has unjust consequences. Aspects of the other, the other's different idiom will have been suppressed, mistranslated, or ignored, in the terms of the agreement. In other words, discourse communities marginalize voices. Likewise, when judgments are made within a general genre of discourse about matters conducted in another genre—for example, legal decisions—the decision will fail to do justice to the different idiom regardless of attempts at inclusion or interpretation of different views.

> [The] powers that be (ideological, political, religious, police, etc.) presuppose that the human beings they are supposed to guide, or at least control, are in possession of something they communicate. Communication is the exchange of messages, exchange [is] the communication of goods. The instances of communication like those of exchange are definable only in terms of property or propriety [*propriété*]: the propriety of information, analogous to the propriety of uses. And just as the flow of uses can be controlled, so can the flow of information (Lyotard 1983, 12).

Lyotard therefore argues that the effort to attain agreement through dialogue always constitutes an unjust suppression of dissent. It is this suppressed, untranslatable rift between genres of discourse that Lyotard identifies as a "differend." The differend is of political significance because when a social dialogue contains various idioms, as it often does, any agreement or decision will be made in terms that favor one idiom and suppress or distort the others. Moreover, there is no way to mediate fairly between various genres of discourse, for any such process would itself merely create new "differends." Injustices of translation occur when "the plaintiff is divested of the means to argue and becomes for that reason a victim," now a victim of the adjudication process as well as the initial crime.

> It is in the nature of a victim not to be able to prove that one has been done a wrong. A plaintiff is someone who has incurred damages and who disposes of the means to prove it. . . . One loses them . . . if the author of the damages turns out directly or indirectly to be one's judge. . . . . [The] "perfect crime" does not consist in killing the victim or the witnesses (that adds new crimes to the first one and aggravates the difficulty of effacing everything), but rather in obtaining the silence of the witnesses, the deafness of the judges, and the inconsistency (insanity) of the testimony (Lyotard 1983, 8).

Lyotard uses the examples of the legal adjudication of the claims of victims of the Holocaust and of disputes between labor and capital to instantiate his argument. He argues that justice cannot be done in these cases, for the claims of the plaintiffs are lost when they have to be expressed in the terms of the law. The claim that one has witnessed a gas chamber is undermined by its very ability to be stated in court. The inability to come up with a law which covers international violations of human rights, particularly of this magnitude. is an extreme example of a general problem with attempts (or pretenses) to respond to unfairness in an evenhanded manner.

Similarly, in disputes over norms regarding labor, a legal system designed to treat labor as another exchangeable commodity cannot countenance claims that the quality of labor is of intrinsic importance to human self-realization. Similar difficulties of presenting proof of injustice and the unfairness of placing the burden of giving proof on the plaintiff have been noted in the crimes of rape, sexual harassment, and discrimination in employment, housing, education, and the like. In each case, justice is impossible because disputes are resolved in terms that favor particular interests: "the 'regulation' of the conflict that opposes [the competing parties] is done in the idiom of one of the parties while the wrong suffered by the other is not signified in that idiom" (Lyotard 1983, 141).

On this view, the goal of political consensus is unattainable and not even desirable in its consequences. The very attempt to reach agreement through rational discourse leads to exclusion or distortion of some claims. Agreements will be reached in idioms that are dominant, and thus will tend not to do justice to the claims of those who speak in a marginal idiom or whose claims are foreign to those who make decisions.

The key to Lyotard's notion of justice is recognizing his refusal to legitimate discursive consensus of a Habermasian type. This does not mean that political discourse—justice talk—is without value or utility. Deliberation opens perspectives on difference and exposes the differends that are the warp and woof of modern complex societies. "In the deliberative politics of modern democracies, the differend is exposed, even though the transcendental appearance of a single finality that would bring it to resolution persists in helping forget the differend, in making it bearable" (Lyotard 1983, 147).

Since incommensurable difference cannot be adjudicated without loss of all that can be expected as "justice," real "justice" means exposing the differends. Exposing—throwing light on, bringing to the light of conscious attentiveness—in some sense harks back to the Greek ideal of truth as *aletheia*—an "uncovering." Lyotard is perhaps correct that justice lies in exposing differences that have been silenced. In the end, however, Lyotard's notion of justice, seems thinly unsatisfying if exposing difference is all that justice is. Lyotard argues that every consensus cannot help but be coercive and so inherently "unjust," but this in itself is an argument, and therefore it must be regarded as being at least on the same playing field with Rousseau, Rawls, and other arguments. In the end, it is still a matter of comparing different arguments with regard to their logical, ontological, and epistemological rigor.

Chapter Thirteen
Privacy and the Public Life

The social contract theories on which the U.S. Constitution was based, as we have seen, generally take the approach of asking what kinds of legitimate justification can be given for warranting any party to the contract giving up freedom. The assumption here is that, in the absence of any such justification, liberty should not be infringed. Traditionally—and increasingly so in recent times—this liberty has been interpreted to include a general *right to privacy*. That is, the government should "leave us alone," and refrain from intruding into our private lives, unless there is some specific justification for doing so. The government leaving us alone is often regarded as an aspect of the government respecting our liberty, as least *prima facie*.

Interpreting just what this "right to privacy" means, what it includes, and how far it extends has been a major controversy in legal and political discussions. Recently, the question has arisen as to whether the President has a right to order surveillance of private citizens' e-mail and phone calls without obtaining a court order and without legislative oversight, on the basis that secret intelligence operatives make a judgment that the person might be suspicious. In the same way, questions have arisen about whether citizens or foreigners can be detained without trial or legal representation, and in some instances tortured or "disappeared" to offshore "torture prisons," if government workers suspect that the person is involved in international terrorism, and that such treatment might be in the interest of national security. Do such actions violate privacy rights of citizens?

In the same way, a woman's right to make reproductive decisions—for example, to have an abortion—has been interpreted to involve the conflict between the woman's privacy rights and the duty of the government to legislate in the interest of unborn children, their fathers, or other parties who have concerns about reproductive issues. The question has often been framed in terms of a basic value decision: at what point does protection of the rights of the unborn fetus or of its father warrant infringing the woman's *prima facie* right to privacy?

This chapter traces the reasoning that has been used about such matters, especially in the context of social contract theory, but also touching on the way feminist philosophers, communitarians, and others approach this issue. We begin with a short history of legal cases to set the agenda for privacy discussions.

1. Cases about Privacy and Publicity

Teachers nationwide in the United States commonly tell students to swap homework, quizzes or other schoolwork and then to correct one another's work as the teacher goes over it aloud. Sometimes, the teacher then has students call out the scores to record them in a gradebook. However, the U.S. Supreme Court in November 2001 decided to hear a case of a mother who claimed that the practice of calling out the scores violated her child's privacy. The boy's mother contended that discussing the work and "calling out" the grades embarrassed her son. A federal district court agreed with the mother that a 1974 federal law designed to protect the privacy of educational records covered her son. Publicizing grades violated his privacy. February 18, 2002, the U.S. Supreme Court reversed the lower court decision. They decided that the practice of students grading the papers of other students did not fall under the privacy provisions of the law regulating personal privacy in education. They did not comment on the merits of the mother's claim that making the scores public was an invasion of privacy.

A proposal by federal government officials to encode finger or eye prints on American drivers' licenses in late 2001 set off a furor of controversy. The suggestion followed the bombing of the World Trade Center as a way to identify potential threats to national security. The opponents of the proposal argued that this would be a move toward a national identification card. Acting to protect what they believe were threats to privacy, they argued that national identification cards violate individuals' privacy, increase the potential of government control over citizens' movements, and characterize totalitarian regimes and police states throughout the world. The proposal was dropped.

In 1997, author Sandra Cisneros painted her house in the historic King William District of San Antonio fuchsia purple because, on her account, the color reflected her taste and her heritage. Her neighborhood association asked her to change the color to something more in keeping with the recent history of the neighborhood. When Cisneros refused to repaint her house, lawyers for the association asked City Council to order the house repainted. Cisneros argued that the house was her private property. She was free to paint the house any color she chose. Moreover, the color of the house was a form of self- and cultural-expression that was in keeping with her Mexican heritage and the distant history of the community. Neighborhood residents argued that the color of the house was not in keeping with the recent historical character of the community. It should be returned to something more in keeping with the neighborhood's more proximate history of the nineteenth century German merchants who occupied the site. Moreover, they found the color tasteless and claimed it lowered their own property values. Several City Council committees asked Cisneros to repaint her house. She continued to refuse. Finally, San Antonio City Council, citing privacy, refused to act to force her to change the color.

In many countries, including the U.S., employees and unions have protested employers monitoring employee e-mail and internet use. Employees argue that reading e-mail and monitoring internet use is a violation of personal privacy. Employers argue that employees are using company resources and time, and therefore such surveillance is justified. In 2001, in London, England, seven lawyers were fired for circulating a colleague's bawdy stories using their firms' e-mail. In court, they argued that e-mail was a form of private communication, like a letter, and should not be subject to employer surveillance. The high court disagreed and upheld the right of employers to read employees e-mails. In the U.S., there has so far been no definitive judicial ruling on the issue. However, practice and precedent suggest that the practice of employer surveillance of employees' private communications in the workplace is acceptable. It is not a violation of privacy.

By the end of 2002, seventeen states have passed laws allowing citizens to register their phone numbers and choose not to receive phone solicitations from telemarketers. Telemarketers must use the lists and refrain from calling households who have registered. These laws were a response to the popular feeling that unsolicited telemarketing calls are annoying intrusions and a violation of privacy. These lists, which are public, are intended to protect the privacy of those who register. However, a federal proposal for a similar national registry is hotly contested by telemarketing firms as a restriction of free speech.

From cases to questions. These cases are just a few examples of the kinds of privacy issues that abound in society today. Many people believe that privacy is threatened in a host of ways. They point to the fact that government agencies and large scale institutions, like businesses, have power to coerce individuals to conform to particular ways of thinking and acting. To balance this unequal distribution of power, some argue, individuals need to be protected from unfair or unjustified intrusions into their private lives. However, one function of such public institutions is to impose conformity of behavior for the good of social order. When a police officer stops someone who is speeding and asks for a driver's license, few would say that the officer is violating the driver's privacy. Most people would in fact argue that because speeding is a potential harm to others, stopping a speeder is justified. However, when a government authority orders a person to repaint his or her house to protect "property values," people are more likely to be uneasy about the legitimacy of the order because the use of private property such as a house, many believe, is not an area subject to the dictates of authorities. Yet it could also be argued that lowering the property values of neighbors is in fact harming them.

Privacy is not just a matter of the power of authority to coerce behavior. Many organizations, not just governmental ones, possess a tremendous amount of information about people. Electronic storage of this information makes this information quickly and readily available. Organizations routinely share medical records, insurance claims, employment history, consumer purchases, internet use, police records, driving records, and credit records, except when specifically prohibited by law. This has led to significant questions about who should have access to this information. Obviously, when a person applies for a mortgage, information about the person's credit history is relevant and important to the bank. However, is the person's driving record equally relevant? Lenders argue it is. Others believe this is an unjustified intrusion on personal privacy.

Information about people's buying habits benefits businesses trying to sell products. However, such information allows businesses to "target" sales and advertising to individuals by phone or e-mail. Such "targeting" intrudes on a person's private time. Think about the last time you received a "courtesy call" at dinnertime. That was a "targeted" call based on information that the business calling had about you. How comfortable are you with businesses knowing your buying habits based on prior credit card purchases? This issue is of such a concern for many that one credit card company as part of its sales pitch says they do not sell "your name" to other companies, though selling such personal information remains a routine business practice.

Some companies routinely read employees' e-mail and monitor their internet use in the work place. Is this an invasion of an employee's privacy? If a person posts a personal letter through the company's mail system, the letter cannot be opened without violating laws protecting privacy. However, if you are overheard complaining about the boss, this is not privileged communication. Is e-mail more like a letter, or like a public conversation?

Many people insist that they have a right to know when a sex offender is living in their neighborhood because the presence of the sex offender affects personal security. Others, especially sex offenders and their lawyers, argue that the "right to privacy" and "to be let alone" covers such information. Should a person's criminal record be a matter of public knowledge? Or do criminals have a right to a "new start" that would be difficult if their criminal record were public knowledge?

These are not easy questions to answer. They also involve surprisingly complicated conceptual and practical issues. When we consider questions about privacy, three things stand out. First, in contemporary Western societies, privacy is a highly prized social value. However, the value placed on privacy is not historically or culturally universal. Second, while many people value privacy, there are no completely satisfactory definitions of what privacy is or what a "right to privacy" includes or excludes. Third, identifying a clear boundary between the private and public realms of human living is difficult because of the complexity of the relationship between individuals and the institutions that constitute the public sphere.

2. Privacy as a Privileged Social Value

Most people desire and expect their privacy to be respected. Americans particularly treat privacy as a "privileged value." A value is "privileged" when it is allowed priority in cases where it conflicts with others values. While we do not treat a privileged value with the same priority that we give an absolute value, we expect it to take priority over other values in most instances. Thus, all things being equal, privacy trumps other competing values.

Take the case of Sandra Cisneros. While many people agreed that her choice of house color was less than tasteful (an aesthetic value) and her unwillingness to respect her neighbors' opinions was rude (a social value), her right to paint her house any color she wanted was finally respected because it was private, not public, property. Similarly, "national security" is an important value, particularly in times of national conflict. However, in the case of the proposal to include finger prints on drivers' licenses, an appeal to privacy took precedence over security.

Most people assume that a person usually should not intrude on the privacy of others. That is, we ought to respect their privacy. Thus, eavesdropping on a conversation, even when it might be in our interest (or just interesting) to know what is said is normally not acceptable conduct. However, a police officer may listen in on another person's conversations to protect public safety, provided there is a warrant from a court.

Likewise, personal information about others should not to be made public unless there are exceptional overriding reasons, such as public health, to do so. Thus, while we have a right to paint our house the color we choose, we cannot allow our house to become a safety or health hazard. So city authorities cannot require a person to paint a house one color or another, but they can require a person to cut the weeds, remove garbage, maintain the house in general good repair, and restrict or monitor public uses such as parties, business, or the like.

As these examples show, when it comes to privacy, we assume that the burden of proof is on those who argue for ignoring privacy in favor of another value. In other words, privacy tends to "trump" other values. When a value is strongly privileged, any other claims are initially suspect and made to jump over many hurdles to "trump" claims of the privileged value. Thus, a policeman must have a warrant (legal authority) to eavesdrop on private conversations. A city must have a court order to enforce health regulations against private homeowners. Even private citizens apologize when they inadvertently violate another person's privacy.

The distinction between the private and public is central to much legal and political thought. In the everyday thinking of most Americans, privacy—the state of being withdrawn from the world, free from public attention, interference or intrusion—is not only a highly prized social value by individuals, but many people think that the right to privacy is foundational to constitutional democracy. Yet philosophically, politically, and legally, many other people seriously challenge the idea of privacy on several grounds. First, privacy connotes secrecy or being hidden from public scrutiny. Thus, privacy can be used to cloak wrongdoing. One of the early court cases dealing with privacy concerned a bookie who used the phone to place bets. Many forms of public corruption thrive on secrecy and privacy. Many forms of racial discrimination were justified until recently by declaring a club, school, or business "private." This permitted members or owners to serve those whom they chose rather than "being open to" the public.

Second, privacy often leads to deceit and hypocrisy, especially in social relations. The characterization "two-faced" is sometimes used to describe people who act one way in their private life and another in their social or public life.

Third, privacy can protect guilty people from taking responsibility for their victims. For example, until recently marital relations were considered a "private affair," which allowed many women and children to suffer physical and emotional harm with no protection by the police, courts or welfare agencies. If the line between the private and the public is too narrowly and tightly drawn, it can increase the risk of harm to vulnerable people by detouring shame and guilt. For example, family violence until recently went unremarked and unaddressed because family relations were private. Many—especially feminists and critical theorists—argue that a private-public distinction is incoherent and open to manipulation to protect the interests of the holders of social power.

Fourth, claims to privacy often block public debate about moral issues. Abortion and sexual discrimination are two examples of issues whose public discussion was retarded because of claims of privacy.

So, while people highly value privacy, there is lack of clarity of what privacy is and what it "protects." Privacy is not an absolute value, even though it is privileged. As we have seen, there are restrictions on both publicity and privacy in social practice. However, debate continues on the degree to which individuals can be or have a right to be shielded from publicity. Thus, privacy issues open questions of what the value represents and whether, in fact, privacy should be valued as highly as it is.

The idea of privacy is not clear cut. Privacy means many different things that vary according to the writer. Privacy has been defined as "self-regarding conduct" (J.S. Mill 1859); "being left alone" (Warren and Brandeis 1890); "autonomy" (Alan Westin 1967); "a voluntary and temporary isolation from others" (Edward Bloustein 1964); "a sphere or realm of action protected from public encroachment, freedom from unauthorized intrusion: state of being let alone, able to keep certain, especially personal, matters to oneself" (*Black's Law Dictionary* 1999); "control of information others have about us" (Charles Fried 1968); and "the realm in which an actor (either a person or a group, such as a couple) can legitimately act without disclosure and accountability to others" (Amitai Etzioni 2000). Many variations of these definitions exist. The definitions are not interchangeable. Each one has significant conceptual problems. This means that no single definition of "privacy" has gained universal acceptance. Moreover, there is not even a consensus about what would constitute an adequate definition. The broad range of issues and a lack of conceptual clarity means the idea of privacy is ambiguous.

In the legal literature, where privacy has been most discussed, "private" means a sphere from which others may be excluded in some meaningful way. When I close the door to my office to be alone, I am asking that others respect my privacy. If I insist that family members not open my mail, then I am insisting that the communication be private. Following this idea, courts have tended to rule that excluding others from one's thoughts, beliefs, dispositions, or actions is a "right." The "right to privacy" constrains, if not prohibits completely, unwarranted crossing or intrusion on a boundary of personal space.

> The right to be let alone; the right of a person to be free from unwarranted publicity. Term "right of privacy" is generic term encompassing various rights recognized to be inherent in concept of ordered liberty, and such right prevents governmental interference in intimate personal relationships or activities, freedoms of individual to make fundamental choices involving himself, his family, and his relationship with others. The right of an individual (or corporation) to withhold himself and his property from public scrutiny, if he so chooses. It is said to exist only so far as its assertion is consistent with law or public policy (*Black's Law Dictionary*, 7th ed., 1999).

Thus "privacy" is a term that designates various rights of the individual to order his or her own life without the intrusion of others, especially civil authorities, except where allowed by law. In essence, privacy is an exercise of freedom of choice or personal autonomy. The idea that privacy is a right of individuals to be free from public interference is basic to legal thinking about privacy, but it does not clearly define what privacy is, or why it should be regarded as a "right." Thus, while it seems clear legally that one's home encompasses a private sphere, it is much less clear whether a student's school work does.

In a search for conceptual clarity, philosophers have depended less on a definition of privacy than defining privacy in relation to other personal properties. Thus, some philosophers stress the importance of privacy to the development and maintenance of intimate relationships such as friendship and trust, to individuality, and to the development of persons from pre-social human beings because of its internal relationship with autonomy, dignity and self-development. Privacy, these writers argue, promotes the moral principle of *"respect for persons."* On this account, privacy is valuable and necessary in the creation, enhancement and maintenance of full human expression, which includes intimate relationships, individuality, autonomy and dignity.

However, these claims leave crucial, underlying questions unanswered. For example, why is privacy necessary for intimacy? Privacy may be important because we connect it with personal autonomy, but why would an autonomous person choose privacy? What is it about privacy, rather than social relations, that promotes or maintains individuality?

Comparative sociological studies show that the scope of what is considered a matter of privacy varies greatly, not only across societies but within societies over time. This means that what people considered private varies with the social and historical context. For example, in Britain claims to privacy are more restricted than in the United States. Camera surveillance of urban public spaces is routine. The police carry out searches of bodies and belongings more readily and more frequently than in the United States. On the other hand, British law protects the privacy of celebrities or "newsworthy persons" to a greater degree than the U.S. On the continent of Europe, people are routinely required to carry some form of identification or identity card and to identify themselves at police request without any special cause. Even Americans are becoming more open to public intrusion into private lives after the terrorist bombing of the World Trade Center in 2001. Thus, there is no "absolute" or "natural" right to privacy that transcends cultures or historical circumstance, as rights like "respect of person" or "autonomy" seem to do.

Alan Westin, in *Privacy and Freedom,* provides one of the most extensive social studies of privacy. His study was motivated by his concern that social, economic, and political changes would diminish the privacy of individuals. He argued that privacy is a basic need derived from the animal world. It was important to people in primitive societies and is found in all cultures, even though its particular forms will vary. Thus, it is universal.

> Needs for individual and group privacy and resulting social norms are present in virtually every society. Encompassing a vast range of activities, these needs affect basic areas of life for the individual, the intimate family group, and the community as a whole. . . . The individual seeks privacy, as well as companionship, in his daily interactions with others; limits are set to maintain a degree of distance at certain crucial times in his life. The family-household unit also institutes limitations on both members of the unit and outsiders to protect various activities within the household. Finally significant rituals and ceremonies in the larger community are also protected by customs which prescribe privacy for these rites within the group. . . . [T]he norms vary, but the functions which privacy serves to perform are crucial for each of these three areas of social life (Westin 1967, 24-25).

Westin defines privacy in individual terms as "the claim of individuals, groups, or institutions to determine for themselves when, how, and to what extent information about them is communicated to others" (7). He concludes that "privacy is an irreducibly critical element in the operation of individuals, groups, and government in a democratic system with a liberal culture"(368). That is, privacy is essential to maintaining liberty and a sense of personal autonomy in the face of large, depersonalizing institutions and social processes. Thus privacy serves broad social functions in liberal democracies, including providing support for religious tolerance, scholarly inquiry, integrity of the electoral system, and limits on police powers (24-25).

While recognizing the social utility of privacy, Westin still links the value of privacy to the individual and each individual's relationship to society.

The individual's desire for privacy is never absolute, since participation in society is an equally powerful desire. Thus each individual is continually engaged in a personal adjustment process in which he balances the desire for privacy with the desire for disclosure and communication of himself and others, in light of the environment conditions and social norms set by the society in which he lives (Westin 1967, 7).

The core of the right to individual privacy is "the right of the individual to decide for himself, with only extraordinary exceptions in the interest of society, when and in what terms his acts should be revealed to the general public" (42). Thus, Westin regards privacy as fundamentally at odds with social interests. There is an inherent conflict between privacy and the public openness demanded by institutions. For Westin, privacy and social participation are competing desires. Each individual establishes a balance between the two that is best for that individual. Obviously, the norms of society set some boundaries on that balance. However, the balance is a "personal adjustment process" in which each individual establishes a unique balance between privacy and social participation.

Anthropological studies have shown that the individual in virtually every society engages in a continuing personal process by which he seeks privacy at some times and disclosure or companionship at other times. This part of the individual's basic process of interaction with those around him is usually discussed by social scientists under the terms "social distance" and "avoidance rules" (Westin 1967, 42).

However, in the balancing process, the individual is at some considerable disadvantage because of social interests through "privacy-invading phenomena" motivated by curiosity, interpersonal social comparisons, and surveillance against "anti-social" behavior.

Any social system that creates norms—as all human societies do—must have mechanisms for enforcing those norms. Since those who break the rules must be detected, every society has mechanisms of watching conduct, investigating transgressions, and determining "guilt" . . . Society also requires certain acts to be done in the presence of others, in recognition that visibility itself provides a powerful method of enforcing social norms.

The importance of recognizing this "social" half of the universal privacy-invading process is similar to the recognition of the individual curiosity—it reminds us that every society which wants to protect its rules and taboos against deviant behavior must have enforcement machinery. Until a society appears in which every individual obeys every rule . . . there will be family heads, group leaders, religious authorities, and tribal-national authorities who will engage in surveillance to see that private conduct stays within a socially determined degree of conformity with the rules and taboos of that culture (Westin 1967, 20-21).

Westin therefore sees privacy as set up by a tension between personal conduct and social surveillance. Social surveillance puts people "under the regard of others" and in some significant sense depersonalizes or objectifies the individual and so diminishes his or her sense of autonomous being. On the other hand, some degree of surveillance is socially required to assure some degree of conformity to social standards required to reduce social conflict. Such surveillance is, however, coercive. It limits "choices" of individuals to reduce social tension. The "privacy-invading phenomena" serve to maintain social norms and enforce social conformity. Privacy, on the other hand, primarily serves individual purposes within the context of organization and democratic society. Privacy is "basically an instrument for achieving individual goals of self-realization" (39). Privacy is a means by which individuals voluntarily or temporarily withdraw from society to pursue their interests and values. Such privacy must be protected for the good and benefit of individuals.

Westin's argument is that the sociological data confirm the classical liberal view of privacy framed on *tension between the individual and society.* "Privacy" is a conceptual and practical constraint against public interests intruding on private interests without justifiable warrant. However, one can criticize Westin in two ways. First, his study starts with the assumption that public institutions *diminish* the autonomy of individuals when one might as well argue that mastering the skills of institutional life in fact *enlarge* personal autonomy. Second, his argument is circular. Privacy is valuable because people value it; and since people value it, it is valuable. Westin's assumptions are not unproblematic. However, they rest on a deeper bedrock of thinking about privacy and the individual in the Western social and political tradition that we can now consider.

3. John Stuart Mill and the Liberal Ideal of Privacy: Freedom from Coercion

John Stuart Mill (1806-1873) was the first philosopher to offer explicit arguments for privacy from society or the public sphere. Chapter Four in *On Liberty* (1859) lays out the *classical liberal* position on the limits to the authority of society over the individual that frame Westin's assumptions. By "classical liberal" in this context, we mean a position in which liberty can never be infringed without a well-justified reason for doing so. On Mill's account, privacy is the sphere of "self-regarding conduct" or, we might say, autonomous action. However, Mill recognized that affirming an individual's autonomy of action in society raises an interesting set of questions about the possible limits of such action: "What, then is the rightful limit to the sovereignty of the individual over himself? Where does society begin? How much of human life should be assigned to individuality, and how much to society?" (Mill 1859, 552) Mill answers: "To the individual should belong the part of life in which it is chiefly the individual that is interested; to society, the part which chiefly interests society" (552).

Mill's principle is grounded on a separation of social benefits and responsibilities. Social living confers distinct benefits to each individual that carry with them distinct responsibilities. Since society is an aggregate (collection) of autonomous individuals, each individual ought to be able to pursue his or her interests in so far as it does not infringe on the freedom of others to do the same. As long as a person's beliefs, values, or activities do not injure others, then each person ought to be able to believe, value, or act as he or she deems best. For example, "free speech" means that we are free to express our opinions, but not to yell "fire" in a crowded stadium because others may be hurt. Society is justified in curbing free speech to protect members of society. Otherwise, neither society nor one's fellow citizens should interfere.

> . . . everyone who receives the protection of society owes a return for the benefit, and the fact of living in society renders it indispensable that each should be bound to observe a certain line of conduct toward the rest. This conduct consists, *first*, in not injuring the interests of one another; or rather certain interests, which, either by express legal provision or tacit understanding, ought to be considered as rights; and *secondly*, in each person's bearing his share . . . of the labors and sacrifices incurred for defending the society or its members from injury and molestation. These conditions society is justified in enforcing, at all costs for those who endeavor to withhold fulfillment (Mill 1859, 552).

This view of society and the individual is not, on Mill's account, a "negative doctrine" in the sense that people should not take any interest in the activities of others.

> . . . It would be a great misunderstanding of this doctrine to suppose that it is one of selfish indifference, which pretends that human beings have no business

with each other's conduct in life, and that they should not concern themselves about the well-doing or well-being of one another. . . . Human beings owe to each other help to distinguish the better from the worse, and encouragement to choose the former and avoid the latter. However . . . neither one person, nor any number of persons, is warranted in saying to another human creature of ripe years, that he shall not do with his life for his own benefit what he chooses to do with it. He is the person most interested in his own well-being (Mill 1859, 553-554).

It does mean, however, that in general people should not interfere with the conduct of others, except when certain limited conditions are met. "When, by conduct of this sort [mischief that harms others] is led to violate a distinct and assignable obligation to any other person or persons, the case is taken out of the self-regarding class, and becomes amenable to moral disapprobation in the proper sense of the term" (Mill 1859, 559). Thus "Whenever . . . there is a definite damage, or a definite risk of damage to an individual or to the public, the case is taken out of the province of liberty, and placed in that of morality or law" (560).

Mill's position can be reduce to two maxims or principles: First, the individual is not accountable to society for his actions, in so far as these concern the interests of no person but himself. "Advice, instruction, persuasion, and avoidance by other people if thought necessary by them for their own good, are the only measures by which society can justifiably express its dislike or disapprobation of his conduct" (Mill 1959, 573).

Secondly, in so far as such actions are prejudicial to the interests of others, the individual is accountable for them. Thus, a person may be subjected either to social or legal punishment, if society thinks the one or the other is requisite for its protection (Mill 1959, 573).

Three basic claims frame Mill's argument for protecting the private sphere of personal action from the public interference. No single claim is sufficient to establish a "right to privacy," but together they provide what Mill believed were sufficient reasons to affirm that an individual's privacy ought to be respected.

1. Each person knows his or her own interests best. When another person undertakes to act for another, he or she does so without full knowledge of the other's real interests. So each individual ought to be allowed to act on his or her interests without public constraint.

2. When society undertakes to act on another's behalf, such interference is based on assumptions that are likely to be false. Given the possibility of mistake regarding assumptions about what is best for each individual, society ought to interfere as little as possible with individual privacy.

> The interference of society to overrule [an individual's] judgment and purposes only in what regards himself must be grounded on general presumptions; which may be altogether wrong, and even if right, are as likely as not to be misapplied

to individual cases, by persons no better acquainted with the circumstances of such cases than those who merely look at them from without. In this department, therefore, of human affairs, individuality has its proper field of action. In the conduct of human beings towards one another it is observed, in order that people may know what they have to expect; but in each person's own concerns his individual spontaneity is entitled to free exercise. . . .All errors which he is likely to commit against advice and warning are far outweighed by the evil of allowing others to constrain him to what they deem his good (Mill 1959, 554).

3. Public interference with the decision and actions of others is most likely to be done in a way that is wrong and in the wrong place. Public acceptance of what is right or ought to be done is often not morally right. Notions of "right"— what is good or bad for others to do—are based on moral sentiment or preference. Others ought not to impose their preferences on others.

The opinion of a . . . majority, imposed as a law on the minority, on questions of self-regarding conduct, is quite as likely to be wrong as right; for in these cases public opinion means, at the best, some people's opinion of what is good or bad for other people. . . .[A] person's taste is as much his own peculiar concern as his opinion or his purse. It is easy for anyone to imagine an ideal republic which leaves the freedom and choice of individuals in all uncertain matters undisturbed, and only requires them to abstain from modes of conduct which universal experience has condemned. . . . But where has there been any such state? (Mill 1959, 562-563).

We can frame these negative arguments into a simple argument:

1. Freedom, or personal autonomy, is the highest (social) good.

2. Respecting the autonomy of the other to decide for himself what he ought to do increases the degree of freedom in society.

3. One ought to act in ways that increase rather than decrease autonomy and freedom.

4. Therefore, individuals ought to be able to decide and act for themselves without public intrusion or interference.

What Mill does is mark off a private sphere of thought, belief, value and action by protecting individual rights to a sphere of personal thought, belief, and action. Thus, the private realm demarcates a domain of autonomy for individuals. This move, then, makes room for a variety of semi-autonomous community associations such as the family, schools, clubs, neighborhood associations, teams, churches, and interest groups, whose private functions ought likewise to be respected and free from public intrusion. Thus, in Western political thinking, such groups came to be regarded as being in the "private sphere" and so protected from public interference.

However, one can insist on one's privacy only up to the point where exercises in the private realm intrude on the liberties of others. Individual rights, including privacy, are limited. Such limitations *are not directly for the common good.* Rather, they are meant to protect the *liberties* and *rights* of others as individuals. Although Mill's overall philosophy was one of utilitarianism, where the common good is the only long-term intrinsic value, he regarded rights and liberties as the most important immediate values to be protected for this purpose. On the whole, the view of privacy is one of a personal sphere protected from the coercive authority of state and society. Privacy and coercive authority, both formal and informal, on this account are often in conflict as a tension between the freedom of the individual and the needs or good of the state or community.

This tension is well illustrated by events after the attack on the World Trade Center. Following this event, the government sought extended powers to tap phones, listen in on lawyer-client relationships, and detain suspects without warrants. Authorities sought these powers to interfere in the privacy of individuals to detour terrorism that requires a significant degree of seclusion and "privacy" to succeed. Others argued, however, that despite the need to detour terrorism, such extended powers to intrude on individuals' privacy was a threat to citizens' rights to privacy, understood as being free from surveillance and intrusion.

What is obvious is that Mill's thinking about the private realm as a sphere of personal liberty was shaped by the central belief that the collective power of society, especially as vested in social institutions like government, needs to be constrained in the face of the more limited power of the individual to protect him or herself from unwanted intrusion. A similar belief underlies the American Bill of Rights and its protection of the private sphere of person, home, and religious belief. However, it is also obvious that the contemporary understanding of what is protected by claims to privacy includes a larger reach than constraining institutions from intruding on private interests.

4. Warren and Brandeis: The Right to Be Left Alone

Thirty years after Mill's essay, a *Harvard Law Review* article by Samuel D. Warren and Louis Brandeis, called "The Right to Privacy" (1890/1984), offered a key turning point in legal thinking about privacy. Its language and arguments served as the basis for hundreds of legal cases in the twentieth century. Consequently, many people think it the most influential law review article ever published. There is little question that it extended the view of the reach of privacy into the public sphere for Americans.

The essay is not original in its thinking. It reflects the classical liberalism of Mill and pieces together a miscellany judicial decisions that had granted jurisprudential relief from unwanted publicity based on defamation of character, the invasion of property rights, and breaches of confidence. Taking the cases as a whole, Warren and Brandeis concluded that these decisions in such cases were based on a broader principle—privacy—that was entitled to recognition in the law. This right, they argued, protects individuals from the intrusion by press and media and its attendant "mental distress."

Warren and Brandeis argued that the right to privacy is conceptually distinct from other freedoms, particularly the right to property. The advance of civilization that had cultivated new sensibilities and vulnerabilities in humans also created new "privacy needs." The need for privacy is not an inherent social need, but develops after society reaches a certain threshold of cultivated sophistication that requires privacy for the good of the individual. The intensity and complexity of modern life makes a person's ability to retreat from the world and exercise *"the right to be let alone"* crucial for maintaining a sense of personal well-being.

In defending the importance of privacy, Warren and Brandeis never define what privacy is—only that it creates a right to be left alone, although it can be inferred that privacy means "being left alone" or in peace free from uninvited intrusion by others. Certainly, their reference to the "precincts of private and domestic life" connects privacy to exercising the capacity to isolate oneself from the public life and the community. They also connect privacy with other values, especially the respect due an individual's "inviolate personality" or individuality that has been a key principle of American thinking about privacy. In any case, Warren and Brandeis build a picture of private sphere as a personal harbor or retreat from the pressures of social life. "The right to be let alone," on their account, is "supreme" and sits apart from other considerations. People can and ought to be let alone as much as they desire—even completely, if they desire. Even if all members of a society were to choose to be let alone, the "common good" would not suffer any ill effect.

Thus, on the Warren and Brandeis argument, privacy is necessary to protect the "inviolate personality," meaning individuality. "Publicity," making public what is private, trivializes and "destroys the robustness of thought and delicacy of feeling." Making private concerns public, on this view, is a "blighting influence" that coarsens feelings, creates unwarranted mental distress, and diminishes the quality of social life itself.

That the individual shall have full protection in person and in property is a principle as old as the common law; but it has been found necessary from time to time to define anew the exact nature and extent of such protection. Political, social, and economic changes entail the recognition of new rights, and the common law, in its eternal youth, grows to meet the demands of society. Thus, in very early times . . . liberty meant freedom from actual restraint; and the right to property secured to the individual his lands and his cattle. . . . [N]ow the right to life has come to mean the right to enjoy life—the right to be let alone; the right to liberty secures the exercise of extensive legal privileges; and the term "property has grown to comprise every form of possession—intangible, as well as tangible. . . .

Recent inventions and business methods call attention to the next step which must be taken for the protection of the person, and for securing to the individual. . .—the right "to be let alone." . . . The press is overstepping in every direction the obvious bounds of propriety and decency. Gossip is no longer the resource of the idle and of the vicious, but has become a trade, which is pursued with industry as well as effrontery. . . . The intensity and complexity of life, attendant upon advancing civilization, have rendered necessary some retreat from the world. . . . When personal gossip attains the dignity of print, and crowds the space available for matters of real interest to the community, what wonder that the ignorant and thoughtless mistake its relative importance. . . .

The common law secures to each individual the right of determining, ordinarily, to what extent his thoughts, sentiments, and emotions shall be communicated to others. Under our system of government, he can never be compelled to express them (except when upon the witness-stand). . . . In every case, the individual is entitled to decide whether that which is his shall be given to the public. No other has the right to publish his productions in any forms without his consent. . . .

No basis is discerned upon which the right to restrain publication . . .can be rested, except the right to privacy, as part of the more general right to the immunity of person—the right to one's personality. . . . The common law has always recognized a man's house as his castle, impregnable, often even to its own officers engaged in the execution of its commands. Shall the courts close the front entrance to constituted authority, and open wide the back door to idle or prurient curiosity? (Waren and Brandeis 1984, 75-103).

Obviously, Warren and Brandeis affirmed that the courts should protect privacy from public intrusion as a fundamental right. Their position expands the classical liberal position that protected the individual from public authority to include intrusion from uninvited social pressure and coercion, especially the power of the media to render public private concerns and interests. Their argument is a considerable expansion of the notion of privacy from Mill's basic idea that privacy defined a sphere of personal autonomy protected from collective coercion. Privacy concerns not just the individual's relation to constituted authorities like the State; it also includes every social relation and interest potentially open to uninvited public regard.

Warren-Brandeis thinking did not immediately change the law. It did, however, start to change legal thinking about privacy as new cases made their way through the courts. Subsequent arguments for privacy held that privacy—especially in terms of one's person and personality—is a kind of property—something to which one had an absolute right of disposal. The Warren-Brandeis formula that privacy is "the right to be left alone" gained currency and acceptance as it appeared in hundreds of briefs and legal decisions.

Jurisprudence and privacy: Enlarging the meaning of privacy. Warren-Brandeis both reaffirmed and enlarged the basic liberal conception of the private sphere that sets normative and empirical limits to political and social power over the individual. In private life, the individual is not and should not be regulated by law or subject to the intrusion of unwanted social pressure. In public life, the individual shares, or at least obeys, the norms and laws governing the individual's relations with others and in so doing accepts social and political authority. While this view continued to dominate thinking about private and public life, beginning in 1960 there were a number of court cases that enlarged the meaning of the private life by limiting the range of what could be considered public. These cases altered, and continue to change, the conceptions of the boundary between the private and the public.

The first major case was a 1964 Supreme Court decision that acknowledged a constitutional right to privacy for the first time. The Bill of Rights does not explicitly recognize a right to privacy *per se,* but dimensions of privacy such as security of person, property, and religious belief are specifically acknowledged, and it is often argued that the right of liberty implies a *prima facie* right to be left alone. Justice William O. Douglas' majority opinion in *Griswold v. Connecticut* argued that privacy is a "penumbra right" that flows from other rights guaranteed in the Constitution (*Griswold v. Connecticut* 1965). In this case, the Supreme Court ruled that a Connecticut law forbidding use of contraceptives was unconstitutional, because it violated the right of marital privacy, an implicit "zone of privacy" guaranteed by the U.S. Constitution.

The foregoing cases suggest that specific guarantees in the Bill of Rights have penumbras, formed by emanations from those guarantees that help give them life and substance. Various guarantees create zones of privacy. The right of association contained in the penumbra of the First Amendment is one, as we have seen. The Third Amendment in its prohibition against the quartering of soldiers "in any house" in time of peace without the consent of the owner is another facet of that privacy. The Fourth Amendment explicitly affirms the "right of the people to be secure in their persons, houses, papers, and effects, against unreasonable searches and seizures." The Fifth Amendment in its Self-Incrimination Clause enables the citizen to create a zone of privacy which government may not force him to surrender to his detriment. The Ninth Amendment provides: "The enumeration in the Constitution, of certain rights, shall not be construed to deny or disparage others retained by the people."

The Fourth and Fifth Amendments were described in *Boyd v. United States,* 116 U.S. 616, 630 , as protection against all governmental invasions "of the sanctity of a man's home and the privacies of life." We recently referred [381 U.S. 479, 485] in *Mapp v. Ohio,* 367 U.S. 643, 656 , to the Fourth Amendment as creating a "right to privacy, no less important than any other right carefully and particularly reserved to the people."

The present case, then, concerns a relationship lying within the zone of privacy created by several fundamental constitutional guarantees. And it concerns a law which, in forbidding the use of contraceptives rather than regulating their manufacture or sale, seeks to achieve its goals by means having a maximum destructive impact upon that relationship. Such a law cannot stand in light of the familiar principle, so often applied by this Court, that a "governmental purpose to control or prevent activities constitutionally subject to state regulation may not be achieved by means which sweep unnecessarily broadly and thereby invade the area of protected freedoms." Would we allow the police to search the sacred precincts of marital bedrooms for telltale signs of the use of contraceptives? The very idea is repulsive to the notions of privacy surrounding the marriage relationship.

　　We deal with a right of privacy older than the Bill of Rights—older than our political parties, older than our school system. Marriage is a coming together for better or for worse, hopefully enduring, and intimate to the degree of being sacred. It is an association that promotes a way of life, not causes; a harmony in living, not political faiths; a bilateral loyalty, not commercial or social projects. Yet it is an association for as noble a purpose as any involved in our prior decisions (*Griswold v. Connecticut* 1965).

Interestingly, Douglas' argument does not define privacy nor does it set parameters to right to privacy established by the majority ruling. It affirms simply that the right to privacy is older than the Bill of Rights and that several constitutional guarantees create a "zone of privacy" for the individual. This "zone of privacy" is an area from which government intrusion or interference is guaranteed. In a later abortion case, Justice Blackmun would refer to privacy in terms of a private sphere of liberty and a "promise" of the American Constitution: "Our cases have long recognized that the Constitution embodies a promise that a certain private sphere of individual liberty will be kept largely beyond the reach of government" (*Thornburgh v. American College of Obstetricians & Gynecologists* 1986).

　　In the same decision, Blackmun also connects privacy and individual autonomy.

Few decisions are more personal and intimate, more properly private, or more basic to individual dignity and autonomy, than a woman's decision—with the guidance of her physician and within the limits specified in *Roe*—whether to end her pregnancy. A woman's right to make that choice freely is fundamental. Any other result, in our view, would protect inadequately a central part of the sphere of liberty that our law guarantees equally to all (*Thornburgh v. American College of Obstetricians & Gynecologists* 1986).

To understand what is at stake here one can imagine the private and public realms as two non-intersecting spheres that include all possible human actions. One sphere "grows" only at the expense of another. The notion of a "zone of privacy" seems to suggest that certain kinds of actions are permanently included within a private sphere which is legally protected from any cooption by the public.

As the fence around my property effectively excludes public regard for what happens within it, so the "right to privacy" secures an effective barrier to public interest in private actions.

In spite of not defining privacy, *Griswold* did intensify jurisprudential interest and analysis of it. Some constitutional scholars debate the legitimacy of Justice Douglas' reasoning in this decision. For example, Justice Black in his dissent called it a "right conjured out of thin air." The right to privacy established in *Griswold* effectively established privacy as a legal right which subsequent courts extended. For example, seven years later, the Court converted this right of married couples, in Griswold, into a right of the individual. In *Eisenstadt v. Baird*, the Court overturned a Massachusetts statute banning distribution of contraceptive devices to unmarried couples: "Whatever the rights of the individual to access to contraceptives may be, the rights must be the same for the unmarried and the married alike" (*Eisenstadt v. Baird* 1972).

> If under *Griswold* the distribution of contraceptives to married persons cannot be prohibited, a ban on distribution to unmarried persons would be equally impermissible. . . . If the right of privacy means anything, it is the right of the individual, married or single, to be free from unwarranted governmental intrusion into matters so fundamentally affecting a person as the decision whether to bear or beget a child.
>
> On the other hand, if *Griswold* is no bar to a prohibition on the distribution of contraceptives, the State could not, consistently with the Equal Protection Clause, outlaw distribution to unmarried but not to married persons. In each case the evil, as perceived by the State, would be identical (*Eisenstadt v. Baird* 1972).

The Supreme Court expressed a similar understanding of the right to privacy in *Roe v. Wade*. The Court interpreted a number of its previous decisions in light of the right to privacy that it had recently recognized in *Griswold v. Connecticut*:

> The Constitution does not explicitly mention any right of privacy. In a line of decisions, however, . . . the Court has recognized that a right of personal privacy, or a guarantee of certain areas or zones of privacy, does exist under the Constitution. . . . These decisions make it clear that only personal rights that can be deemed "fundamental" or "implicit in the concept of ordered liberty," are included in this guarantee of personal privacy. They also make it clear that the right has some extension to activities relating to marriage, procreation, contraception, family relationships, and child rearing and education (*Roe v. Wade* 1973).

However, the ambit of privacy as the sphere individual liberty extended its farthest in 1992 when Justice Kennedy, writing for the majority, affirmed that personal liberty extends to each individual's right to define the universe for himself.

Our law affords constitutional protection to personal decisions relating to marriage, procreation, contraception, family relationships, child rearing, and education. Our cases recognize the right of the individual, married or single, to be free from unwarranted governmental intrusion into matters so fundamentally affecting a person as the decision whether to bear or beget a child *(Eisenstadt v. Baird)*. . . . "These matters, involving the most intimate and personal choices a person may make in a lifetime, choices central to personal dignity and autonomy, are central to the liberty protected by the Fourteenth Amendment. At the heart of liberty is the right to define one's own concept of existence, of meaning, of the universe, and of the mystery of human life. Beliefs about these matters could not define the attributes of personhood were they formed under compulsion of the State *(Planned Parenthood of Southeastern Pennsylvania vs. Casey, Governor of Pennsylvania* 1992).

Kennedy's claim that the heart of liberty is the right of each individual to define concepts of existence, the universe, etc. without compulsion from the State tightly links privacy, person, and autonomy together as a single moral unity that requires protection from public coercion. It represents, perhaps, in spite of some ambiguity, the fullest expression of the liberal view of privacy.

Thus, jurisprudential reasoning extended the range of privacy by restricting social intrusion into private life. However, case law does not clarify what privacy is. What it shows is that the analysis of privacy is complex because it entails multiple entwined strands. One of these is the distinction between privacy as a political notion and privacy as a social notion developed in liberal political theory. In liberal political theory, the private realm is the area of human life in which the state may not legitimately intervene. By analogy, this reasoning carries over from the political to the social realm. Thus some writers think privacy is as essential to human development as autonomy, and they equated liberty and autonomy, making both synonymous to privacy.

In a similar way, others have argued that privacy is intimately connected to persons' most deeply held values, their understanding of what it means to be an autonomous moral agent capable of self-reflection and choice. A violation of privacy is "demeaning to the individuality [and] an affront to personal dignity" (Bloustein 1964, 975). Bloustein argues that a person completely subject to public scrutiny will lose his uniqueness as an individual, his autonomy, and his sense of himself as an individual, meaning his moral personality. Such an individual will conform to other's expectations and become a wholly conventional being—part of an undifferentiated herd. Protection of privacy is, thus, necessary to protect individuality and autonomy, two essential characteristics of moral personality. On this account then, privacy is not just a legal right, it is also a moral obligation.

The classical liberal position frames the issue of privacy in terms of protecting as wide a range of freedom for the individual as possible. It assumes that the public sphere always in some measure constrains the individual. Thus it argues that we protect the freedom of the individual by protecting the private sphere from intrusion by the public. Others have contested this position, especially when its application is to the broadly social, not just the narrowly political dimension of public life. They argue that the society is not a *constraint* on freedom, but an *enabler* of it. Society is essential to full development as a human being, and active participation in a public sphere contributes to the vitality of democratic societies. On these accounts, the protection of privacy has extended too far, to the detriment of a vital public sphere. It is worthwhile considering some of the positions that argue for a privileged *public* sphere.

4. Hannah Arendt: The Loss of the Public Sphere

Hannah Arendt (1906-1974) is one of the leading political thinkers of the twentieth century. One of her fundamental concerns, based on her personal experience of fascism and political chaos before and after World War II, was *totalitarianism*. She argued that totalitarianism was successful because it mobilized fragmented masses around a simple ideology, and devised a form of rule in which bureaucratically-minded officials performed murderous deeds with a clear conscience. The personal and social fragmentation that is a necessary condition of totalitarianism is due in some measure to a devitalized public sphere in which individuals over-valorized privacy over social participation. The only way to avoid totalitarianism is to establish a well-ordered political community that encourages public participation and institutionalized political freedom.

Thus the private-public distinction figured significantly in her work, especially in her masterwork, *The Human Condition* (1958), in which she argues that the modern notion of privacy—as a withdrawal from public life—played a key role in the rise of twentieth century totalitarianism. Arendt starts with a comparison of classical and modern views about privacy.

Greek and medieval society valued public life, and private life was viewed as a deprivation—the lack of something essentially humanizing. Arendt prefers classical public life to the enlarged private sphere of modernity, because the enlarged private sphere of modernity has contributed to the loss of meaning of personal lives necessary to support vital public discourse and political association.

Arendt affirms that language reveals the difference between classical and modern notions of privacy. In classical Greece, "privacy" carried negative connotations. It implied the absence of full participation in the accepted social order. The Greek word for "private," *idios* means "one's own," or "pertaining to oneself," and so, "personal" or "private." *Demios*, the Greek for public, means "having to do with the people." Another widely used term for public, *koinos*, means "common," as in "shared in common," and differentiated public interest from private property or private interests. The Greek use of the words expressed a bias against the private in favor of sharing what is public.

Arendt explained how the rise of the social sphere has affected our notion of the private.

> The emergence of society—the rise of housekeeping, its activities, problems, and organizational devices—from the shadowy interior of the household into the public sphere, has not only blurred the old borderlines between private and political, it has also changed almost beyond recognition the meaning of the two terms and their significance for the life of the individual citizen (Arendt 1958, 38).

At first glance, Arendt's position appear quixotic. For example, few modern people would agree with the Greeks that a life spent in the privacy of one's self (*idios*), outside the common world, is "idiotic" or "idiosyncratic." For us, privacy is "sane," "rational," and "desired by everyone." Nor would we agree with the Romans, to whom privacy offered only a temporary refuge from the business of the *res publica*—the community service which views that the highest fulfilment of a human life is one of public participation in the roles and institutions of "civic life." On our view, "public life" is a sacrifice. "Public service" diminishes the highly valued private life.

However, careful study of the Greco-Roman culture shows that both the Greeks and the Romans scarcely recognized a "private life." Privacy, on Arendt's account, is a distinctly modern value. "We call private today a sphere of intimacy whose beginnings we may be able to trace back to late Roman, though hardly to any period of Greek antiquity, but whose peculiar manifoldness and variety were certainly unknown to any period prior to the modern age" (Arendt 1958, 38). Furthermore, "In antiquity, 'privacy' denoted a state of being deprived of something. A man who lived on a private life, who was like the slave, was not permitted to enter the public realm, or like the barbarians had chosen not to establish such as a realm, was not fully human" (Arendt 1958, 38).

For moderns, private life is at least as interesting and fulfilling, if not more so, as the old public life. Our transformed notion of privacy puts a sharp division between the private and the public that was unknown in the classical world. "The decisive historical fact is that modern privacy in its most relevant function, to shelter the intimate, was discovered as the opposite not of the political sphere, but of the social, to which it is therefore more closely and authentically related" (Arendt 1958, 38).

Arendt attributed the change to the rise of *individualism*—the philosophy that privileges the individual and his or her interests above other interests. She argues that the rise of modern individualism removed the aspect of privation from the idea of "privacy." Nonetheless, a life removed, by choice or plan, from the public realm is still a deprived life. The word "public," she said, signifies two closely related, but not identical phenomena: first that everything that appears in public can be seen and heard by everybody and has the widest possible publicity; second, that public means the world itself, in so far as it is common to all of us and distinguished from our privately owned places in it. . . . Compared with the reality which comes from being seen and heard, even the greatest forces of intimate life—the passions of the heart, the thought of the mind, and the delights of the senses—lead an uncertain, shadowy kind of existence unless and until they are transformed, deprivatized, and deindividualized, as it were, into a shape to fit them for public appearance (Arendt 1958, 50-51).

Arendt, however, did not reject a "private life" or the notion of "privacy." She did reject the tendency to exclude the public from the private, which in effect enlarges the private sphere at the expense of the public.

This is unfortunate or deleterious, on Arendt's account, because the private is *dependent on* the vitality of the public. This is true because, she argues, it is through the "presence of others" (the public sphere) that we learn the "reality of the world" as well as the "reality of ourselves," and where intimacy is fully developed (50). Thus, Arendt counters the popular notion that the development of intimacy requires the private. It is, in fact, the other way around. The capacity for closeness is actualized through interaction in a community of others. Even though some aspects of human living, such as love as distinct from friendship, cannot stand the "implacable bright light of the constant presence of others," nonetheless, a meaningful life *includes* a meaningful public dimension. In other words, the public sphere is valuable to private life.

Contesting Arendt. Arendt's position on the relationship of the private and public is a sharp contrast to classical liberalism. Liberalism argues that the social good is served only when society protects the private realm from the social. Arendt, on the other hand, argues that the public sphere must be protected against erosion from the private. This dialectic is worth thinking about to understand many of the contemporary controversies about privacy and the public sphere.

Charles Fried, a Harvard professor and former jurist, does not contest Arendt's thesis directly. However, in a seminal law review article "Privacy" (*Yale Law Review* 1968), he develops a position that is sufficiently contrary to Arendt's to provide a critical contrast to Arendt's position that contests the position of classical liberalism. Fried defends privacy as the only way to protect those personal qualities that Arendt claims can develop only through participation in the public sphere.

Fried defends the legal protection of the right to privacy and an enlarged private sphere based on the importance of individuality and moral personality. He argues that privacy has many practical and instrumental functions; however, it also relates to basic aspects of individual integrity and moral and social personality. In defining oneself, the individual must be able to exercise discretion in selecting which thoughts about the self to present to others. This freedom to chose what one reveals is, on Fried's account, central to an individual's ability to be a certain kind of person.

Equally important to the development of an individual's moral and social personality is the capacity to form important intimate relationships that involve love, friendship, and trust. These relationships require relinquishing parts of the inner self to another. This capacity for sharing oneself presupposes possession of those features and control of information about oneself in the first place. Privacy, as constitutive of a sense of the self and title to oneself, is a necessary condition for love, friendship, and trust that implies sharing oneself with another. Without being able to control access to one's inner self, important personal relationships could not emerge.

> Privacy is closely implicated in the notion of respect and self-respect, and of love, friendship, and trust. Quite apart from any philosophical analysis this is intuitively obvious. . . . it is my thesis that in developed social contexts love, friendship, and trust are only possible if persons enjoy and accord to each other a certain measure of privacy (Fried 1968, 482).

Fried's notion of privacy is intuitive—privacy is controlling how much of the knowledge of one's intimate self that others have access too.

It is helpful to sharpen the idea of privacy just a bit. As a first approximation, privacy seems to be related to secrecy, to limiting the knowledge of others about oneself. However, as Fried admits, it is not true, for instance, that the less that is known about us the more privacy we have. Privacy is not a mere absence of information about a person in the minds of others. Rather, it is the *control* a person has over the information about oneself.

> To refer for instance to the privacy of a lonely man on a desert island would be to engage in irony. The person who enjoys privacy is able to grant or deny access to others. Even when one considers private situations into which outsiders could not possibly intrude, the context implies some alternative situation where the intrusion is possible. A man's house may be private, but that is because it is constructed—with doors, windows, window shades—to allow it to be private, and because the law entitles a man to exclude unauthorized persons. And even the remote vacation hide-away is private just because one resorts to it in order—in part—to preclude access to unauthorized persons (Fried 1968, 482-483).

On Fried's view, then, privacy is control over knowledge about oneself by others. Such control, however,

> . . . .is not simply control over the quantity of information abroad; there are modulations in the quality of knowledge as well. We may not mind that a person

knows a general fact about us, and yet feel our privacy invaded if he knows the details. For instance, a casual acquaintance may comfortably know that I am sick, but it would violate my privacy if he knew the nature of my illness. Or a good friend may know what particular illness I am suffering from, but it would violate my privacy if he were actually to witness my suffering from some symptom which he must know is associated with the disease (Fried 1968, 483).

For Fried, the legal protection of privacy reflects the "rules" of privacy that are embedded in the organization of society. Many of the social structures by which persons express their respect for the privacy of others are informal and implicit. The sanctions for violating the expectations set up by these structures, if they exist at all, are often subtle and informal, too. Law renders explicit what is implicit.

> But legal rules also play a large part in establishing the social context of privacy. These rules guarantee to a person the claim to control certain areas, his home, perhaps his telephone conversations, etc., and back this guarantee with enforceable sanctions. Now these legal norms are more or less incomprehensible without some understanding of what kind of a situation is sought to be established with their aid. Without this understanding we cannot surmise the changing law they demand in changing circumstances (Fried 1968, 483).

What is less obvious is that law is not just an instrument for protecting privacy. In our culture, it is an essential element of the institution of privacy itself. In other words, the law does not merely reflect existing (if informal) rules of privacy: it also helps create the sense of entitlement to privacy. Thus Fried argues:

> The concept of privacy requires. . . .a sense of control and a justified acknowledged power to control aspects of one's environment. But in most developed societies the only way to give a person the full measure of both the sense and the fact of control is to give him legal title to control. A legal title to control is control which is the least open to question and argument; it is the kind of control we are most serious about:
> . . . .[P]rivacy is not just an absence of information abroad about ourselves; it is a feeling of security in control over information. By using the fully impersonal and ultimate institution of law to grant persons this control, we at once put the right to control as far beyond question as we can and at the same time show how seriously we take that right (Fried 1968, 483).

Thus, on Fried's account, "man feels that invasion of that right [to privacy] injures them in their very humanity" (475). Privacy is not just one possible means among others to insure some other value. It is necessarily related to ends and relations of the most fundamental sort: respect, love, friendship, and trust. Privacy is not merely a good technique for furthering these fundamental relations. Without privacy, they are simply inconceivable; because they require a context of privacy for their existence. Fried's argument can be framed in this simple form:

1. Love, friendship and trust are a system of individual dispositions, beliefs and attitudes.
2. These dispositions, beliefs and attitudes are organized according to identifiable principles.
3. They build on a common conception of personality and its entitlements.
4. These entitlements comprise a moral conception of corresponding duties of persons in regard to each other that yield a basic principle of respect for persons.
5. Respect for persons recognizes that all persons are accounted equal rights.

The only qualification to equal rights is what is required to ensure equal protection of the same rights as others. In the absence of adequate qualification, the privacy of others ought to be respected.

Fried's argument is similar to Mill's, except, unlike Mill, Fried attaches privacy to the development of the individual's capacity for love, friendship, and trust rather than autonomy. *Self-development,* one might say, is the condition of the possibility of meaningful *autonomy.* Thus, on Fried's account, privacy is necessary for the individual *as* an individual to manifest the qualities of unique personality valued by all individuals. The value of personal (i.e., individual) development sets up the framework of social entitlement and reciprocal duties and responsibilities.

What Fried seems to undervalue, however, is what Arendt brings into focus. Society is not a container of individuals pursuing their private life plans. Society provides the materials from which individuals shape their moral personality. It is in "the presence of others" that we come to know ourselves as individuals. One's presence "in" society and to others is as valuable as being able to withdraw or seclude oneself from society. Thus, Fried does not address the nexus of public-private dichotomy that seems to be at the heart of the debate.

Back to Arendt again. Fried argues that privacy is control of what others know about us. This control is basic to the development of oneself as a moral being. Consequently, a sphere secure from public scrutiny and knowledge is required to develop and maintain personality (i.e., individuality), which on Fried's view is the basis of moral existence. In so far as moral existence is fundamental to human well-being, freedom *from* the public sphere is essential to human well-being.

Arendt, however, argues the opposite: the central features of personality (i.e. individuality) can only be developed *in* a robust social or public sphere. So, the private and public spheres are *interdependent* and to some degree inseparable.

> The public realm, as the common world, gathers us together and yet prevents our falling over each other. What makes mass society so difficult to bear is not the number of people involved . . . .but the fact that the world between them has lost

its power to gather them together, to relate and to separate them (Arendt 1958, 52-53).

Arendt's argument stands against the liberal position that shapes thinking about privacy. Arendt's argument is compelling because it gathers together a view of human living that contains and allows for the privacies of life as well as the futility of individual life lived in isolation from others. Her position stands against the traditional liberal argument by reintroducing a robust social sphere as a key term in defining the private. On the liberal account, protection of the private sphere aims to accommodate diversity of beliefs, thoughts, values, and dispositions. However, Arendt argues that this ideal did not achieve its goal. The social has lost its ability and desire to accommodate diversity and commonality—public commitment and private interests. The fractured public sphere easily yields to the enforced commonality of totalitarian solutions. "Only where things can be seen by many in a variety of aspects without changing their identity, so that those who are gathered around them know they see sameness in utter diversity, can worldly reality truly and reliably appear" (57).

Thus Arendt argues for a closer conception of the private and public spheres. The individual and community are interdependent. When individual privacy leads to isolation, people are deprived of seeing and hearing others, of being seen and heard by them. One's personal identity is impoverished because it is only turned in on itself—its own subjective presence. "They are imprisoned in the subjectivity of their own singular experiences, which does not cease to be singular if the same experience is multiplied innumerable times" (58).

So, on Arendt's account, to be obsessed with privacy, a condition of later modernity, is to live a life deprived of objective relationships, devoid of any intermediary element, and destructive of aspirations more permanent than life itself.

5. Communitarian Contributions to the Private-public Discourse

Communitarian theorists take a position similar to Arendt's. Amitai Etzioni, for example, argues that privacy leads to a breakdown of social order by providing a type of social permission or license that exempts certain kinds of acts from public judgment. "Privacy is the realm in which an actor (either a person or a group, such as a couple) can legitimately act without disclosure and accountability to others. Privacy thus is a social license that exempts a category of acts (including thoughts and emotions) from communal, public, or governmental scrutiny" (Etzioni 2000, 196). Thus, privacy is understood as a particular kind of relationship within the social or common good. On the communitarian account, privacy is a "balance" between individual action and common or public goods.

Privacy is not an absolute. It is contextual and subjective. . . . moreover, the privacy interests at stake in any given situation may vary from the profound to the trivial, and that valuation will depend significantly on who is making it. For example, if privacy protects the combination to my safe or the location of a key to my house, it is extraordinarily valuable to me and, in most circumstances, to society more broadly, which shares my interest in avoiding theft and other criminal conduct. . . . If, however, privacy permits me to avoid paying taxes or obtain employment for which I am qualified, it may be valuable time, but extremely costly to society as a whole. It is clear, therefore, that neither privacy values nor costs are absolute. . . . What is needed is a balance, of which privacy is a part. Determining what that part is in any specific context requires a careful evaluation of subjective, variable, and competing interests (Cate 1997, 31).

The communitarian position is based on the view that personality—the thoughts, beliefs, and values that are determinative of the self—are inextricably embedded in social relationships that *precede* the individual. Thus, the community—understood as a robust public sphere—is essential to the development of the self. There is empirical evidence that this view is in fact correct. However, this does not deal with the liberal claim that privacy is essential for the development and maintenance of democratic institutions.

Habermas and the public sphere. Jürgen Habermas is another thinker who thinks the public sphere is an individual and social good. In the *Structural Transformations of the Public Sphere* (1991, originally published 1962), Habermas traced the growth and decline of the *bourgeois* ("civic" or "middle class") public sphere. For Habermas, the *"public sphere"* is a collection of private individuals who come together to discuss matters of common or collective concern and thereby form public opinion. The public sphere was not, as on the classic liberal account, inherently political, but it did contribute to vital, robust democratic political institutions.

On Habermas' account, this public sphere originated in the eighteenth century as a result of the rise of the bourgeoisie or commercial-mercantile middle class. During this time, a large number of associations, clubs, coffeehouses and salons came into existence patronized by members of the French, English and German middle class. These were public places, like coffeehouses, where people discussed philosophy, science, art, literature, and, most importantly, contemporary political, social and cultural affairs freely amongst themselves. Gradually, discussion of issues of politics, polity and governance grew in importance.

The bourgeois public sphere may be conceived above all as the sphere of private people coming togther as a public. They soon claimed the public sphere as regulated from above against the public authorities themselves, to engage them in a debate over the general rules governing relations in the basically privatized but publicly relevant sphere of commodity exchange and social labor. The medium of this political confrontation was peculiar with historical precedent: people's public use of their reason (Habermas 1991, 27).

These associations opposed the absolutist monarchical governments that had no form of mediation between the state and society, between the sovereign and individuals. What these associations did, according to Habermas, was open or mediate a "space" between individuals in society and the state though the creation of "public opinion." Public opinion, then, mediated between government and society.

Habermas, like Arendt, sees similarities between the middle class public sphere and institutions in classical, particularly Greek, culture. According to Habermas, the idea of a public sphere drew upon the idea of free discussion among citizens in the Athenian *agora*. The agora was the marketplace of ancient democratic Athens, where people gathered informally to discuss common matters and to disclose and defend their opinions. However, the eighteenth century bourgeois public sphere added to the Greek ideal the belief that public discourse, if it were sufficiently public, could achieve a form of universality and social-political consensus that trumped individual interests.

The idea of universality derives from Enlightenment social philosophy. The emerging middle class, as avid followers of the Enlightenment, believed in the centrality of human reason and the ability of autonomous, reasoning people to attain knowledge of truth and collective goods *through discussion*. The idea was that if humans are freely reasoning and autonomous beings, and if they have adequate information, and if their beliefs and opinions could be freely discussed and tested in a public arena, then they would eventually be able to attain truth and the collective good.

Thus, on Habermas' account, the public sphere was first a *mediating* sphere *between* individuals or society and the state, which made claims for full disclosure (or publicity) on matter of public importance. Because of the existence of the public sphere, the State could not operate in the *closed, secretive* manner of previous absolutist regimes. It was claimed that free information and knowledge of state activities was required in order for them to be tested, accepted, and thus legitimated. At the same time, the public sphere became an arena of free discussion on collective matters where private individuals were expected to temporarily put aside their private interests and to deliberate about truth and the collective good.

The idea was that if this discussion were truly to be ruled by the principle of publicity or *public disclosure,* the *information could not be private* or hidden from publicity. If there was *free information* and if people's opinions were subject to the scrutiny of public discussion, then a universal "public opinion" would emerge. It would be a universal public opinion because it would have an element of universal truth to it and would have to be listened to by any political state which was truly legitimate.

A political consciousness developed in the public sphere of civil society, . . .
[demanded a] general and abstract law and . . . ultimately came to assert itself
(i.e., public opinion) as the only legitimate source of this law. In the course of the
eighteenth century public opinion claimed the legislative competent for those
norms whose polemical-rationalist conception it had provided to begin with.

The criteria of generality and abstractness characterizing legal norms had
to have a peculiar obviousness for privatized individuals who, by communicating
with each other in the public sphere of the world of letters, confirmed each
other's subjectivity as it emerged from their spheres of intimacy. For as a public
they were already under the implicit law of the parity of all cultivated persons,
whose abstract universality afforded the sole guarantee that the individuals
subsumed under it in an equally abstract fashion, as "common human beings,"
were set free in their subjectivity precisely by this parity. The clichés of
"equality" and "liberty," not yet ossified into revolutionary bourgeois propaganda
formulae, were still imbued with life. The bourgeois public's critical public
debate took place in principle without regard to all preexisting social and
political rank and in accord with universal rules. These rules, because they
remained strictly external to the individuals as such secured space for the
development of these individuals' interiority by literary means. These rules,
because universally valid, secured a space for the individual person; because they
were objective, they secured a space for what was most subjective; because they
were abstract, for what was more concrete. . . . Intrinsic to the idea of a public
opinion born of the power of the better argument was the claim to that morally
pretentious rationality that strove to discover what was at once just and right
(Habermas 1991, 54).

The public sphere, on Habermas' account, was a form of social life that affected
the political by forcing the political to justify its rules and actions to the "public"
via publicity and public discussion. The public sphere was, thus, a *forum* for
exchanging views of importance to the common good. This public discussion
formed public opinion. Public opinion mediated between the desires of society and
the will of government. So, one may say, this public sphere comes into being when
people gather to discuss issues of political concern.

Habermas' concept of the public sphere describes a space of institutions and
practices between the private interests of everyday life in civil society and the
realm of state power. The public sphere mediates between the domains of the
family and the workplace—where private interests prevail—and the state which
often exerts arbitrary forms of power and domination. What Habermas called the
"bourgeois public sphere" consisted of social spaces where individuals gathered
to discuss their common public affairs and to organize against arbitrary and
oppressive forms of social and public power.

The line between state and society, fundamental in our context, divided the
public sphere from the private realm. The public sphere was co-extensive with
public authority, and we consider the court a part of it. Included in the private
realm was the authentic "public sphere," for it was a public sphere constituted

by private people. . . . The private sphere comprised civil society in the narrower sense, that is to say, the realm of commodity exchange and of social labor; imbedded in it was the family with its interior domain (intimate sphere). The public sphere in the political realm evolved from the public sphere in the world of letters; through the vehicle of public opinion it put the state in touch with the needs of society (Habermas 1991, 31).

Habermas' model of the private and public sphere is more nuanced than the simple dichotomy of public and private interests of classical liberal theory. He makes an important distinction between the state-governed political realm's public sphere and citizen-governed life-world's public sphere. While the political sphere exercises potentially coercive authority, the public sphere is an arena of critical rational discourse in which consensus, not coercion, plays the key role. Most importantly, the public sphere was the place where private individuals could collectively influence the policy and direction of the political sphere.

Private individuals participate in the public sphere via reading, writing and talking to each other. This public discussion formed a "public opinion" on the issues of the day. Public opinion, based on rational consensus, influenced political policy. The public sphere mediated between private interests and "will" of the political sphere. It became harder, and less effective, for the "political sphere" to assert its will on private interests.

An example of the operation of Habermas' notion of a public sphere are the "committees of correspondence" in the American colonies, who provided for a unified response to the effort of the British crown to impose taxation without representation by colonists who were separated from each other by geographical, economic, religious, and cultural differences. It was a cultivated "public sphere" that demanded, extended and protected citizens' freedoms, not a simple aggregate of collective private interests.

What Habermas' work shows is how, historically, a space emerged where, for the first time, people had an opportunity and place to meet to discuss and contribute to political discourse. This development emancipated people from authority, as the public forum for discussion played a key role in "the process in which the state-governed public sphere was appropriated by the public of private people" (Habermas 1991, 51). Privatized individuals came together to form a public and also "they formed the public sphere of a rational-critical debate in the world of letters" (51).

The public of "human beings" engaged in rational-critical debate was constituted into one of "citizens" wherever there was communication concerning the affirms of the "commonwealth." Under the "republican constitution" this public sphere in the political realm became the organizational principle of the liberal constitutional state. Within its framework, civil society was established as the sphere of private autonomy (everyone was to be permitted to pursue his "happiness" in any way he thought useful). The citizen's liberties were safeguarded by general laws; corresponding to the freedom of the "human being" was the equality of all citizens before the law (the elimination of all "rights by birth"). Legislation itself was traced back to the "popular will that has its source in reason"; for laws empirically had their origin in the "public agreement" of the public engaged in critical debate (Habermas 1991,106-107).

By the mid-nineteenth century, however, this "public sphere" of rational-critical debate declined. The rise of the welfare-state, consumerism, and the technologies of mass society each contributed to the decline. Public relations, the formation of public opinion via media, first in newspapers and magazines and later through radio and television, replaced genuine public discourse on issues of public importance. As events absorbed the public sphere, the private realm diminished and the "authority" of the political sphere expanded.

> Along the path from a public critically reflecting on its culture to one that merely consumes it, the public sphere in the world of letters, which at one time could still be distinguished from that in the political realm, has lost its specific character. For the "culture" propagated by the mass media is a culture of integration. It not only integrates information with critical debate and the journalistic format with the literary forms of the psychological novel into a combination of entertainment and "advice" governed by the principle of "human interest"; at the same time it is flexible enough to assimilate elements of advertising, indeed, to serve itself as a kind of super slogan that, if it did not already exist, could have been invented for the purpose of public relations serving the cause of the status quo. The public sphere assumes advertising functions. The more it can be deployed as a vehicle for political and economic propaganda, the more it becomes unpolitical as a whole and pseudo-privatized (Habermas 1991,175).

The collapse of the public sphere meant the loss of the mediating function of the public sphere and a "return" to the co-option of the citizen to the political will, albeit in a new form.

> Along with its communal basis, the public sphere lost its place. It lost its clear boundary over against the private sphere on the one hand and the "world public" on the other; it lost its transparency and no longer admitted of a comprehensive view. There arose as an alternative to class parties, that "integration party" whose form was usually not clearly enough distinguished from them. It "took hold" of the voters temporarily and moved them to provide acclamations without attempting to remedy their political immaturity. Today this kind of mass-based party trading on surface integration has become the dominant type. For such parties the decisive issue is who has control over the coercive and educational means for ostentatiously or manipulatively influencing the voting behavior of the population. The parties are the instrument for the formation of an effective political will; they are not, however, in the hands of the public but in the hands of those who control the party apparatus (Habermas 1991. 205).

According to Habermas, the existence of a real public sphere is crucial for democratic societies because it contributes to human liberty. The importance of these institutions of the public sphere lies in the process of discussion that must take the form of rational critical debate. Criticism is also vital to this process, so that the proposals being put forward can be tested, but also so that participants can discover a meaning together as a result of the process itself. In Habermas' conception of the public sphere, it operates in favor of "the common good." This notion of the public sphere however, assumes that there is one undifferentiated public for whom a common good is possible; that there is only one public arena that works for everyone; and that this is a desirable state of affairs. In summary, Habermas' ideal public sphere is a sphere of rational discussion and deliberation about public policy (political will). It mediates between private individuals and the institutions of the political sphere:

1. It involves autonomous, rational, non-interested participants. The public sphere is not an association for further private or personal interests but to achieve consensus about what is true and (ultimately) worthwhile or "good."

2. It involves discussion over common concerns by "disinterested" actors (i.e those without private interests at play).

3. It produces true public opinion and allows for critique of the structures and processes of domination and coercion.

Many writers, especially post-modern theorists, are critical of Habermas' key assumption that a single, unitary public sphere is possible. These critics argue that a single, unitary public sphere does not exist and never has. Rather there are multiple public spheres or interest groups whose interests at times conflict and other times coincide, whose shifting oppositions and alliances move public interests forward. Examples of such "spheres of interests" are political action committees (PACs), special interest groups such as the Sierra Club or the National Rifle Association, lobbyists, unions, and politically oriented "think tanks."

On this account, what is necessary to a democratic society requires providing opportunities for subordinate groups to convince dominant groups that their concerns are legitimate and worthy of debate. In a society where there are different subgroups with different status, participatory equality is achieved more effectively through numerous public spheres—even though it can be argued that a "politics of interests" allows authority to play interests against each other. Spheres of interests are less than a public opinion, as Habermas describes it.

6. The Feminist Critique of the Private-public Dichotomy

Feminist theorists have been highly critical of the private-public dichotomy. They point out that the public-private distinction is more than a distinction between the state and civil society, or between the general interest and particular interests, or between a person's public life as a citizen and private life as an autonomous individual. It is also a distinction between men and women, between the public world of business and industry and the private, domestic world of the family. They argue that the association of *men* with the *public* sphere of business and politics, and *women* with the *private* sphere of the home is essential, not accidental, to the institutionalized forms of *patriarchal society* that subordinate women to men. This dichotomy of the public and private that privileges the value of privacy works to the advantage of dominant social classes and to the detriment of subordinate groups.

By guaranteeing a right to privacy in the private sphere to all citizens, the liberal state legitimates an area in which inequalities of power based on resources, knowledge, and symbolic attributions can act with impunity (MacKinnon 1989). The family is often used as a prime example in which male heads of households control, without scrutiny or surveillance, subordinate members. How power is allocated in the private sphere is not merely personal or individual, it is political. Thus, feminist theorists affirm that "The personal is political." What they mean is that not only is the personal political in the sense that the private sphere contains power relations that mirror those outside it, but also, systemic power influences the right to privacy. *The socially powerful maintain their power through control of the private sphere.* The arbitrariness of the boundary between public and private subjects the private to the influence of social power. Nancy Fraser set up the critique in these terms:

> Take the role of the worker. In male-dominated, classical capitalist societies, this role is the masculine. . . . Masculinity is in large part a matter of leaving home each day for a place of paid work and returning with a wage that provides for one's dependents. It is this internal relation between being a man and being a provider that explains why in capitalist societies unemployment is often not just economically but also psychologically devastating for men. It also sheds light on the centrality of the struggle for a "family wage" in the history of workers and trade-union movements of the nineteenth and twentieth centuries . . . a conception, of course, that legitimized the practice of paying women less for equal or comparable work.
>
> What, then, of the citizen role, which [Habermas] claims connects the public system of the administrative state with the public lifeworld sphere of political opinion and will formation? This role, too, is a gendered role in classical capitalism, indeed, a masculine role—and not simply in the sense that women did not win the vote in the United States and Britain (for example) until the twentieth century. . . . As Habermas understands it, the citizen is centrally a

participant in political debate and public opinion formation. This means that citizenship, in his view, depends crucially on the capacities for consent and speech, the ability to participate on a par with others in dialogue. But these are capacities that are connected with masculinity in male-dominated, classical capitalism . . . . [E]ven today . . . in most jurisdictions there is no such thing as marital rape. That is, a wife is legally subject to her husband. . . . [E]ven outside of marriage the legal test of rape often boils down to whether a "reasonable man" would have assumed that the woman had consented. It means, says Carol Pateman, that "women find their speech . . . persistently and systematically invalidated in the crucial matter of consent, a matter that is fundamental to a democracy. [But] if women's words about consent are consistently reinterpreted, how can they participate in the debate among citizens? (Fraser 1998, 124-127).

Fraser's criticism of Habermas articulates the heart of the feminist critique of the private-public dichotomy. First, the private-public dichotomy is incoherent because it ignores the gendered relationships that inhere in the basic schematization. Women "belong" to the private (domestic sphere), men to the public (political) sphere. This conceptual dichotomy systematically ignores women's voices and women's public roles. The dichotomy fosters a continuation of sexism and discrimination against women because it closes the "private sphere" off from public critical scrutiny and closes the "private" off from "interference" or criticism.

Many feminists argue that noninterference in the "private" sphere has the effect of reinforcing power and powerlessness (MacKinnon 1989). Formal political equality (having the vote, holding public offices) fails to bring about real equality. Indeed, public privileges reinforce inequality, because power relations from the public realm operate with impunity in the arena of nonintervention—the private sphere. Thus children, women and the dependent become identified with "private" life—the non-political private sphere. It is the feminine sphere of "care-giving." Socially constructed roles are institutionalized as gender dichotomies. In turn, the "gendered" dichotomies—equality and difference, reason and emotion, independence and dependence—lead to "cultural gendering."

Many feminists are not content merely to criticize current thinking about social roles. They believe that by taking "gendered-relations" seriously it is possible to develop a more complete theory that overcomes the inequalities that inhere in the notion of a dichotomized private-public sphere. Fraser argues:

[A better theory] would need to take as its starting point the multivalent, contested character of the categories of privacy and publicity with their gendered and racialized subtexts. . . . [I]n highly stratified late capitalist societies, not everyone stands in the same relation to privacy and publicity; some have more power than others to draw and defend the line. Further, an adequate theory of the public sphere would need to distinguish . . . official governmental public spheres, mass mediated mainstream public spheres, counter-public spheres, and informal public spheres in everyday life. It would also need to show how some of these publics marginalize others. Such a theory would certainly help us better understand discursive struggles like the Thomas/Hill confrontation. Perhaps it could also help inspire us to imagine, and to fight for, a more egalitarian and democratic society (Fraser 1998, 334).

On Fraser's account, as long as structural social inequality exists, there will be unequal access to the public sphere. Social inequalities enter the public sphere first through *cultural "distinctions."* That is, groups—for example women, workers, and racial minorities—develop their own characteristic ways of thinking and acting. They become socially distinct. Social distinctions become a way to *categorize* differences. Differences become the basis to categorize and marginalize those who do not share the characteristics of the dominant culture. The marginalized are not socially equal. When there is social inequality, differences become a means of subtle and informal distinction between classes and groups.

Drawing on the work of recent historians, Fraser suggests that the culture of the original bourgeois public sphere in the eighteenth century was never a universal culture that only failed to formally incorporate women and workers. Rather, it implicitly demanded a whole set of cultural practices and assumptions that were particular to the male bourgeoisie. In acting in the public sphere, bourgeois men were basically engaging in a process of class formation, separating themselves from the aristocracy and the peasantry and working classes, while claiming to be "universal." The fact was they aspired to culture-social hegemony. What was actually the case, on her account, was the existence of many public spheres which were set up *in opposition to* the bourgeois one—popular peasant associations, women's associations, working class associations, etc., all formed "counter-publics."

Fraser argues that cultures, along with our theories about culture, are fragmenting. So is the public sphere, or at least how we understand it. So, against the liberal ideal of a singular, unitary public sphere, Fraser takes as a given the radical ideal of a *proliferation* of public spheres that contribute to a vital public discourse about issues of public concern. It is through a *diversity* of public spheres that society is able to suppose a pluralism of meaning and values. The liberal ideal of a single, unitary, and universally valid set of meanings and values was only an ideal, never the real.

Fraser's thesis of multiple public spheres contrasts sharply to Habermas' view of a single, unitary public sphere. Fraser's ideal of multiple public spheres affirms:

1. The public spheres are "places"—cultural regions—of discourse and identity formation. The private and public spheres are interwoven, not distinct spheres of deliberating and acting.

2. Public discourse is not wholly rational. It involves processes of affective and psychological identification with one's communities. One's thoughts, beliefs,

dispositions, desires (i.e., one's person, individuality) are not merely private, but are present in one's various public spheres.

3. Public discourse discussion takes place within and between spheres, including contestation over the nature of the collectivity or group. An individual's "private sphere" is embedded in implicit and explicit publics.

4. Multiple public spheres produce the conditions of more open contestation and debate that allows for the ongoing reformation of public policy (political will) for critiques of particular exclusions, injustices, and inequalities.

While a great deal divides Habermas' critical theory and his feminist critics, both agree that the public sphere plays a central role in the formation of persons and citizens. A discourse that gives voice to all the constitutive publics of society is essential to democratic action. Thus, a robust public sphere as a locus of full participation in the social and political life of a community is essential to democratic institutions. On their account, public policies that privilege the private at the expense of the public are deleterious, if not overtly dangerous, to democratic institutions.

What are the issues? Obviously, there are significant problems in our thinking about the relationship of the private and public dimensions of human living. Nevertheless, dealing with the issues is unavoidable if one is to think at all about the nature and function of society. Part of the problem is the diversity and complexity of social associations. Another is our ambivalence about social associations. On the one hand, we recognize the value and benefit of the forms of cooperation that social living offers. On the other hand, the maintenance of the forms of cooperation requires submerging individual interests to public interests. The "rules of society," to adapt Fried's characterization, are often coercive and intrusive.

Take education as an example. Many students say that their pursuit of education is an effort to satisfy personal interests in being educated, the joy of learning, satisfying curiosity, preparing for employment, and the like. To the degree that education satisfies personal interests, our participation is voluntary—a free act of a self-determining, autonomous individual. However, once we enter the structure and routines of education—the roles and rules that make it what it is—our degree of freedom is considerably constrained. There are times when the multifarious demands seem unremitting, unfair, and unsolvable. How can one "balance" personal needs and desires against the demands of life lived with others?

Classical liberal theory sets up a dichotomy between the private and the public that is in a constant state of tension because of potential conflict between private desires and interests and the collective will with its power to coerce conformity to the will of the group. Some thinkers, like Arendt, try to reduce the tension by arguing that the public or social sphere is not inimical to privacy, but constitutive of the good of individuals—especially for the full development of the self. Others, like Habermas, acknowledge a tension between the private sphere of individuals and the power of the political sphere. However, they argue that a vital public sphere mediates or ameliorates tension. The relationship of private individuals and political collectives is not the simple dichotomy of liberal theory. Yet others, like Nancy Fraser, argue that the distinction between the private and public is incoherent, misleading, and distorting and try to reduce this tension by eliminating the private-public distinction or reconfiguring the theory in the direction of multiple public spheres.

The weight of the evidence suggests that the private-public sphere is not dichotomous, but a complementarity. To great degree, dichotomizing private individuals and public collectivities risks seeing the relationship of the private and public as a permanently conflicted relationship. It is no accident that the adversarial procedures of the courts dealt with the issue of privacy more consistently than did public policy or private reflection by philosophers.

Second, however, many of the complex issues involved in contemporary notions of privacy are the result of a lack of conceptual clarity about both the private and the public. It is not easy to draw a line between what is private and what is public, as classical liberal theory assumes. Recent work has shown that the public sphere is more likely a plurality of spheres than a single, unitary sphere. Thus, the value of privacy relates to multiple, not singular, spheres and so undoubtedly to multiple dimensions of personality. In other words, privacy, or a private life, as a value incorporates a social as well as a personal dimension. To a significant degree, privacy can only be understood in relation to the social or public.

This view contrasts with traditional philosophical and legal notions about privacy and publicity rooted in traditional liberal thinking that privacy inheres in the individual as an individual, and is important to the individual for self-development or for the establishment of intimate or human relationships. The classical liberal view emphasizes privacy as a negative value and sets in place a conflict between the individual and society. This fails to take into account the power invested in large social and economic organizations that create systems of unequal, but often unacknowledged, power and authority.

A central theme running through the literature on privacy and the public sphere concerns the issue of *power*. Mill's essay that explored the limits of the public or social sphere on the private sphere can be viewed as a response to the asymmetrical power relationship between individuals and social institutions. Habermas argued that the bourgeois public sphere emerged in the eighteenth century as a means of mediating between the needs of private individuals and the coercive power of the political sphere. Thus there is a degree to which thinking about the public sphere means thinking about the meaning of legitimate power and authority.

In the West, at least since the Enlightenment, this thinking has been antagonistic. That is, institutional power has been viewed as the adversary of individual autonomy. Undergirding this view, however, is the assumption that power exists independently of human beings. It is a "force" invested in institutions. but we can also argue that institutional power is *derivative from* human acting and valuing. Thus, social institutions, the routinized roles and rules of social cooperation, are empowered by those who participate in them. If this is true, a new direction of thinking about the private-public nexus is required that shifts from a relation between private individual and public institution, to the meaning of empowerment. This is possible by gathering up several strains of thinking that we have studied about the private-public nexus in a last view of the public sphere as the expression of civil society.

Mediating structures: A theory of civil society. Peter Berger and Richard John Neuhaus provide a significant rethinking of the meaning of private-public nexus by starting with the meaning of social institutions rather than individuals. In their short but influential essay, *To Empower People: The Role of Mediating Structures in Public Policy* (1977/1996), Berger and Neuhaus suggest that the direction of thinking about the relationship of individuals and society needs to be reversed from how to protect individuals *from* interference with their liberty to how to empower people to act *on* their liberty in value-generating institutions. This is necessary because "one of the most debilitating results of modernization is a feeling of powerlessness in the face of institutions controlled by those whom we do not know and whose values we often do not share" (7).

Berger and Neuhaus' essay is an argument that public policy should foster institutions, such as families, neighborhoods, religious and volunteer organizations, that contribute to a civil society that can enable human beings to satisfy their need and desire to participate and co-ordinate human activities in a social milieu. Civil society, on their account, is the space between the individual and the large-scale structures of society, such as the state, and " ... the large conglomerates of capitalist enterprise, big labor, and the growing bureaucracies that administer wide sectors of the society . . . . " (Berger and Neuhaus 1996, 2). This sphere of society is composed of institutions of individual association such as families, churches, neighborhoods, and voluntary associations. These are "mediating structures" because they stand "between the individual and his private life and the large institutions of public life" (Berger and Neuhaus 1996, 3). They claim that a new attentiveness to mediating structure is necessary because modernization has exacerbated the private-public dichotomy with a resulting loss of personal meaning and value.

Modernization brings about an historically unprecedented dichotomy between public and private life. The most important and large institutions in the ordering of modern society is the modern state itself. In addition, there are large economic conglomerates of capitalist enterprise, big labor, and the growing bureaucracies that administer wide sectors of the society, such as in education and the organized professions. All these institutions we call megastructures.

Then there is that modern phenomenon called private life. It is a curious kind of preserve left over by the large institutions and in which individuals carry on a bewildering variety of activities with only fragile institutional supports.

For the individual in modern society, life is an ongoing migration between these two spheres, public and private. The megastructures are typically alienating, that is, they are not helpful in providing meaning and identity for individual existence. Meaning, fulfillment, and personal identity are to be realized in the private sphere. While the two spheres interact in many ways, in private life the individual is left very much to his own devices, and thus is uncertain and anxious. Where modern society is "hard," as in the megastructures, it is personally unsatisfying; where it is "soft," as in private life, it cannot be relied upon. Compare, for example, the social realities of employment and those of marriage.

The dichotomy poses a double crisis. It is a crisis for the individual who must carry on a balancing act between the demands of the two spheres. It is a political crisis because megastuctures (notably the state) come to be devoid of personal meaning and are therefore viewed as unreal or even malignant. Not everyone experiences this crisis in the same way. Many who handle it more successfully than most have access to institutions that *mediate* between the two spheres. Such institutions have a private face, giving private life a measure of stability, and they have a public face, transferring meaning and value to the megastructures. Thus, mediating structures alleviate each facet of the double crisis of modern society. Their strategic position derives from their reducing both the anomic precariousness of individual existence in isolation from society and the threat of alienation to the public order. . . .

Without institutionally reliable processes of mediation, the political order becomes detached from the values and realities of individual life. Deprived of its moral foundation, the political order is "delegitimated." When that happens the political order must be secured by coercion rather than consent. And when that happens, democracy disappears. . . . The attractiveness of totalitarianism . . . is that it overcomes the dichotomy of private and public existence by imposing on life one comprehensive meaning (Berger and Neuhaus 1996, 2-3).

Berger and Neuhaus do not claim originality for their idea of "mediating structures." They attribute it to Edmund Burke and Alexis de Tocqueville. Burke argued that the source of civil affection and public order was "love for our 'little platoon'," or social sub-group of family and social associations. Berger and Neuhaus return to the classical liberal sources for their inspiration, but with a twist. The private sphere does not exist independently of the public, but within it. Thus, the idea of mediating structures echoes Habermas' notion of a public sphere. However, unlike Habermas, Berger and Neuhaus connect the notion of mediating structures to a cultivated pluralism and diversity.

Every world within this society, whether it calls itself a subculture or a supra culture or simply the American culture, is in fact a subculture, is but part of the whole. . . . The subculture that envisages its values as universal and its style as cosmopolitan is no less a subculture for that. . . .Pluralism means the lively interaction among inherited particularities, and, through election, the evolution of new particularities. The goal of public policy in a pluralistic society is to sustain as many particularities as possible (Berger and Neuhaus 1996, 43-44).

Thus, they deny Habermas' insistence that a vital public sphere is universal and singular. But they also deny Fraser's contention that pluralism is a context of contestation and critique of power. Mediating structures augment power—they are empowering—rather than defusing or countervailing existing power.

For Berger and Neuhaus, social justice and the long-term survival of a democratic society are in large measure based on the strength of the mediating institutions. These institutions do not only give individuals meaning in their lives, but they provide the moral foundation on which the political society and social reform are legitimized. Without these institutions, political order is reached by coercion rather than consent, and democratic society becomes susceptible to the forces of tyranny:

. . . mediating structures are the value-generating and value maintaining agencies in society. Without them, values become another function of the megastructures, notably of the state and this is a hallmark of totalitarianism. In the totalitarian case, the individual becomes the object rather than the subject of the value-propagating process of this society (Berger and Neuhaus 1996, 3).

What Berger and Neuhaus argue is that public life—the concrete operation of the social cooperative schemes of coordinated human action—requires a civic sphere. The civic sphere, expressed most obviously in civic associations, *ad hoc* associations for public action, recreation and leisure groups, volunteer activities, and some dimensions of family and school, is the training ground of the virtues and values of the civil society, or the *civitas*. In these groups and associations, values are enacted, expressed, in-formed, critiqued, transformed, and finally coordinated with the larger associations and communities of socio-political life.

Social living—the public sphere—is structured in some manner. How we choose to understand that structuring and human relationships to it is essential, not incidental, to our understanding of society and politics. The consequences of how people choose to think about the relationship of private and public dimensions of human living have their effect on the actual concrete institutions of society. Thus the issue raised by question of privacy, rights and public life merges with questions about justice, or what is fair or equitable or normative, about the structures of social living.

References

Andenaes, Johannes. 1974. *Punishment and deterrence*. Ann Arbor: University of Michigan Press.

Arendt, Hannah. 1958. *The human condition*. Chicago: University of Chicago Press.

Aristotle. 1962. *Nicomachean ethics*. Martin Ostwald, ed. Indianapolis: Bobbs-Merrill.

Aristotle. 1974. *Politics*. Ernest Barker, ed. London: Oxford University Press.

Aristotle. 1984. *The Politics*. Carnes Lord, trans. Chicago: University of Chicago Press.

Ayer, A. J. 1936. *Language, truth, and logic*. New York: Dover.

Beccaria, Cesare. 1963. *On crimes and punishments*. Henri Peolucci, trans. New York: Bobbs-Merrill.

Benedict, Ruth. 1958. *Patterns of culture*. New York: Houghton Mifflin.

Benhabib, Seyla. 2000. *Situating the self*. London: Routledge.

Bentham, Jeremy. 1948. *An introduction to the principles of morals and legislation*. New York: Hafner.

Berger, Peter, and Richard John Neuhaus. 1977/1996. *To empower people: The role of mediating structures in public policy*. Washington: American Enterprise Institute.

Black, Henry Campbell. 1999. Privacy, right of. *Black's Law Dictionary*, 7th ed., s.v. St. Paul, Minn.: St. Paul Press.

Bloom, Allan. 1968. *The republic of Plato, translated, with notes and an interpretive essay*. New York: Basic Books.

Bloustein, Edward J. 1964. Privacy as an aspect of human dignity. *New York University Law Review* 39: 975.

Bornschier, Volker. 1981. Multinational corporations, economic policy and national development in the world system. *International Social Science Journal* 81: 158-172.

Bottomore, T.B. 1963. *Karl Marx: Early writings*. New York: McGraw-Hill.

Boxill, Bernard. 1992. *Blacks and social justice*. New York: Rowman and Littlefield.

Brandt, Richard. 1971. Some merits of one form of rule-utilitarianism. In Thomas Hearn, ed. *Studies in utilitarianism*. New York: Appleton-Century-Croft.

Brightman, Edgar. 1945. *Nature and values*. New York: Holt.

Cannon, James P. 1978. *America's road to socialism*. New York: Pathfinder.

Cate, Fred H. 1997. *Privacy in the information age*. Washington: Brookings Institution Press.

Clark, Andrew. 1986. Philosophies at war in law schools. *Time*, September 29: 30.

Cornell, Drucilla. 1995. *The imaginary domain: Abortion, pornography, and sexual harrassment*. New York: Routledge.

Cornell, Drucilla. 1998. *At the heart of freedom*. Princeton: Princeton University Press.

Cress, Donald (trans. and ed.). 1987. *Basic political writings of Jean-Jacques Rousseau*. Indianapolis: Hackett Publishing Co.

Cross, Theodore. 1984. *Black power imperative*. New York: Faulkner Press.

DeFronzo, James. 1983. Economic assistance to impoverished Americans. *Criminology* 21: 119-136.

Dobbs, Darrell. 1985. The justice of Socrates' philosopher kings. *American Journal of Political Science* 29: 809-826.

Ellis, Ralph D. 1998. *Just results: Ethical foundations for policy analysis*. Washington: Georgetown University Press.

Ellis, Ralph D., and Carol S. Ellis. 1989. *Theories of criminal justice: A critical reappraisal*. Wolfeboro, N.H.: Longwood Academic.

Eisenstadt v. Baird, 405 U.S. 438, 453-54 (1972)] (Brennan, J.).

Etzioni, Amitai, 2000. *The right to privacy*. New York: Basic Books.

Foucault, Michel. 1965. Madness and civilization. Richard Howard, trans. New York: Random House.

Foucault, Michel. 1977. *The birth of the prison*. Alana Sheridan, trans. New York: Partheon Books.

Foucault, Michel. 1974a. Human nature: Justice and power. In *Reflective waters*. Fons Elder, ed. London: Souvenir Press.

Foucault, Michel. 1974b. *Power/Knowledge: Selected Interviews and Other Writings 1972-1974*, New York: Pantheon.

Fraser, Nancy. 1989. *Unruly practice: Power, discourse, and gender in contemporary social theory*. Minneapolis: University of Minnesota Press.

Fraser, Nancy. 1998. Sex, lies, and the public sphere: Reflections on the confirmation of Clarence Thomas. In Joan B. Landes, ed. *Feminism, the public and the private*. Oxford: Oxford University Press.

Fried, Charles. 1968. Privacy. *Yale Law Review* 77.

Gilligan, Carol. 1982. *In a different voice: Psychological theory and women's development*. Cambridge, Mass.: Harvard University Press.

Goldstein, Kurt. 1938. *The organism*. New York: American Books.

Griswold v. Connecticut, 381 U.S. 479 (1965).

Gutman, Amy. 1986. Communitarian critics of liberalism. *Philosophy and Public Affairs* 15: 308-322.

Habermas, Jürgen. 1990a. *Moral consciousness and communicative action*. Cambridge, Mass.: MIT Press.

Habermas, Jürgen. 1990b. Reconciliation through the public use of reason: Remarks on John Rawls's *Political Liberalism*. *Journal of Philosophy* 92: 3.

Habermas, Jürgen. 1990c. *Die nachgholende Revolution, Kleine Politische Schriften*. Frankfurt: Suhrkamp.

Habermas, Jürgen. 1991. *The structural transformations of the public sphere*. Boston: MIT Press.

Habermas, Jürgen. 1995. Multiculturalism and the liberal state. *Stanford Law Review* 47 (May 1995).

Hearn, Thomas, ed. 1971. *Studies in utilitarianism*. New York: Appleton-Century-Croft.

Hegel, G.W.F. 1971. *Philosophy of mind*. A.V. Miller, trans. Oxford: Oxford University Press.

Held, Virginia. 1989. *Rights and goods: Justifying social action*. Chicago: University of Chicago Press.

Hobbes, Thomas. 1968. *Leviathan*. New York/London: Penguin.

Ibn Khaldun. 1969. *The muqaddimah*, abridged. F. Rosenthal, trans. Princeton: Princeton University Press.

Kamenka, Eugene. 1969. *Marxism and ethics*. London: Macmillan.

Kant, Immanuel. 1981. *Grounding of the metaphysics of morals*. James W. Ellington, trans. Indianapolis: Hackett Publishing Company.

Kautsky, Karl. 1936. *The economic doctrines of Karl Marx*. London: M.C.L.C. Publishing Society.

Lessnoff, Michael. 1986. *Social contract*. Atlantic Highlands, N.J.: Humanities Press International.

Locke, John. 1690/1960. *Second treatise of government*. C.B. Macpherson, ed. Indianapolis: Hackett.

Linton, Ralph. 1954. The problem of universal values. In R.F. Spencer, ed. *Method and perspective in anthropology*. Minneapolis: University of Minnesota Press, 145-68.

Lyotard, Jean-Francois. 1983. *The differend: Phrases in dispute*. George Van Den Abbeele, trans. Minneapolis: University of Minnesota Press.

Lyotard, Jean-Francois. 1984. *The postmodern condition: A report on knowledge*. Geoff Bennington and Brian Massume, trans. Minneapolis: University of Minnesota Press.

MacIntyre, Alisdair. 1981. *After virtue*. Notre Dame: University of Notre Dame Press.

MacIntyre, Alasdair. 1989. *Whose justice? Which rationality?* Notre Dame: University of Notre Dame Press.

Catherine MacKinnon. 1989. *Toward a feminist theory of the state*. Cambridge, Mass.: Harvard University Press.

Mandel, Ernst. 1971. *Marxist economic theory*. London: Merlin.

Manning, Rita. 1992. Just caring. In Eve Browning Cole and Susal Coultrap-McQuin, eds. *Explorations in feminist ethics*. Bloomington: University of Indiana Press.

Marx, Karl. 1848/1906. *Capital*. New York: Modern Library.

Mayer, Hellmuth. 1936. *Das Strafrecht des deutschen Volkes*. Stuttgart: Duncker & Humbolt.

Maschner, Horst. 1969. *Individual and technostructure*. Bad Nauheim: Buchdruckerei und Verlag Ludwig Wagner.

McPheters, Lee. 1976. Criminal behavior and gains from crime. *Criminology* 14: 137-152.

Mill, John Stuart. 18591895/1947. *On liberty*. New York. E.P. Dutton.

Miller, Walter. 1978. Some characteristics of present-day delinquency. Cited from C.B. Horton, *The sociology of social problems*. Englewood Cliffs: Prentice-Hall, 155.

Moore, G.E. 1900/1956. *Principia ethica*. Cambridge: Cambridge University Press.

Myrdal, Gunnar. 1962. *Challenge to affluence*. New York: Random House.

Nozick, Robert. 1974. *Anarchy, state, and utopia*. New York: Basic Books.

Okin, Susan Moller. 1989. *Justice, gender and the family*. New York: Basic Books.

Outlaw, Thurnel. 1996. *On race and philosophy*. New York: Routledge.

Perkins, Robert. 2004. *Confessions of an economic hit man*. New York: Penguin.

Planned Parenthood of Southeastern Pennsylvania vs. Casey, Governor of Pennsylvania, 505 U.S. 833 (1992).

Plato. 1979. *The republic.* Raymond Larson, trans. Arlington Heights, Il.: Crofts Classics.

Railton, Peter. 1985. Locke, stock, and peril: Natural property rights, pollution, and risk. In Mary Gibson, ed. *To breathe freely.* Center for Philosophy and Public Policy, College Park, Md.: Rowman and Allanheld.

Rawls, John. 1971. *A theory of justice.* Cambridge, Mass.: Harvard University Press.

Rawls, John. 1982. The basic liberties. In Sterling McMurrin, ed. *The Tanner lectures on human values,* III, 1-87. Salt Lake City: University of Utah Press; Cambridge: Cambridge University Press.

Rawls, John. 1989. The domain of the political and overlapping consensus. *New York University Law Review* 64(2): 233-255.

Reiss, Hans (ed.). 1970. *Kant: Political writings.* H.B. Nisbett, trans. Cambridge: Cambridge University Press.

Ricoeur, Paul. 1995. *Oneself as another.* Kathleen Blamey, trans. Chicago: University of Chicago Press.

Ricoeur, Paul. 1997. Ethique et politique. In *Ideologie et Utopie.* Paris: Seiul.

Ricoeur, Paul. 2003. *The just.* David Pellauer, trans. Chicago: University of Chicago Press.

Ring, Harry. 1977. *Socialism and individual freedom.* New York: Pathfinder.

Roe v. Wade, 410 U.S. 113, 152-53 (1973)] (Blackmun, J.).

Ross, David. 1965. *The right and the good.* Oxford: Clarenden.

Rousseau, Jean-Jacques. 1862/1977. *The social contract.* New York: Penguin.

Sandel, Michael. 1982/1998. *Liberalism and the limits of justice.* New York: Cambridge University Press.

Sandel, Michael. 1984. *Liberalism and its critics.* New York: New York University Press.

Sankowski, Edward. 1985. Paternalism and social policy. *American Philosophical Quarterly* 22: 1-12.

Schaff, Adam. 1970. *Marxism and the human individual.* New York: McGraw-Hill.

Schweickart, David. 1978. Should Rawls be a socialist? *Social Theory and Practice* 4: 1-27.

Shaw, Clifford. *Delinquency Areas.* Chicago: University of Chicago Press.

Short, James. 1980. *An investigation of the relation between crime and business cycles.* New York: Arno.

Smith, Alexander, and Harriet Pollack. 1972. *Crime and justice in a mass society.* New York: Rinehart.

Sommers, Christina Hoff. 2001. *The war against boys: How misguided feminism is harming our young men.* New York: Simon and Schuster.

Sterba, James. 1980. *The demands of justice.* Notre Dame: University of Notre Dame Press.

Strauss, Leo. 1953. *Natural right and history.* Chicago: University of Chicago Press.

Sumner, William G. 1909/2002. *Folkways: A study of mores, manners, customs and morals.* New York: Dover.

Sutherland, Edwin, and Donald Cressey. 1974. *Criminology.* Philadelphia: J.B. Lippencott, 95ff.

Taylor, Charles. 1982. *Utilitarianism and beyond.* A. Sen and B. Williams, eds. Cambridge: Cambridge University Press.

Thornburgh v. American College of Obstetricians & Gynecologists, 476 U.S. 747, 772 (1986) (Blackmun. J.).

Tocqueville, Alexis de. 1945. *Democracy in America*. New York: Alfred Knopf/Random House.

Tucker, Robert. 1971. *Philosophy and myth in Karl Marx*. Cambridge: Cambridge University Press.

Walzer, Michael. 1994. *Thick and thin: Moral argument at home and abroad*. Notre Dame: Notre Dame University Press.

Warren, Samuel D., and Louis Brandeis. 1890/1984. The right to privacy. *Harvard Law Review* 4: 289-320. Reprinted in F.D. Schoeman, ed. *The philosophical dimension of privacy*. Cambridge: Cambridge University Press, 75-103.

West, Cornel. 2001. *Race matters*. New York: Vintage.

Westermarck, Edward. 1932. *Ethical relativity*. New York: Harcourt-Brace.

Westin, Alan. 1967. *Privacy and freedom*. Atheneum.

Young, Iris Marion. 1997. *Intersecting voices*. Princeton: Princeton University Press.

Young, Iris Marion. 2000. *Inclusion and democracy*. Oxford: Oxford University Press.

Index

abortion, 8
Adorno, Theodor, 238, 241
aggression, military, 3
aletheia, 276
alienation, 156, 158
al-Qaida, 1-3
anomie, 6
American Revolution, 3
Aquinas, Thomas, 33
Arendt, Hannah, 297ff
Aristotle, 12-13, 19, 20, 33, 36, 63ff
assassination (of political leaders), 9-
    10, 11
atomism, 64
atomistic individualism, 71, 298
autonomos individual, 81ff, 139, 298
Ayer, A.J., 12

Beccaria, Cesare, 6, 31-2, 166
Benedict, Ruth, 12
Benhabib, Seyla, 251
Berger, Peter, 215-17
Black power, 38
Bloom, Alan, 60
Bonhoffer, Dietrich, 10
Boxill, Bernard, 38
Brandeis, Louis, 290ff
Brandt, Richard, 25
Brightman, Edgar, 6

Calvinists, 31
campaign contributions, 16
care ethics, 208ff, 215ff

Castro, Fidel, 23
categorical imperative, 141
cave allegory, 58
censorship, in Aristotle, 67
child protection, 7, 13, 24, 36
Civil Rights Movement, 38, 129, 241
communalism, in Plato, 53
communicative action, 243
communicative ethics, 242
communitarianism, 6-7, 33-6, 62, 68,
    182, 219ff
commutative justice, 180
consent, tacit, 4-7, 8-9, 26, 78
constructivism (social), 229, 271
contextualism, 219
contractarianism, 4-7, 26, 34
conventionalism, 74, 77
Cornell, Drucilla, 208ff
cost-benefit analysis, 23-4
critical theory, 237ff
cultural pluralism, 19

de-capitalization, 15
dehumanization of workers (Marx),
    156, 159
depression, 35
Descartes, René, 76-7
desert, moral, 28-9, 31, 225
determinism, 156ff, 252
deterrence of crime, 22, 24, 28
dialectic, 160
dialectical materialism, 160
difference principle (Rawls), 186

differend (Lyotard), 268ff
dignity, 141
discourse ethics, 242ff
distributive justice, 26, 31-6, 180
division of labor, 124ff
duty, 11-12, 34, 140, 144

egoism, 12, 14, 46
egoism, Aristotle's rejection of, 67
eidos, 58
Eisenstadt v. Baird, 295-6
elasticity, 196
electronic surveillance, 25-6
emotion, in Hobbes, 74
emotivism, 12
enlightened self-interest, 84, 99
entitlement, 180, 192ff
epistemology, 3-4, 12, 177
equality, interpretations of, 259
equal protection clause (of U.S.
    Constitution), 129
essence, 58
ethical relativism, 12, 19-22
Etzioni, Amitai, 303-4
eudaimonia, 50
ever-increasing profit (Marx), 160
external *versus* internal goods, 223-4
extrinsic value, 24-5, 48

factions, 130
failed state, 37, 41
fairness, 1832ff
false advertising, 13
false cause fallacy, 15-16
family, as basic institution, 36, 205
feminism, 33, 182, 201ff, 310ff
Ferri, Enrico, 158, 166-7
Foucault, Michel, 166ff
Frankfort School, 238ff
Fraser, Nancy, 310-13
freedom of conscience, 34-5
Fried, Charles, 299-302

game theory, 189
gender inequality, 202ff
general will, 22, 126
Geneva Convention, 2

Gilligan, Carol, 210ff
good, conceptions of, 177ff, 255
good *versus* right, 177, 234
Great Depression, 35
Griswold v. Connecticut, 293
Gutman, Amy, 6

Habermas, Jürgen, 241ff
health care, 8, 10-11
hedonism, 12, 46
Hegel, G.W.F., 71-2, 237-8
Held, Virginia, 214ff
hermeneutic circle, 39-40
Hisballah, 10
Hitler, Adolphe, 9-11
Hobbes, Thomas, 5, 26, 31
holism, 64
holocaust, 9, 11
Horkheimer, Max, 238
hypothetical imperative, 141

Ibn Khaldun, 6
illegal surveillance, 25-6
illegitimate government, 6
immanent (internal) criticism, 240
impartialism, 180ff
imperialism, 40-41, 161
inalienable rights, 20ff
industrial reserve army (Marx), 161
instrumental rationality, 238
internal *versus* external goods, 223-4
international relations, 147
intrinsic value, 24-6, 28-9, 31, 48
Islamic Jihad, 10
is-ought problem, 21

just acquisition and transfer (Nozick),
    194ff
justice, contemporary theories, 175ff
justice, types of, 180
just war, 147

Kant, Immanuel, 137ff
Khaldun, Ibn, 6
King, Martin Luther, 39, 241
kingdom of ends, 141
Kohlberg, Lawrence, 210-11

law, 4-10, 24-5, 30, 32-5
legitimate state, 1-6, 13, 26-7, 31-2
liberalism (classical), 5, 8, 198, 287
liberal *versus* conservative, 197ff
liberty, 5, 125ff
limited government, 31ff, 100ff
Locke, John, 26, 30-2, 95ff
logical empiricism, 12-13
Lycophron, 12, 19-20
Lyotard, Jean-Francois, 267ff

macro- *versus* micro-fairness, 29
MacIntyre, Alasdair, 34-5, 220ff
marginalization (social), 253
majoritarianism, 127
Manning, Rita, 215ff
Marx, Karl, 155ff, 237-8
Marxism, 14, 35
maximin rule, 187ff
mechanistic worldview, 71-3
medical care, 10, 11
merit, 225
Mill, John Stuart, 24ff, 37-8
money, 106
monopolies, 13
Moore, G.E., 70
moral desert, 28-9, 31
moral development, 211ff
multinational corporations, 14-15, 40
Muslim political theory, 6
mutual self-interest, 8, 16, 20, 22
Myrdal, Gunnar, 35

narratives, 268ff
natural (moral) law, 102
Natural wholes, 64
naturalistic fallacy, 70
Neuhaus, Richard, 315-17
Nicomachean Ethics, 63, 67
Nozick, Robert, 26, 192ff

obligations, 178
Okin, Susan, 201ff
ontology, 3-4
organicism (Aristotle), 64
original position, 26-30, 183ff
Outlaw, Lucius, 39

overbearing majority, 6, 20ff

Palestinian refugees, 10
passions (Aristotle), 67
paternalism, 35ff, 69
patriarchal society, 310
peace, 147
Pentagon, 1ff
Perkins, Robert, 40-41
personal development, 208
personalism, 33ff, 208, 257ff
philosophy of history, 148
Plato, 12, 33, 36, 44ff
plea bargaining, 24, 29-30
pluralism, in philosophy, 40
pluralism of values, 18-19, 241ff
political animal (Aristotle), 65
political rights, 5, 8, 11-13, 19-26, 28,
    30-35,
pollution, 8
postmodernism, 265ff
practices (Macintyre), 223
pre-Socratic philosophy, 73
preventive war, illegitimacy of, 147
price fixing, 13
prima facie value, 21-2
privacy, 28, 277ff
procedural justice, 99, 184, 188, 248,
    255
property, private, 124
property rights, 8, 16, 31-2, 34-5, 106
Protagoras, 12
psyche, 65
public life, 298
public parks, 8
Puritans, 31

Qu'ran, 6

racial inequality, 20-2, 36, 129
race/ethnicity, in social organization,
    36ff
rational animal, 66
rational self-interest, 185
Rawls, John, 25ff, 177ff
rehabilitation, 6, 35
religious freedom, 8

republican government, 141
respect for persons (and privacy), 284
retributive justice, 30-32, 180
revolution, 112, 173-4
Ricoeur, Paul, 257ff
right of free trade, 13-14
Right of Nature, 86ff
rights, 8, 9-12, 177
rights, natural, 86
rights, inalienable, 20ff, 146
rights of accused, 5, 22-3, 31
rights of potential victims, 31
right *versus* good, 177, 234
ring of Gyges, 48
risk analysis, 27-8, 190
Roe v. Wade, 295-6
Roosevelt, Theodore, 34-5
Rousseau , Jean-Jacques, 22, 26, 32-4,
   117ff
Ruddick, Sara, 216ff
rules, 25-6
rule utilitarianism, 25

Sandel, Michael, 5, 6, 33-5, 234-5
segregation, 21-2
self, in liberalism and
   communitarianism, 233
self, thin view of, 234. 255
Short, James, 34
simple majoritarianism, 20-22
slavery, 68, 105
Smart, J.J.C., 25
social constructivism, 229, 271
social contract, 3ff, 48
social determinism, 160, 252
Socrates, 12, 43
Sommers, Christina Hoff, 213ff
Sophists, 12, 44
soul (Aristotle), 65
sovereign, 83ff
sphere corruption (Waltzer), 229
sphere sovereignty (Waltzer), 229
state of nature, 4, 5ff, 77ff
Sterba, James, 30
Strauss, Leo, 106
Sumner, William, 12
surveillance, electronic, 25

tacit consent, 4-7, 8-9, 26, 78
Taliban, 1ff
taxes, 5, 8, 15, 31-2, 35, 111
Taylor, Charles, 235
teleology, 65, 73
terrorism, 1ff
theocracy, 6
Third World, 13-15
*Thornburgh v. American College of
   Obstetricians and Gynecologists*,
   294
totalitarianism, 297
tradition (MacIntyre), 221
tribal organization, 37
tripartite theory of state (Plato), 49ff
Truman, Harry, 3, 10
trusts and cartels, 13
tyranny of majority, 106

unemployment compensation, 8, 34
universalism, 180ff
utilitarianism, 11-12, 23ff

value assumptions, 8
value pluralism, 18-19, 241ff
veil of ignorance, 184
Viet Nam war, 7-8
virtue, 141ff, 224ff

Waltzer, Michael, 227ff
Warren, Samuel, 290ff
war of all against all, 81-2, 99
welfare benefits, 6
West, Cornel, 37-8
Westermarck, Edward, 12
Westin, Alan, 284ff
wiretapping, without warrant, 24-5
work of freedom (Ricoeur), 261ff
World Health Organization, 13-14
World Trade Center, 1ff

Young, Iris Marion, 251ff

About the Authors

Ralph D. Ellis received his PhD in philosophy at Duquesne University (1975) and a postdoctoral M.S. in Public Affairs at Georgia State University (1985). He has written many books on ethics, social and political philosophy, and philosophical psychology, including *An Ontology of Consciousness* (Kluwer, 1986), *Theories of Criminal Justice* (Longwood 1989), *Coherence and Verification in Ethics* (University Press of America, 1992), *Questioning Consciousness* (John Benjamins, 1995), *Eros in a Narcissistic Culture* (Kluwer, 1996), *Just Results: Ethical Foundations for Policy Analysis* (Georgetown University Press, 1998), *The Caldron of Consciousness* (John Benjamins, 2000), *Love and the Abyss* (Open Court, 2004), *Curious Emotions* (John Benjamins 2005), and a critical thinking textbook, *The Craft of Thinking* (Kendall/Hunt, 2000/2004). He teaches philosophy at Clark Atlanta University, and earlier worked as a social worker — both in the liberal state of Pennsylvania and in the "red state" of Georgia.

Norman Fischer received his Ph.D. in philosophy at Emory University (2000) after doing graduate work in both philosophy and political science. He has published articles in Ancient and Modern Philosophy, particularly on Plato and Nietzsche, as well as the philosophy of sport. He has an abiding interest in the history of political and ethical thought, as well as in the philosophy of literature and art. He is currently an assistant professor at Clark Atlanta University.

James R. Sauer is professor of philosophy at St. Mary's University (San Antonio). He specializes in ethics, social and political philosophy, and philosophy of social science. His work has appeared in numerous journals and book chapters including *Scottish Journal of Philosophy, Humanomics, International Journal of Social Economics,* and *Personalist Forum.* His books include *Faithful Ethics* and *A Commentary on Lonergan's Method in Theology.*